A Kodansha Comics Trade Paperback Original
Rent-A-Girlfriend 1 copyright © 2017 Reiji Miyajima
English translation copyright © 2020 Reiji Miyajima

Published in the United States by Kodansha Comics, an imprint of Kodansha USA Publishing, LLC, New York.

Publication rights for this English edition arranged through Kodansha Ltd., Tokyo.

First published in Japan in 2017 by Kodansha Ltd., Tokyo as *Kanojo, okarishimasu*, volume 1.

ISBN 978-1-63236-997-0

Original cover design by Kohei Nawata Design Office

Printed in the United States of America.

www.kodanshacomics.com

9 8 7 6 5 4
Translation: Kevin Gifford
Lettering: Paige Pumphrey
Kodansha Comics edition cover design by Phil Balsman

Publisher: Kiichiro Sugawara
Vice president of marketing & publicity: Naho Yamada

Director of publishing services: Ben Applegate
Associate director of operations: Stephen Pakula
Publishing services managing editor: Noelle Webster
Assistant production manager: Emi Lotto, Angela Zurlo
Logo and character art ©Kodansha USA Publishing, LLC

Rent-A-Girlfriend

In recent years, a particular business has blossomed in Japan—
"renting" the chaste companionship of a professional for a few hours or
a day. Rental services offer endless possibilities: One might rent a father,
grandmother, sibling...or even a girlfriend! We asked the editor of Rent-A-
Girlfriend to share his thoughts about rental culture and the author, Reiji
Miyajima's, new manga that centers on this relatively new phenomenon.

– Kodansha Comics

The protagonist of this manga, *Rent-A-Girlfriend*, is a helpless 20-year-old
college student named Kazuya Kinoshita. His first-ever girlfriend cheats
on him, and, feeling like he will turn anywhere to ease the pain, he
decides to use a so-called "girlfriend rental" service. However, his whole
life begins to turn around after meeting his rental girlfriend—
Chizuru Mizuhara.

The "girlfriend rental" featured in this manga is a service where you pay
an hourly fee for the "ideal girlfriend." Here's a little introduction for
what you can expect from such an "ideal" date:

CUTE AS AN IDOL.

First, her looks. You are paying to go on a date with a woman so
beautiful that, wherever she goes, heads are constantly turning.

A WOMAN IN CHARGE.

It's OK to be a little nervous. Her easy-going conversation, peppered
with jokes and that sense of intimacy one only gets from a lover, will set
you right at ease. While you're laughing and gazing at her winning smile,
it will feel like time is flying between you and your girlfriend.

A FUN DATE.

She'll hold your hand, go where you want to go, take pictures, and share
meals—making your dream date come to life. And if you can't conjure
these dreams, she'll be there to do it for you.

How does this all sound? A girlfriend you can rent, who's cute and cool,
and will create once-in-a-lifetime memories with you. If any of this has
piqued your interest, I recommend you read *Rent-A-Girlfriend*, and join
Kazuya on his journey to get to know his "ideal girlfriend."

– Editor (Tokyo, Japan)

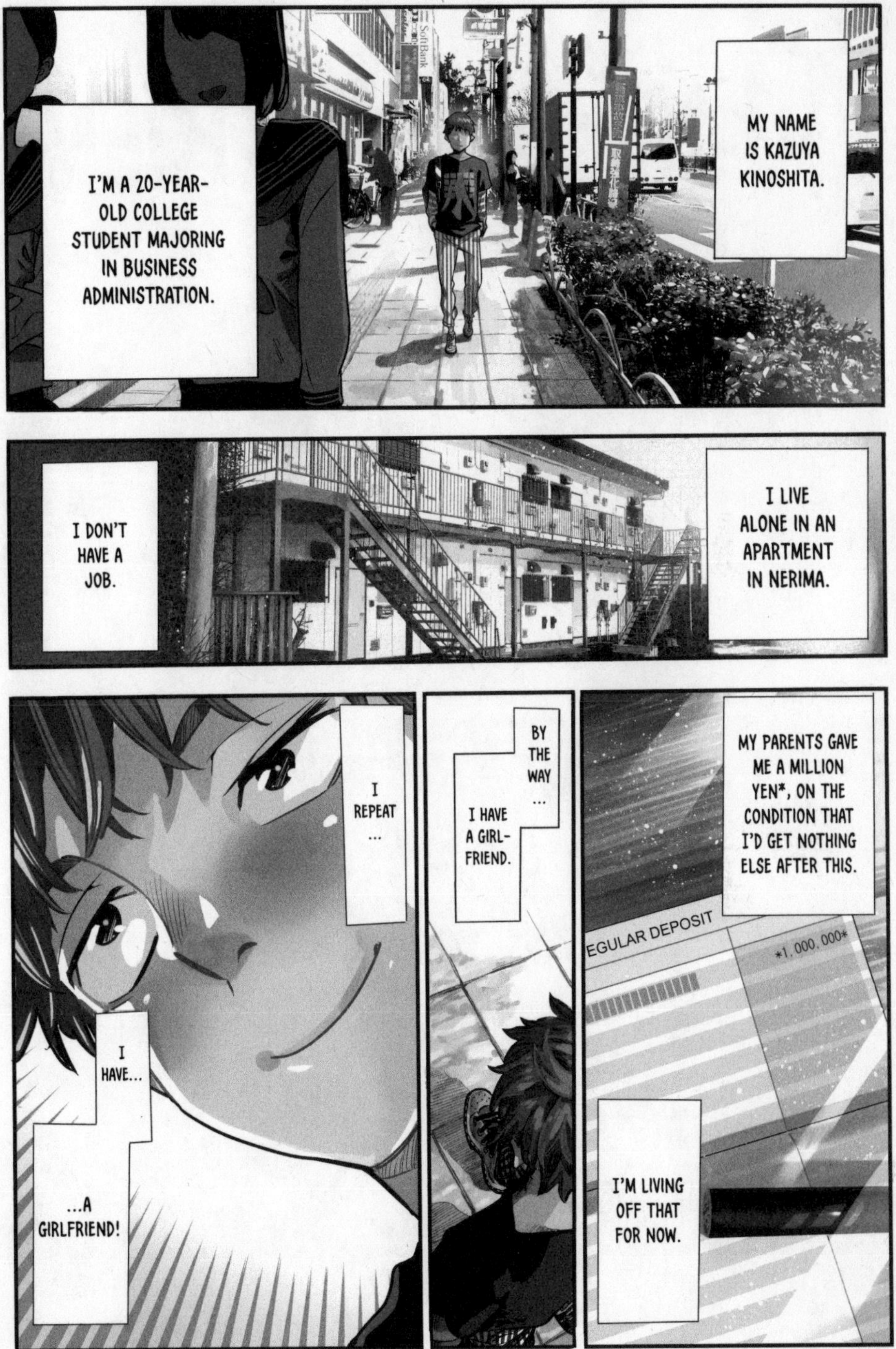
MY NAME IS KAZUYA KINOSHITA.
I'M A 20-YEAR-OLD COLLEGE STUDENT MAJORING IN BUSINESS ADMINISTRATION.
I LIVE ALONE IN AN APARTMENT IN NERIMA.
I DON'T HAVE A JOB.
MY PARENTS GAVE ME A MILLION YEN*, ON THE CONDITION THAT I'D GET NOTHING ELSE AFTER THIS.
EGULAR DEPOSIT
1,000,000
I'M LIVING OFF THAT FOR NOW.
BY THE WAY...
I HAVE A GIRL-FRIEND.
I REPEAT...
I HAVE...
...A GIRLFRIEND!

*ABOUT $9400

RENT-A-GIRLFRIEND

VOLUME 1

REIJI MIYAJIMA

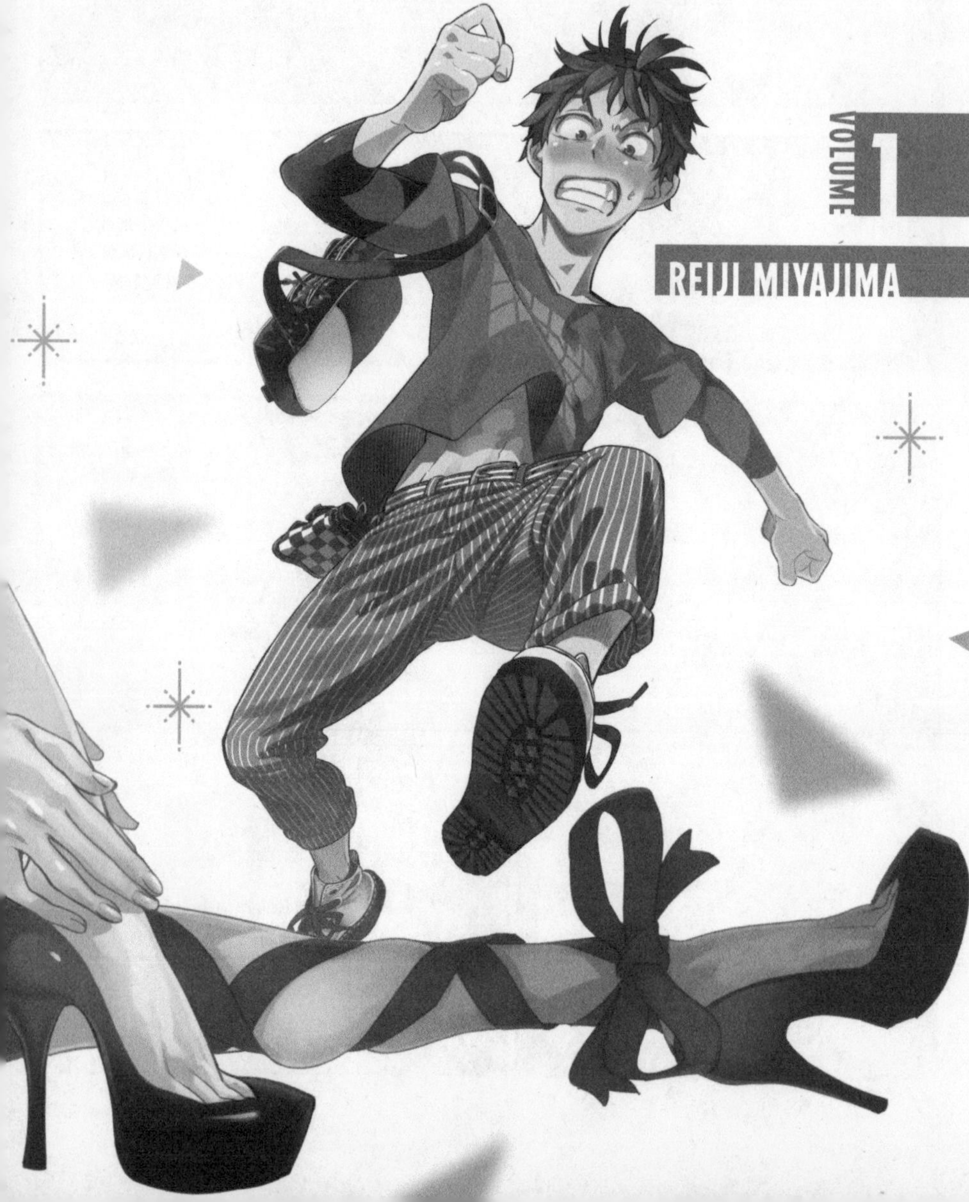

RATING 1
MY "GIRLFRIEND," CHIZURU MIZUHARA

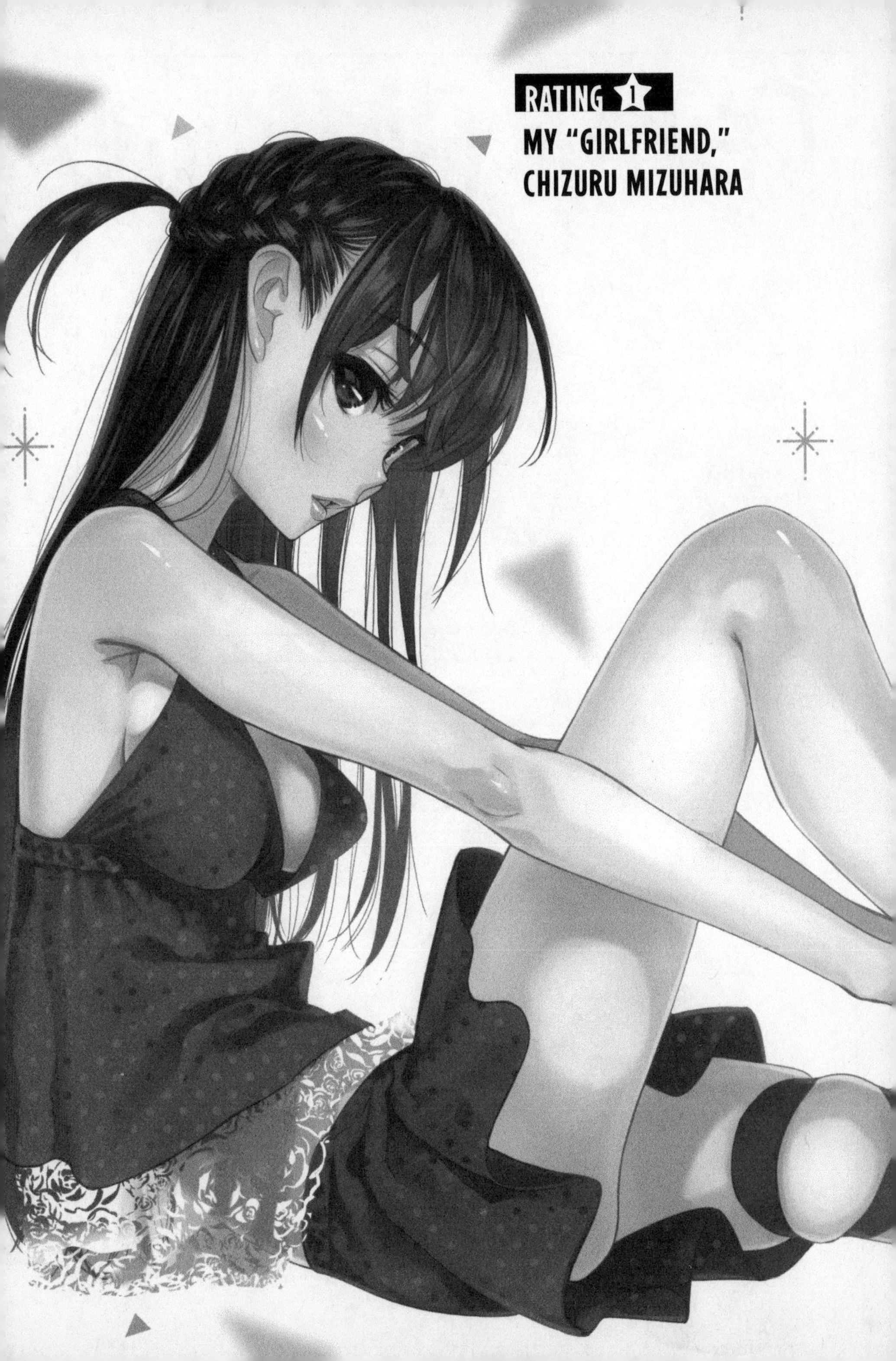

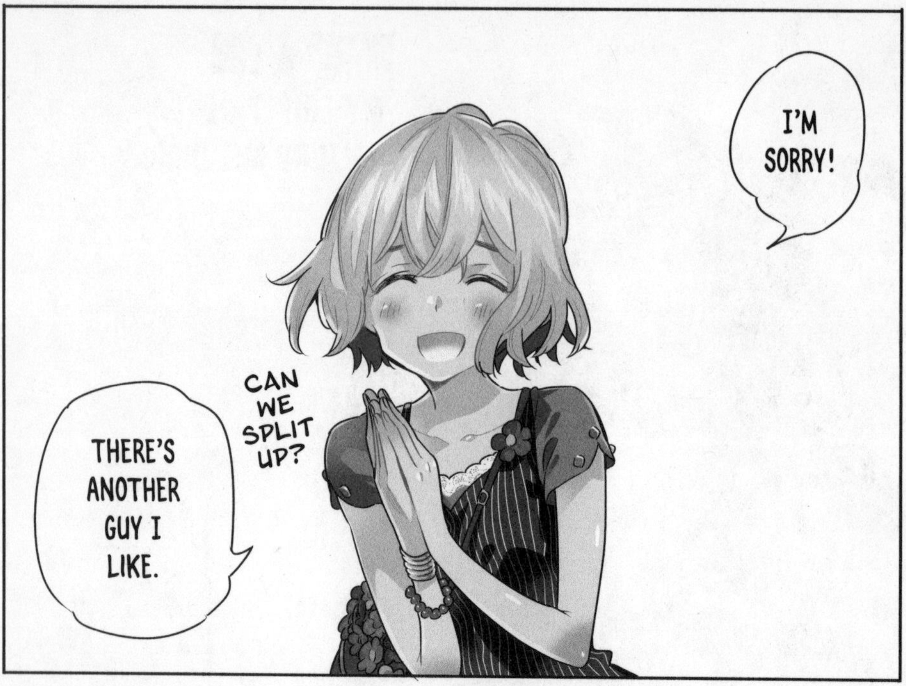
I'M SORRY!
CAN WE SPLIT UP?
THERE'S ANOTHER GUY I LIKE.
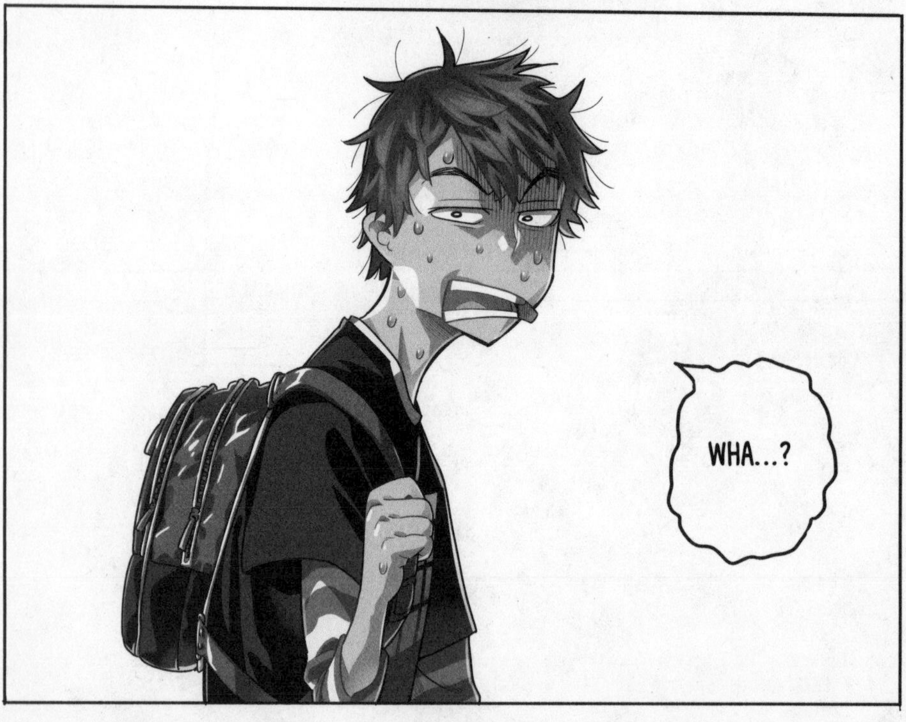
WHA...?

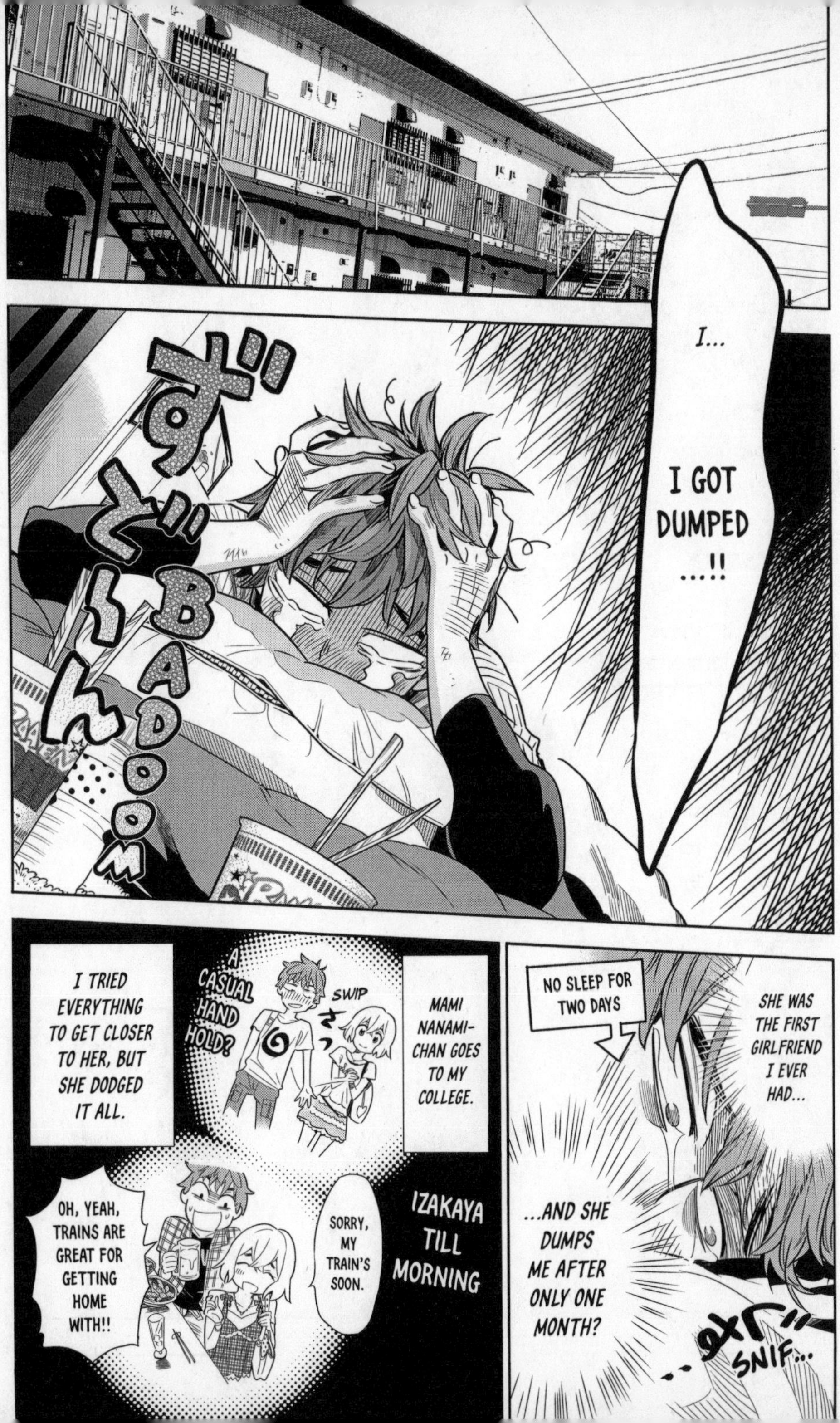
I...
I GOT DUMPED ...!!
ずどん
BADOOM
NO SLEEP FOR TWO DAYS
SHE WAS THE FIRST GIRLFRIEND I EVER HAD...
...AND SHE DUMPS ME AFTER ONLY ONE MONTH?
SNIF...
MAMI NANAMI-CHAN GOES TO MY COLLEGE.
A CASUAL HAND HOLD?
SWIP
I TRIED EVERYTHING TO GET CLOSER TO HER, BUT SHE DODGED IT ALL.
IZAKAYA TILL MORNING
SORRY, MY TRAIN'S SOON.
OH, YEAH, TRAINS ARE GREAT FOR GETTING HOME WITH!!

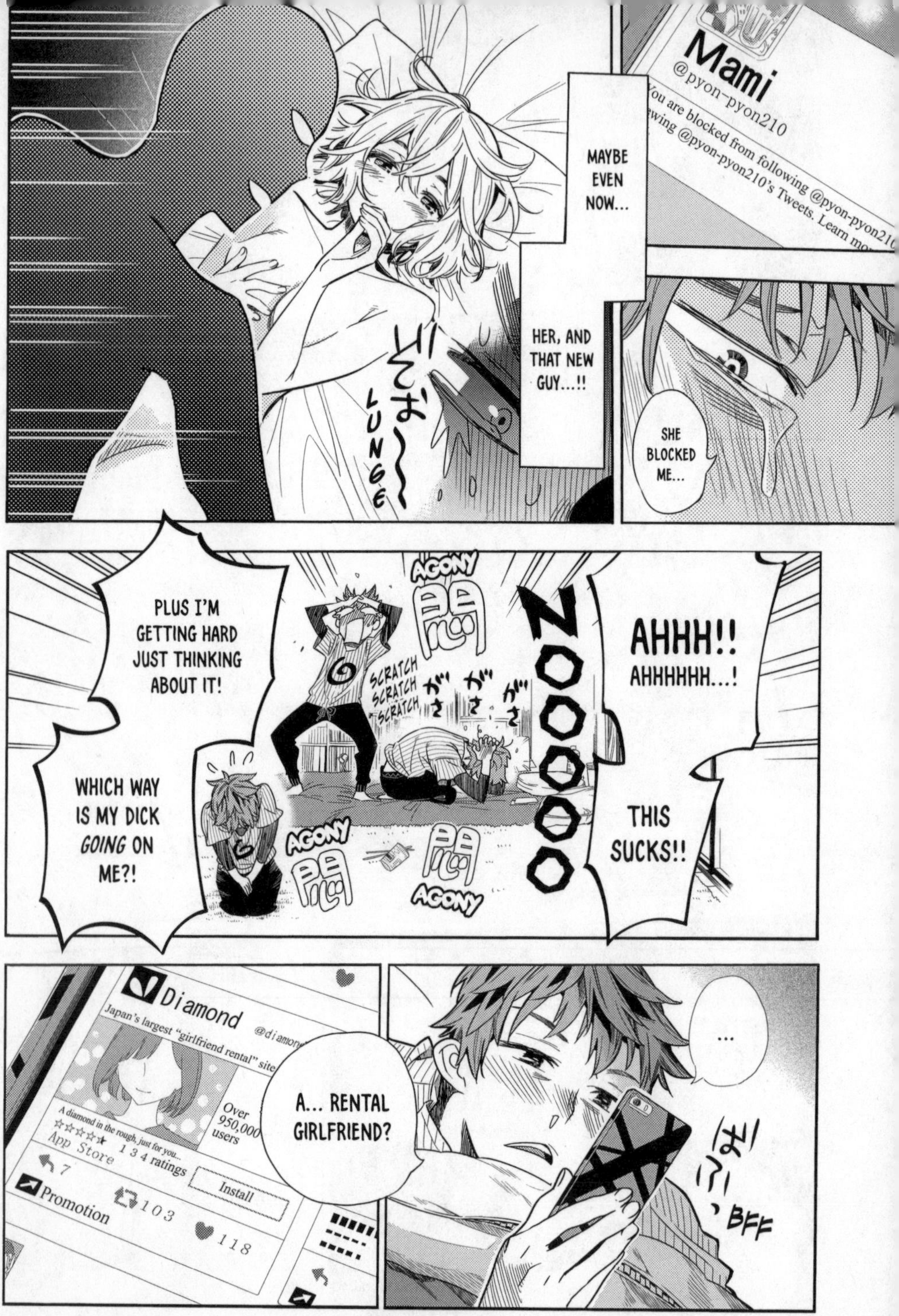

Mami
@pyon-pyon210
You are blocked from following @pyon-pyon210's Tweets. Learn mo
SHE BLOCKED ME...
MAYBE EVEN NOW...
HER, AND THAT NEW GUY...!!
どさぁ~ LUNGE
AHHH!! AHHHHHH...!
NOOOOO
THIS SUCKS!!
AGONY
SCRATCH SCRATCH SCRATCH
PLUS I'M GETTING HARD JUST THINKING ABOUT IT!
WHICH WAY IS MY DICK *GOING* ON ME?!
AGONY
AGONY
...
ぱふ BFF
A... RENTAL GIRLFRIEND?
Diamond
@diamond
Japan's largest "girlfriend rental" site
Over 950,000 users
A diamond in the rough, just for you...
App Store
1 3 4 ratings
Install
Promotion
7
103
118

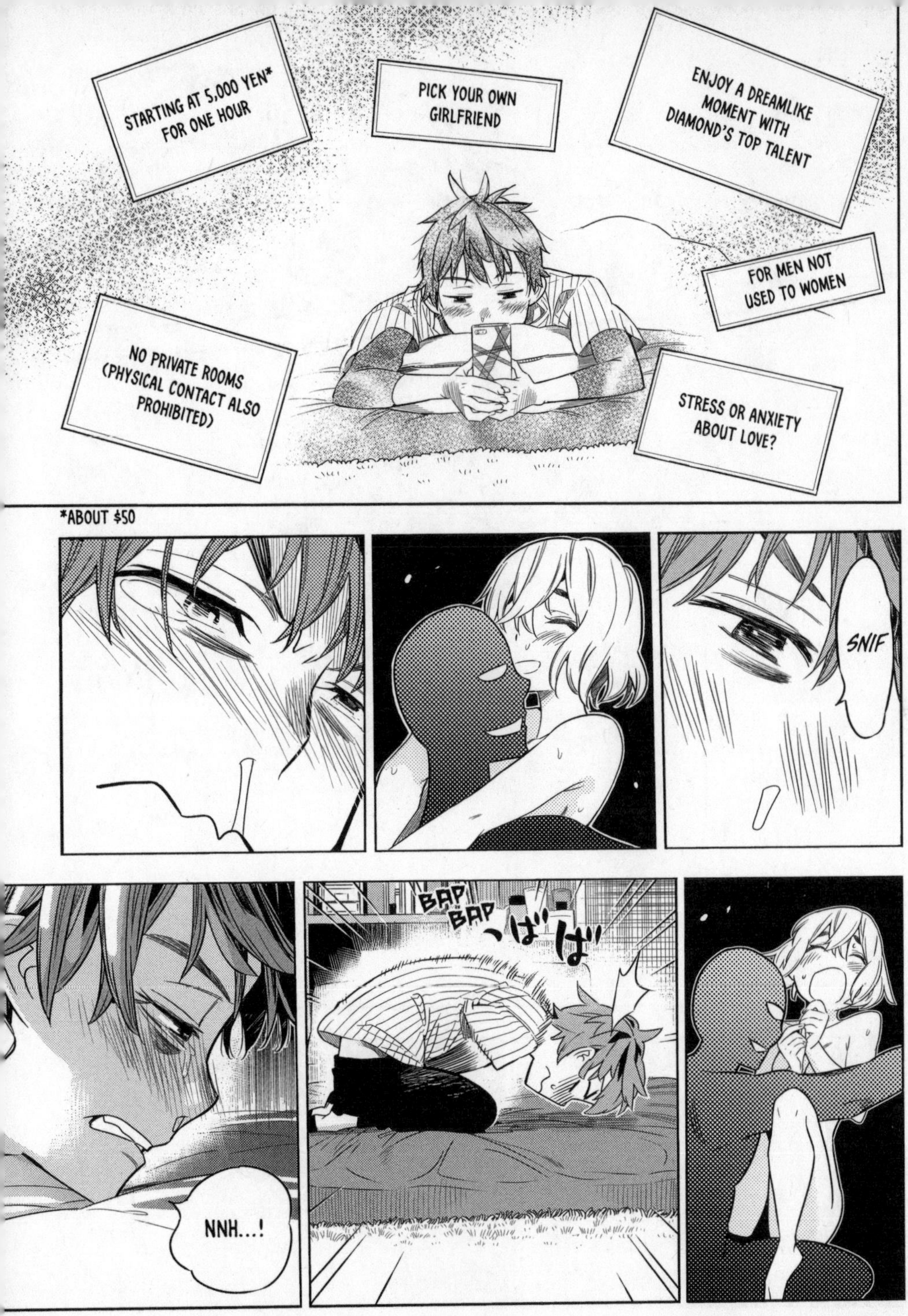
ENJOY A DREAMLIKE MOMENT WITH DIAMOND'S TOP TALENT
PICK YOUR OWN GIRLFRIEND
STARTING AT 5,000 YEN* FOR ONE HOUR
FOR MEN NOT USED TO WOMEN
STRESS OR ANXIETY ABOUT LOVE?
NO PRIVATE ROOMS (PHYSICAL CONTACT ALSO PROHIBITED)
SNIF
BAP BAP ばば
NNH...!

*ABOUT $50

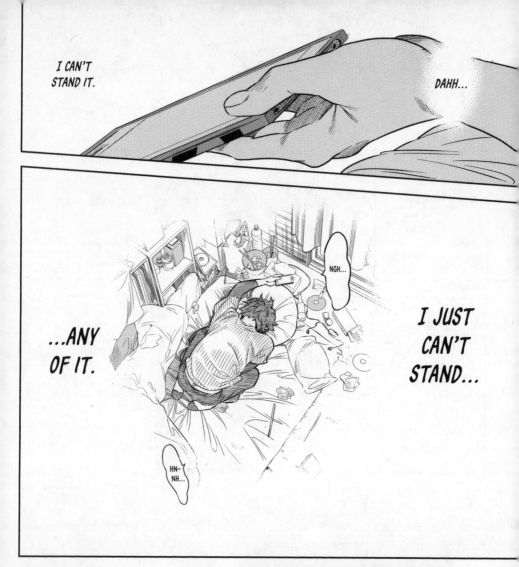

I CAN'T
STAND IT.

DAHH...

NGH...

...ANY
OF IT.

I JUST
CAN'T
STAND...

HN-
NH...

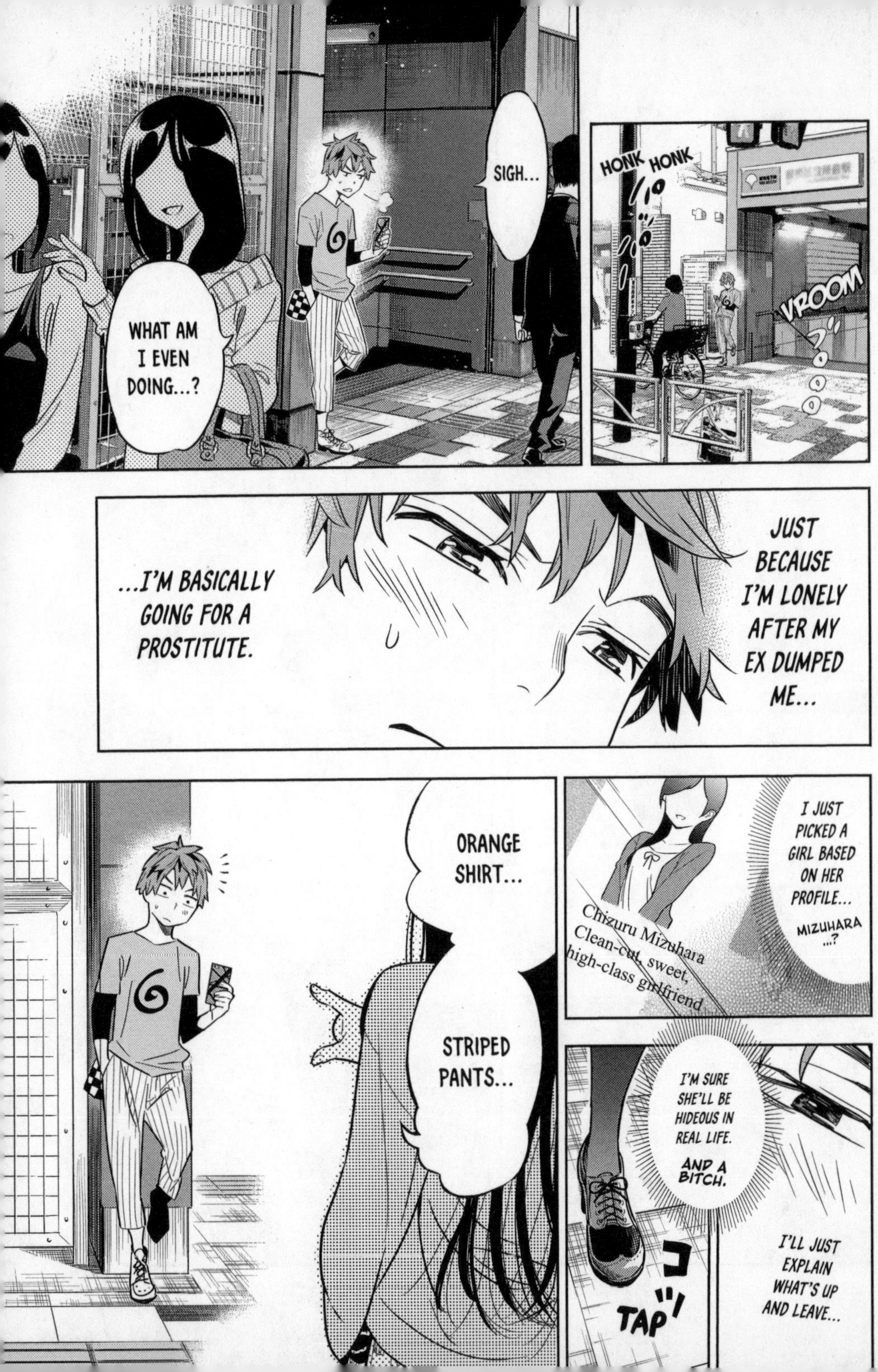
HONK HONK
VROOM
SIGH...
WHAT AM I EVEN DOING...?
JUST BECAUSE I'M LONELY AFTER MY EX DUMPED ME...
...I'M BASICALLY GOING FOR A PROSTITUTE.
I JUST PICKED A GIRL BASED ON HER PROFILE...
MIZUHARA ...?
Chizuru Mizuhara
Clean-cut, sweet,
high-class girlfriend
I'M SURE SHE'LL BE HIDEOUS IN REAL LIFE.
AND A BITCH.
I'LL JUST EXPLAIN WHAT'S UP AND LEAVE...
TAP
ORANGE SHIRT...
STRIPED PANTS...

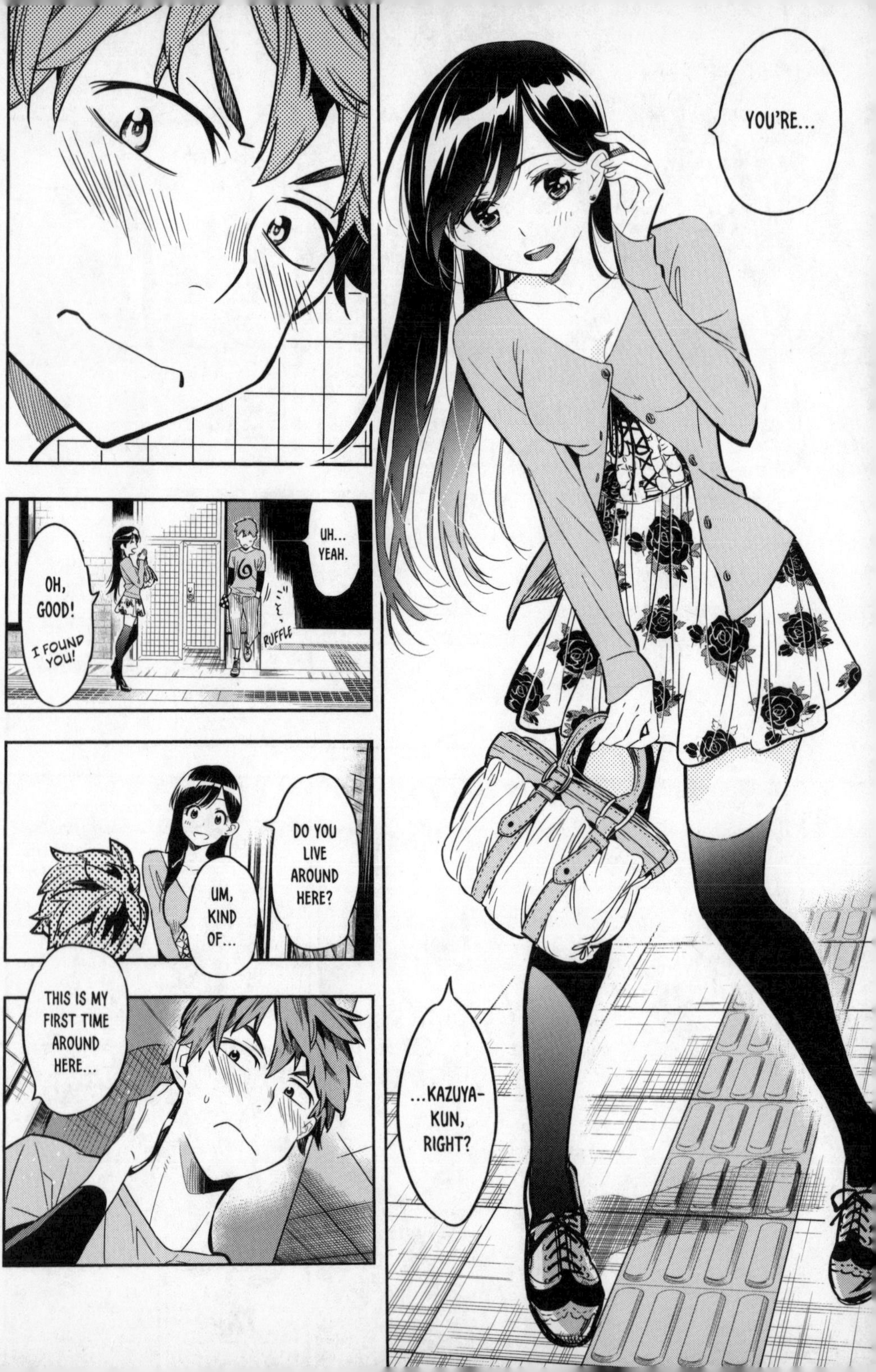
YOU'RE...
...KAZUYA-KUN, RIGHT?
UH... YEAH.
OH, GOOD!
I FOUND YOU!
RUFFLE
DO YOU LIVE AROUND HERE?
UM, KIND OF...
THIS IS MY FIRST TIME AROUND HERE...

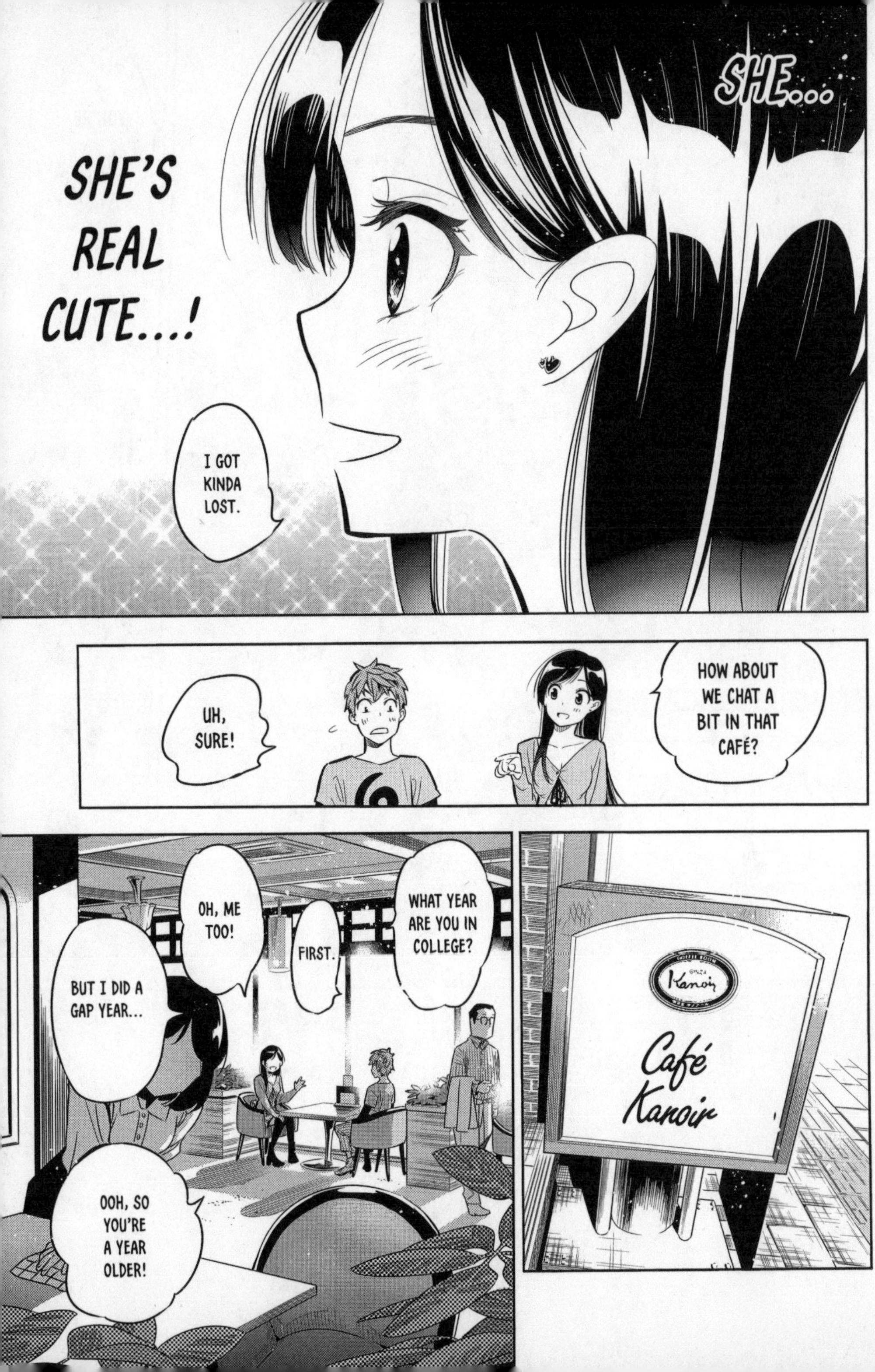
SHE...
SHE'S REAL CUTE...!
I GOT KINDA LOST.
HOW ABOUT WE CHAT A BIT IN THAT CAFÉ?
UH, SURE!
Kanoir
Café Kanoir
WHAT YEAR ARE YOU IN COLLEGE?
FIRST.
OH, ME TOO!
BUT I DID A GAP YEAR...
OOH, SO YOU'RE A YEAR OLDER!

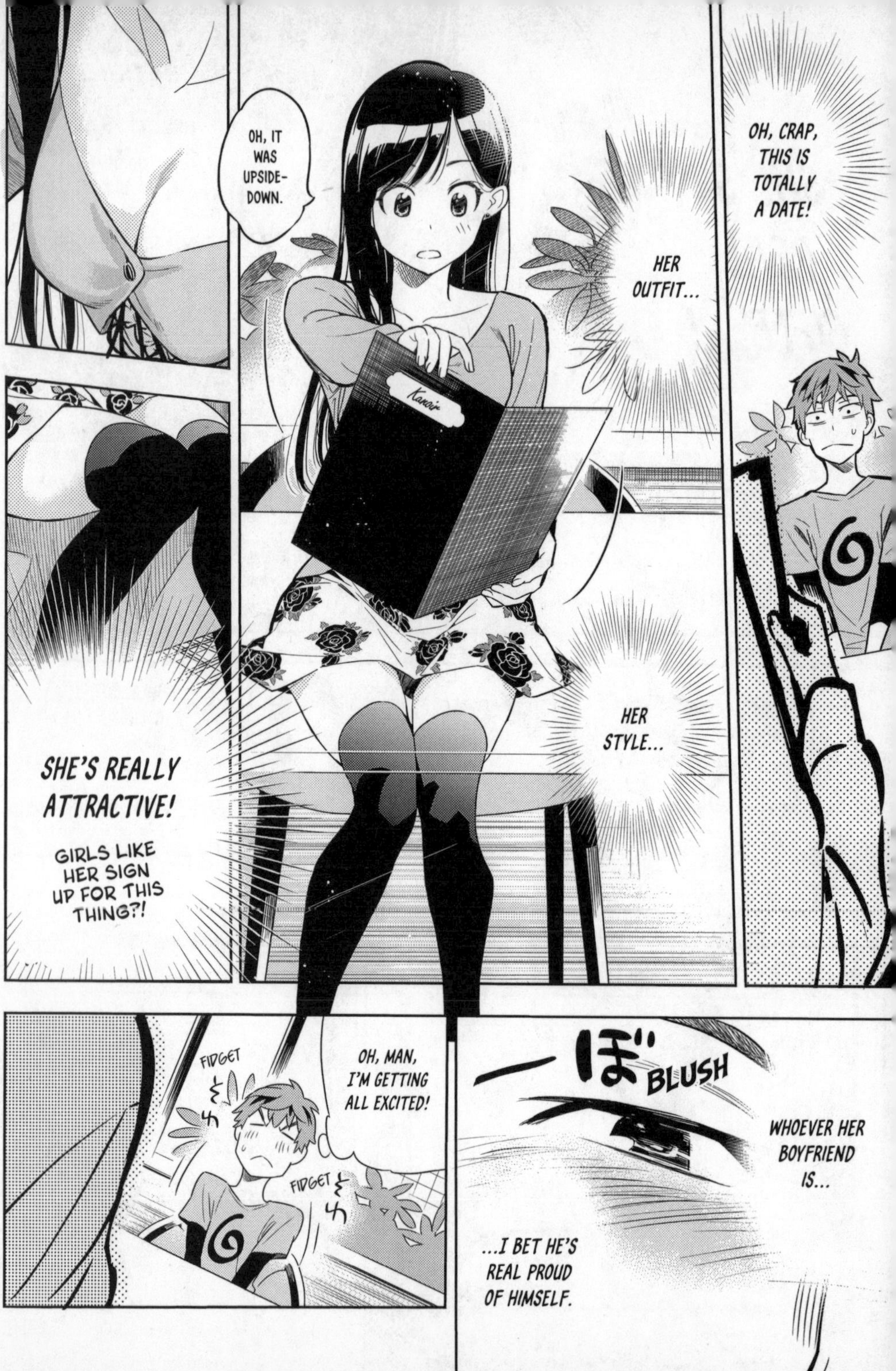
OH, CRAP, THIS IS TOTALLY A DATE!
OH, IT WAS UPSIDE-DOWN.
HER OUTFIT...
HER STYLE...
SHE'S REALLY ATTRACTIVE!
GIRLS LIKE HER SIGN UP FOR THIS THING?!
ぼ
BLUSH
WHOEVER HER BOYFRIEND IS...
...I BET HE'S REAL PROUD OF HIMSELF.
OH, MAN, I'M GETTING ALL EXCITED!
FIDGET
FIDGET

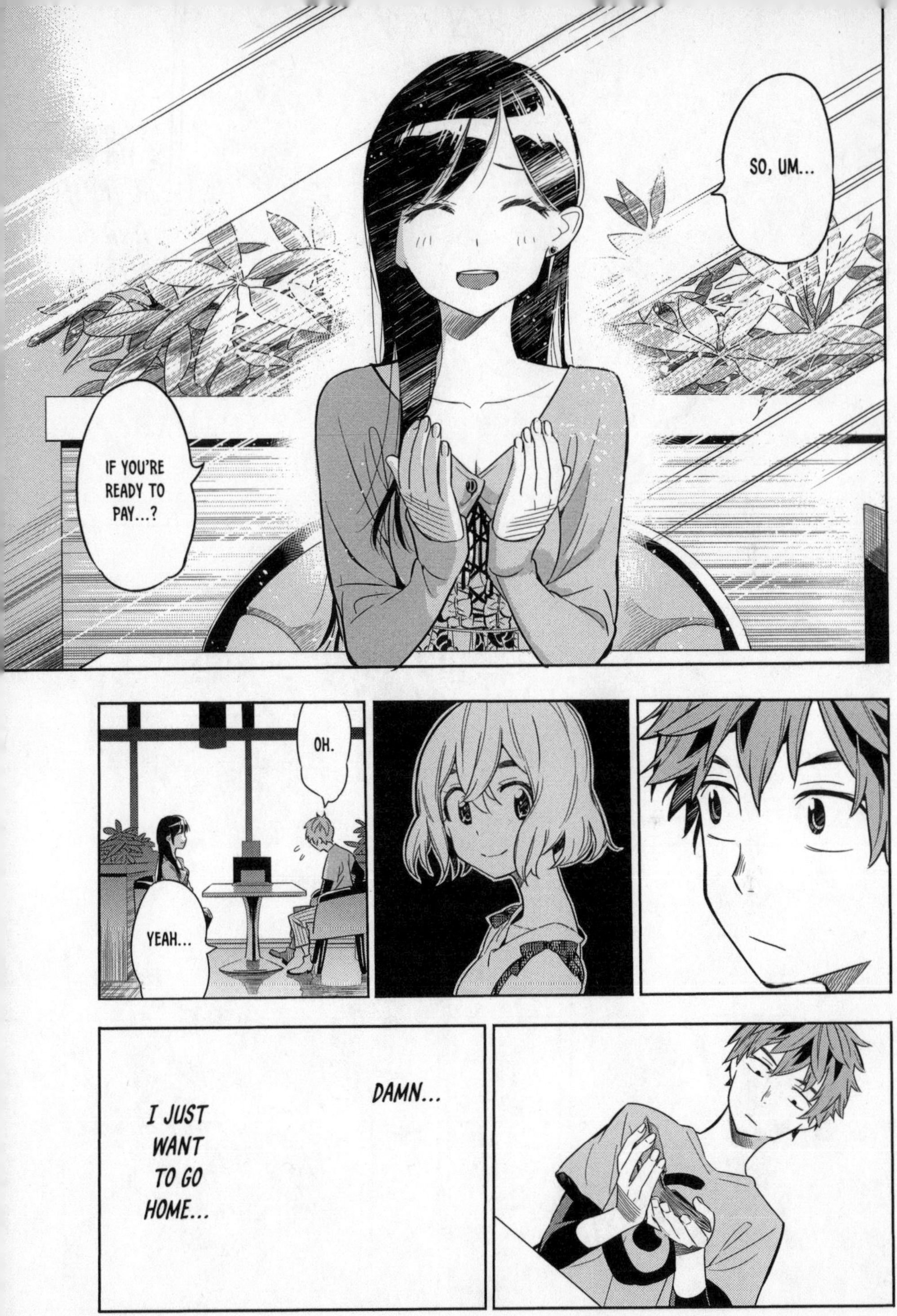
SO, UM...
IF YOU'RE READY TO PAY...?
OH.
YEAH...
DAMN...
I JUST WANT TO GO HOME...

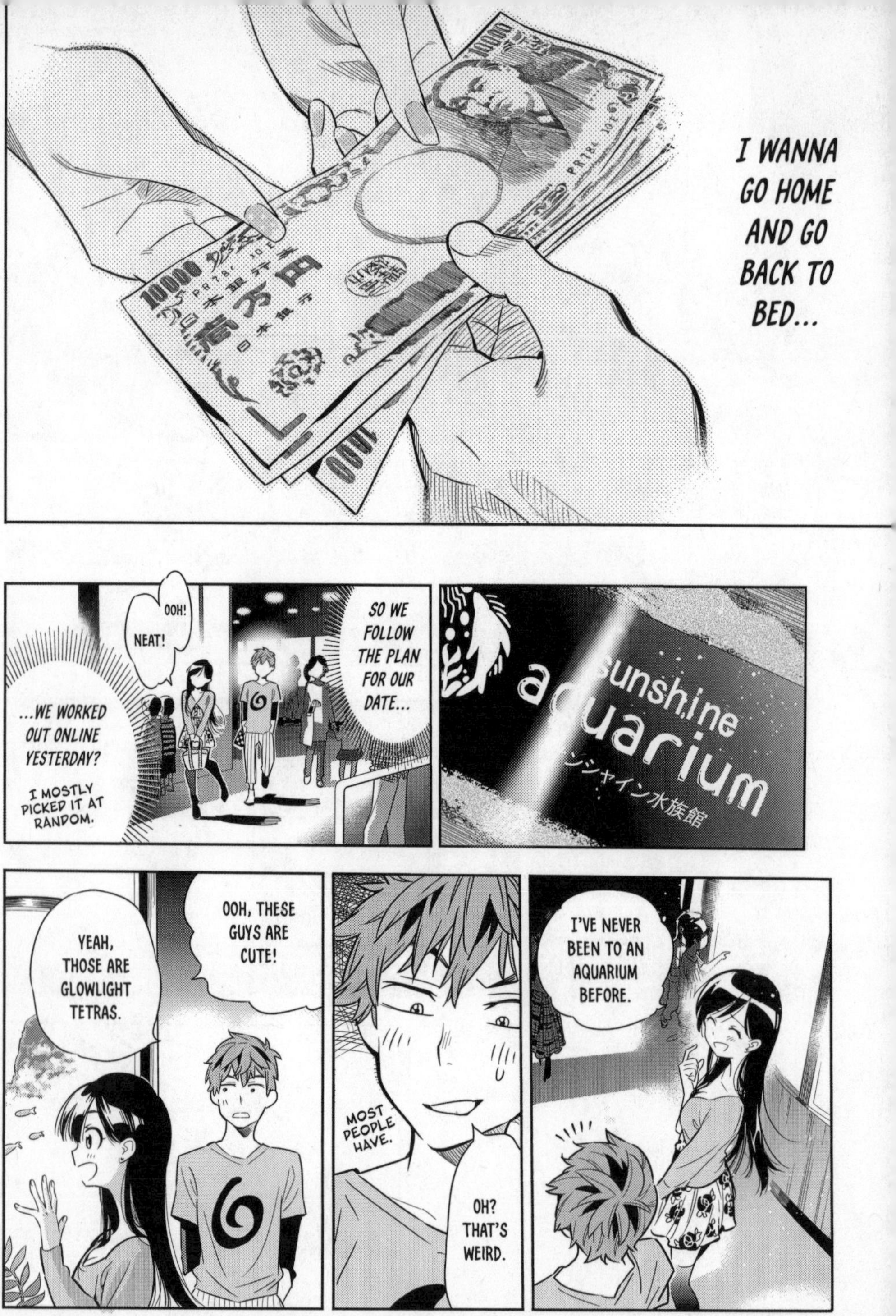
I WANNA GO HOME AND GO BACK TO BED...
sunshine aquarium
ンシャイン水族館
SO WE FOLLOW THE PLAN FOR OUR DATE...
OOH! NEAT!
...WE WORKED OUT ONLINE YESTERDAY?
I MOSTLY PICKED IT AT RANDOM.
I'VE NEVER BEEN TO AN AQUARIUM BEFORE.
OH? THAT'S WEIRD.
MOST PEOPLE HAVE.
OOH, THESE GUYS ARE CUTE!
YEAH, THOSE ARE GLOWLIGHT TETRAS.

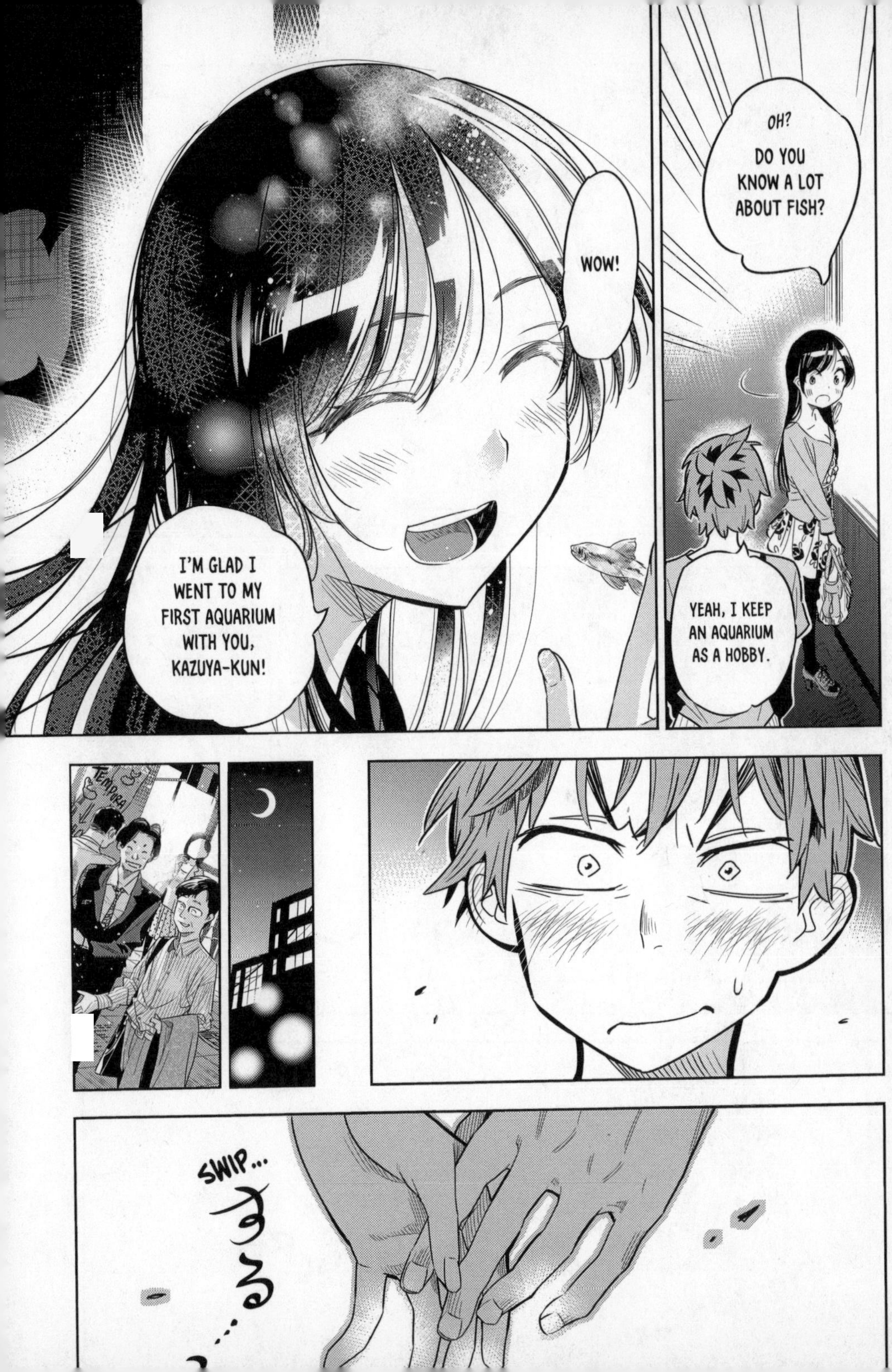
OH? DO YOU KNOW A LOT ABOUT FISH?
YEAH, I KEEP AN AQUARIUM AS A HOBBY.
WOW!
I'M GLAD I WENT TO MY FIRST AQUARIUM WITH YOU, KAZUYA-KUN!
TEMPURA
SWIP...
する...

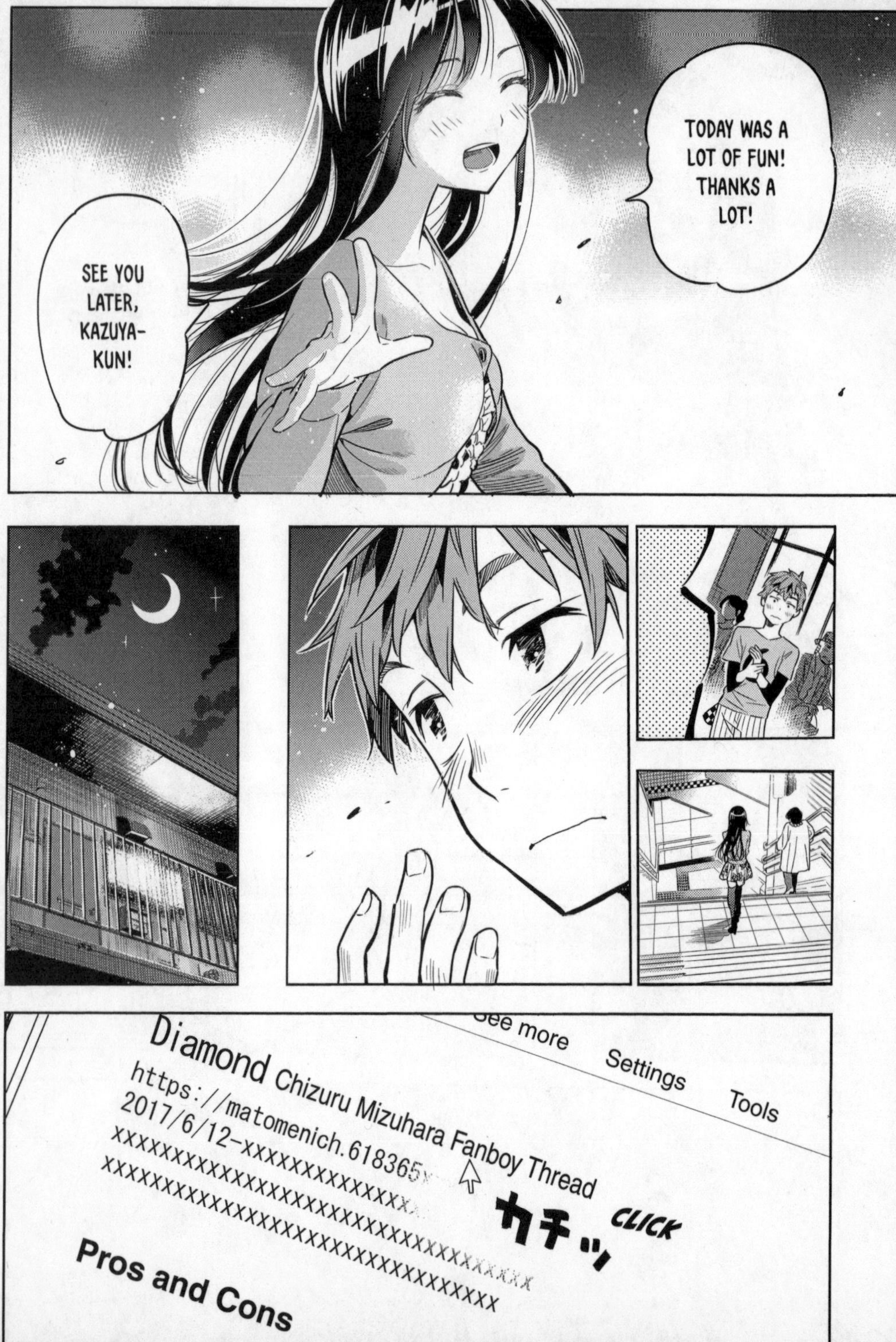
TODAY WAS A LOT OF FUN! THANKS A LOT!
SEE YOU LATER, KAZUYA-KUN!
See more
Settings
Tools
Diamond Chizuru Mizuhara Fanboy Thread
https://matomenich.618365
2017/6/12-
Pros and Cons
カチッ
CLICK

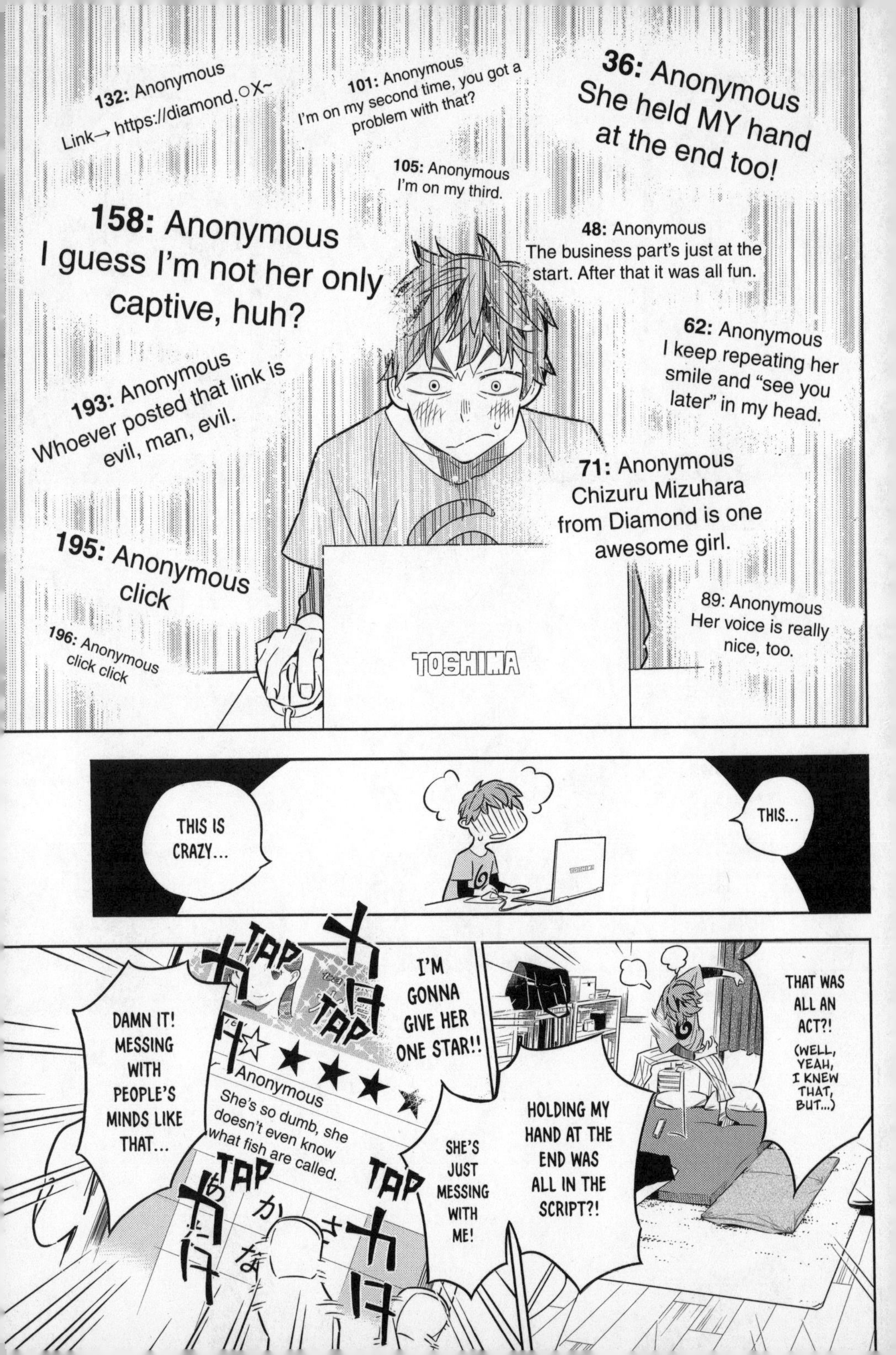
36: Anonymous
She held MY hand at the end too!
101: Anonymous
I'm on my second time, you got a problem with that?
132: Anonymous
Link→ https://diamond.○X~
105: Anonymous
I'm on my third.
48: Anonymous
The business part's just at the start. After that it was all fun.
158: Anonymous
I guess I'm not her only captive, huh?
62: Anonymous
I keep repeating her smile and "see you later" in my head.
193: Anonymous
Whoever posted that link is evil, man, evil.
71: Anonymous
Chizuru Mizuhara from Diamond is one awesome girl.
195: Anonymous
click
89: Anonymous
Her voice is really nice, too.
196: Anonymous
click click
TOSHIMA
THIS...
THIS IS CRAZY...
THAT WAS ALL AN ACT?!
(WELL, YEAH, I KNEW THAT, BUT...)
HOLDING MY HAND AT THE END WAS ALL IN THE SCRIPT?!
SHE'S JUST MESSING WITH ME!
I'M GONNA GIVE HER ONE STAR!!
TAP
TAP
☆★★★★
Anonymous
She's so dumb, she doesn't even know what fish are called.
TAP
TAP
DAMN IT! MESSING WITH PEOPLE'S MINDS LIKE THAT...

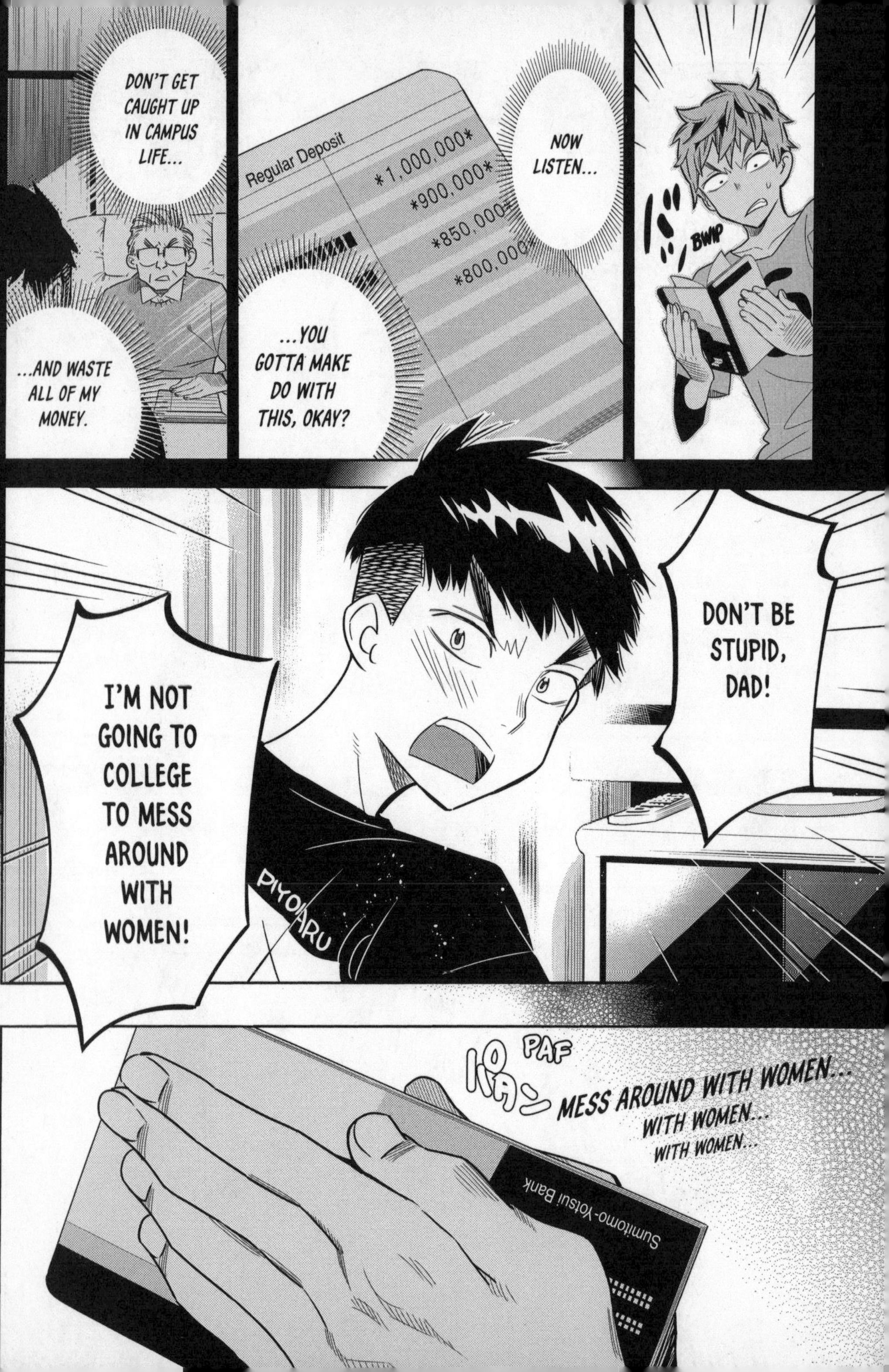
BWIP
NOW LISTEN...
Regular Deposit
1,000,000
900,000
850,000
800,000
...YOU GOTTA MAKE DO WITH THIS, OKAY?
DON'T GET CAUGHT UP IN CAMPUS LIFE...
...AND WASTE ALL OF MY MONEY.
DON'T BE STUPID, DAD!
I'M NOT GOING TO COLLEGE TO MESS AROUND WITH WOMEN!
PAF
MESS AROUND WITH WOMEN...
WITH WOMEN...
WITH WOMEN...
Sumitomo-Yotsui Bank

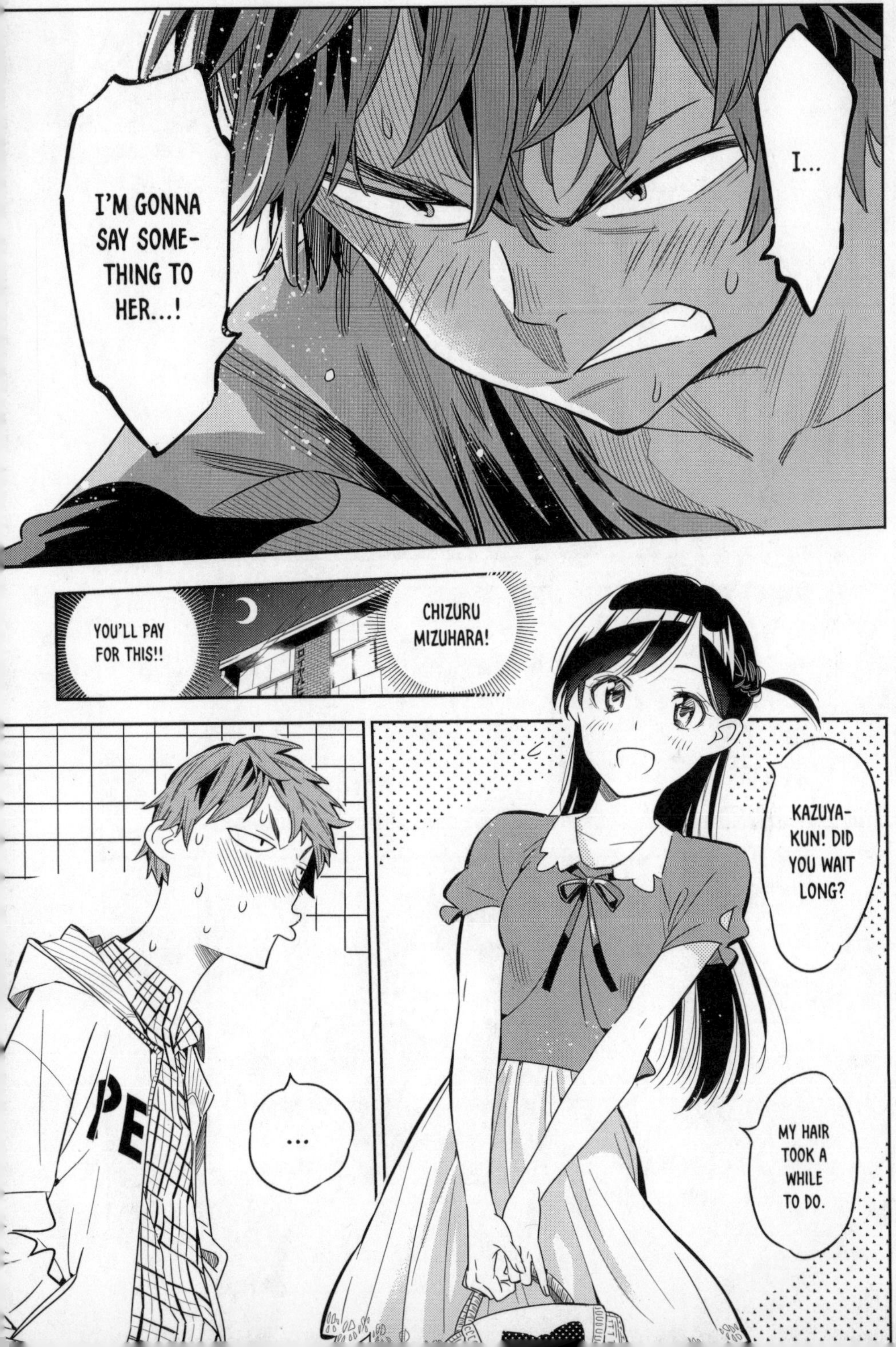
I...
I'M GONNA SAY SOME-THING TO HER...!
CHIZURU MIZUHARA!
YOU'LL PAY FOR THIS!!
KAZUYA-KUN! DID YOU WAIT LONG?
MY HAIR TOOK A WHILE TO DO.
...
PE

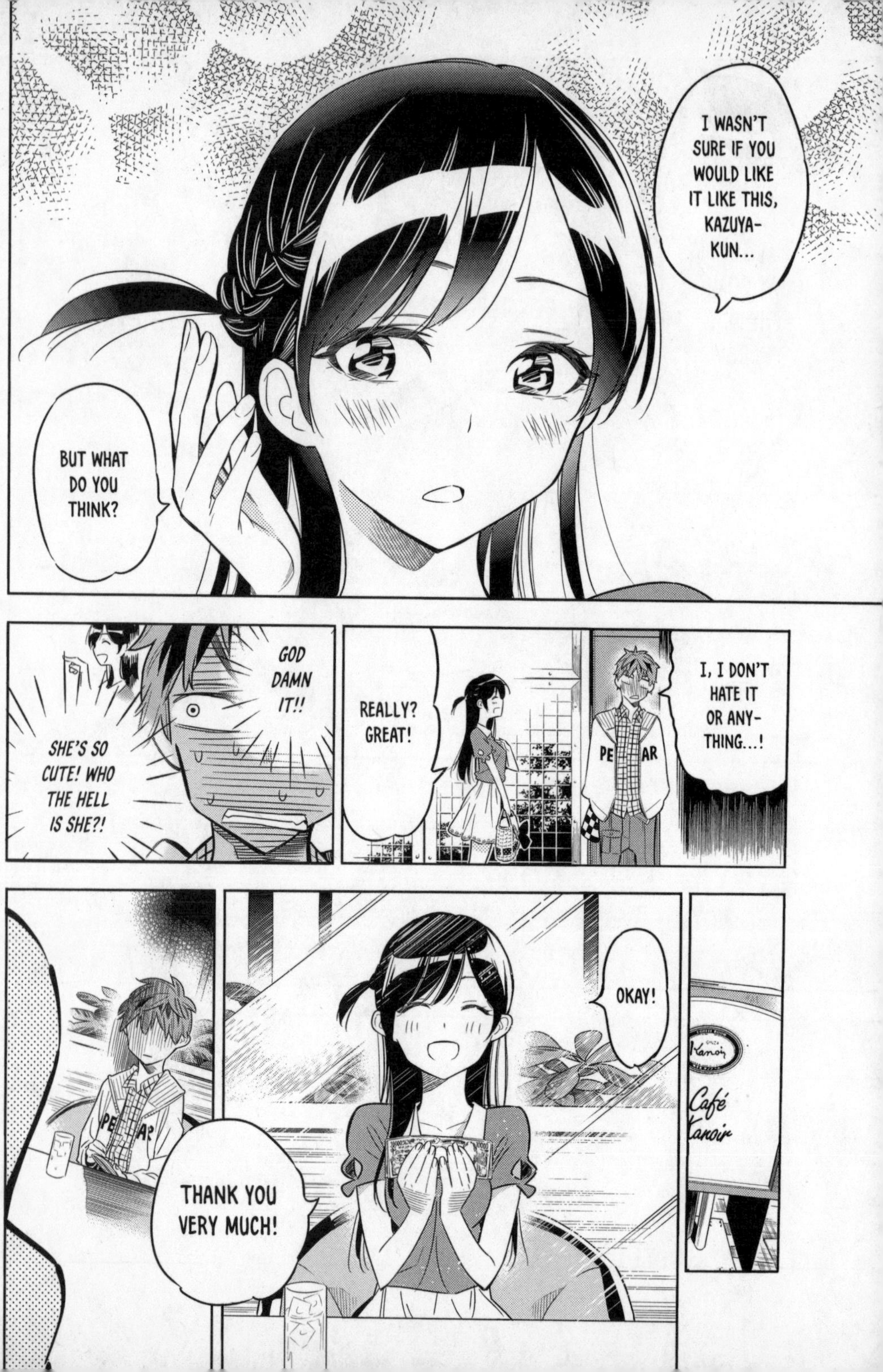
I WASN'T SURE IF YOU WOULD LIKE IT LIKE THIS, KAZUYA-KUN...
BUT WHAT DO YOU THINK?
I, I DON'T HATE IT OR ANY-THING...!
REALLY? GREAT!
GOD DAMN IT!!
SHE'S SO CUTE! WHO THE HELL IS SHE?!
Café Kanoir
OKAY!
THANK YOU VERY MUCH!

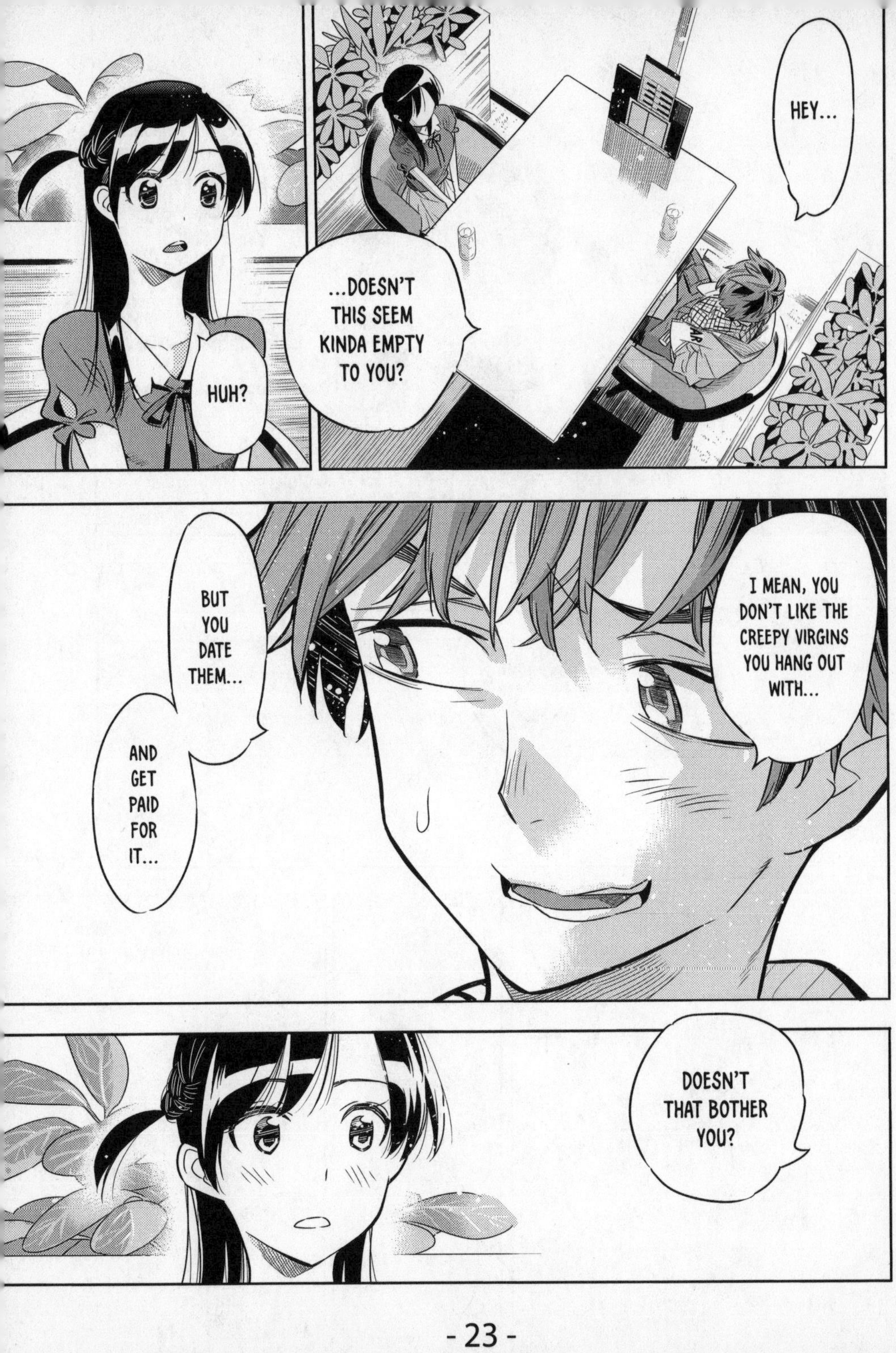
HEY...
...DOESN'T THIS SEEM KINDA EMPTY TO YOU?
HUH?
I MEAN, YOU DON'T LIKE THE CREEPY VIRGINS YOU HANG OUT WITH...
BUT YOU DATE THEM...
AND GET PAID FOR IT...
DOESN'T THAT BOTHER YOU?

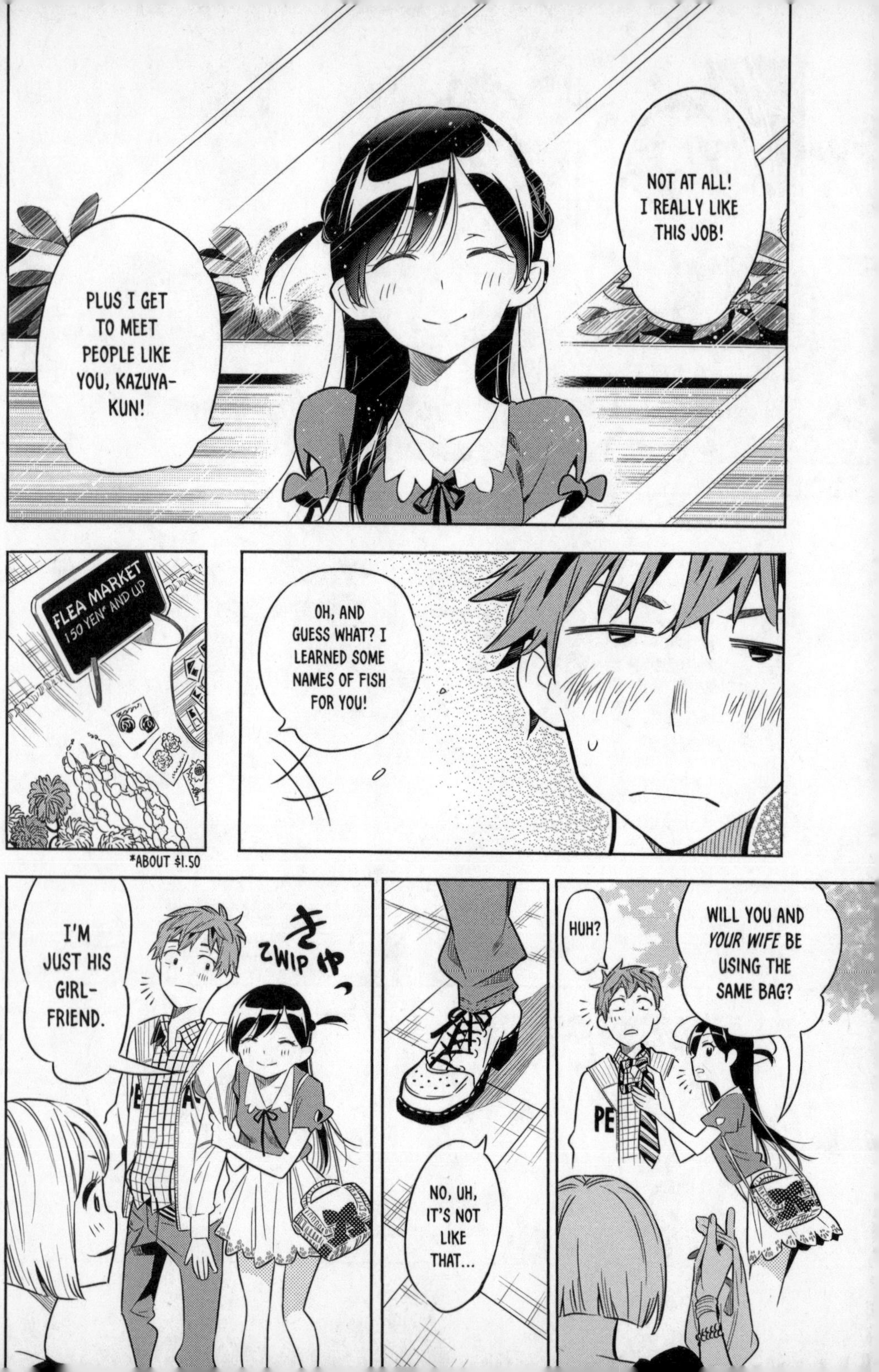
NOT AT ALL! I REALLY LIKE THIS JOB!
PLUS I GET TO MEET PEOPLE LIKE YOU, KAZUYA-KUN!
OH, AND GUESS WHAT? I LEARNED SOME NAMES OF FISH FOR YOU!
FLEA MARKET 150 YEN* AND UP
WILL YOU AND *YOUR WIFE* BE USING THE SAME BAG?
HUH?
NO, UH, IT'S NOT LIKE THAT...
ZWIP
I'M JUST HIS GIRL-FRIEND.
*ABOUT $1.50

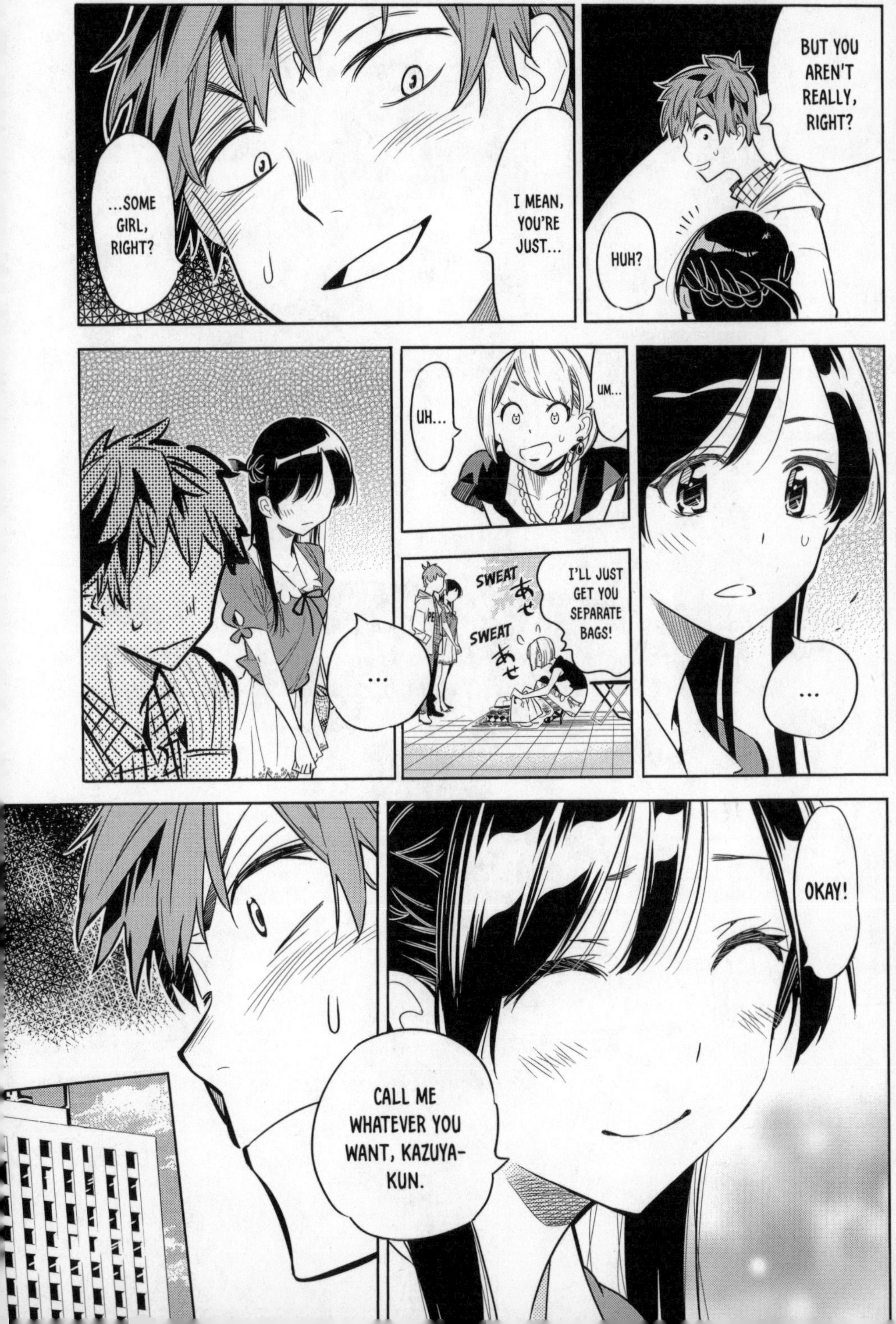
BUT YOU AREN'T REALLY, RIGHT?
HUH?
I MEAN, YOU'RE JUST...
...SOME GIRL, RIGHT?
...
UM...
UH...
I'LL JUST GET YOU SEPARATE BAGS!
SWEAT あせ
SWEAT あせ
...
OKAY!
CALL ME WHATEVER YOU WANT, KAZUYA-KUN.

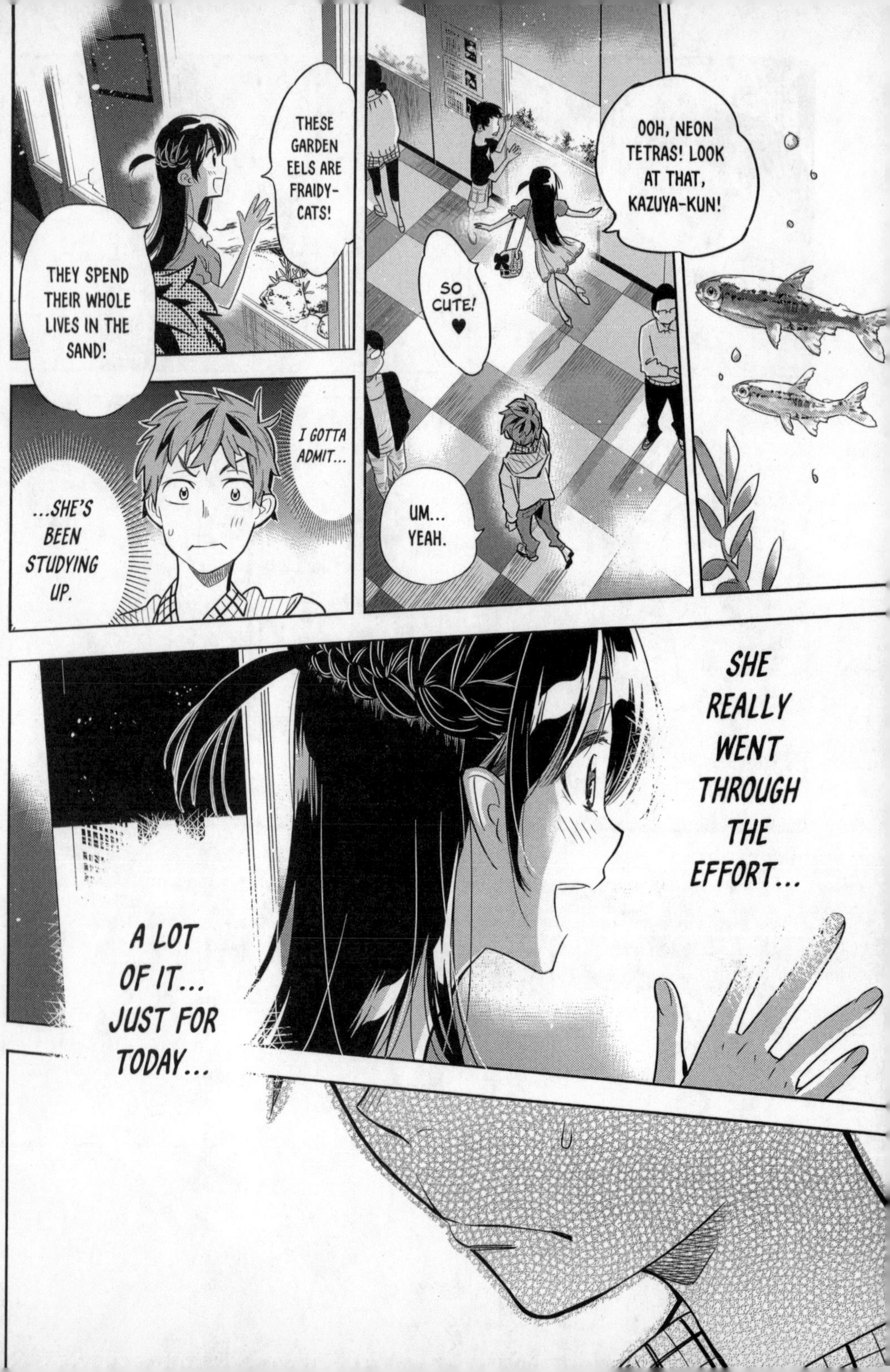
OOH, NEON TETRAS! LOOK AT THAT, KAZUYA-KUN!
SO CUTE! ♥
UM... YEAH.
THESE GARDEN EELS ARE FRAIDY-CATS!
THEY SPEND THEIR WHOLE LIVES IN THE SAND!
I GOTTA ADMIT...
...SHE'S BEEN STUDYING UP.
SHE REALLY WENT THROUGH THE EFFORT...
A LOT OF IT... JUST FOR TODAY...

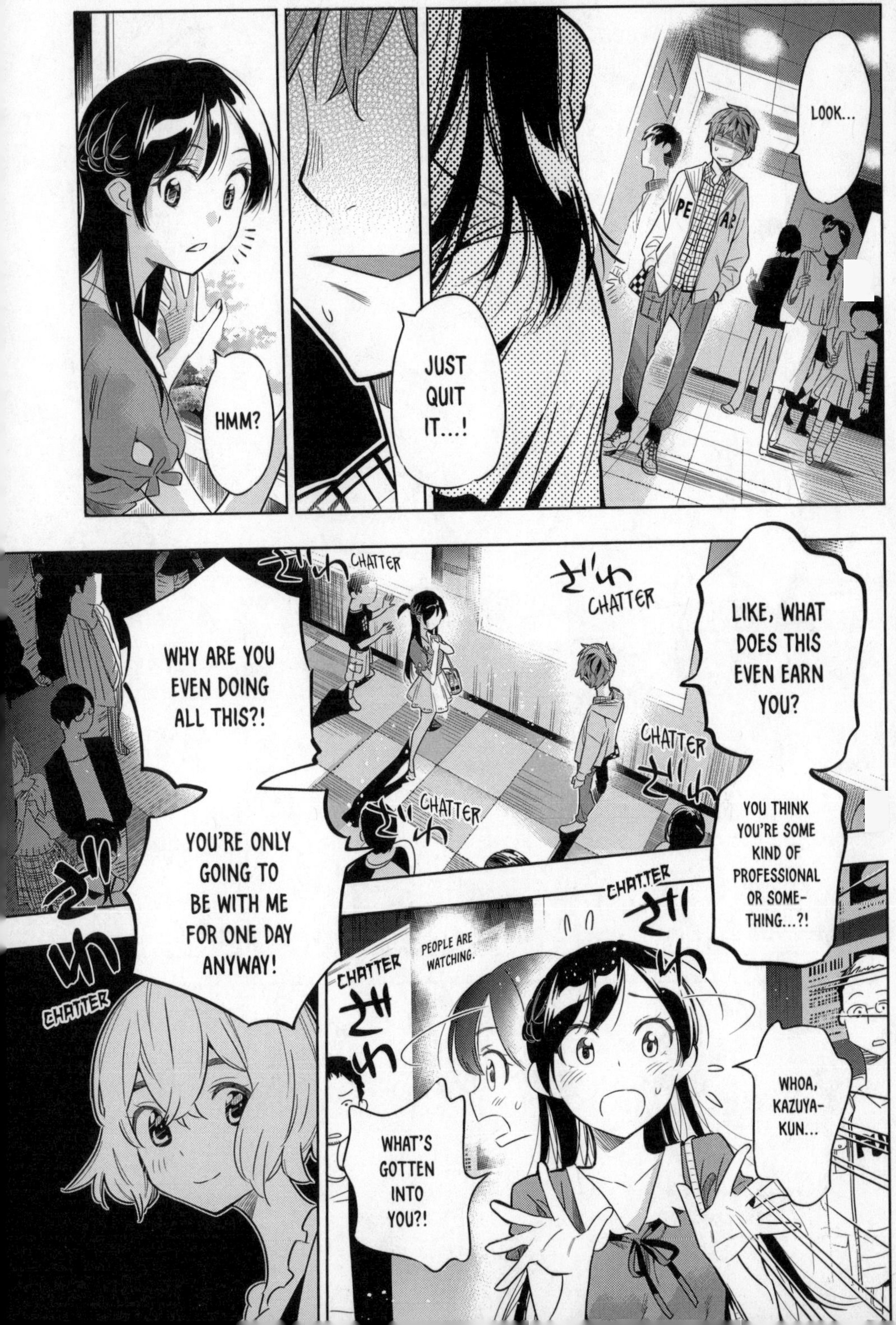
LOOK...
JUST QUIT IT...!
HMM?
LIKE, WHAT DOES THIS EVEN EARN YOU?
ざわ
CHATTER
CHATTER
ざわ
CHATTER
WHY ARE YOU EVEN DOING ALL THIS?!
ざわ
CHATTER
YOU THINK YOU'RE SOME KIND OF PROFESSIONAL OR SOME-THING...?!
YOU'RE ONLY GOING TO BE WITH ME FOR ONE DAY ANYWAY!
ざわ
CHATTER
CHATTER
ざわ
WHOA, KAZUYA-KUN...
PEOPLE ARE WATCHING.
CHATTER
ざわ
WHAT'S GOTTEN INTO YOU?!

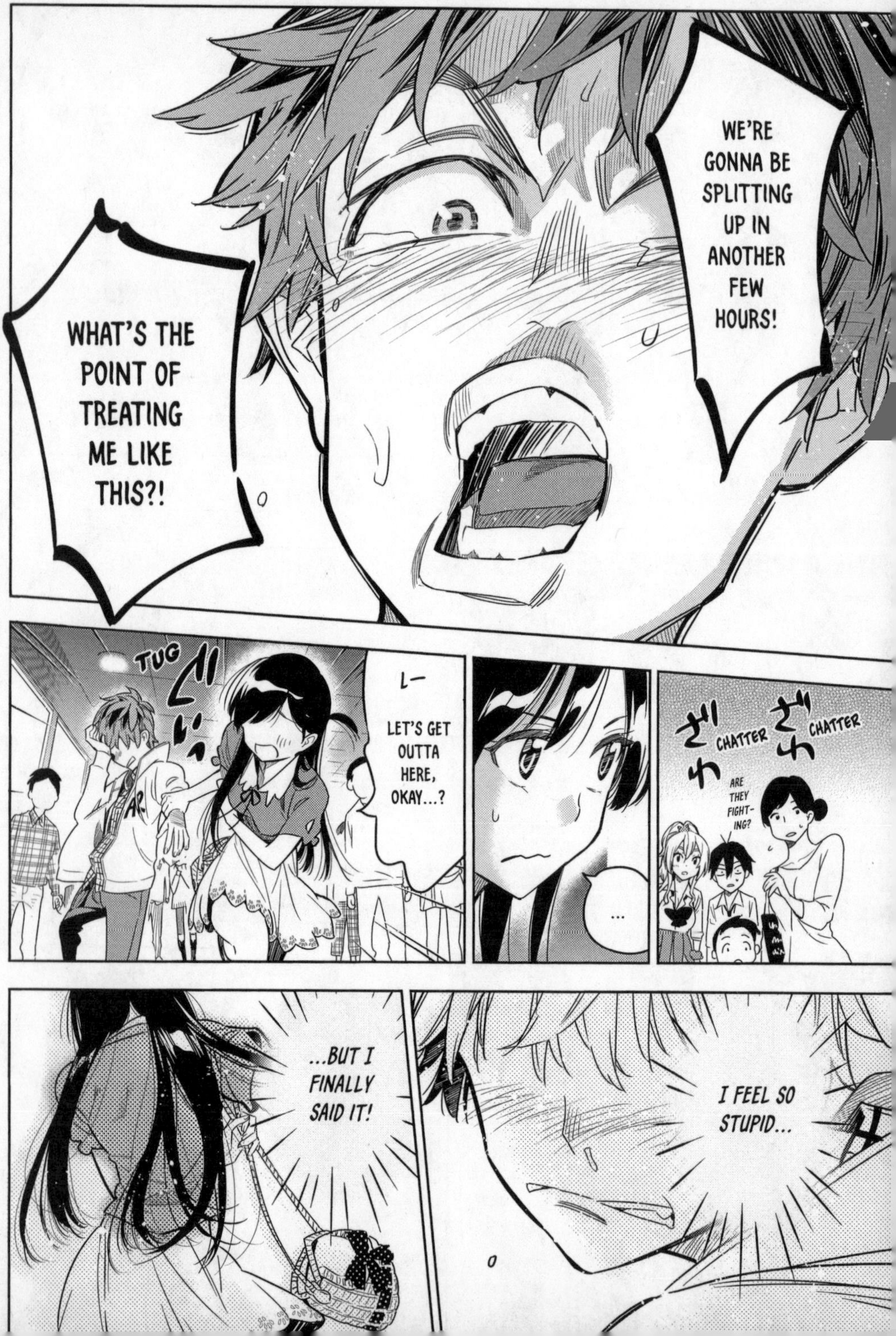
WE'RE GONNA BE SPLITTING UP IN ANOTHER FEW HOURS!
WHAT'S THE POINT OF TREATING ME LIKE THIS?!
ざわ CHATTER
ざわ CHATTER
ARE THEY FIGHT-ING?
...
LET'S GET OUTTA HERE, OKAY...?
TUG
I FEEL SO STUPID...
...BUT I FINALLY SAID IT!

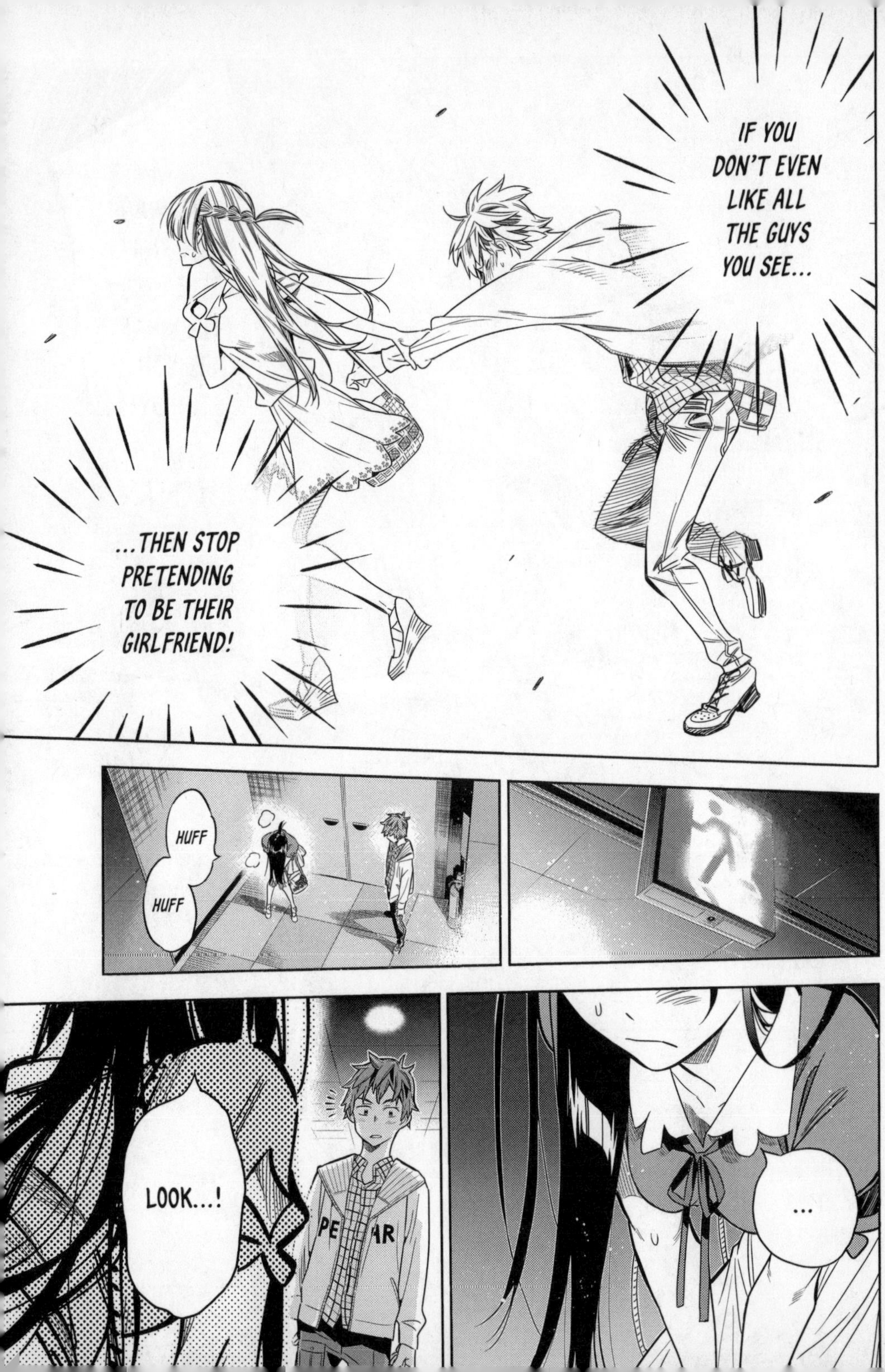
IF YOU DON'T EVEN LIKE ALL THE GUYS YOU SEE...
...THEN STOP PRETENDING TO BE THEIR GIRLFRIEND!
HUFF
HUFF
...
LOOK...!

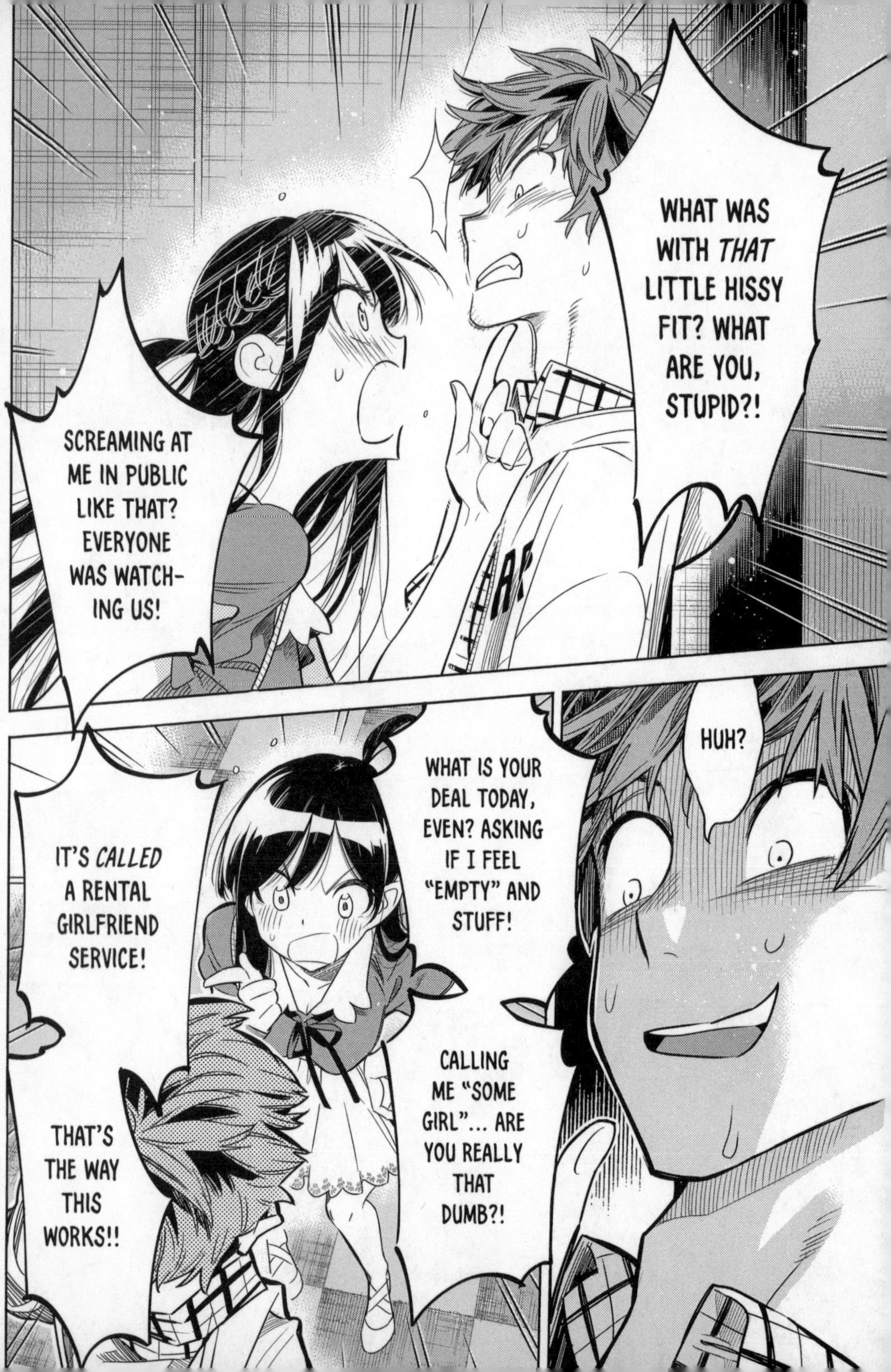
WHAT WAS WITH *THAT* LITTLE HISSY FIT? WHAT ARE YOU, STUPID?!
SCREAMING AT ME IN PUBLIC LIKE THAT? EVERYONE WAS WATCH-ING US!
HUH?
WHAT IS YOUR DEAL TODAY, EVEN? ASKING IF I FEEL "EMPTY" AND STUFF!
CALLING ME "SOME GIRL"... ARE YOU REALLY THAT DUMB?!
IT'S *CALLED* A RENTAL GIRLFRIEND SERVICE!
THAT'S THE WAY THIS WORKS!!

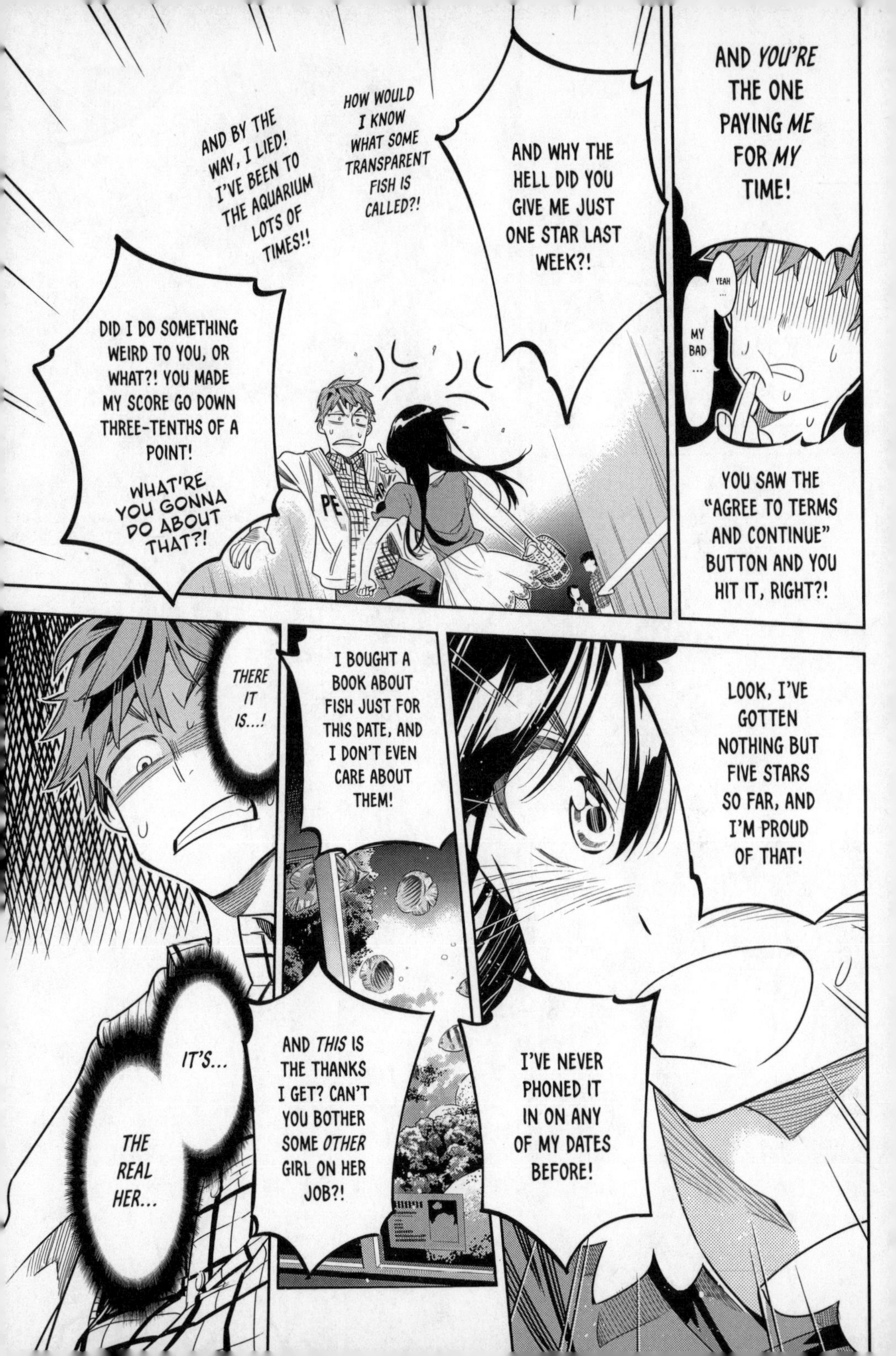

AND *YOU'RE* THE ONE PAYING *ME* FOR *MY* TIME!
YEAH...
MY BAD...
YOU SAW THE "AGREE TO TERMS AND CONTINUE" BUTTON AND YOU HIT IT, RIGHT?!
AND WHY THE HELL DID YOU GIVE ME JUST ONE STAR LAST WEEK?!
HOW WOULD I KNOW WHAT SOME TRANSPARENT FISH IS CALLED?!
AND BY THE WAY, I LIED! I'VE BEEN TO THE AQUARIUM LOTS OF TIMES!!
DID I DO SOMETHING WEIRD TO YOU, OR WHAT?! YOU MADE MY SCORE GO DOWN THREE-TENTHS OF A POINT!
WHAT'RE YOU GONNA DO ABOUT THAT?!
LOOK, I'VE GOTTEN NOTHING BUT FIVE STARS SO FAR, AND I'M PROUD OF THAT!
I'VE NEVER PHONED IT IN ON ANY OF MY DATES BEFORE!
I BOUGHT A BOOK ABOUT FISH JUST FOR THIS DATE, AND I DON'T EVEN CARE ABOUT THEM!
AND *THIS* IS THE THANKS I GET? CAN'T YOU BOTHER SOME *OTHER* GIRL ON HER JOB?!
THERE IT IS...!
IT'S...
THE REAL HER...

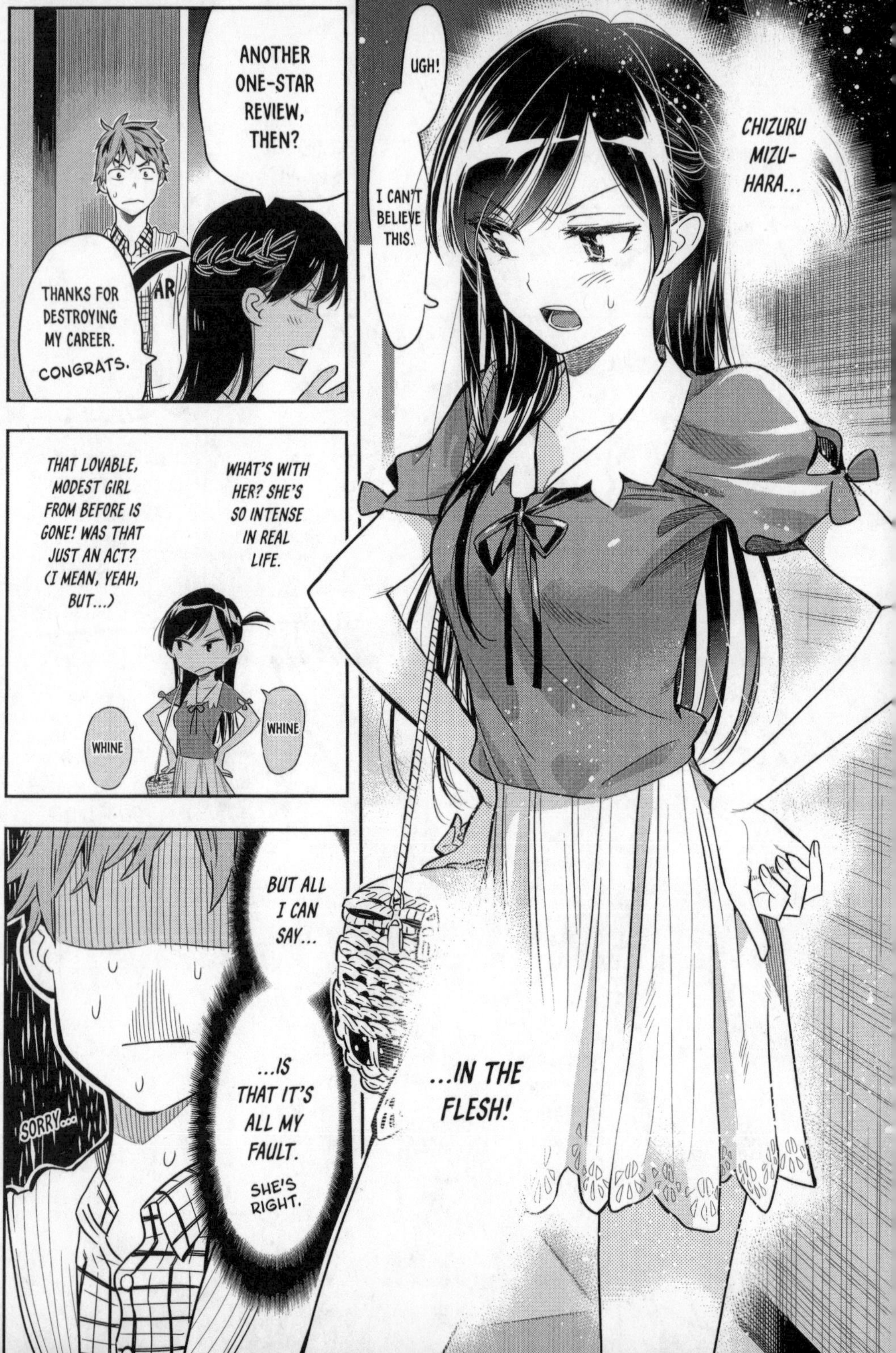
CHIZURU MIZUHARA...
UGH!
I CAN'T BELIEVE THIS.
...IN THE FLESH!
ANOTHER ONE-STAR REVIEW, THEN?
THANKS FOR DESTROYING MY CAREER. CONGRATS.
WHAT'S WITH HER? SHE'S SO INTENSE IN REAL LIFE.
THAT LOVABLE, MODEST GIRL FROM BEFORE IS GONE! WAS THAT JUST AN ACT? (I MEAN, YEAH, BUT...)
WHINE
WHINE
BUT ALL I CAN SAY...
...IS THAT IT'S ALL MY FAULT.
SHE'S RIGHT.
SORRY...

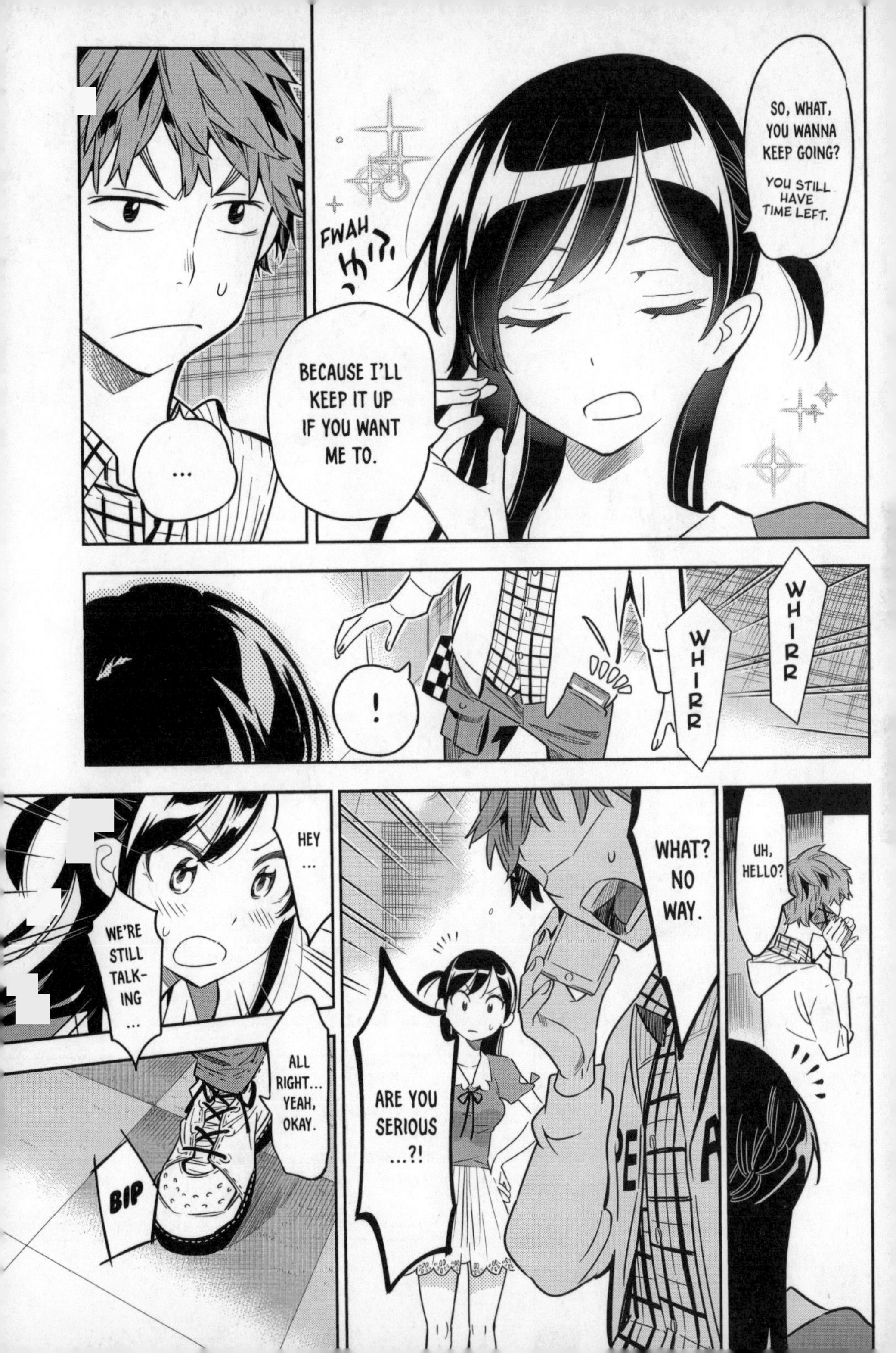
SO, WHAT, YOU WANNA KEEP GOING?
YOU STILL HAVE TIME LEFT.
FWAH
BECAUSE I'LL KEEP IT UP IF YOU WANT ME TO.
...
WHIRR
WHIRR
!
UH, HELLO?
WHAT? NO WAY.
ARE YOU SERIOUS ...?!
HEY ...
WE'RE STILL TALKING ...
ALL RIGHT... YEAH, OKAY.
BIP

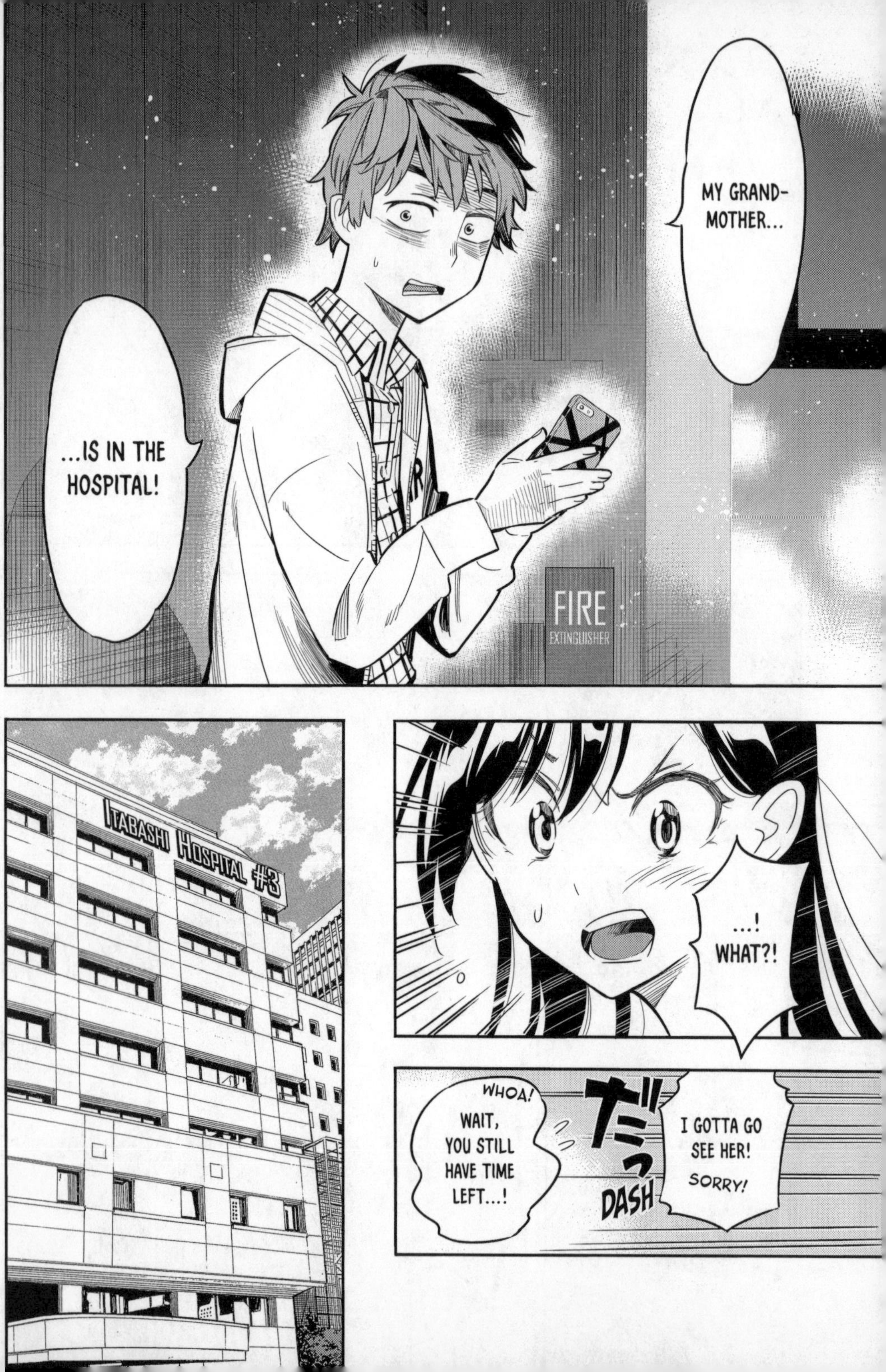
MY GRAND-MOTHER...
...IS IN THE HOSPITAL!
FIRE
EXTINGUISHER
...! WHAT?!
I GOTTA GO SEE HER!
SORRY!
DASH
WHOA!
WAIT, YOU STILL HAVE TIME LEFT...!
ITABASHI HOSPITAL #3

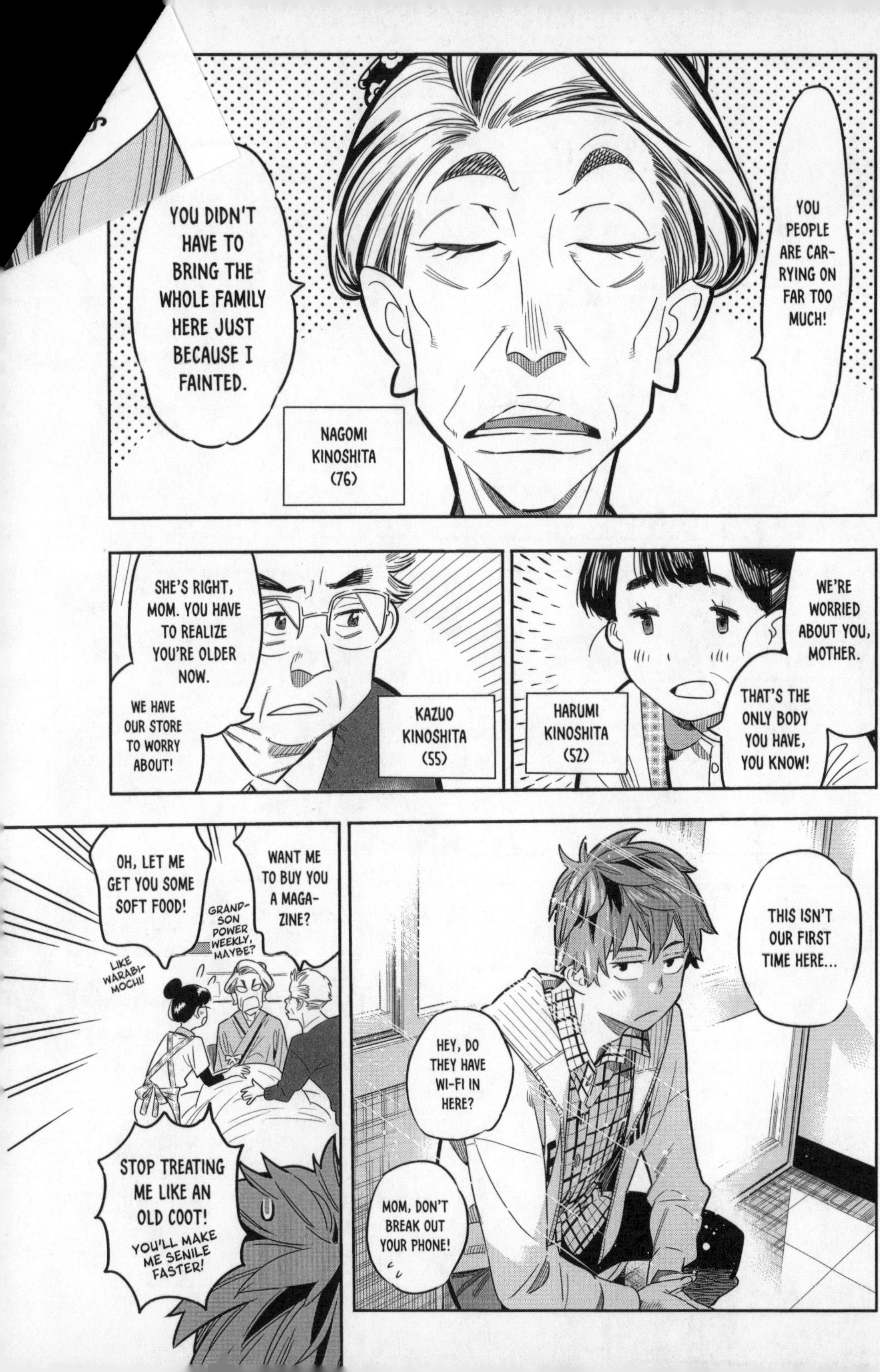
YOU PEOPLE ARE CAR-RYING ON FAR TOO MUCH!
YOU DIDN'T HAVE TO BRING THE WHOLE FAMILY HERE JUST BECAUSE I FAINTED.
NAGOMI KINOSHITA (76)
WE'RE WORRIED ABOUT YOU, MOTHER.
THAT'S THE ONLY BODY YOU HAVE, YOU KNOW!
HARUMI KINOSHITA (52)
SHE'S RIGHT, MOM. YOU HAVE TO REALIZE YOU'RE OLDER NOW.
WE HAVE OUR STORE TO WORRY ABOUT!
KAZUO KINOSHITA (55)
THIS ISN'T OUR FIRST TIME HERE...
HEY, DO THEY HAVE WI-FI IN HERE?
MOM, DON'T BREAK OUT YOUR PHONE!
WANT ME TO BUY YOU A MAGA-ZINE?
GRAND-SON POWER WEEKLY, MAYBE?
OH, LET ME GET YOU SOME SOFT FOOD!
LIKE WARABI-MOCHI!
STOP TREATING ME LIKE AN OLD COOT!
YOU'LL MAKE ME SENILE FASTER!

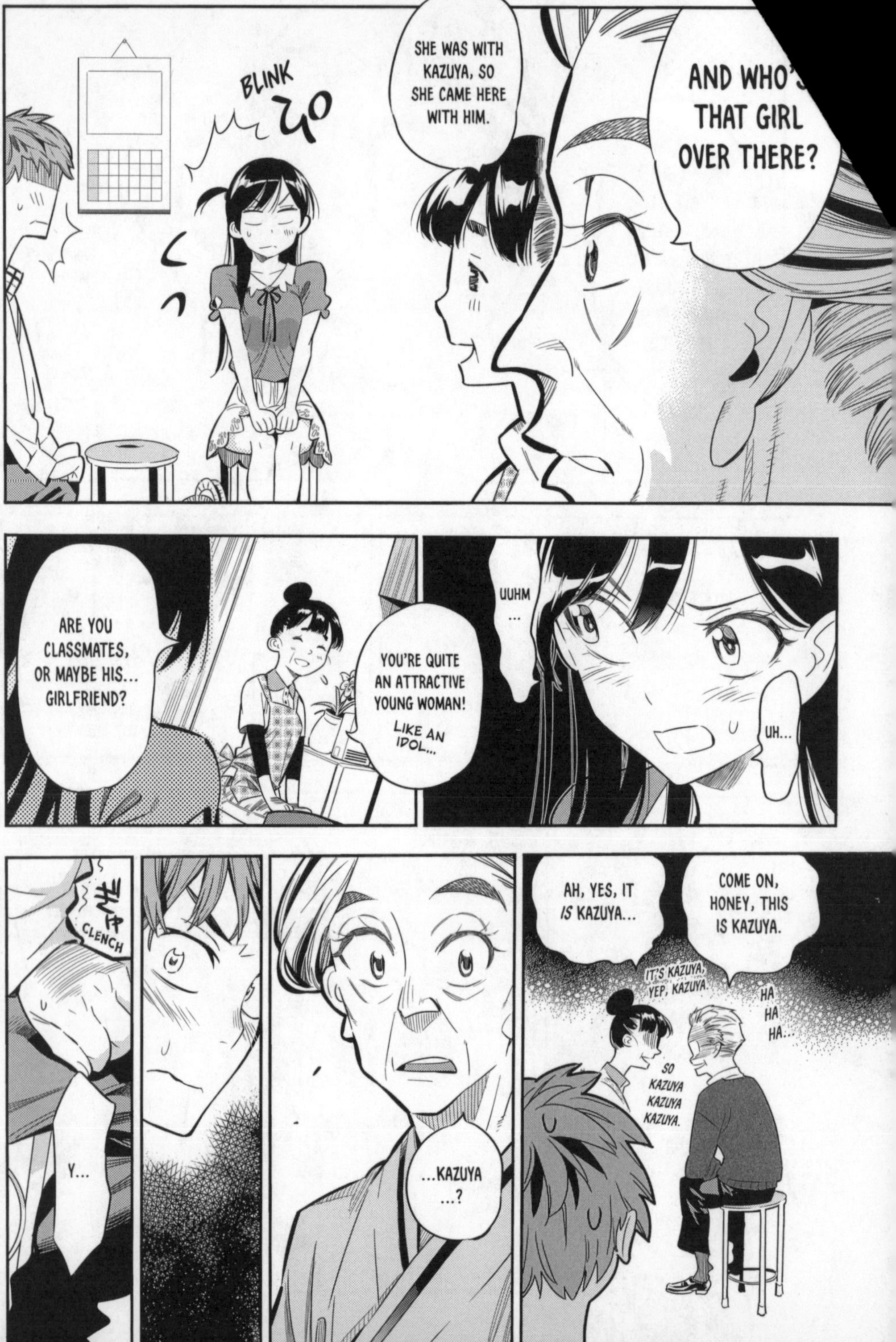
AND WHO'S THAT GIRL OVER THERE?
SHE WAS WITH KAZUYA, SO SHE CAME HERE WITH HIM.
BLINK
UUHM ...
UH...
YOU'RE QUITE AN ATTRACTIVE YOUNG WOMAN!
LIKE AN IDOL...
ARE YOU CLASSMATES, OR MAYBE HIS... GIRLFRIEND?
COME ON, HONEY, THIS IS KAZUYA.
AH, YES, IT *IS* KAZUYA...
HA HA HA...
IT'S KAZUYA, YEP, KAZUYA.
SO KAZUYA KAZUYA KAZUYA.
...KAZUYA ...?
CLENCH
Y...

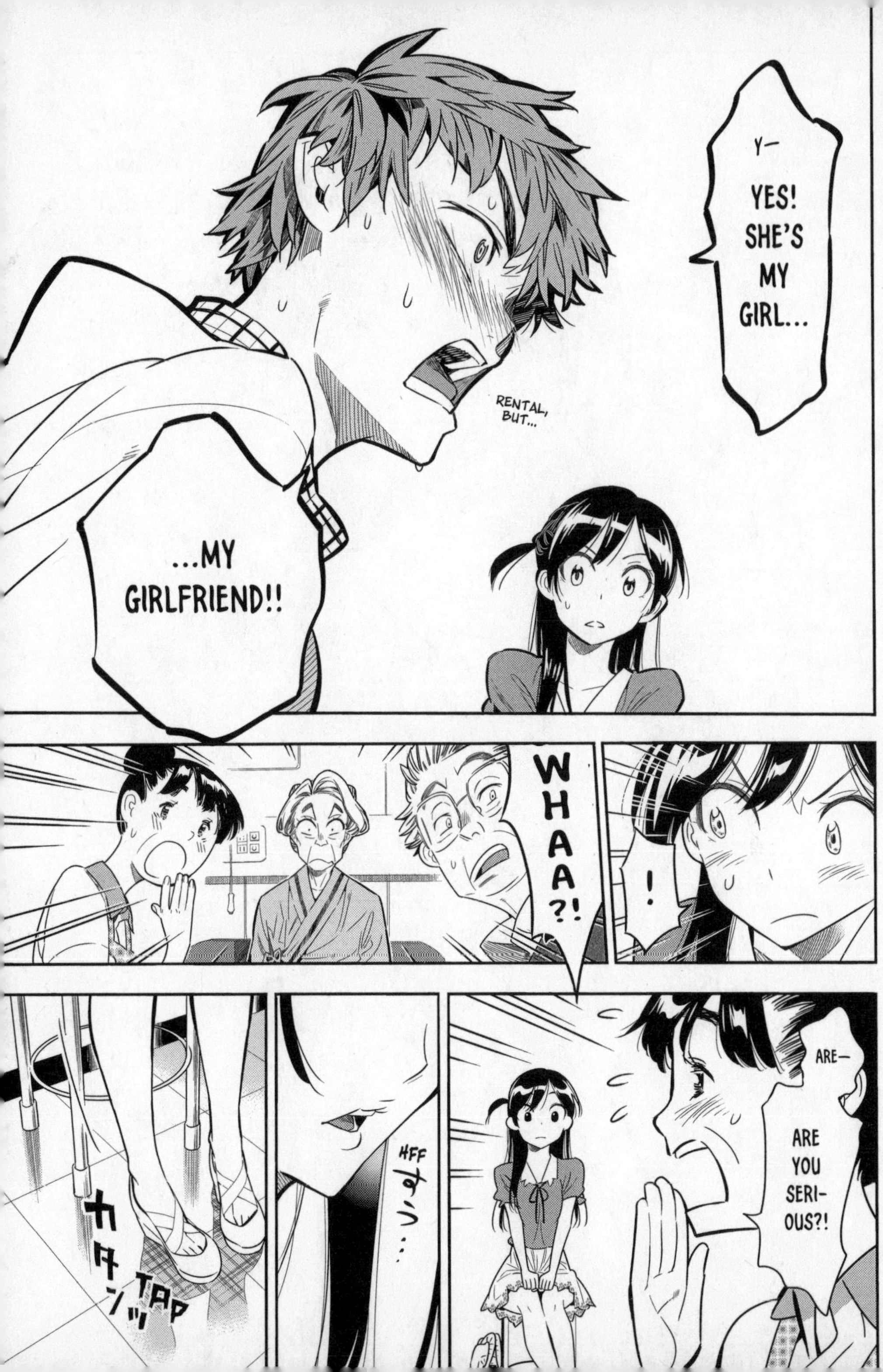
Y—
YES! SHE'S MY GIRL...
RENTAL, BUT...
...MY GIRLFRIEND!!
!
WHAAA?!
ARE—
ARE YOU SERI-OUS?!
HFF
すぅ…
カタンッ
TAP

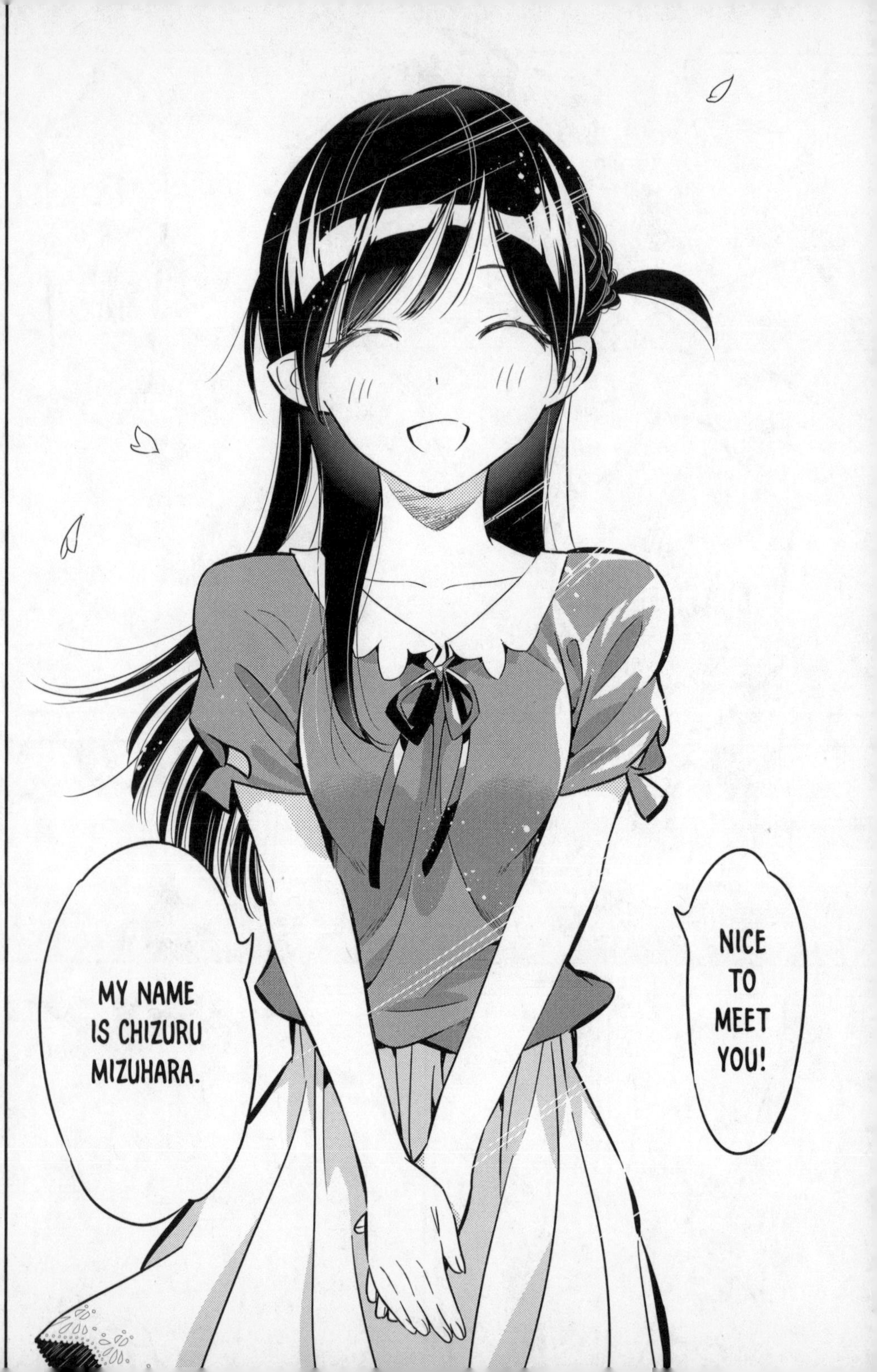
NICE TO MEET YOU!
MY NAME IS CHIZURU MIZUHARA.

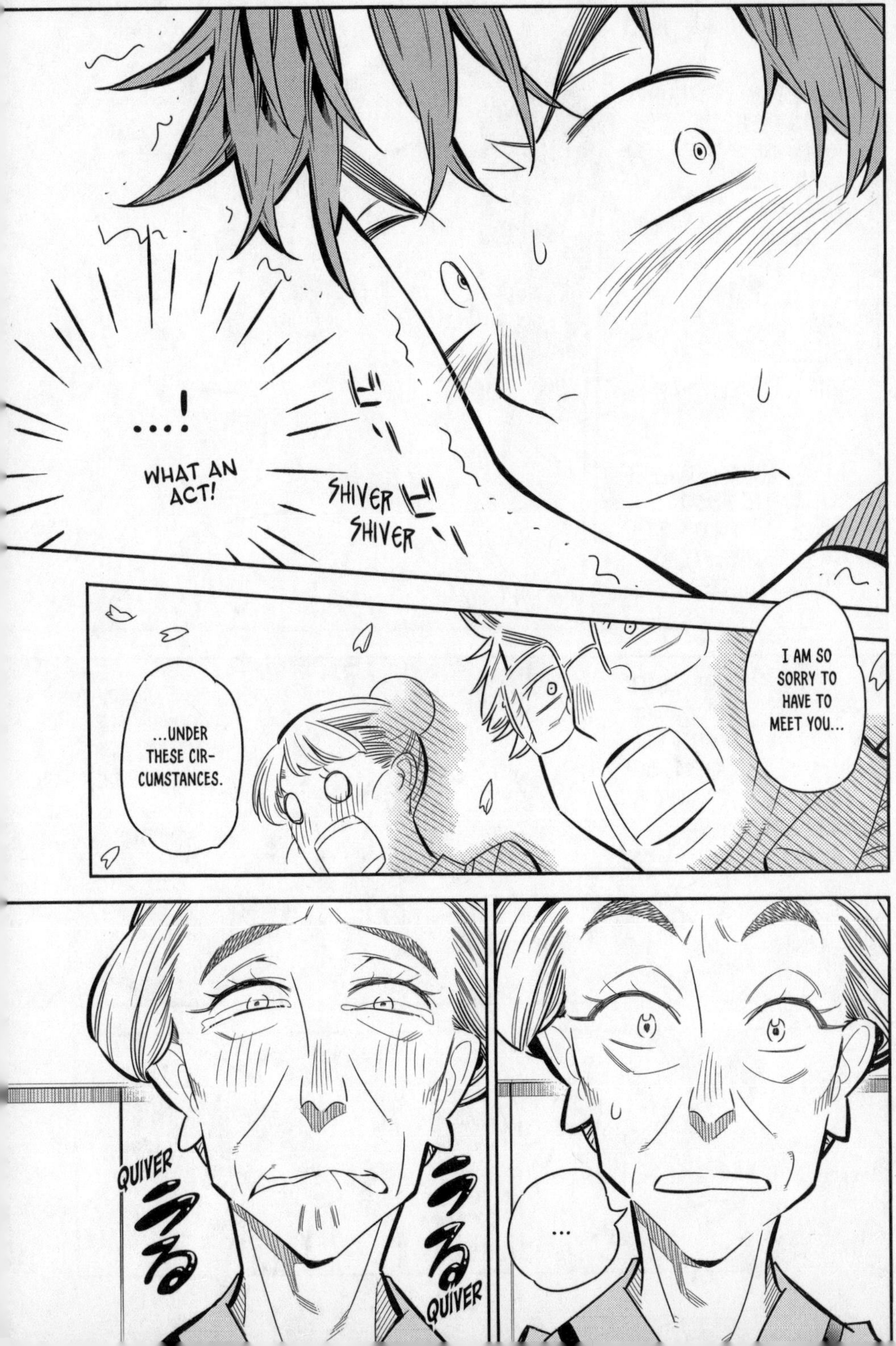
...!
WHAT AN ACT!
SHIVER SHIVER
I AM SO SORRY TO HAVE TO MEET YOU...
...UNDER THESE CIR-CUMSTANCES.
...
QUIVER
QUIVER

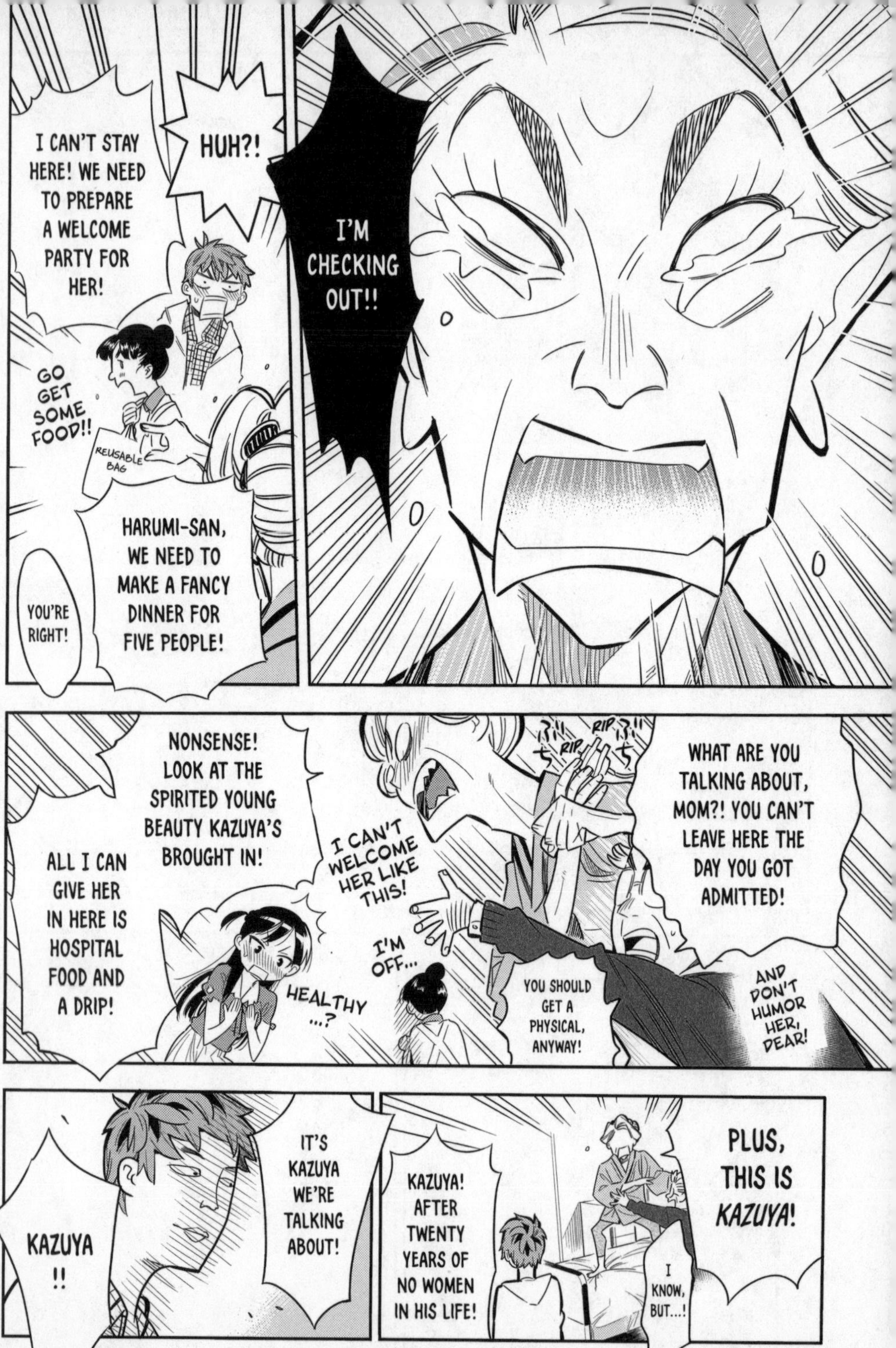
I'M CHECKING OUT!!
HUH?!
I CAN'T STAY HERE! WE NEED TO PREPARE A WELCOME PARTY FOR HER!
GO GET SOME FOOD!!
REUSABLE BAG
HARUMI-SAN, WE NEED TO MAKE A FANCY DINNER FOR FIVE PEOPLE!
YOU'RE RIGHT!
WHAT ARE YOU TALKING ABOUT, MOM?! YOU CAN'T LEAVE HERE THE DAY YOU GOT ADMITTED!
RIP
RIP
AND DON'T HUMOR HER, DEAR!
YOU SHOULD GET A PHYSICAL, ANYWAY!
I CAN'T WELCOME HER LIKE THIS!
I'M OFF...
NONSENSE! LOOK AT THE SPIRITED YOUNG BEAUTY KAZUYA'S BROUGHT IN!
ALL I CAN GIVE HER IN HERE IS HOSPITAL FOOD AND A DRIP!
HEALTHY ...?
PLUS, THIS IS *KAZUYA*!
I KNOW, BUT...!
KAZUYA! AFTER TWENTY YEARS OF NO WOMEN IN HIS LIFE!
IT'S KAZUYA WE'RE TALKING ABOUT!
KAZUYA !!

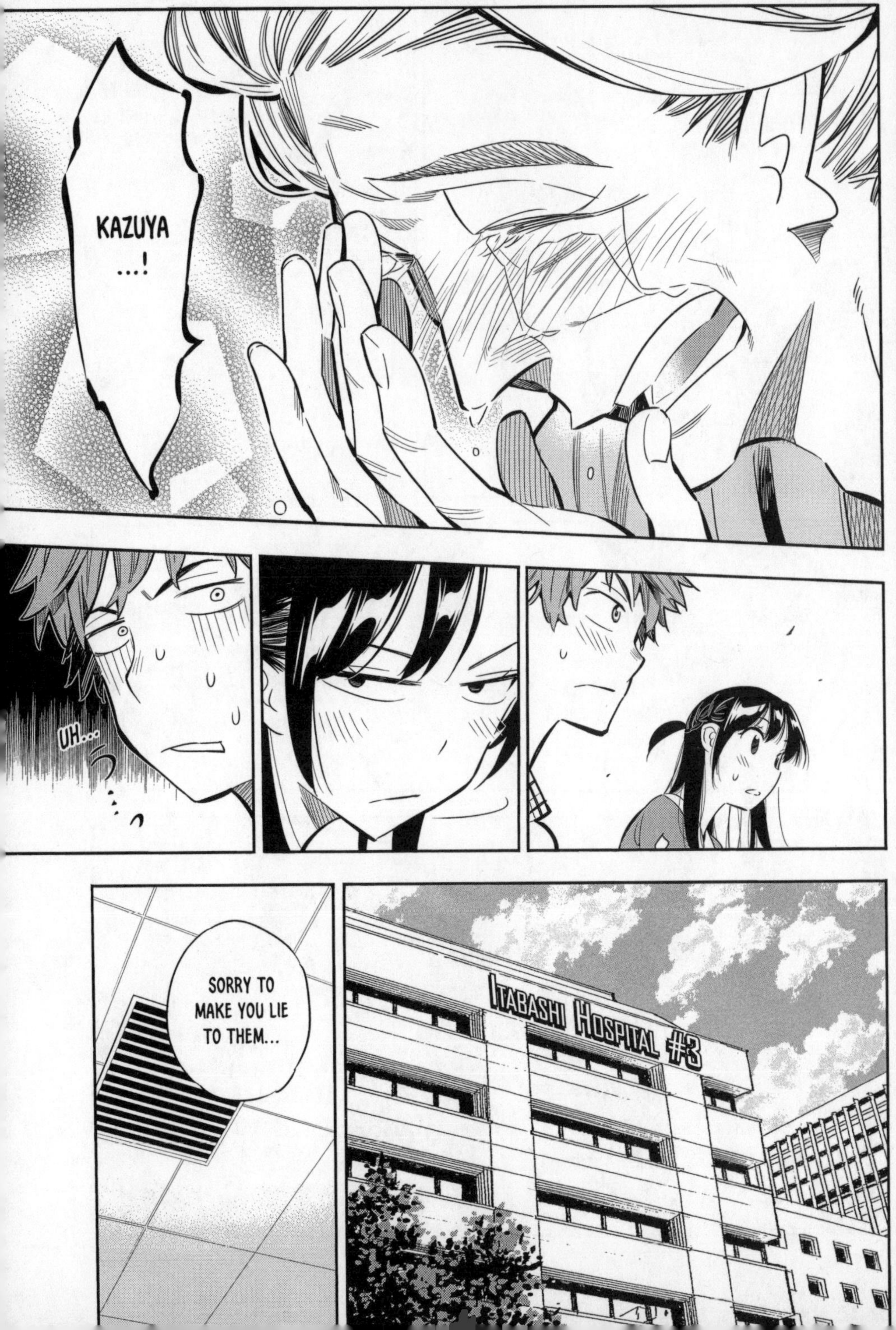
KAZUYA ...!
UH...
ITABASHI HOSPITAL #3
SORRY TO MAKE YOU LIE TO THEM...

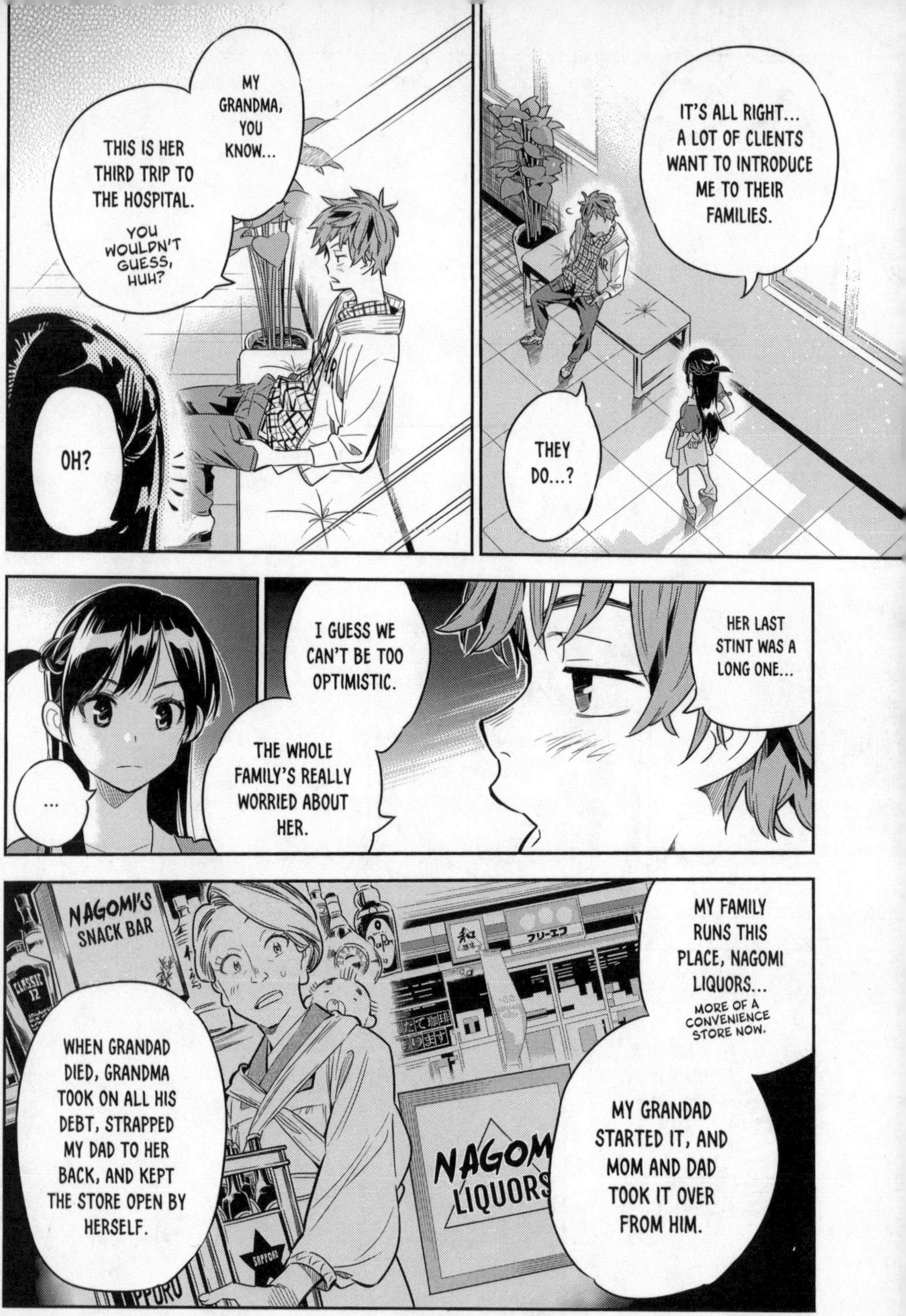

IT'S ALL RIGHT... A LOT OF CLIENTS WANT TO INTRODUCE ME TO THEIR FAMILIES.
THEY DO...?
MY GRANDMA, YOU KNOW...
THIS IS HER THIRD TRIP TO THE HOSPITAL.
YOU WOULDN'T GUESS, HUH?
OH?
HER LAST STINT WAS A LONG ONE...
I GUESS WE CAN'T BE TOO OPTIMISTIC.
THE WHOLE FAMILY'S REALLY WORRIED ABOUT HER.
...
MY FAMILY RUNS THIS PLACE, NAGOMI LIQUORS...
MORE OF A CONVENIENCE STORE NOW.
MY GRANDAD STARTED IT, AND MOM AND DAD TOOK IT OVER FROM HIM.
WHEN GRANDAD DIED, GRANDMA TOOK ON ALL HIS DEBT, STRAPPED MY DAD TO HER BACK, AND KEPT THE STORE OPEN BY HERSELF.
NAGOMI'S SNACK BAR

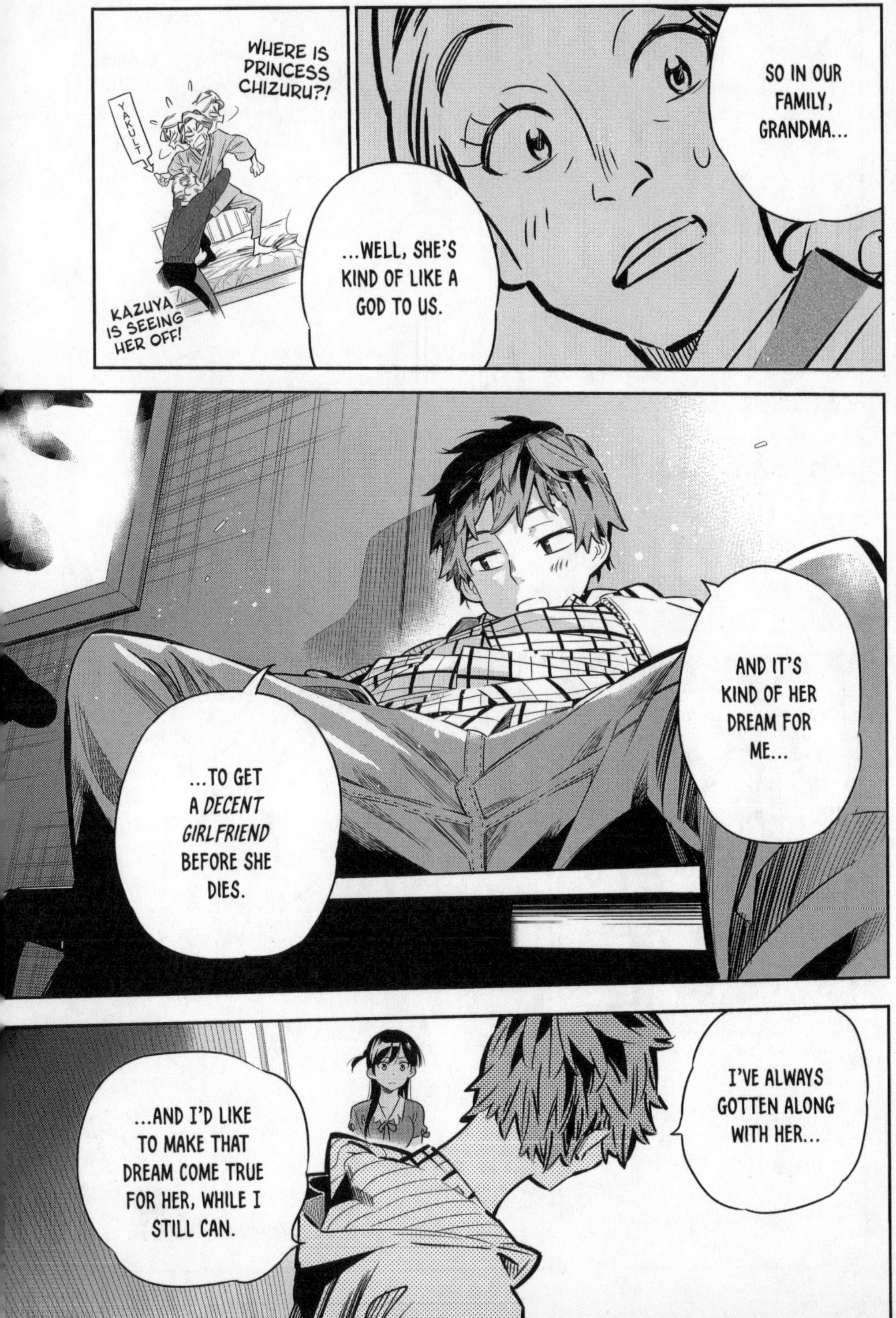
SO IN OUR FAMILY, GRANDMA...
...WELL, SHE'S KIND OF LIKE A GOD TO US.
WHERE IS PRINCESS CHIZURU?!
YAKULT
KAZUYA IS SEEING HER OFF!
AND IT'S KIND OF HER DREAM FOR ME...
...TO GET A *DECENT GIRLFRIEND* BEFORE SHE DIES.
I'VE ALWAYS GOTTEN ALONG WITH HER...
...AND I'D LIKE TO MAKE THAT DREAM COME TRUE FOR HER, WHILE I STILL CAN.

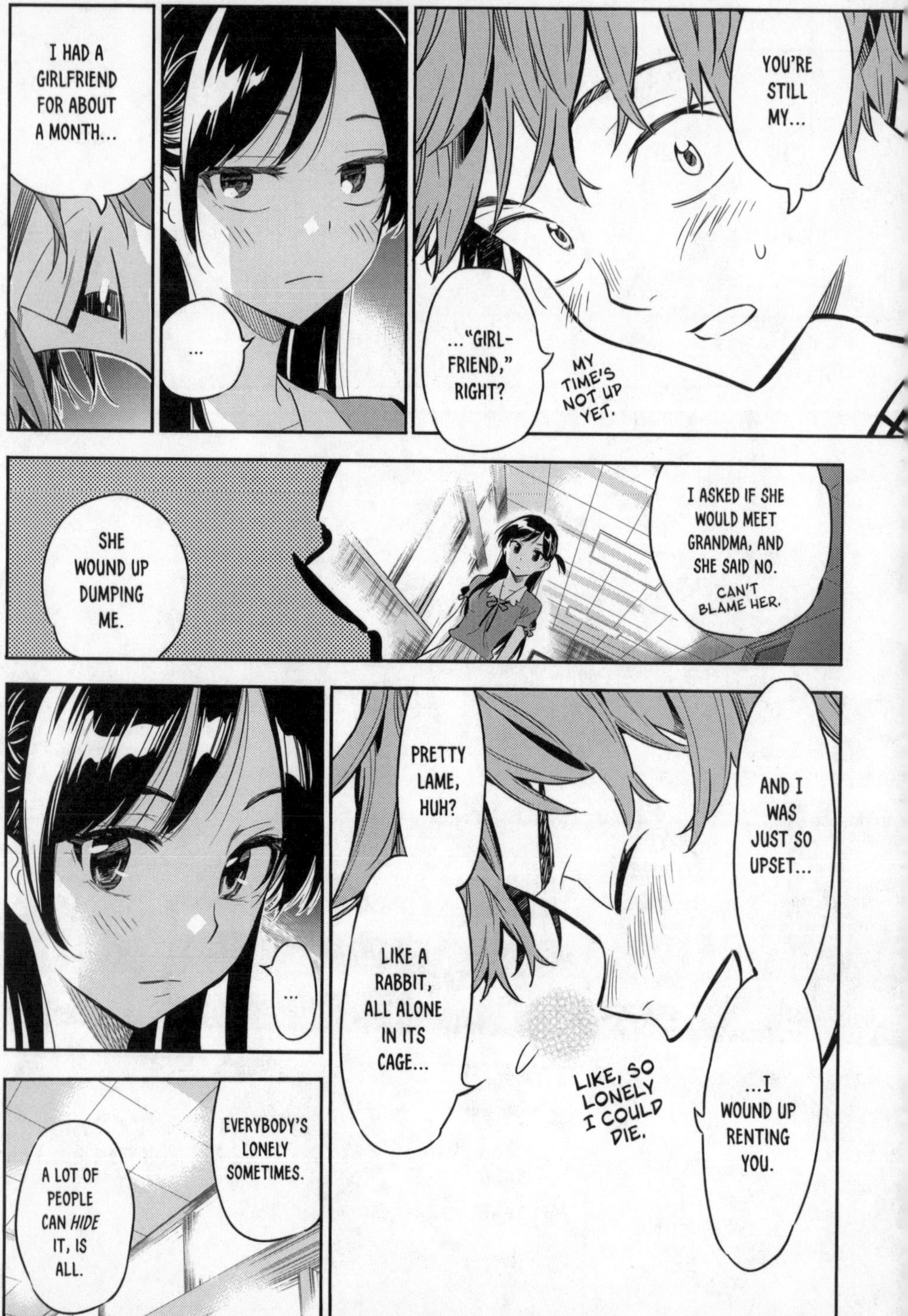
YOU'RE STILL MY...
..."GIRL-FRIEND," RIGHT?
MY TIME'S NOT UP YET.
...
I HAD A GIRLFRIEND FOR ABOUT A MONTH...
I ASKED IF SHE WOULD MEET GRANDMA, AND SHE SAID NO.
CAN'T BLAME HER.
SHE WOUND UP DUMPING ME.
AND I WAS JUST SO UPSET...
PRETTY LAME, HUH?
...I WOUND UP RENTING YOU.
LIKE, SO LONELY I COULD DIE.
LIKE A RABBIT, ALL ALONE IN ITS CAGE...
...
EVERYBODY'S LONELY SOMETIMES.
A LOT OF PEOPLE CAN *HIDE* IT, IS ALL.

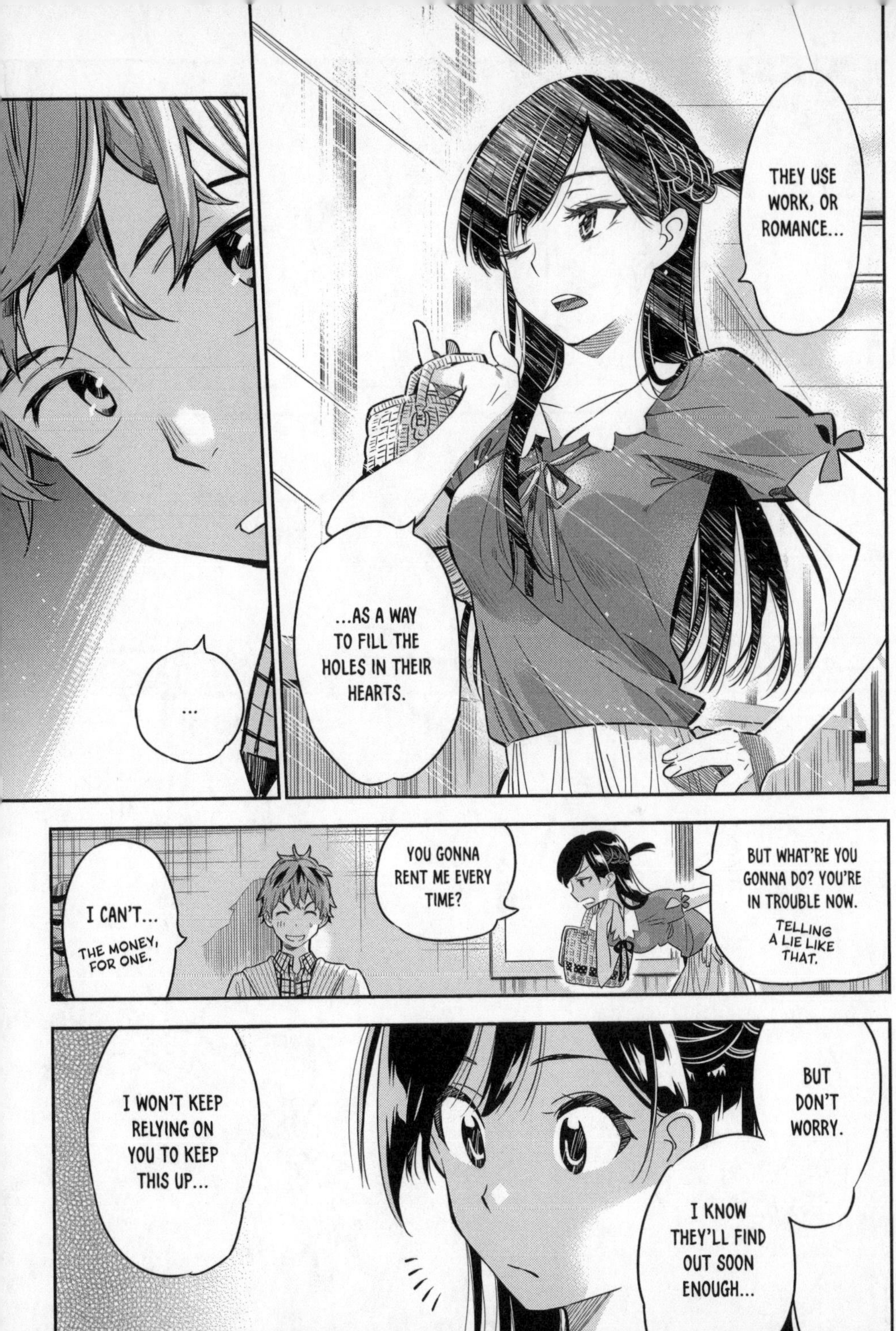
THEY USE WORK, OR ROMANCE...
...AS A WAY TO FILL THE HOLES IN THEIR HEARTS.
...
BUT WHAT'RE YOU GONNA DO? YOU'RE IN TROUBLE NOW.
TELLING A LIE LIKE THAT.
YOU GONNA RENT ME EVERY TIME?
I CAN'T...
THE MONEY, FOR ONE.
BUT DON'T WORRY.
I KNOW THEY'LL FIND OUT SOON ENOUGH...
I WON'T KEEP RELYING ON YOU TO KEEP THIS UP...

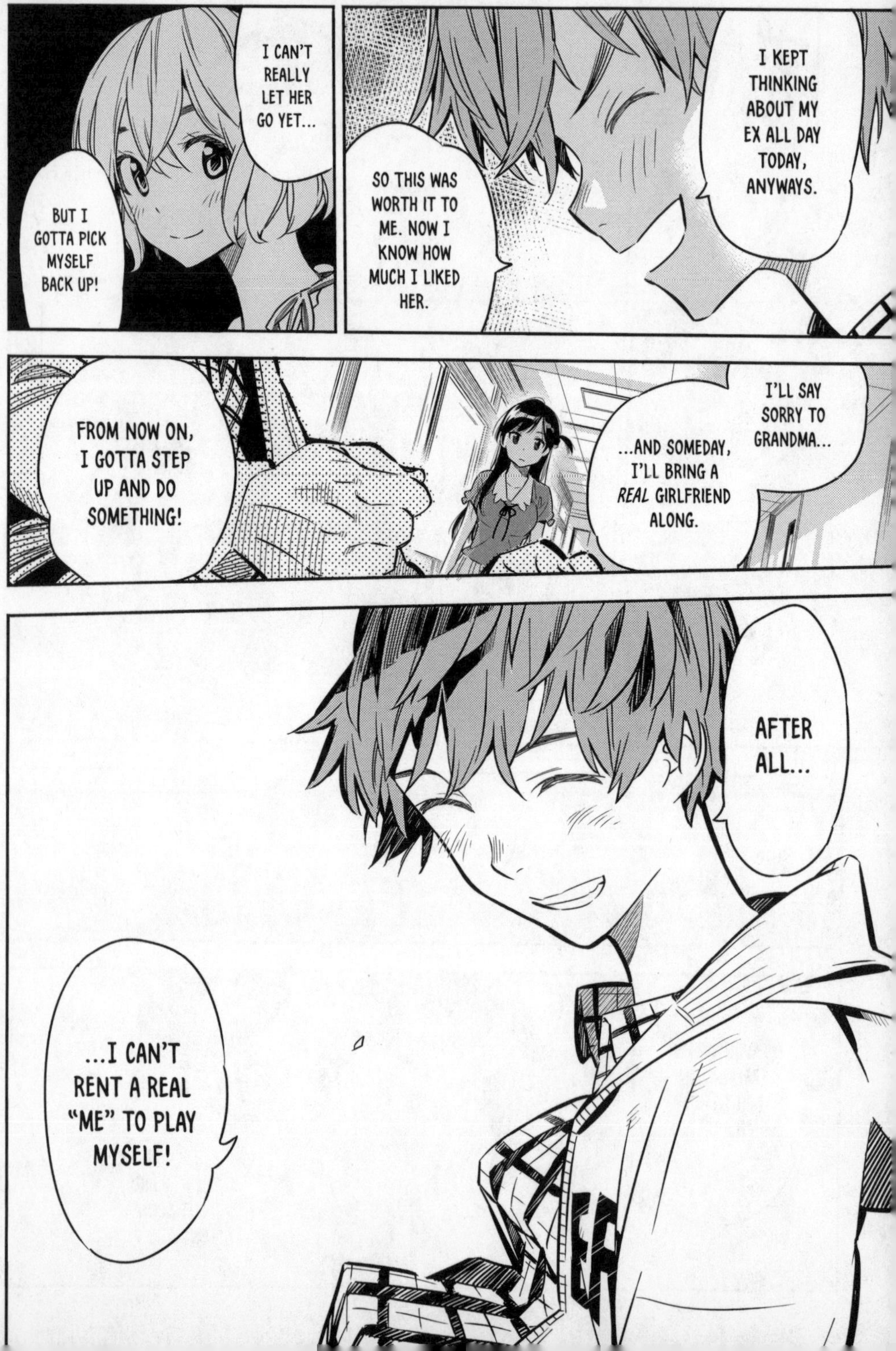
I KEPT THINKING ABOUT MY EX ALL DAY TODAY, ANYWAYS.
SO THIS WAS WORTH IT TO ME. NOW I KNOW HOW MUCH I LIKED HER.
I CAN'T REALLY LET HER GO YET...
BUT I GOTTA PICK MYSELF BACK UP!
I'LL SAY SORRY TO GRANDMA...
...AND SOMEDAY, I'LL BRING A *REAL* GIRLFRIEND ALONG.
FROM NOW ON, I GOTTA STEP UP AND DO SOMETHING!
AFTER ALL...
...I CAN'T RENT A REAL "ME" TO PLAY MYSELF!

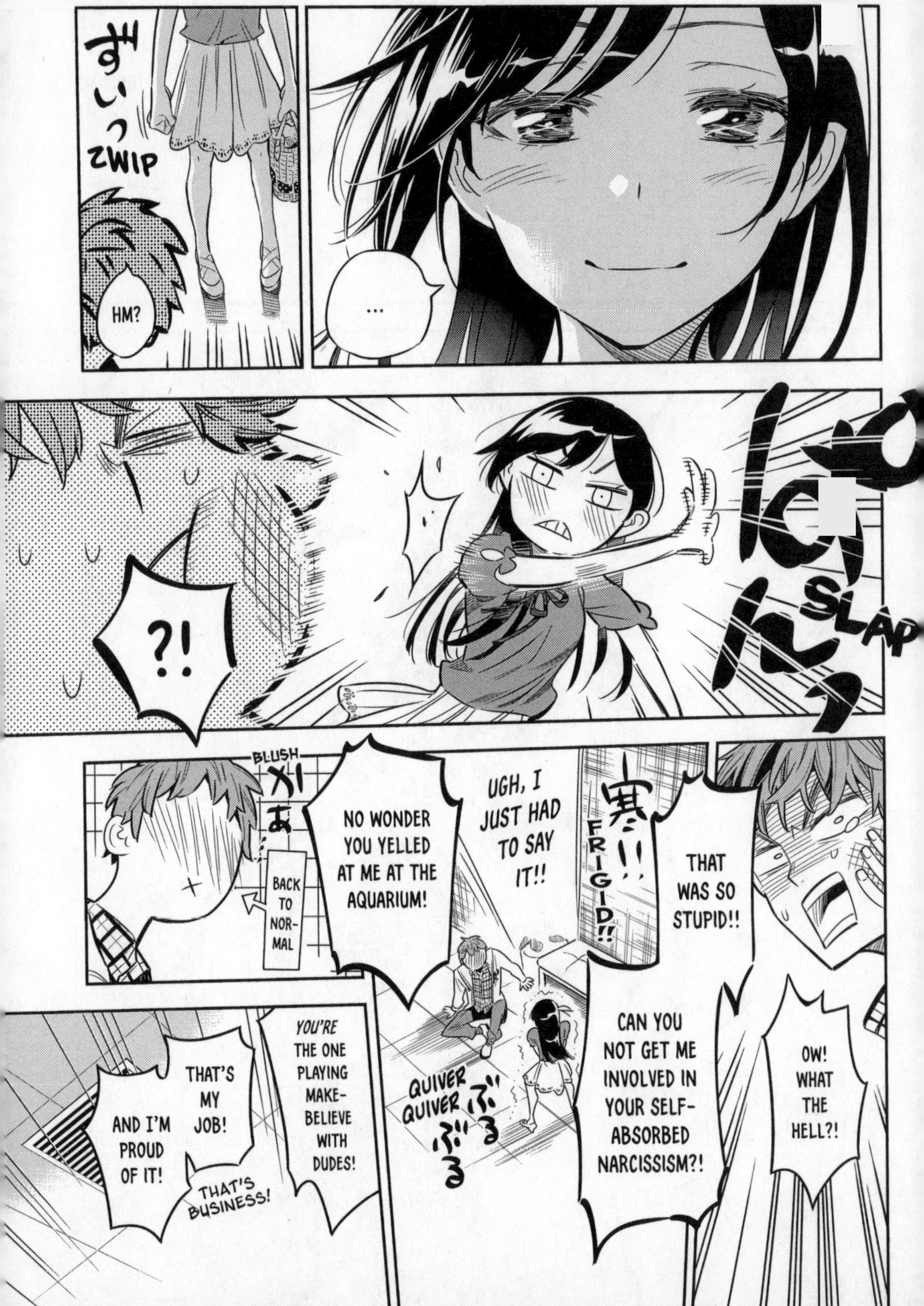
...
ずいっ
ZWIP
HM?
SLAP
?!
THAT WAS SO STUPID!!
寒!!
FRIGID!!
UGH, I JUST HAD TO SAY IT!!
NO WONDER YOU YELLED AT ME AT THE AQUARIUM!
BLUSH
BACK TO NORMAL
OW! WHAT THE HELL?!
CAN YOU NOT GET ME INVOLVED IN YOUR SELF-ABSORBED NARCISSISM?!
QUIVER QUIVER
ぶるぶる
YOU'RE THE ONE PLAYING MAKE-BELIEVE WITH DUDES!
THAT'S MY JOB!
THAT'S BUSINESS!
AND I'M PROUD OF IT!

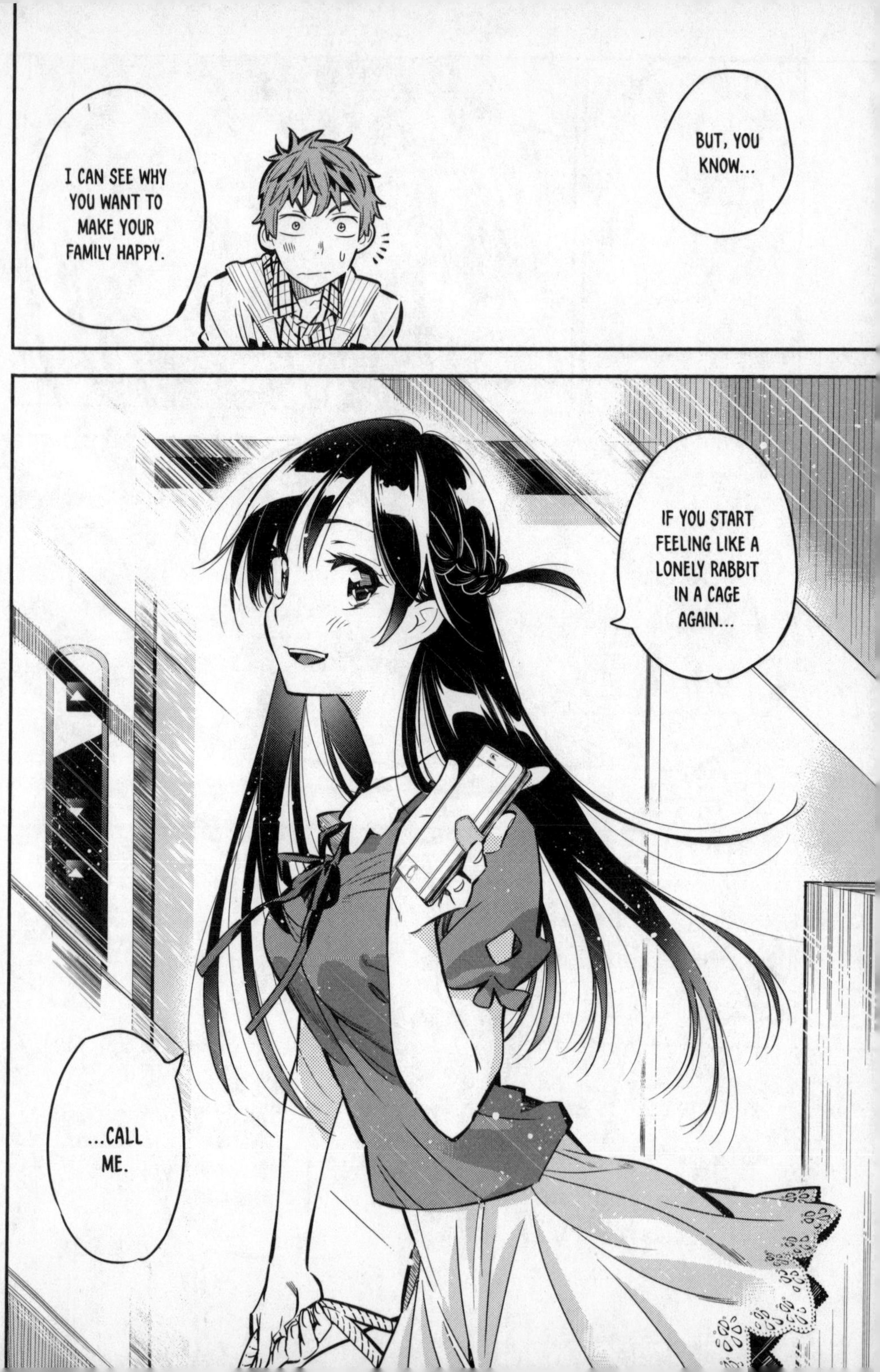
BUT, YOU KNOW...
I CAN SEE WHY YOU WANT TO MAKE YOUR FAMILY HAPPY.
IF YOU START FEELING LIKE A LONELY RABBIT IN A CAGE AGAIN...
...CALL ME.

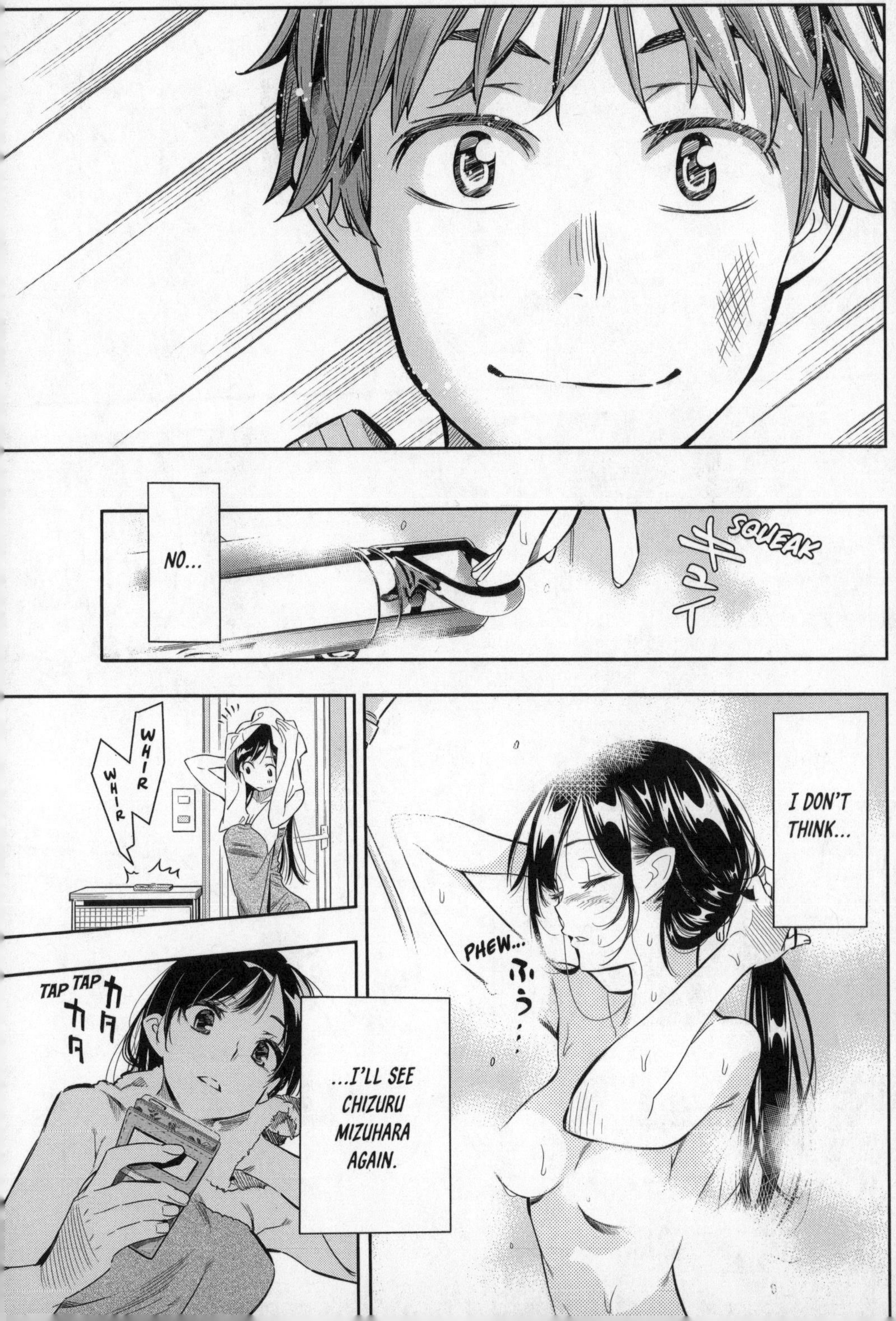
SQUEAK
キュイ
NO...
I DON'T THINK...
PHEW...
ふう...
WHIR WHIR
TAP TAP
カタカタ
...I'LL SEE CHIZURU MIZUHARA AGAIN.

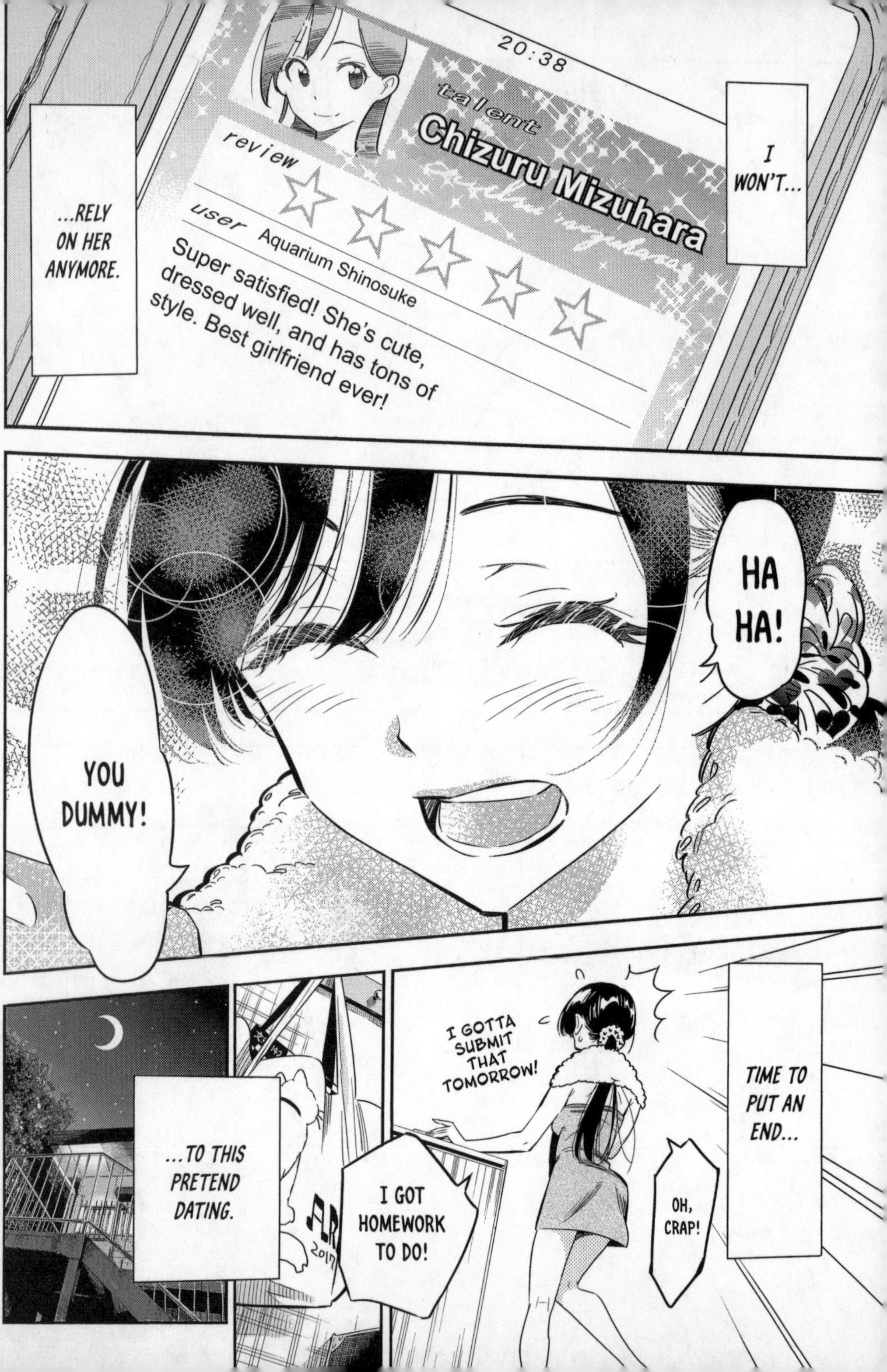
I WON'T...
20:38
talent
Chizuru Mizuhara
review
user Aquarium Shinosuke
Super satisfied! She's cute, dressed well, and has tons of style. Best girlfriend ever!
...RELY ON HER ANYMORE.
HA HA!
YOU DUMMY!
TIME TO PUT AN END...
OH, CRAP!
I GOTTA SUBMIT THAT TOMORROW!
I GOT HOMEWORK TO DO!
...TO THIS PRETEND DATING.

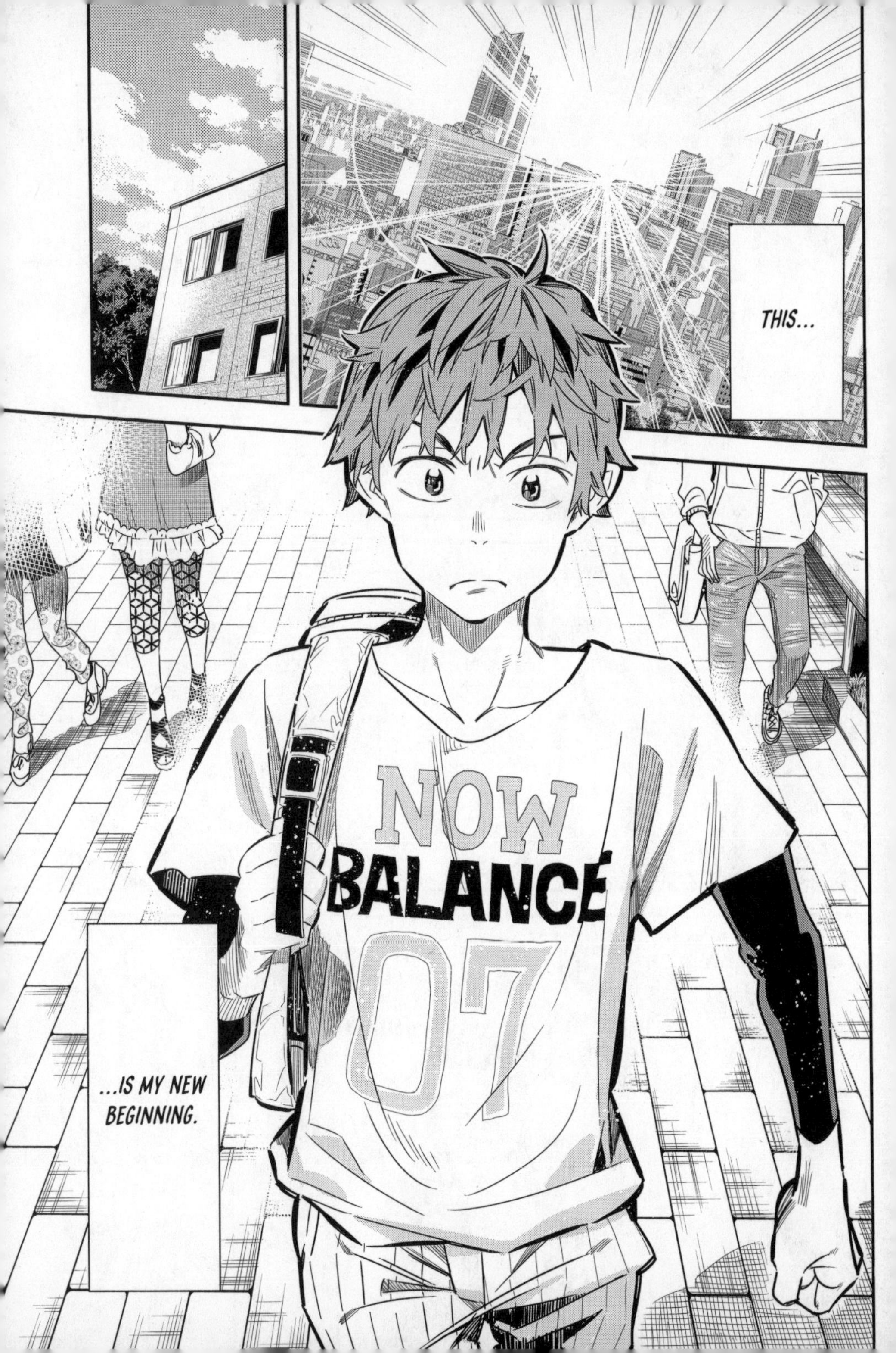
THIS...
NOW
BALANCE
07
...IS MY NEW BEGINNING.

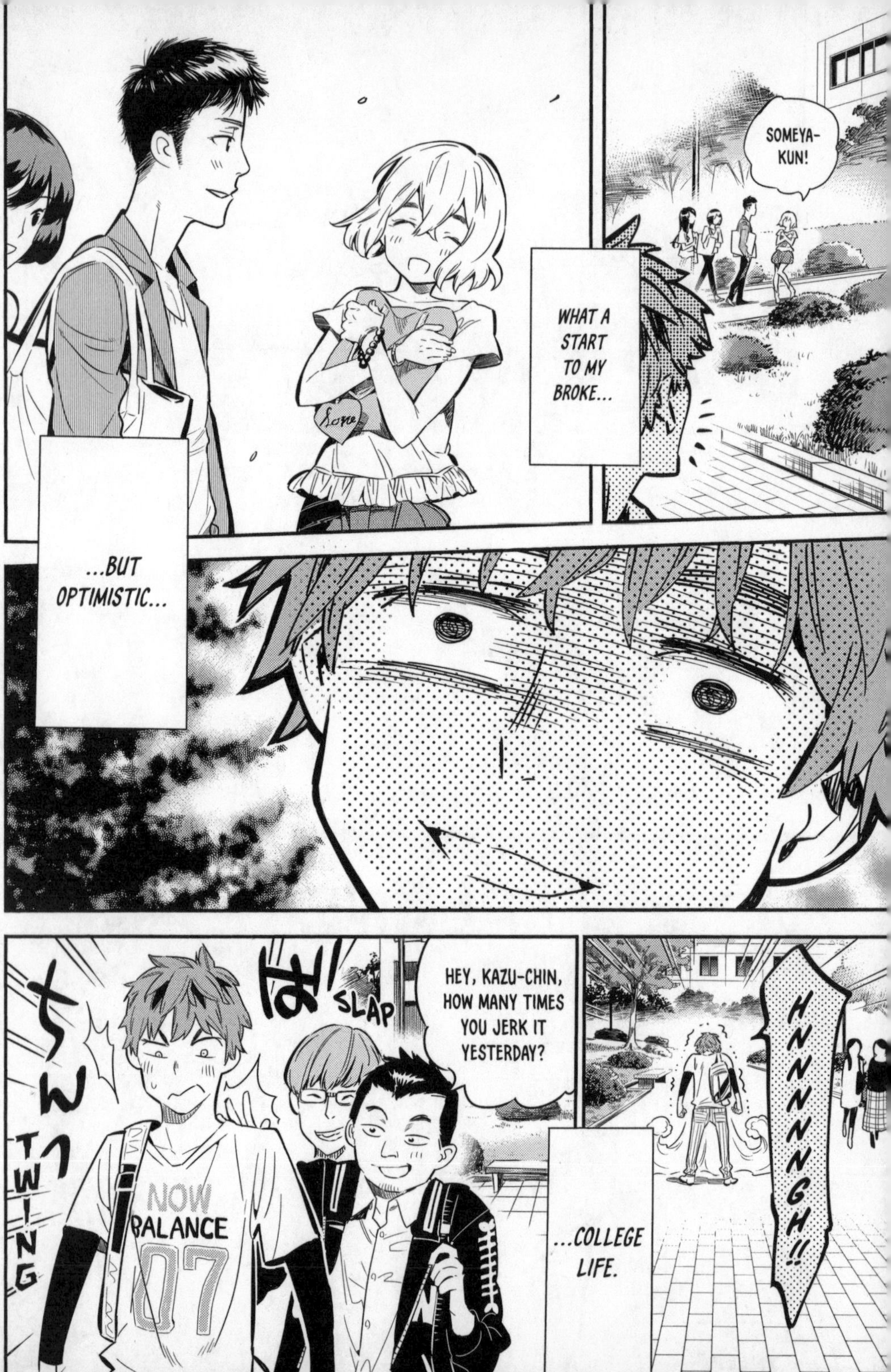
SOMEYA-KUN!
WHAT A START TO MY BROKE...
...BUT OPTIMISTIC...
HNNNNGH!!
...COLLEGE LIFE.
HEY, KAZU-CHIN, HOW MANY TIMES YOU JERK IT YESTERDAY?
SLAP
TWING

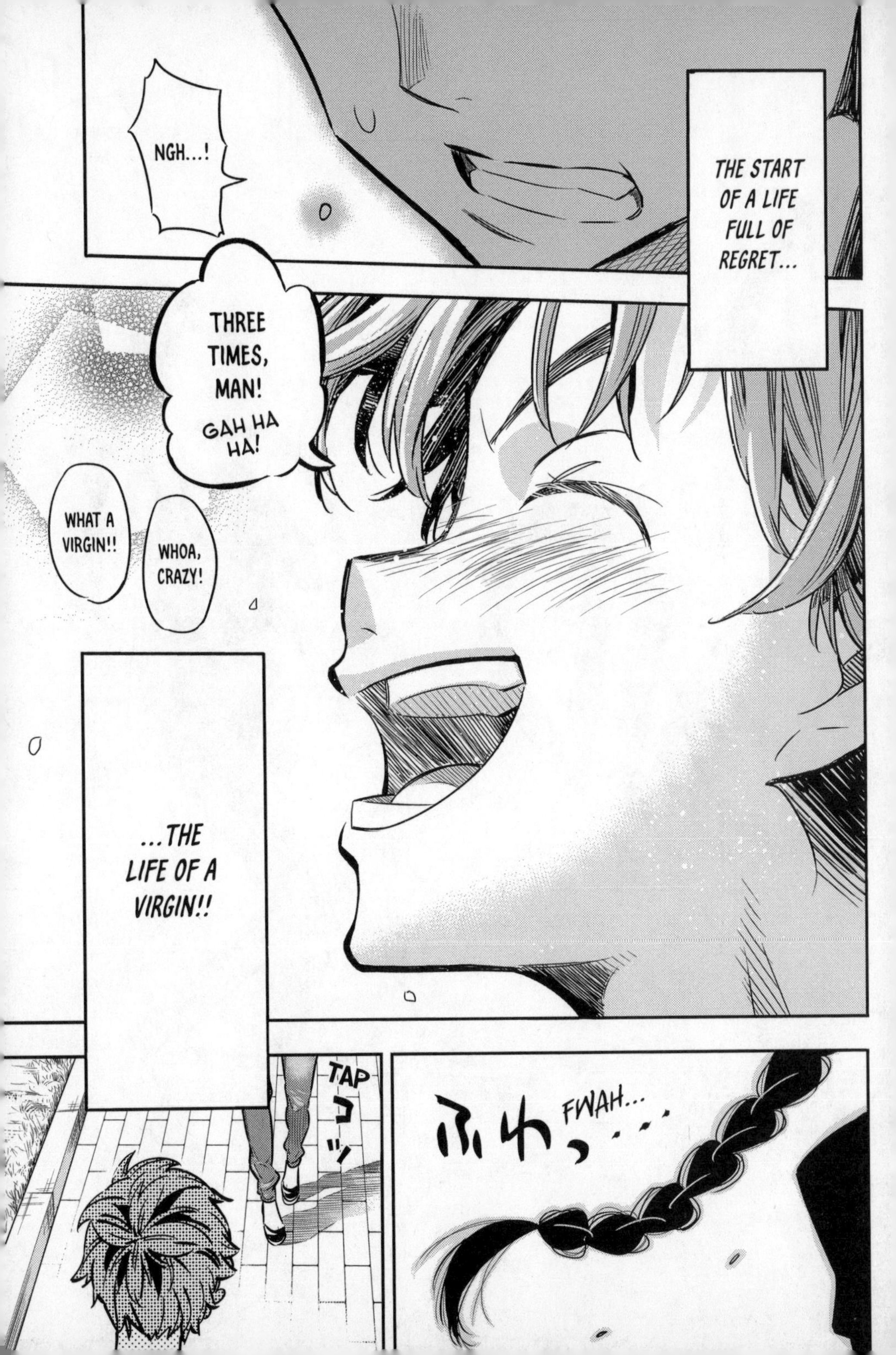
THE START OF A LIFE FULL OF REGRET...
NGH...!
THREE TIMES, MAN!
GAH HA HA!
WHOA, CRAZY!
WHAT A VIRGIN!!
...THE LIFE OF A VIRGIN!!
ふわっ
FWAH...
TAP
コッ

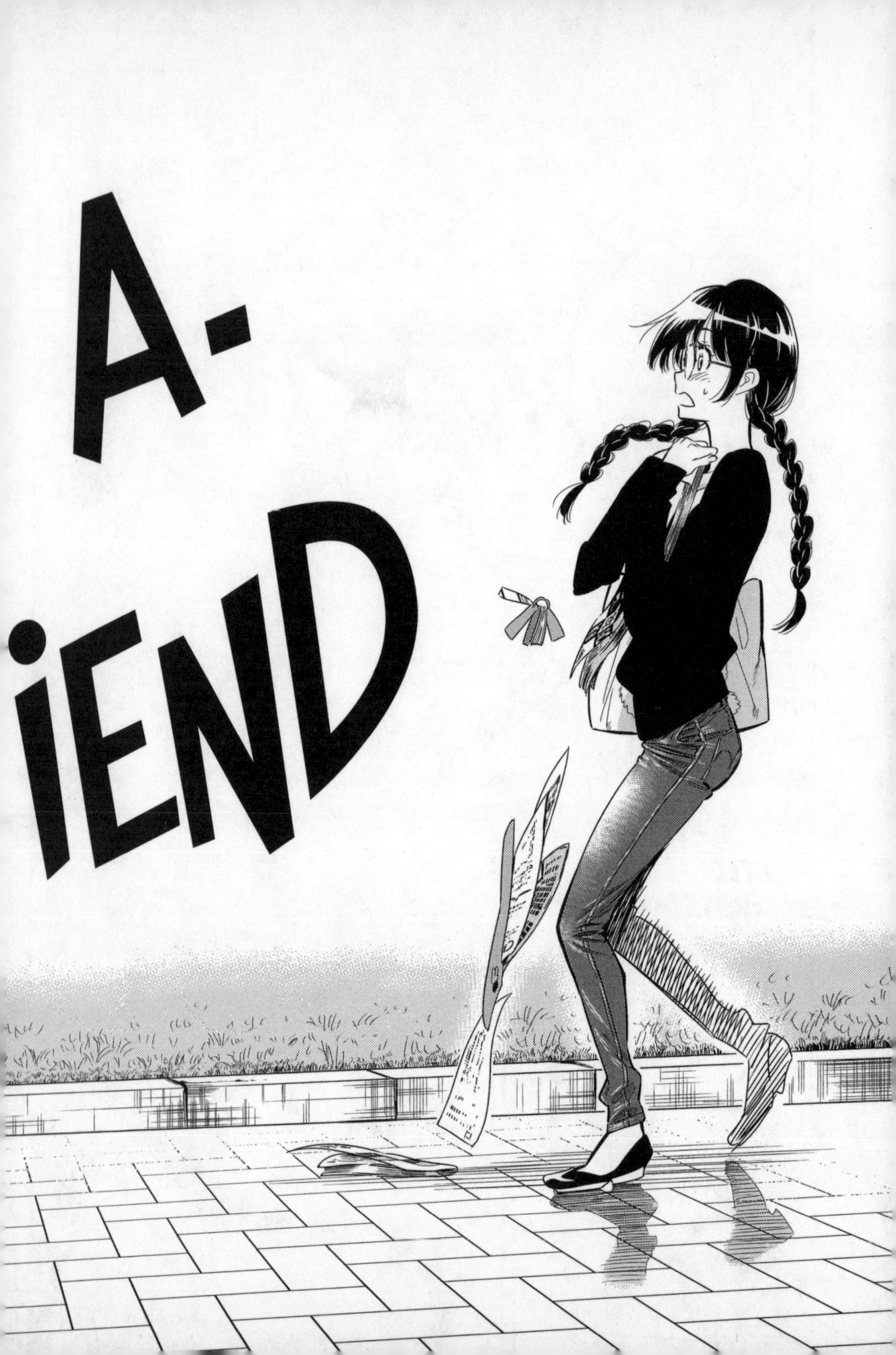
A-
iEND

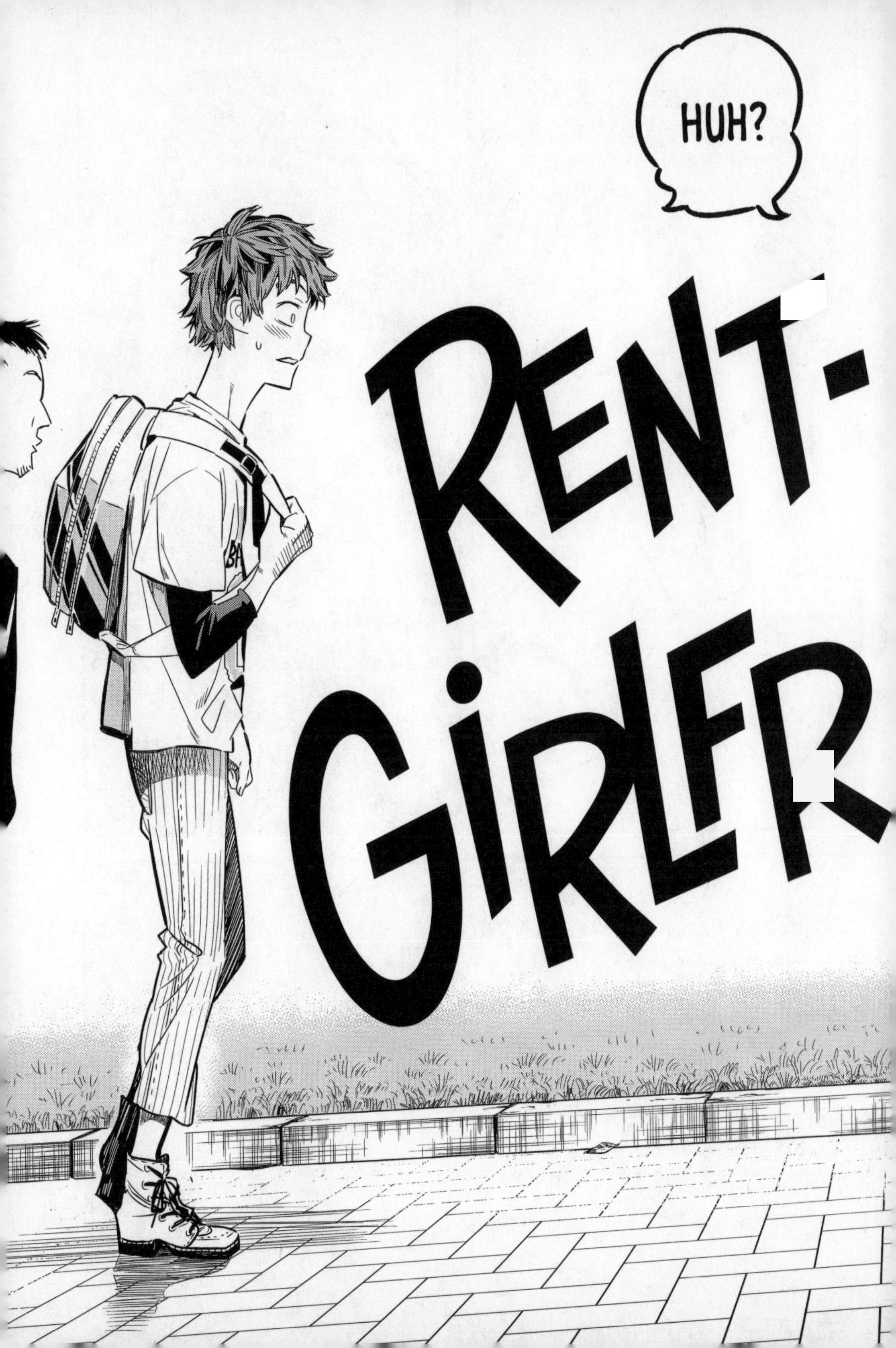
HUH?
RENT-
GIRLFR

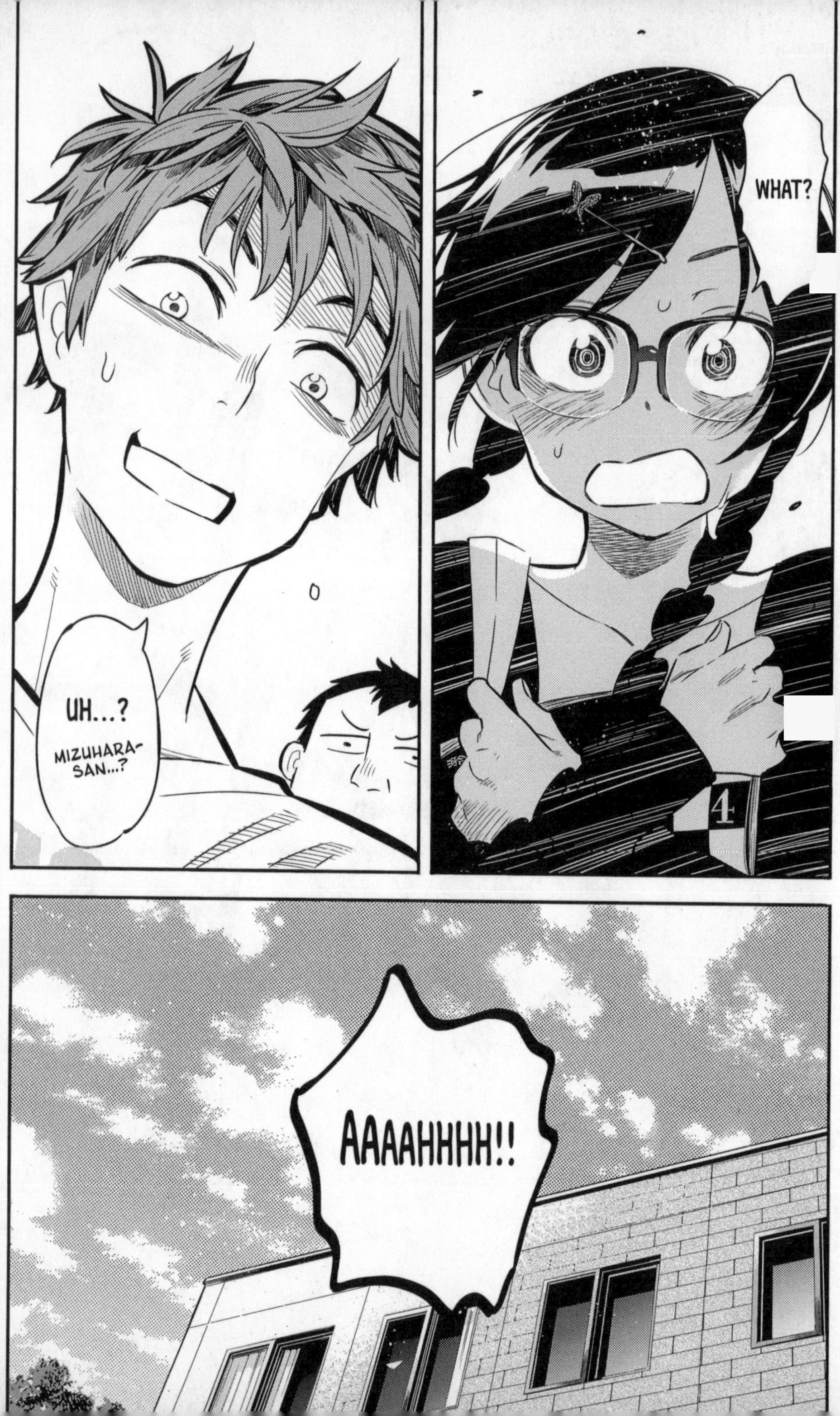
WHAT?
UH...? MIZUHARA-SAN...?
AAAAHHHH!!

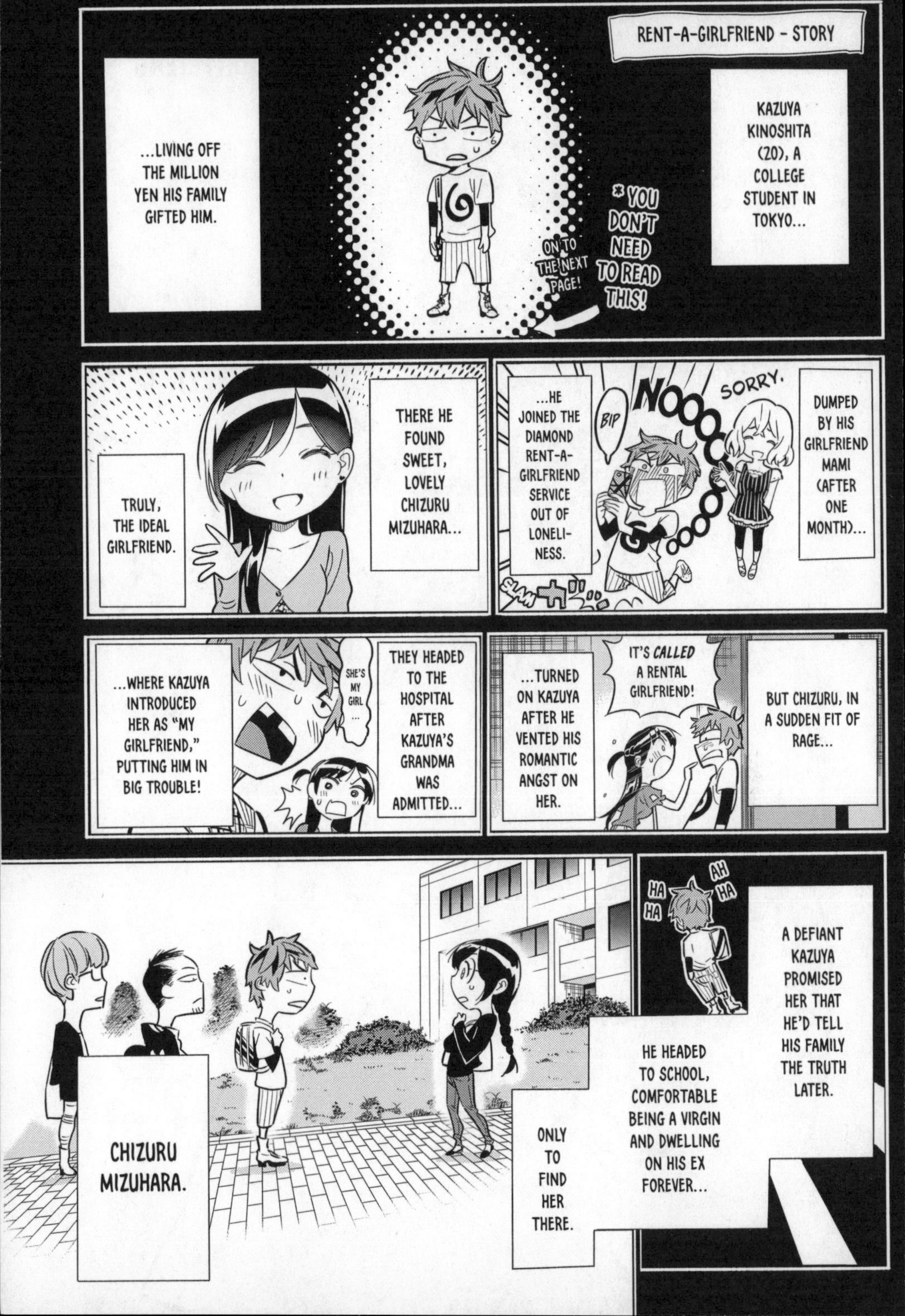
RENT-A-GIRLFRIEND - STORY
KAZUYA KINOSHITA (20), A COLLEGE STUDENT IN TOKYO...
* YOU DON'T NEED TO READ THIS!
ON TO THE NEXT PAGE!
...LIVING OFF THE MILLION YEN HIS FAMILY GIFTED HIM.
DUMPED BY HIS GIRLFRIEND MAMI (AFTER ONE MONTH)...
SORRY.
NOOOOOOOOOOOO
BIP
...HE JOINED THE DIAMOND RENT-A-GIRLFRIEND SERVICE OUT OF LONELINESS.
SLAM
THERE HE FOUND SWEET, LOVELY CHIZURU MIZUHARA...
TRULY, THE IDEAL GIRLFRIEND.
BUT CHIZURU, IN A SUDDEN FIT OF RAGE...
IT'S *CALLED* A RENTAL GIRLFRIEND!
...TURNED ON KAZUYA AFTER HE VENTED HIS ROMANTIC ANGST ON HER.
THEY HEADED TO THE HOSPITAL AFTER KAZUYA'S GRANDMA WAS ADMITTED...
SHE'S MY GIRL...
...WHERE KAZUYA INTRODUCED HER AS "MY GIRLFRIEND," PUTTING HIM IN BIG TROUBLE!
AH HA
HA HA
A DEFIANT KAZUYA PROMISED HER THAT HE'D TELL HIS FAMILY THE TRUTH LATER.
HE HEADED TO SCHOOL, COMFORTABLE BEING A VIRGIN AND DWELLING ON HIS EX FOREVER...
ONLY TO FIND HER THERE.
CHIZURU MIZUHARA.

RATING 2
MY GIRLFRIEND

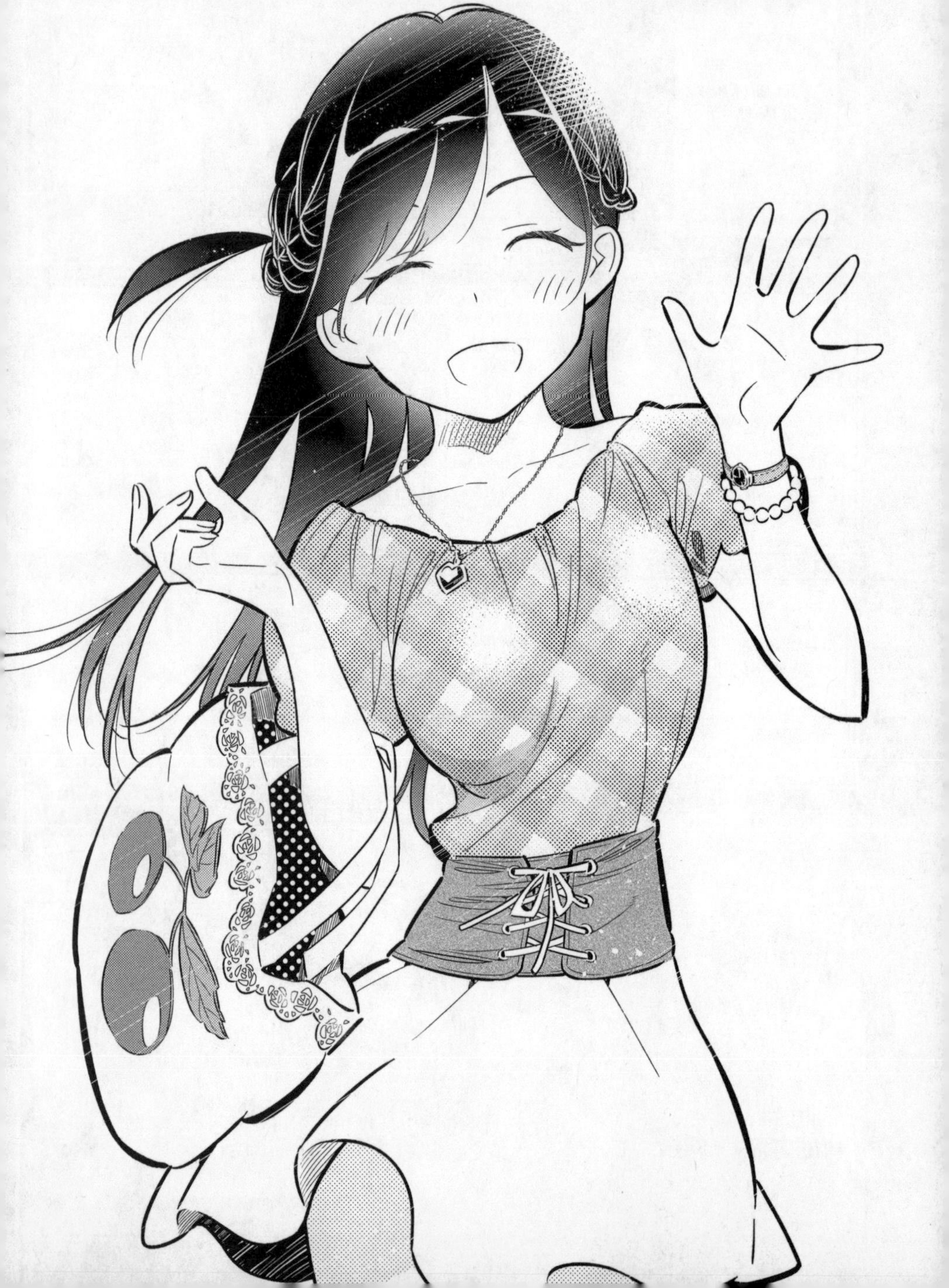

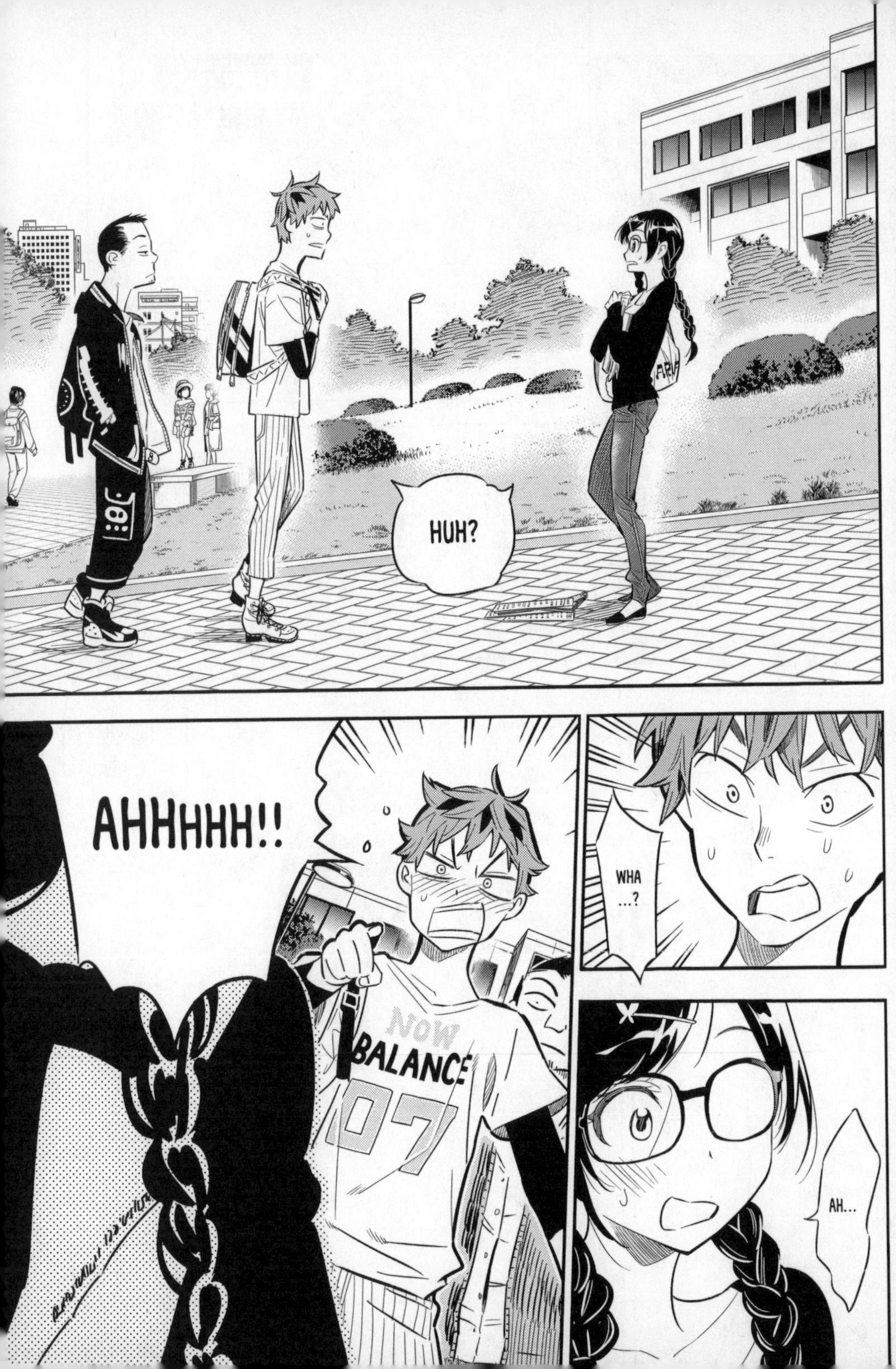
HUH?
WHA ...?
AH...
AHHHHH!!
NOW BALANCE 07

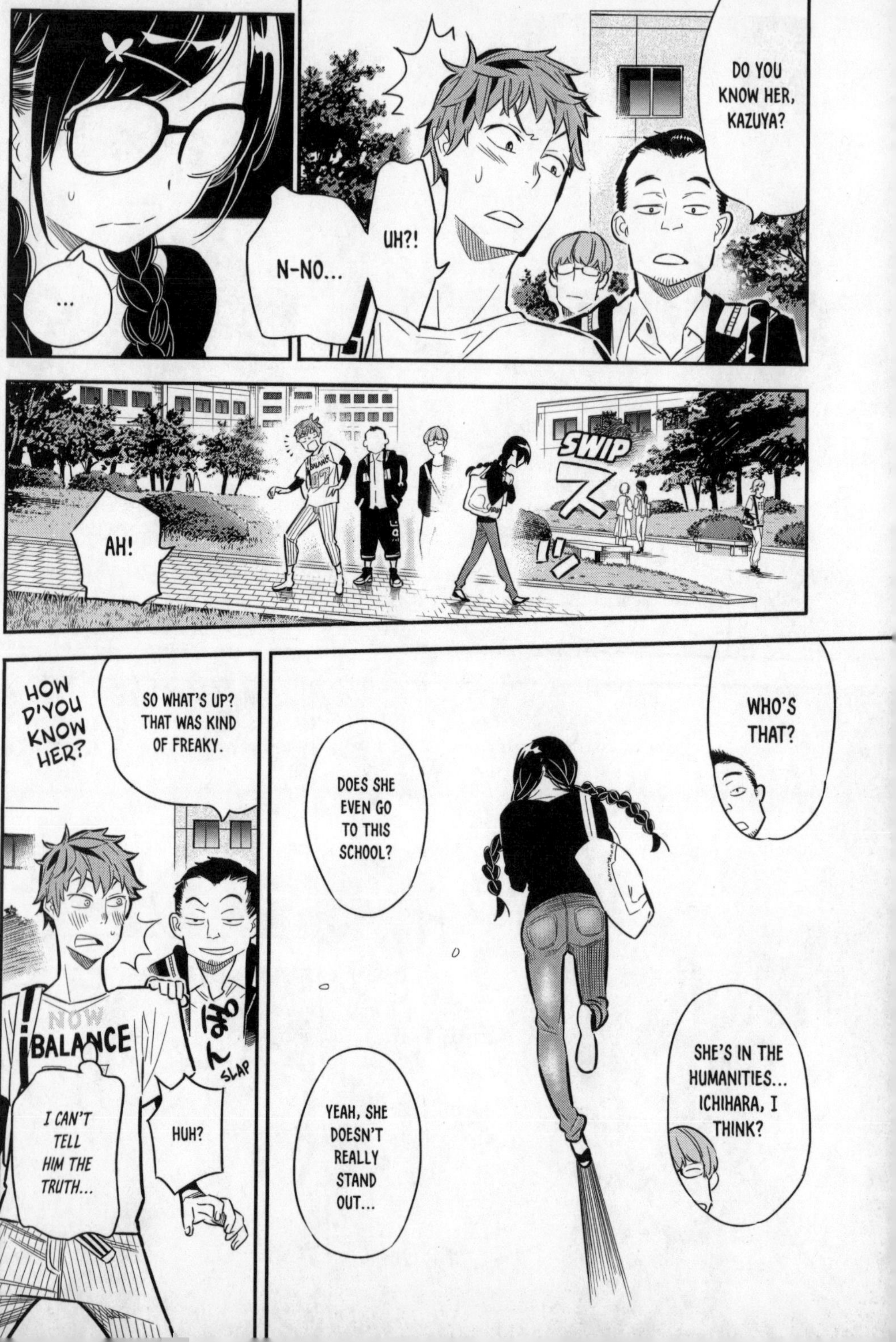
DO YOU KNOW HER, KAZUYA?
UH?!
N-NO...
...
SWIP
ス
AH!
WHO'S THAT?
DOES SHE EVEN GO TO THIS SCHOOL?
SHE'S IN THE HUMANITIES... ICHIHARA, I THINK?
YEAH, SHE DOESN'T REALLY STAND OUT...
SO WHAT'S UP? THAT WAS KIND OF FREAKY.
HOW D'YOU KNOW HER?
ぽん
SLAP
HUH?
I CAN'T TELL HIM THE TRUTH...

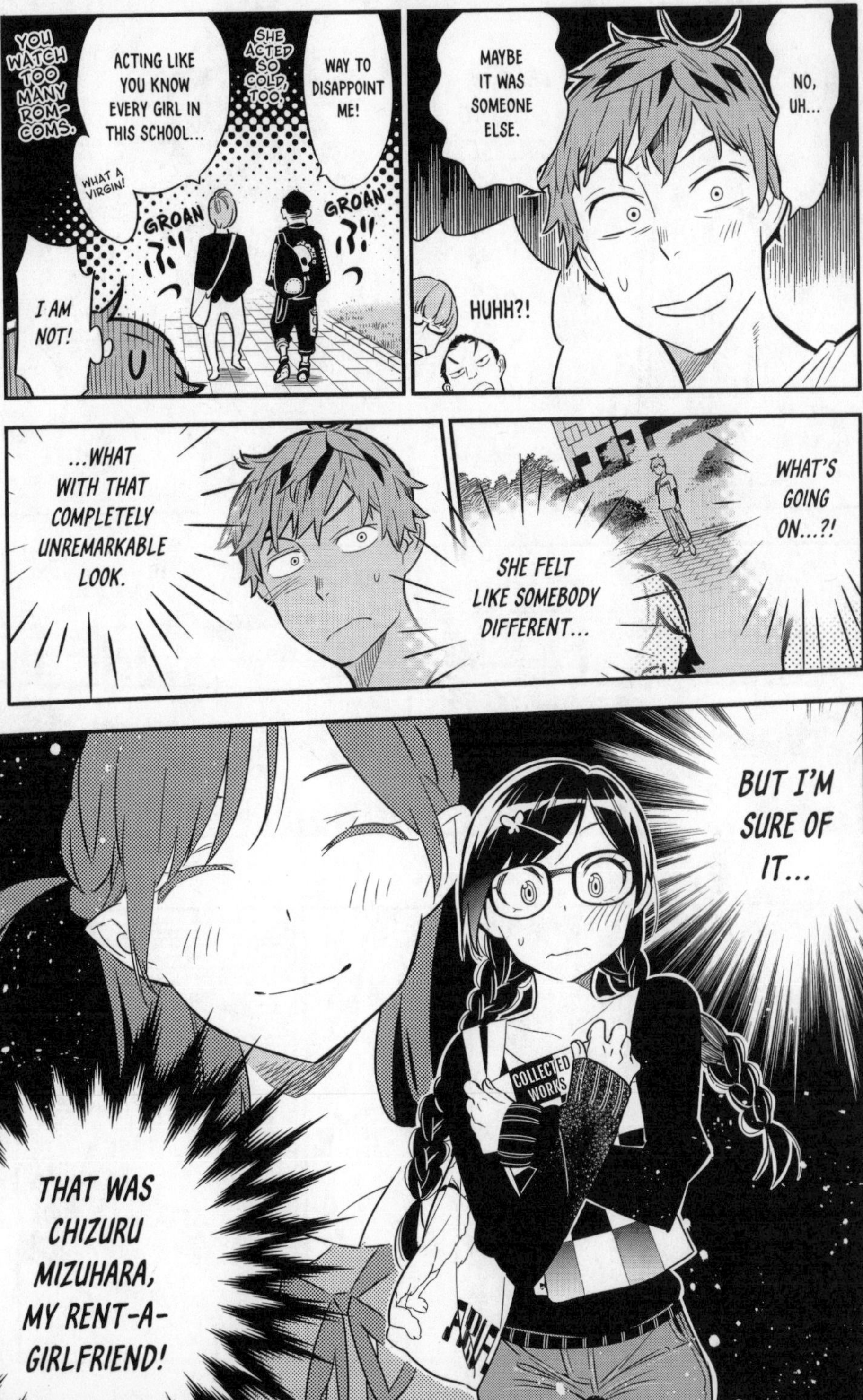
NO, UH...
MAYBE IT WAS SOMEONE ELSE.
HUHH?!
WAY TO DISAPPOINT ME!
SHE ACTED SO COLD, TOO.
ACTING LIKE YOU KNOW EVERY GIRL IN THIS SCHOOL...
YOU WATCH TOO MANY ROM-COMS.
WHAT A VIRGIN!
GROAN
GROAN
I AM NOT!
WHAT'S GOING ON...?!
SHE FELT LIKE SOMEBODY DIFFERENT...
...WHAT WITH THAT COMPLETELY UNREMARKABLE LOOK.
BUT I'M SURE OF IT...
COLLECTED WORKS
THAT WAS CHIZURU MIZUHARA, MY RENT-A-GIRLFRIEND!

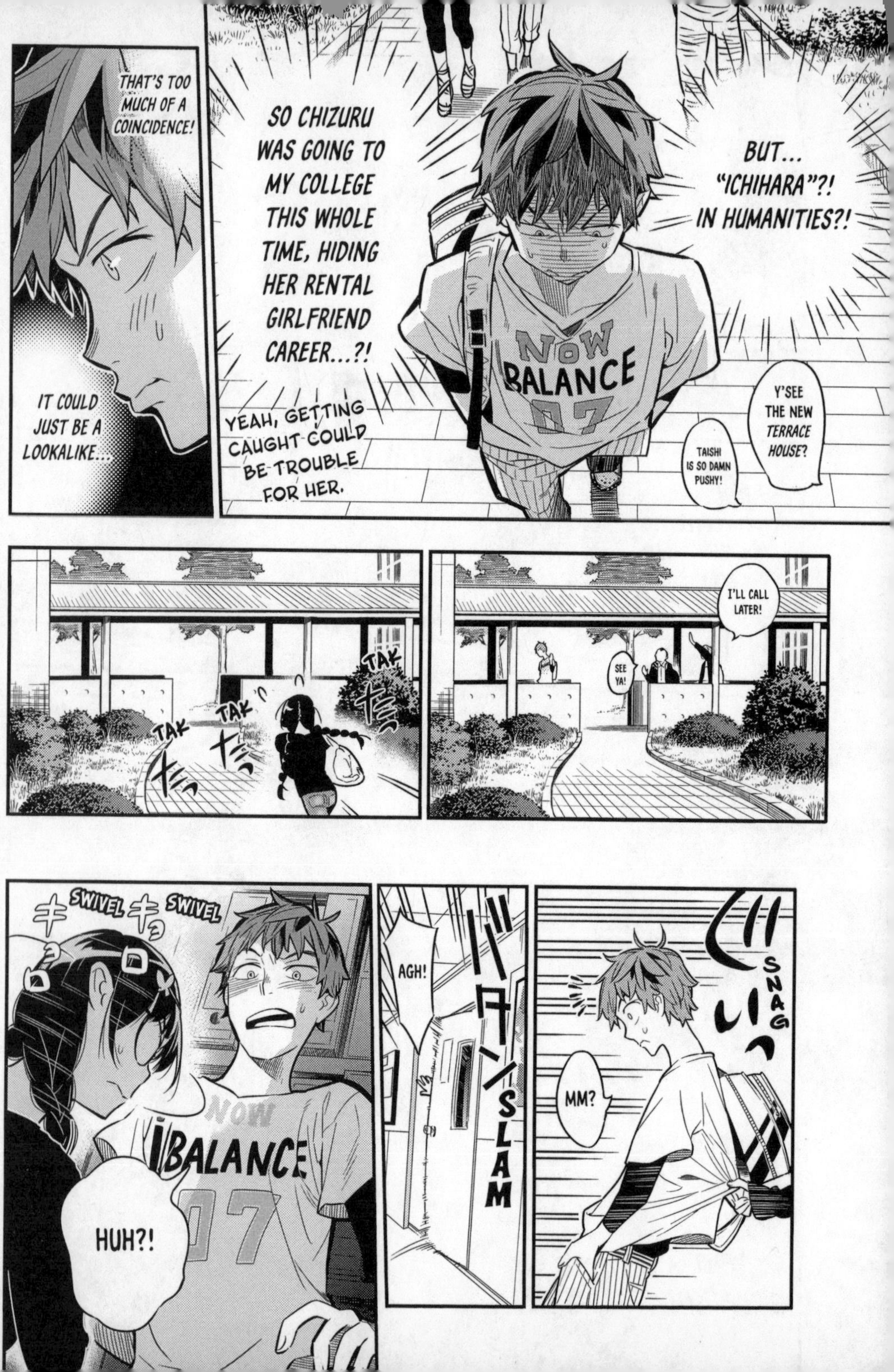
BUT... "ICHIHARA"?! IN HUMANITIES?!
SO CHIZURU WAS GOING TO MY COLLEGE THIS WHOLE TIME, HIDING HER RENTAL GIRLFRIEND CAREER...?!
Y'SEE THE NEW TERRACE HOUSE?
TAISHI IS SO DAMN PUSHY!
YEAH, GETTING CAUGHT COULD BE TROUBLE FOR HER.
THAT'S TOO MUCH OF A COINCIDENCE!
IT COULD JUST BE A LOOKALIKE...
I'LL CALL LATER!
SEE YA!
TAK
TAK
TAK
SNAG
MM?
AGH!
SLAM
SWIVEL SWIVEL
HUH?!

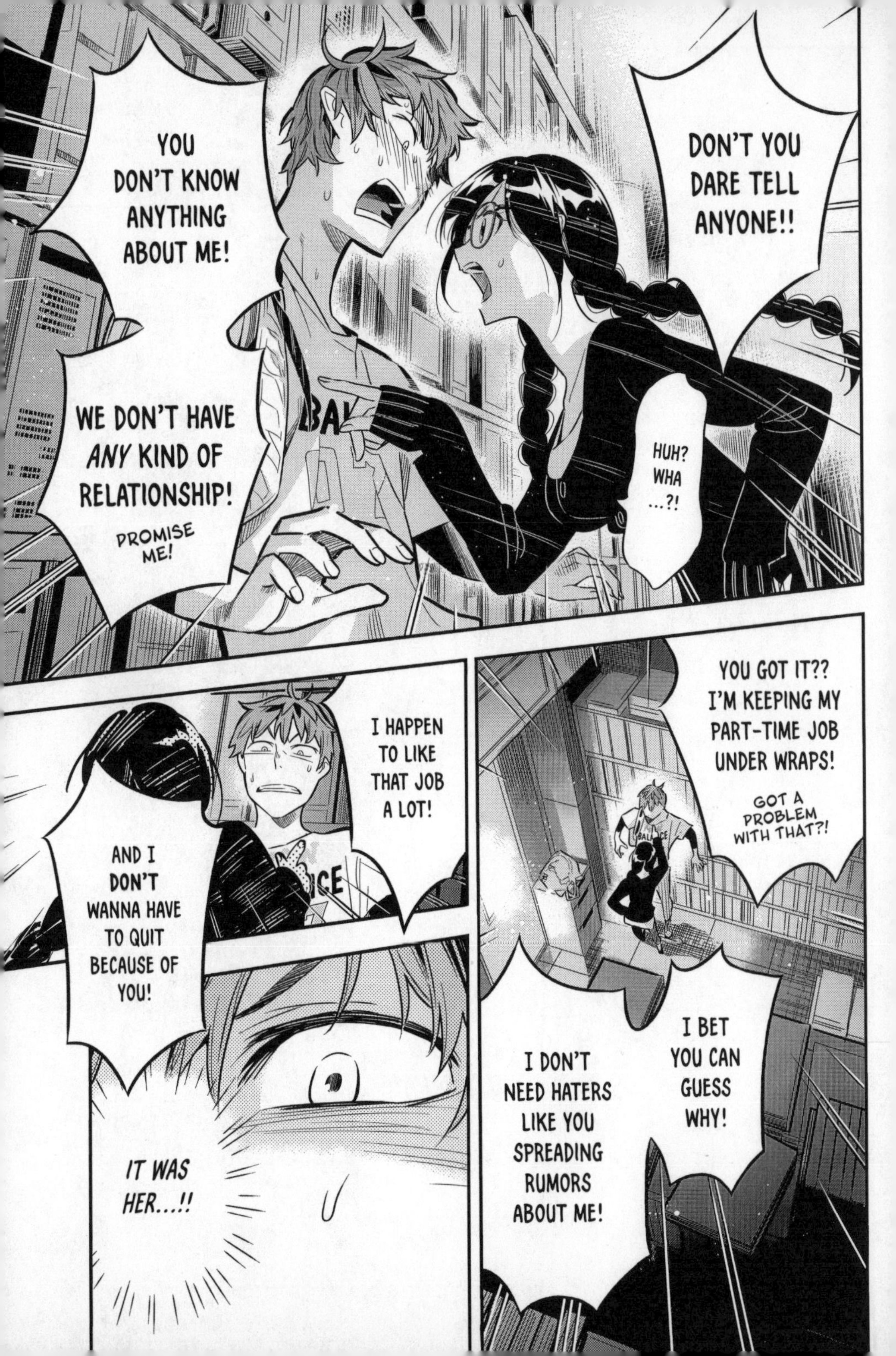
DON'T YOU DARE TELL ANYONE!!
YOU DON'T KNOW ANYTHING ABOUT ME!
HUH? WHA ...?!
WE DON'T HAVE *ANY* KIND OF RELATIONSHIP!
PROMISE ME!
YOU GOT IT?? I'M KEEPING MY PART-TIME JOB UNDER WRAPS!
GOT A PROBLEM WITH THAT?!
I BET YOU CAN GUESS WHY!
I DON'T NEED HATERS LIKE YOU SPREADING RUMORS ABOUT ME!
I HAPPEN TO LIKE THAT JOB A LOT!
AND I DON'T WANNA HAVE TO QUIT BECAUSE OF YOU!
IT WAS HER...!!

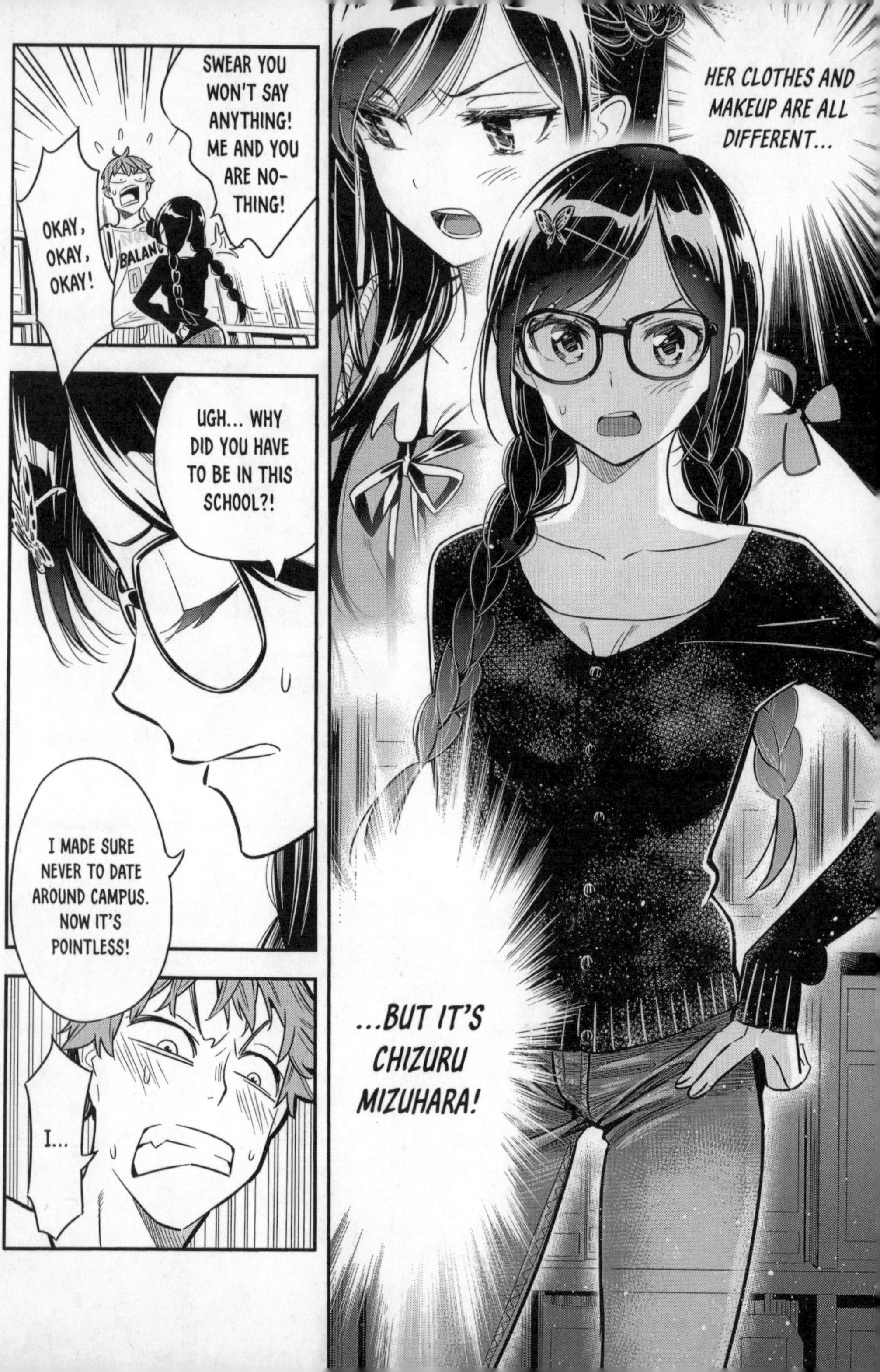
HER CLOTHES AND MAKEUP ARE ALL DIFFERENT...
...BUT IT'S CHIZURU MIZUHARA!
SWEAR YOU WON'T SAY ANYTHING! ME AND YOU ARE NO-THING!
OKAY, OKAY, OKAY!
UGH... WHY DID YOU HAVE TO BE IN THIS SCHOOL?!
I MADE SURE NEVER TO DATE AROUND CAMPUS. NOW IT'S POINTLESS!
I...

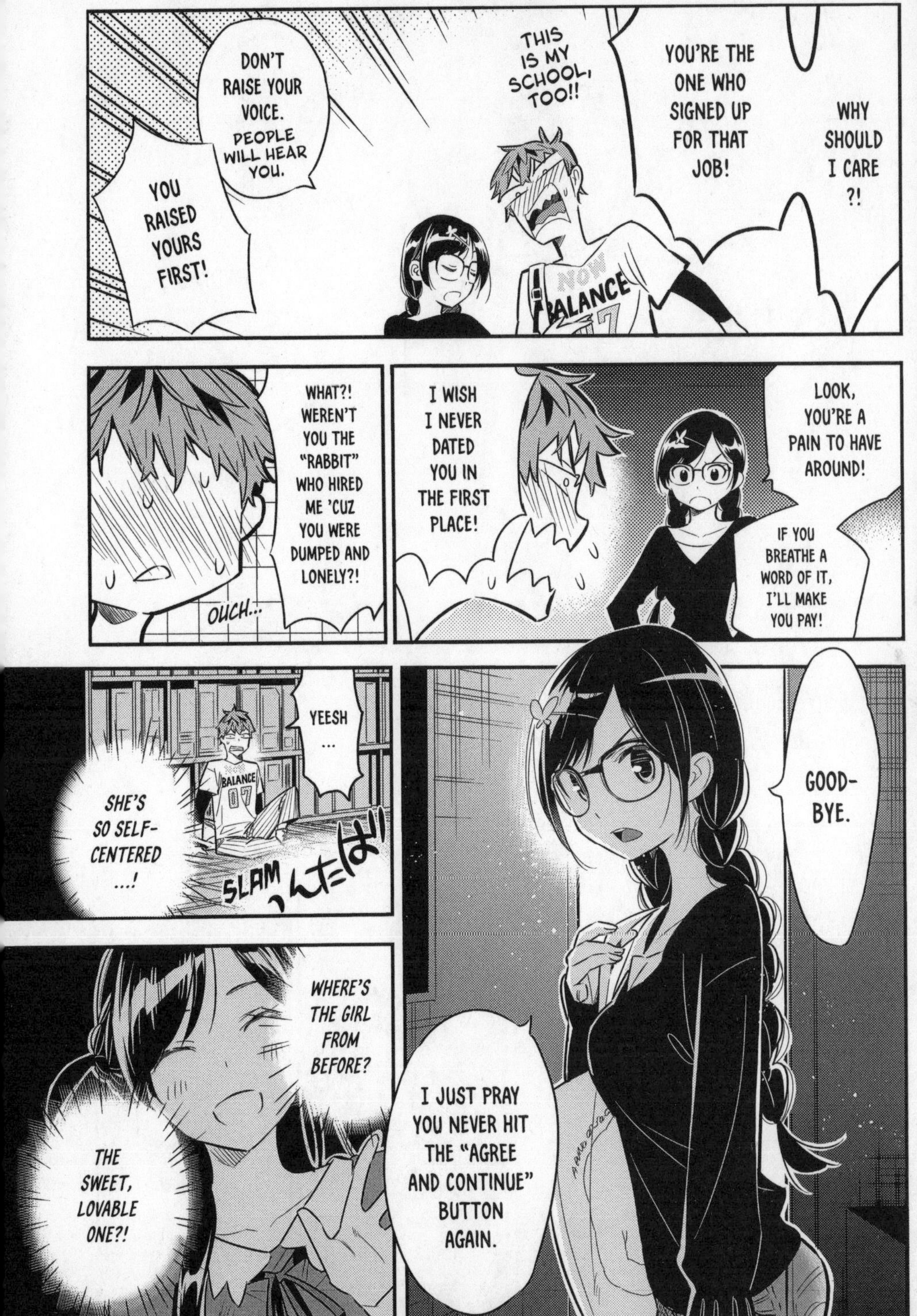
WHY SHOULD I CARE ?!
YOU'RE THE ONE WHO SIGNED UP FOR THAT JOB!
THIS IS MY SCHOOL, TOO!!
DON'T RAISE YOUR VOICE. PEOPLE WILL HEAR YOU.
YOU RAISED YOURS FIRST!
LOOK, YOU'RE A PAIN TO HAVE AROUND!
IF YOU BREATHE A WORD OF IT, I'LL MAKE YOU PAY!
I WISH I NEVER DATED YOU IN THE FIRST PLACE!
WHAT?! WEREN'T YOU THE "RABBIT" WHO HIRED ME 'CUZ YOU WERE DUMPED AND LONELY?!
OUCH...
GOOD-BYE.
I JUST PRAY YOU NEVER HIT THE "AGREE AND CONTINUE" BUTTON AGAIN.
YEESH ...
SHE'S SO SELF-CENTERED ...!
SLAM
WHERE'S THE GIRL FROM BEFORE?
THE SWEET, LOVABLE ONE?!

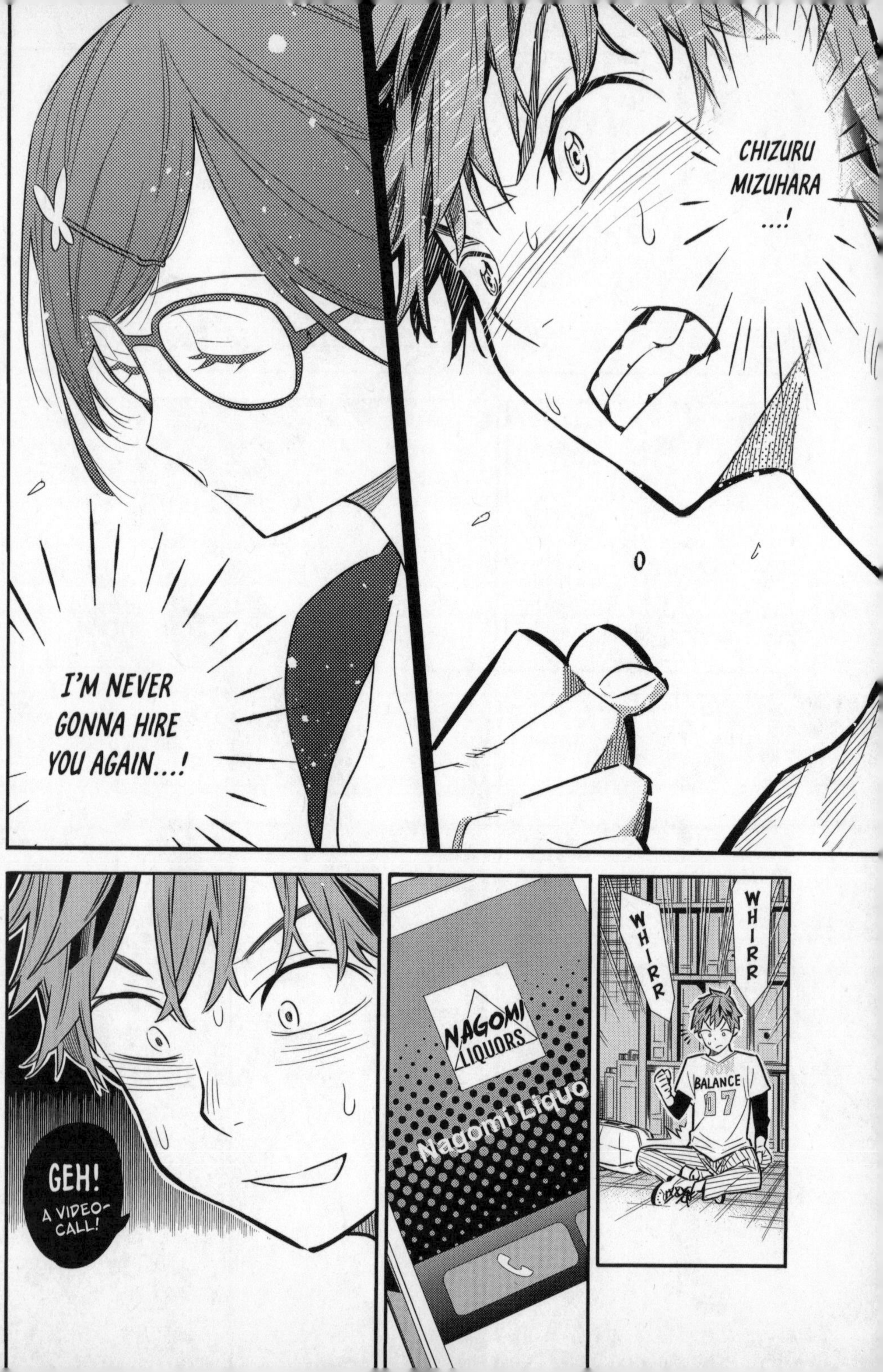
CHIZURU MIZUHARA ...!
I'M NEVER GONNA HIRE YOU AGAIN...!
WHIRR
WHIRR
BALANCE 07
NAGOMI LIQUORS
Nagomi Liquo
GEH! A VIDEO-CALL!

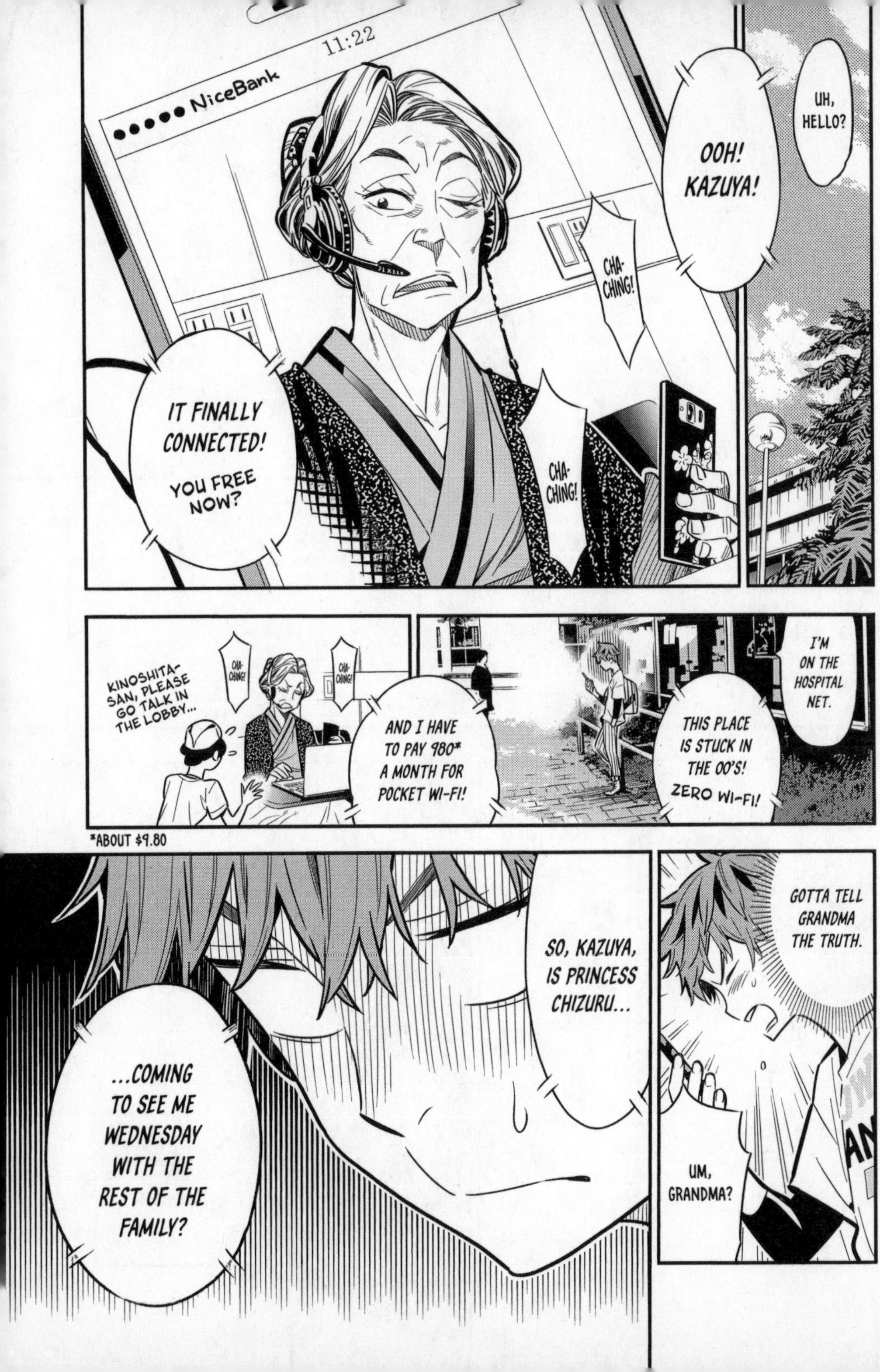
UH, HELLO?
OOH! KAZUYA!
11:22
NiceBank
CHA-CHING!
IT FINALLY CONNECTED!
YOU FREE NOW?
CHA-CHING!
I'M ON THE HOSPITAL NET.
THIS PLACE IS STUCK IN THE 00'S! ZERO WI-FI!
AND I HAVE TO PAY 980* A MONTH FOR POCKET WI-FI!
CHA-CHING!
CHA-CHING!
KINOSHITA-SAN, PLEASE GO TALK IN THE LOBBY...
GOTTA TELL GRANDMA THE TRUTH.
UM, GRANDMA?
SO, KAZUYA, IS PRINCESS CHIZURU...
...COMING TO SEE ME WEDNESDAY WITH THE REST OF THE FAMILY?

*ABOUT $9.80

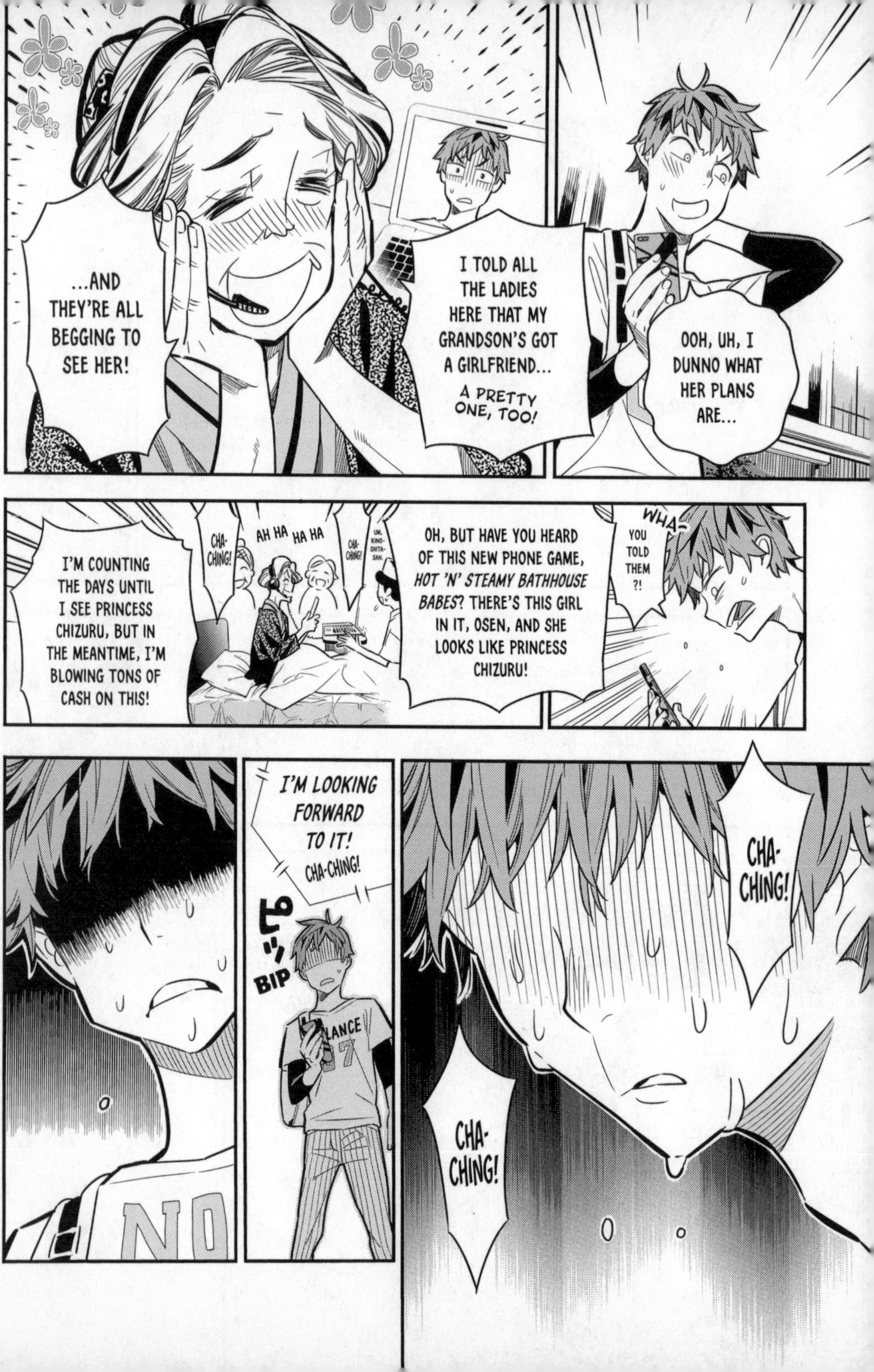
OOH, UH, I DUNNO WHAT HER PLANS ARE...
I TOLD ALL THE LADIES HERE THAT MY GRANDSON'S GOT A GIRLFRIEND...
A PRETTY ONE, TOO!
...AND THEY'RE ALL BEGGING TO SEE HER!
WHA-
YOU TOLD THEM?!
OH, BUT HAVE YOU HEARD OF THIS NEW PHONE GAME, *HOT 'N' STEAMY BATHHOUSE BABES*? THERE'S THIS GIRL IN IT, OSEN, AND SHE LOOKS LIKE PRINCESS CHIZURU!
UM, KINO-SHITA-SAN.
CHA-CHING!
HA HA
AH HA
CHA-CHING!
I'M COUNTING THE DAYS UNTIL I SEE PRINCESS CHIZURU, BUT IN THE MEANTIME, I'M BLOWING TONS OF CASH ON THIS!
CHA-CHING!
CHA-CHING!
I'M LOOKING FORWARD TO IT!
CHA-CHING!
ピッ
BIP
LANCE
NO

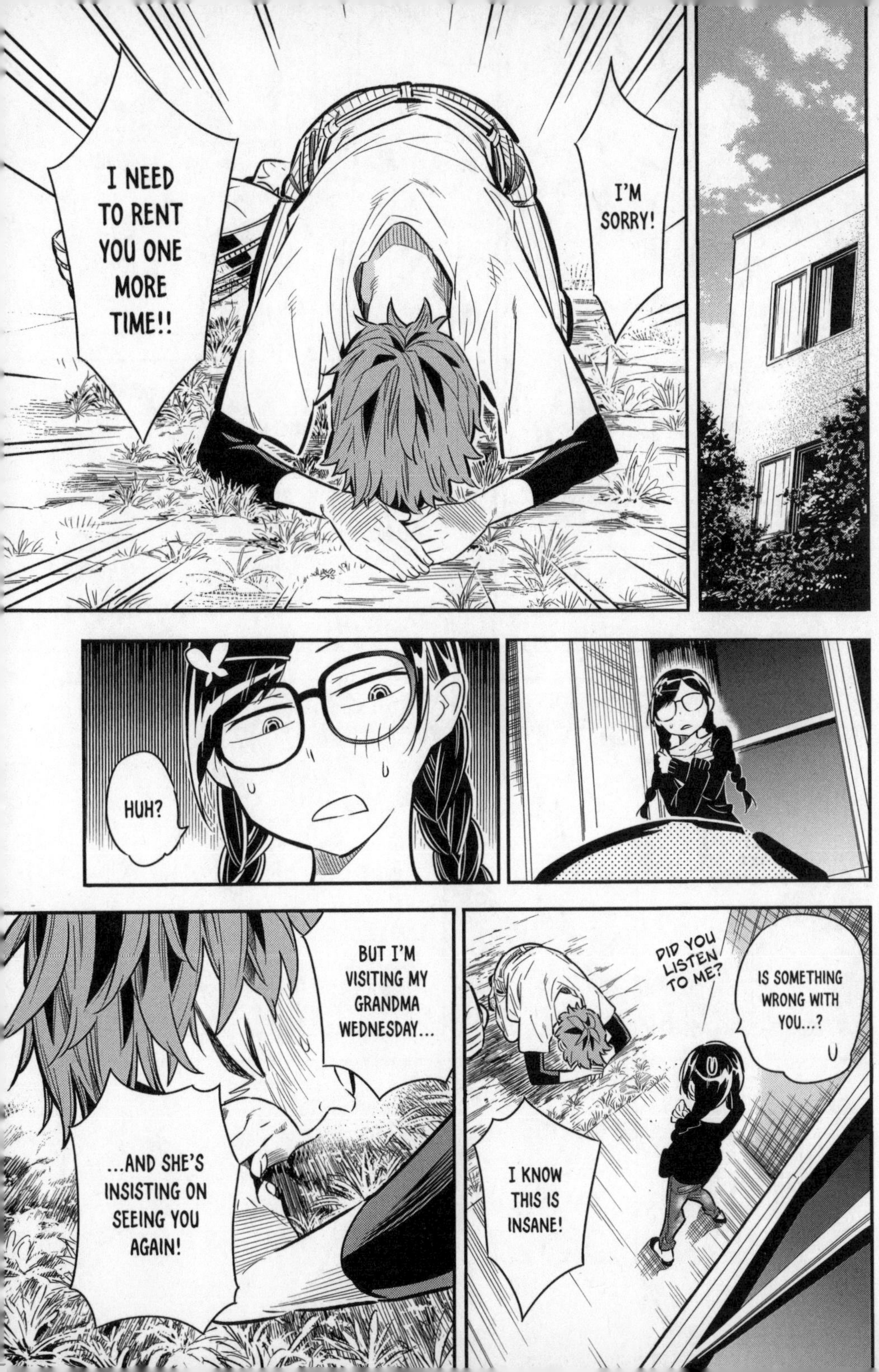
I'M SORRY!
I NEED TO RENT YOU ONE MORE TIME!!
HUH?
IS SOMETHING WRONG WITH YOU...?
DID YOU LISTEN TO ME?
I KNOW THIS IS INSANE!
BUT I'M VISITING MY GRANDMA WEDNESDAY...
...AND SHE'S INSISTING ON SEEING YOU AGAIN!

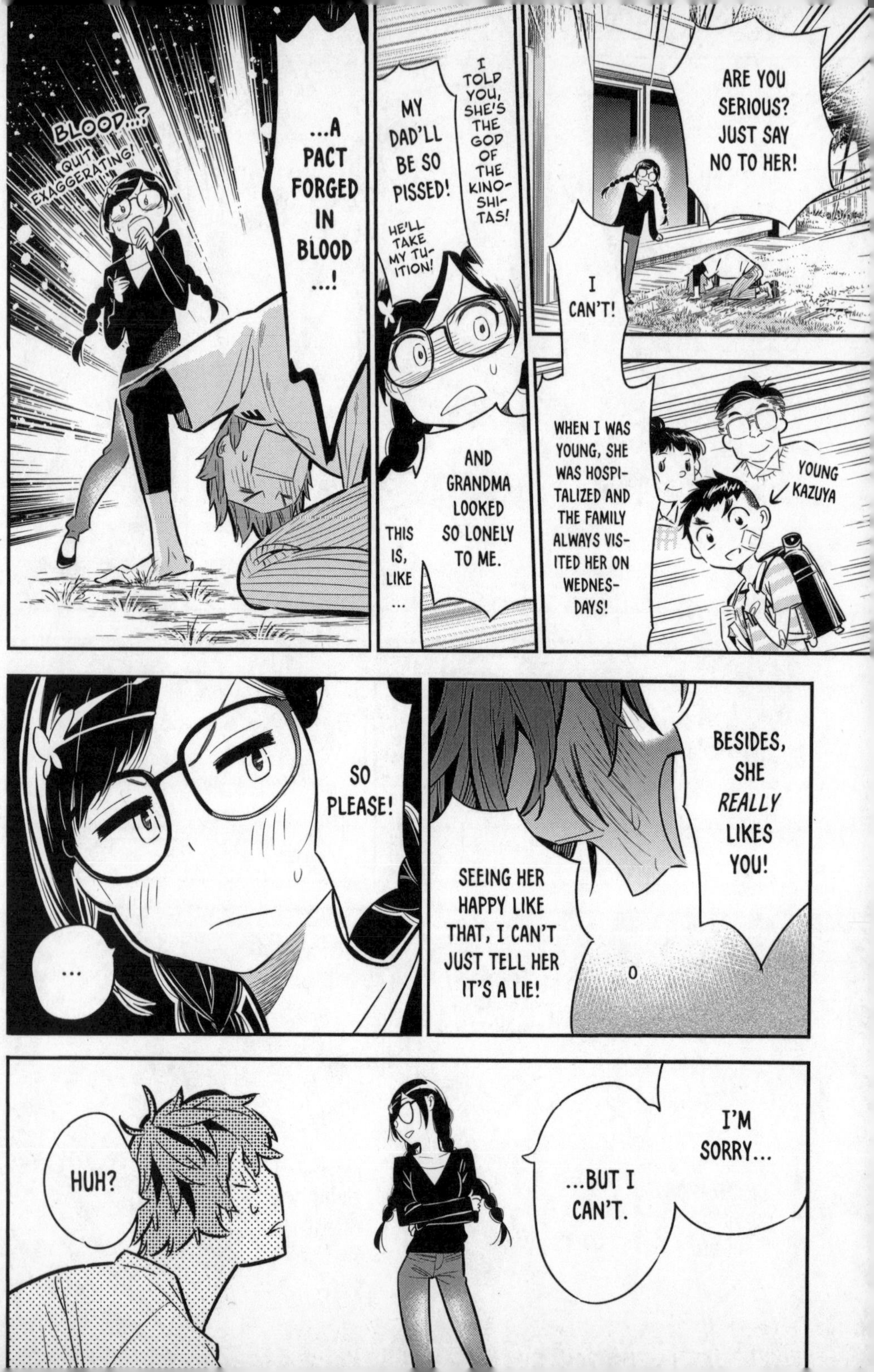
ARE YOU SERIOUS? JUST SAY NO TO HER!
I CAN'T!
WHEN I WAS YOUNG, SHE WAS HOSPITALIZED AND THE FAMILY ALWAYS VISITED HER ON WEDNESDAYS!
YOUNG KAZUYA
I TOLD YOU, SHE'S THE GOD OF THE KINOSHITAS!
MY DAD'LL BE SO PISSED!
HE'LL TAKE MY TUITION!
AND GRANDMA LOOKED SO LONELY TO ME.
THIS IS, LIKE ...
...A PACT FORGED IN BLOOD ...!
BLOOD...?
QUIT EXAGGERATING!
BESIDES, SHE REALLY LIKES YOU!
SEEING HER HAPPY LIKE THAT, I CAN'T JUST TELL HER IT'S A LIE!
SO PLEASE!
...
I'M SORRY...
...BUT I CAN'T.
HUH?

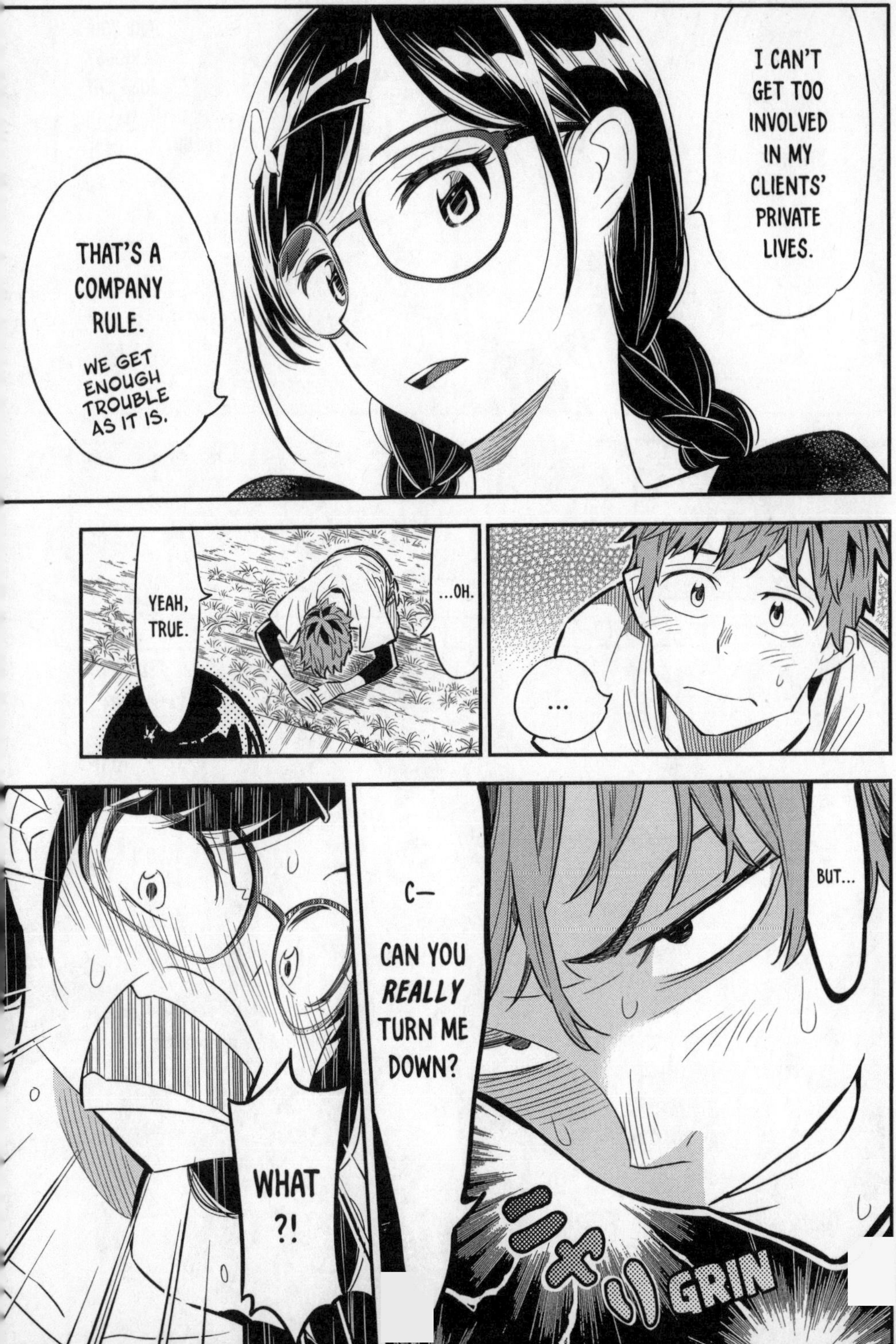
I CAN'T GET TOO INVOLVED IN MY CLIENTS' PRIVATE LIVES.
THAT'S A COMPANY RULE.
WE GET ENOUGH TROUBLE AS IT IS.
...
...OH.
YEAH, TRUE.
BUT...
GRIN
C—
CAN YOU *REALLY* TURN ME DOWN?
WHAT?!

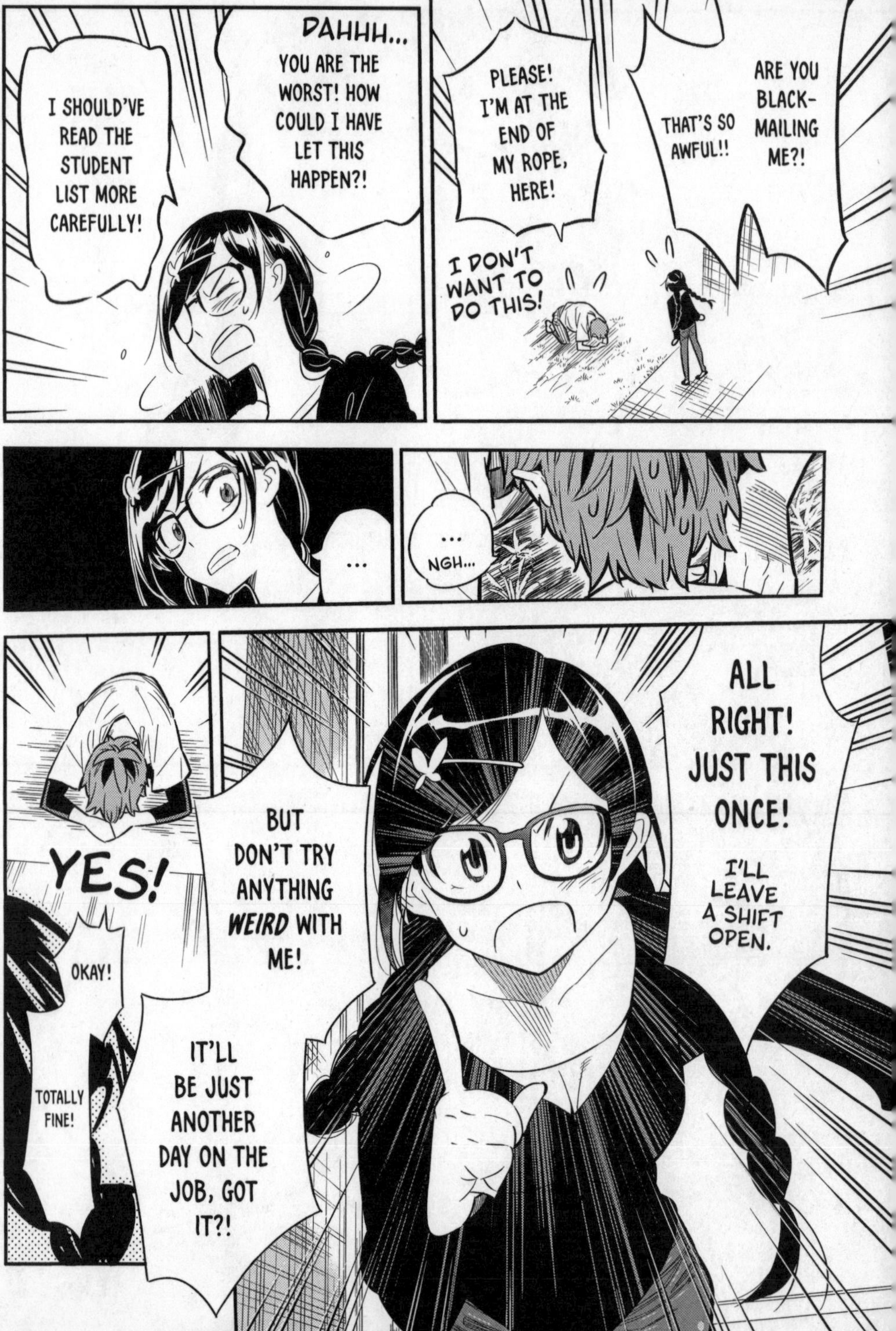
ARE YOU BLACK-MAILING ME?!
THAT'S SO AWFUL!!
PLEASE! I'M AT THE END OF MY ROPE, HERE!
I DON'T WANT TO DO THIS!
DAHHH... YOU ARE THE WORST! HOW COULD I HAVE LET THIS HAPPEN?!
I SHOULD'VE READ THE STUDENT LIST MORE CAREFULLY!
... NGH...
...
ALL RIGHT! JUST THIS ONCE!
I'LL LEAVE A SHIFT OPEN.
BUT DON'T TRY ANYTHING *WEIRD* WITH ME!
IT'LL BE JUST ANOTHER DAY ON THE JOB, GOT IT?!
YES!
OKAY!
TOTALLY FINE!

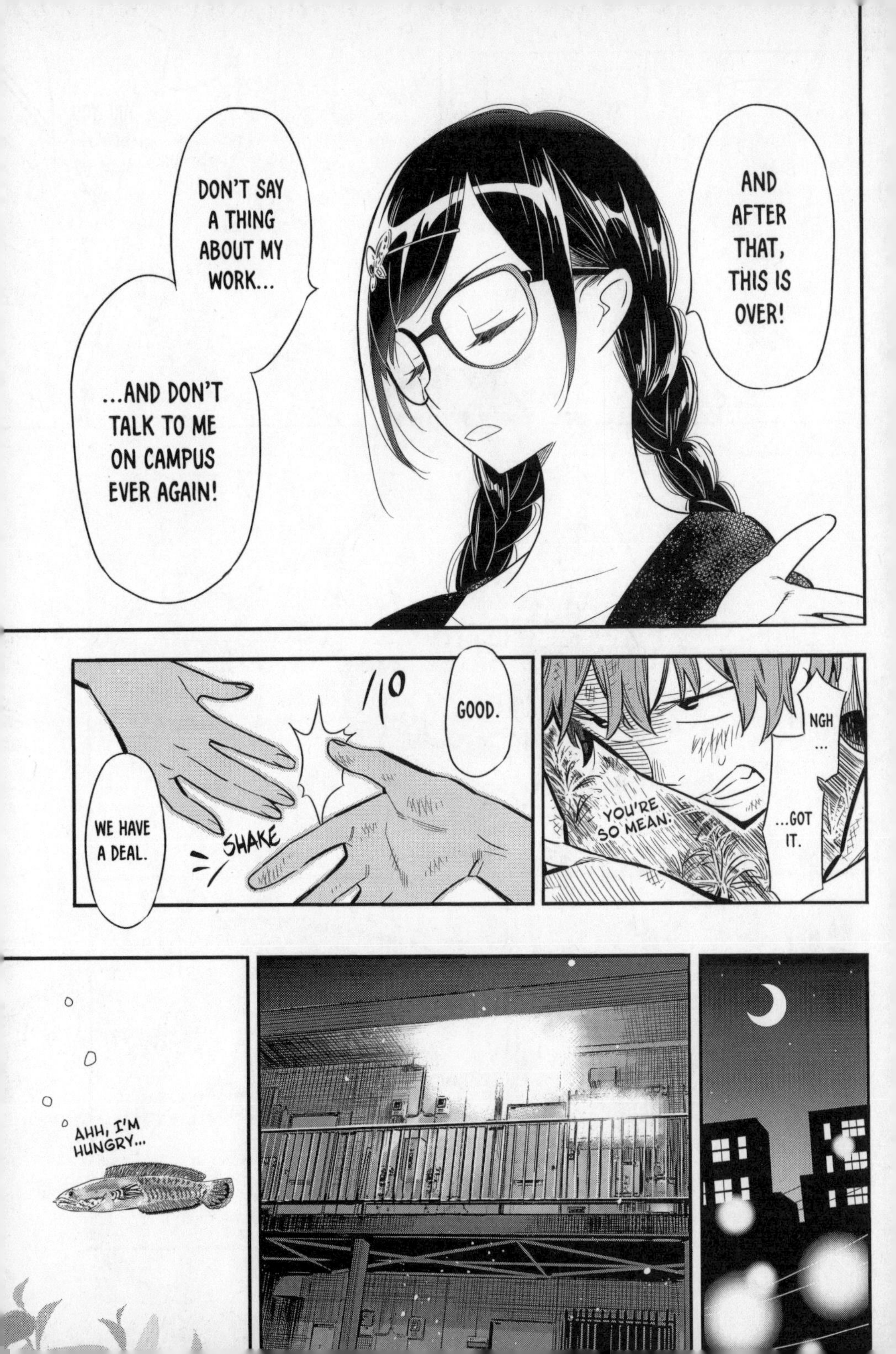
AND AFTER THAT, THIS IS OVER!
DON'T SAY A THING ABOUT MY WORK...
...AND DON'T TALK TO ME ON CAMPUS EVER AGAIN!
NGH...
YOU'RE SO MEAN.
...GOT IT.
GOOD.
WE HAVE A DEAL.
SHAKE
AHH, I'M HUNGRY...

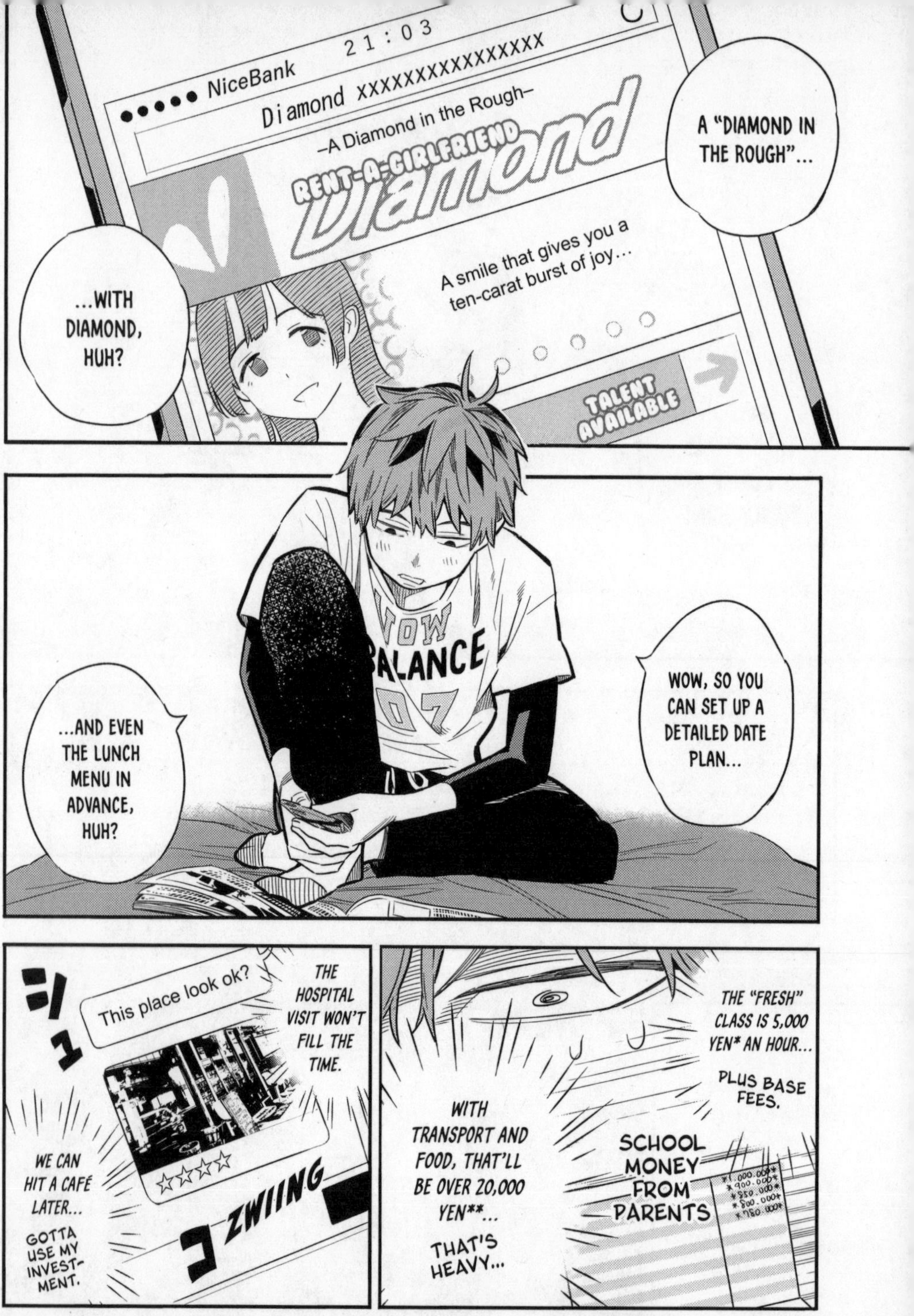
21:03
NiceBank
Diamond xxxxxxxxxxxxxxx
–A Diamond in the Rough–
RENT-A-GIRLFRIEND Diamond
A smile that gives you a ten-carat burst of joy...
TALENT AVAILABLE
A "DIAMOND IN THE ROUGH"...
...WITH DIAMOND, HUH?
WOW, SO YOU CAN SET UP A DETAILED DATE PLAN...
...AND EVEN THE LUNCH MENU IN ADVANCE, HUH?
THE "FRESH" CLASS IS 5,000 YEN* AN HOUR...
PLUS BASE FEES.
SCHOOL MONEY FROM PARENTS
WITH TRANSPORT AND FOOD, THAT'LL BE OVER 20,000 YEN**...
THAT'S HEAVY...
THE HOSPITAL VISIT WON'T FILL THE TIME.
This place look ok?
ZWIING
WE CAN HIT A CAFÉ LATER...
GOTTA USE MY INVEST-MENT.

** ABOUT $180

*ABOUT $50

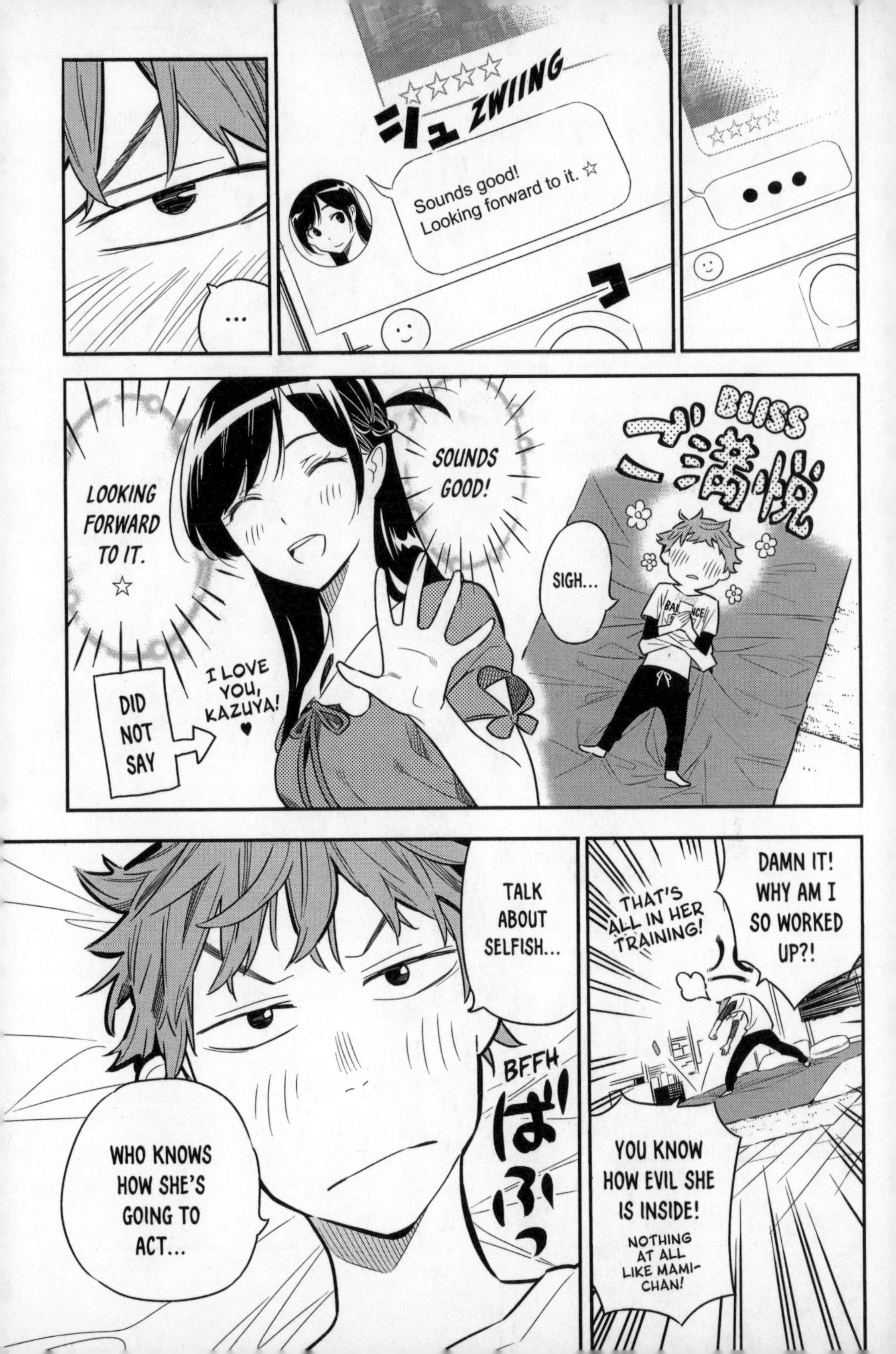
•••
シュ ZWIING
Sounds good! Looking forward to it. ☆
...
ご満悦 BLISS
SIGH...
SOUNDS GOOD!
LOOKING FORWARD TO IT. ☆
I LOVE YOU, KAZUYA! ♥
DID NOT SAY
DAMN IT! WHY AM I SO WORKED UP?!
THAT'S ALL IN HER TRAINING!
YOU KNOW HOW EVIL SHE IS INSIDE!
NOTHING AT ALL LIKE MAMI-CHAN!
TALK ABOUT SELFISH...
BFFH ぱふっ
WHO KNOWS HOW SHE'S GOING TO ACT...

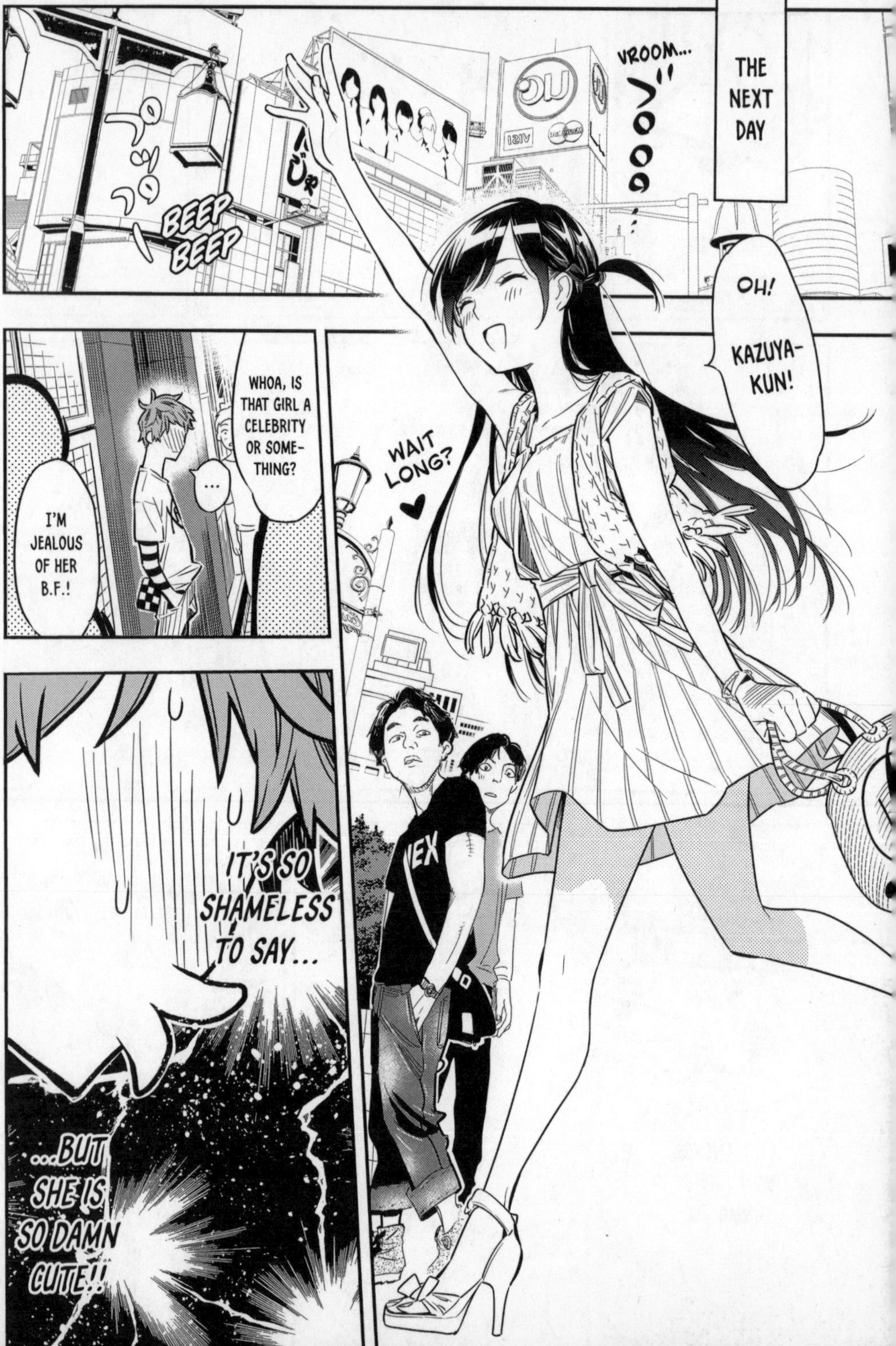
THE NEXT DAY
VROOM...
BEEP BEEP
OH! KAZUYA-KUN!
WAIT LONG? ♥
WHOA, IS THAT GIRL A CELEBRITY OR SOMETHING?
...
I'M JEALOUS OF HER B.F.!
IT'S SO SHAMELESS TO SAY...
...BUT SHE IS SO DAMN CUTE!!

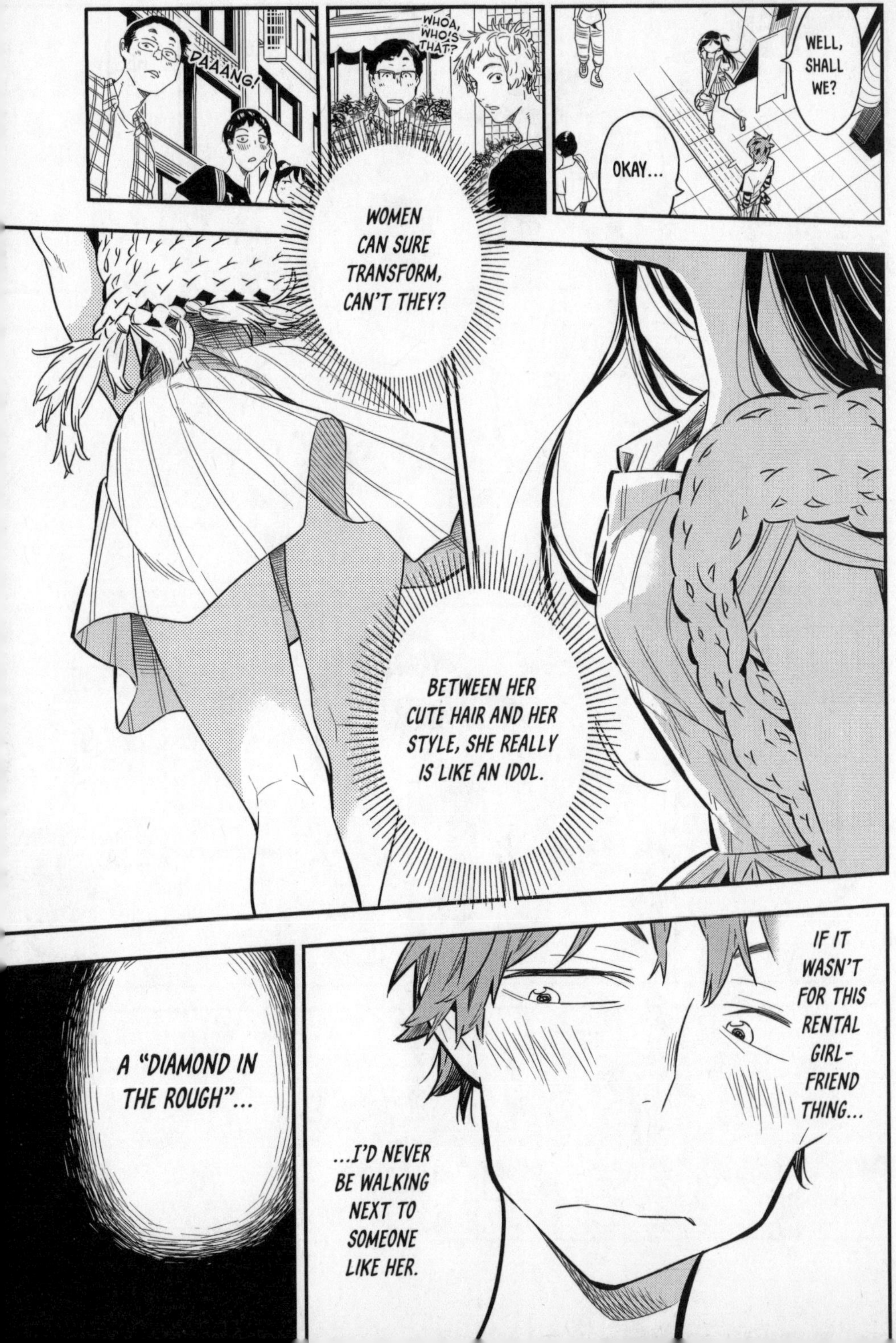
WELL, SHALL WE?
OKAY...
WHOA, WHO'S THAT?
DAAANG!
WOMEN CAN SURE TRANSFORM, CAN'T THEY?
BETWEEN HER CUTE HAIR AND HER STYLE, SHE REALLY IS LIKE AN IDOL.
IF IT WASN'T FOR THIS RENTAL GIRL-FRIEND THING...
...I'D NEVER BE WALKING NEXT TO SOMEONE LIKE HER.
A "DIAMOND IN THE ROUGH"...

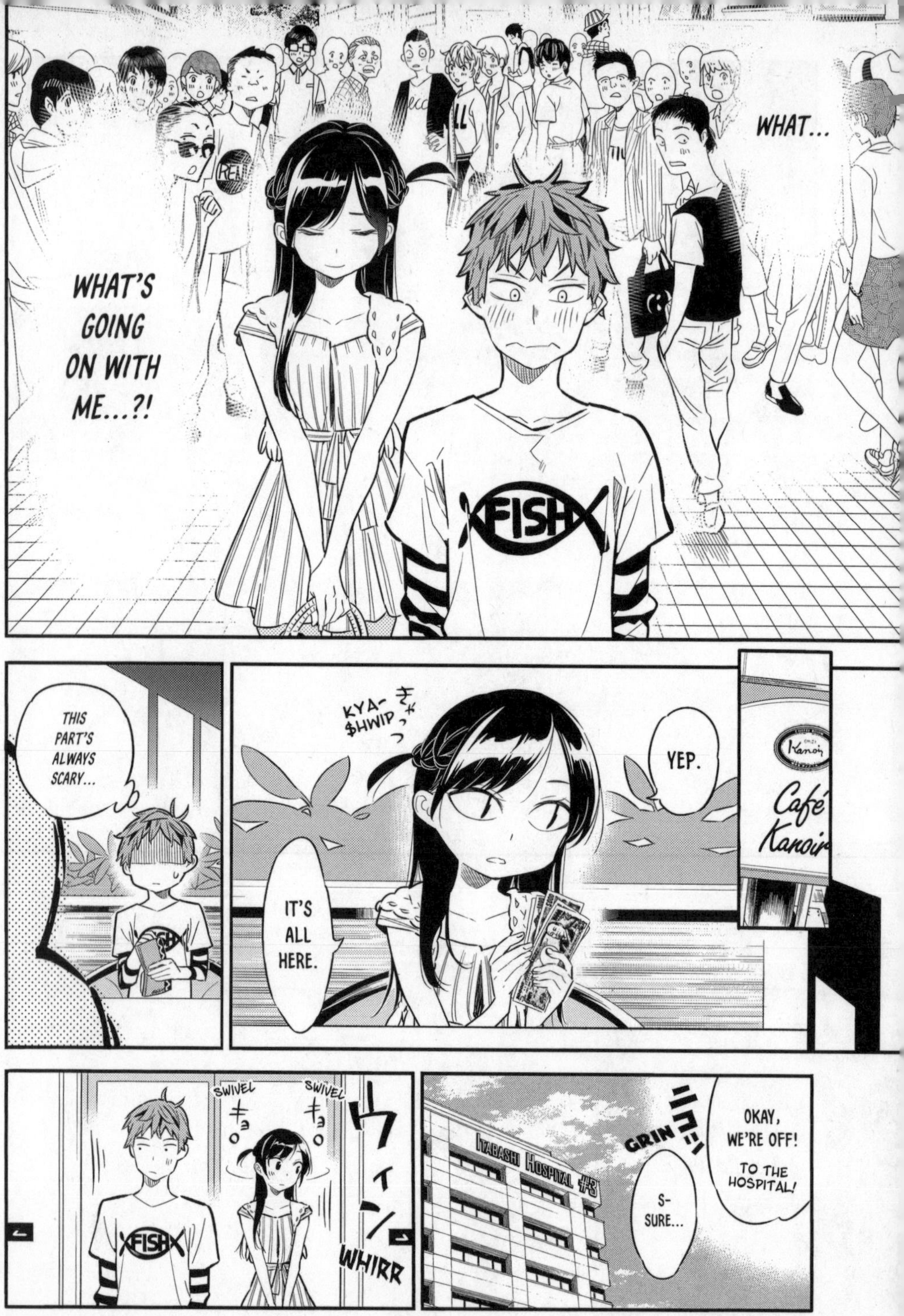
WHAT...
WHAT'S GOING ON WITH ME...?!
Café Kanoir
YEP.
KYA-$HWIP
IT'S ALL HERE.
THIS PART'S ALWAYS SCARY...
OKAY, WE'RE OFF!
TO THE HOSPITAL!
GRIN
S-SURE...
ITABASHI HOSPITAL #3
WHIRR
SWIVEL
SWIVEL

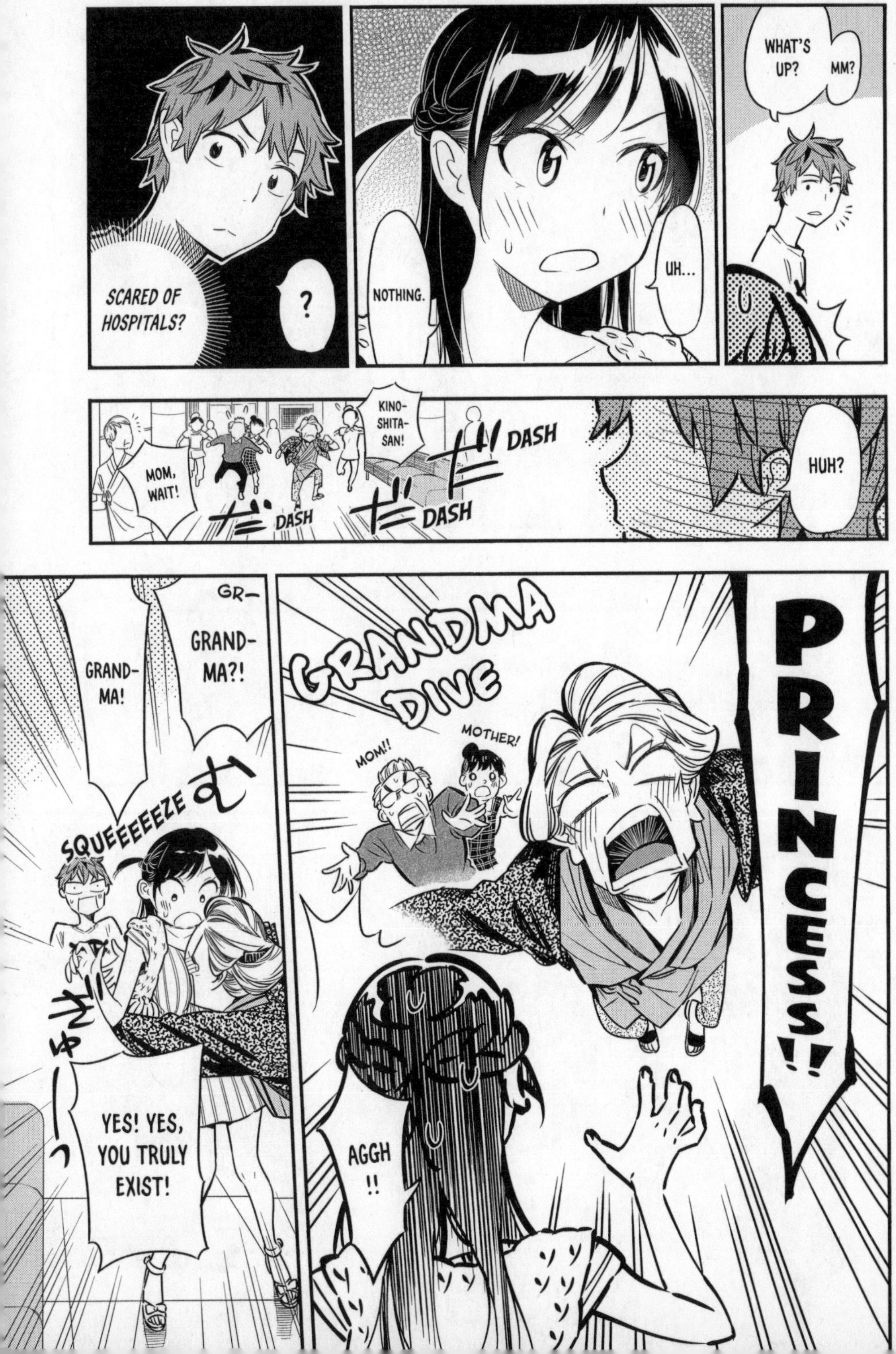
MM?
WHAT'S UP?
UH...
NOTHING.
?
SCARED OF HOSPITALS?
HUH?
DASH
KINO-SHITA-SAN!
DASH
DASH
MOM, WAIT!
PRINCESS!!
GRANDMA DIVE
MOTHER!
MOM!!
AGGH !!
GR- GRAND-MA?!
GRAND-MA!
SQUEEEEEZE
YES! YES, YOU TRULY EXIST!

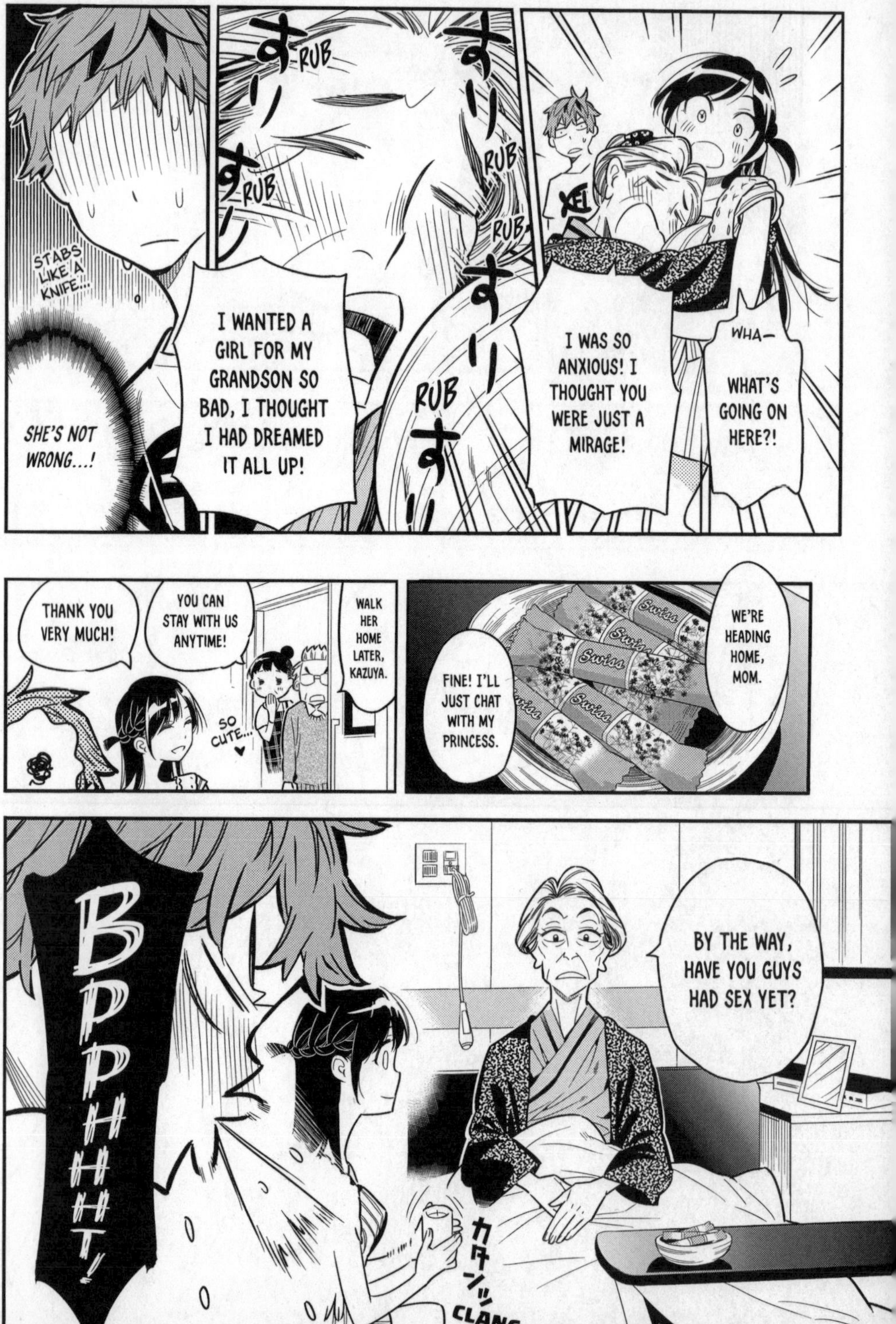
WHA—
WHAT'S GOING ON HERE?!
I WAS SO ANXIOUS! I THOUGHT YOU WERE JUST A MIRAGE!
RUB
RUB
RUB
RUB
RUB
I WANTED A GIRL FOR MY GRANDSON SO BAD, I THOUGHT I HAD DREAMED IT ALL UP!
STABS LIKE A KNIFE...
SHE'S NOT WRONG...!
WE'RE HEADING HOME, MOM.
FINE! I'LL JUST CHAT WITH MY PRINCESS.
Swiss
WALK HER HOME LATER, KAZUYA.
YOU CAN STAY WITH US ANYTIME!
SO CUTE...
THANK YOU VERY MUCH!
BY THE WAY, HAVE YOU GUYS HAD SEX YET?
カタンッ
CLANG
BPPHHHHT!

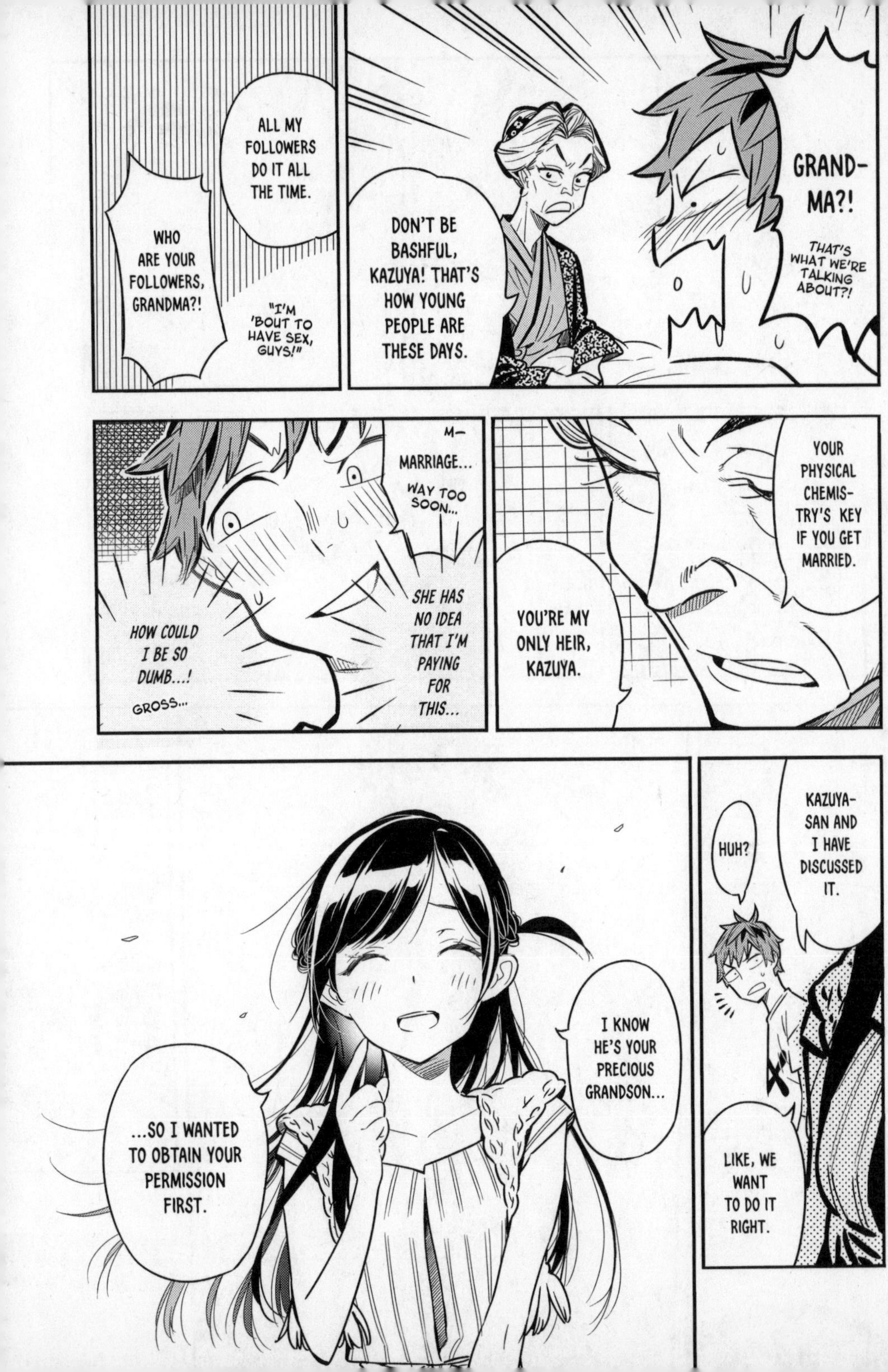
GRAND-MA?!
THAT'S WHAT WE'RE TALKING ABOUT?!
DON'T BE BASHFUL, KAZUYA! THAT'S HOW YOUNG PEOPLE ARE THESE DAYS.
ALL MY FOLLOWERS DO IT ALL THE TIME.
WHO ARE YOUR FOLLOWERS, GRANDMA?!
"I'M 'BOUT TO HAVE SEX, GUYS!"
YOUR PHYSICAL CHEMIS-TRY'S KEY IF YOU GET MARRIED.
YOU'RE MY ONLY HEIR, KAZUYA.
M— MARRIAGE...
WAY TOO SOON...
SHE HAS NO IDEA THAT I'M PAYING FOR THIS...
HOW COULD I BE SO DUMB...!
GROSS...
KAZUYA-SAN AND I HAVE DISCUSSED IT.
HUH?
LIKE, WE WANT TO DO IT RIGHT.
I KNOW HE'S YOUR PRECIOUS GRANDSON...
...SO I WANTED TO OBTAIN YOUR PERMISSION FIRST.

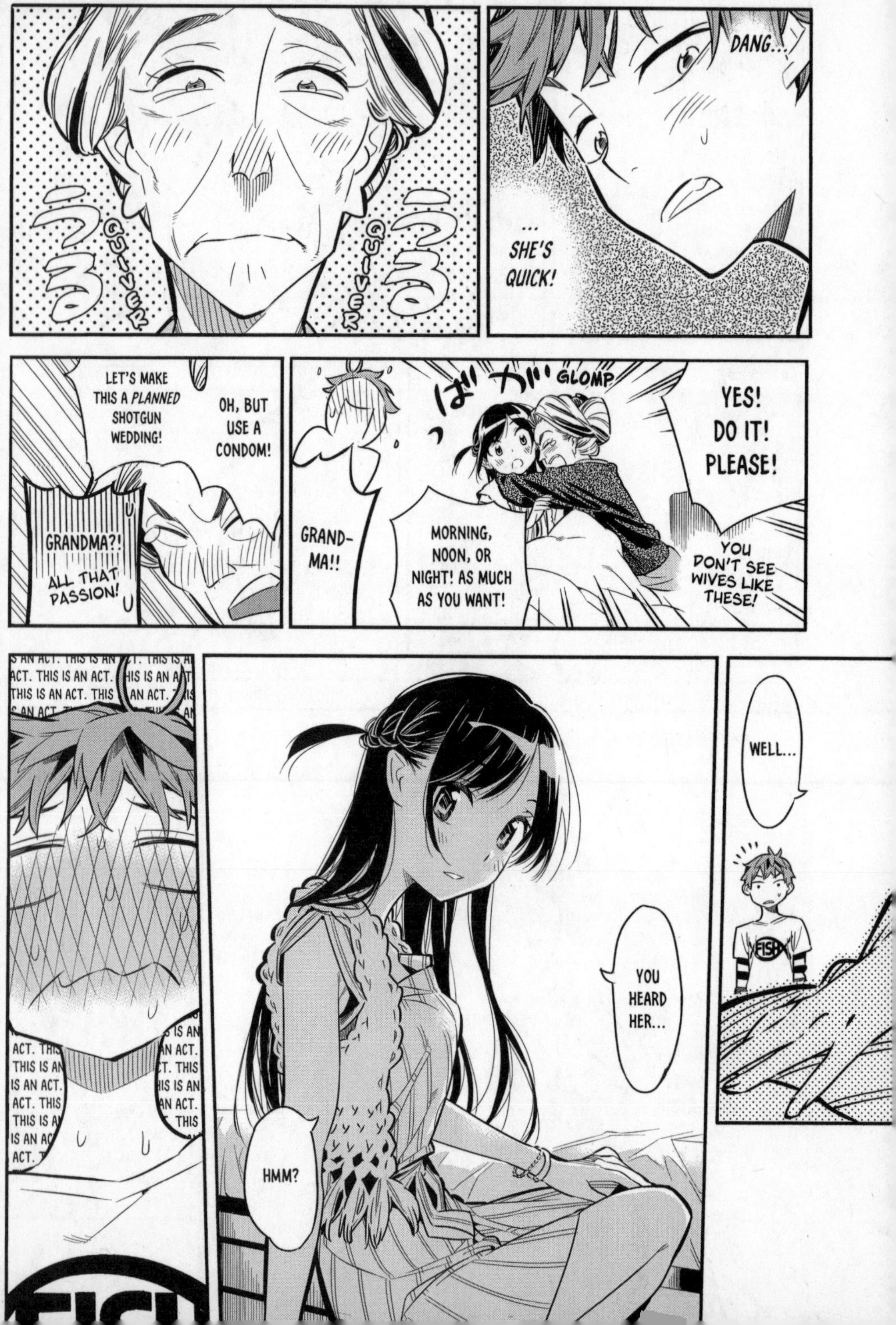
DANG...
... SHE'S QUICK!
うる
QUIVER
うる
QUIVER
YES! DO IT! PLEASE!
YOU DON'T SEE WIVES LIKE THESE!
GLOMP
MORNING, NOON, OR NIGHT! AS MUCH AS YOU WANT!
GRAND-MA!!
OH, BUT USE A CONDOM!
LET'S MAKE THIS A PLANNED SHOTGUN WEDDING!
GRANDMA?! ALL THAT PASSION!
WELL...
YOU HEARD HER...
HMM?
THIS IS AN ACT. THIS IS AN ACT. THIS IS AN ACT. THIS IS AN ACT. THIS IS AN ACT.

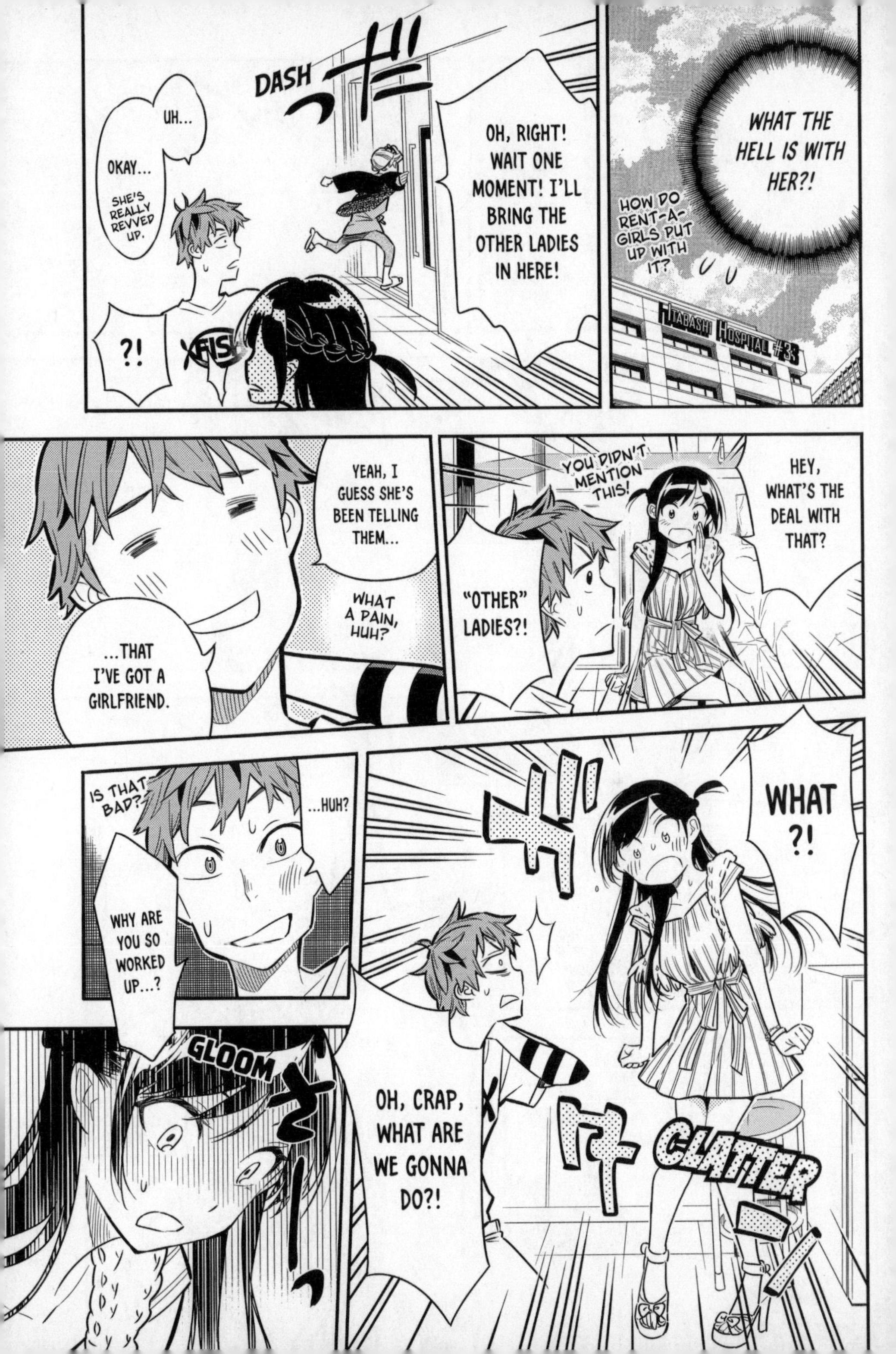
WHAT THE HELL IS WITH HER?!
HOW DO RENT-A-GIRLS PUT UP WITH IT?
ITABASHI HOSPITAL
OH, RIGHT! WAIT ONE MOMENT! I'LL BRING THE OTHER LADIES IN HERE!
DASH
?!
UH...
OKAY...
SHE'S REALLY REVVED UP.
HEY, WHAT'S THE DEAL WITH THAT?
YOU DIDN'T MENTION THIS!
"OTHER" LADIES?!
YEAH, I GUESS SHE'S BEEN TELLING THEM...
...THAT I'VE GOT A GIRLFRIEND.
WHAT A PAIN, HUH?
WHAT ?!
...HUH?
IS THAT BAD?
WHY ARE YOU SO WORKED UP...?
CLATTER
GLOOM
OH, CRAP, WHAT ARE WE GONNA DO?!

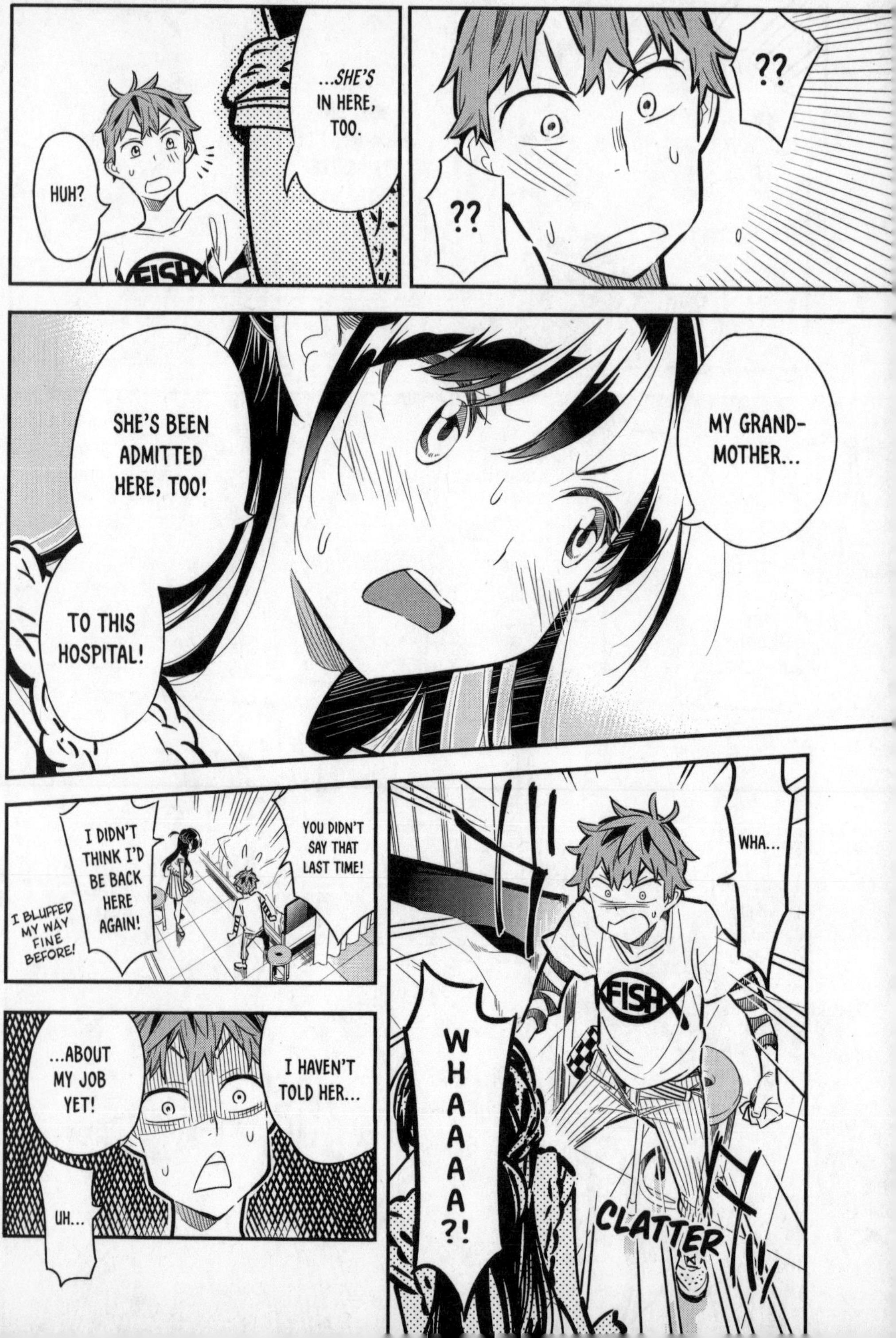

??
??
...SHE'S IN HERE, TOO.
HUH?
MY GRAND-MOTHER...
SHE'S BEEN ADMITTED HERE, TOO!
TO THIS HOSPITAL!
WHA...
WHAAAAA?!
CLATTER
YOU DIDN'T SAY THAT LAST TIME!
I DIDN'T THINK I'D BE BACK HERE AGAIN!
I BLUFFED MY WAY FINE BEFORE!
I HAVEN'T TOLD HER...
...ABOUT MY JOB YET!
UH...

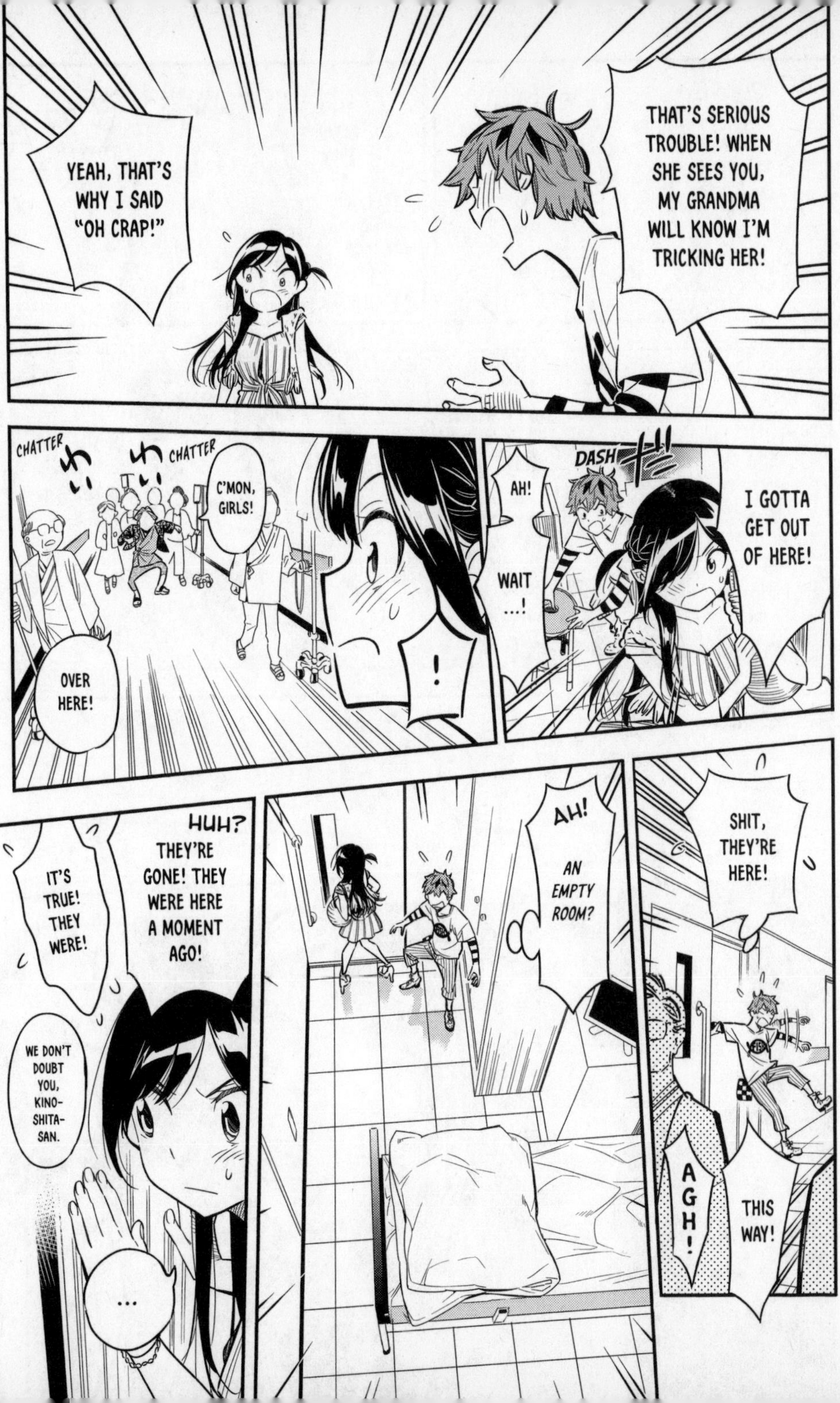
THAT'S SERIOUS TROUBLE! WHEN SHE SEES YOU, MY GRANDMA WILL KNOW I'M TRICKING HER!
YEAH, THAT'S WHY I SAID "OH CRAP!"
DASH
I GOTTA GET OUT OF HERE!
AH!
WAIT ...!
!
C'MON, GIRLS!
CHATTER
CHATTER
OVER HERE!
SHIT, THEY'RE HERE!
THIS WAY!
AGH!
AH!
AN EMPTY ROOM?
HUH?
THEY'RE GONE! THEY WERE HERE A MOMENT AGO!
IT'S TRUE! THEY WERE!
WE DON'T DOUBT YOU, KINO-SHITA-SAN.
...

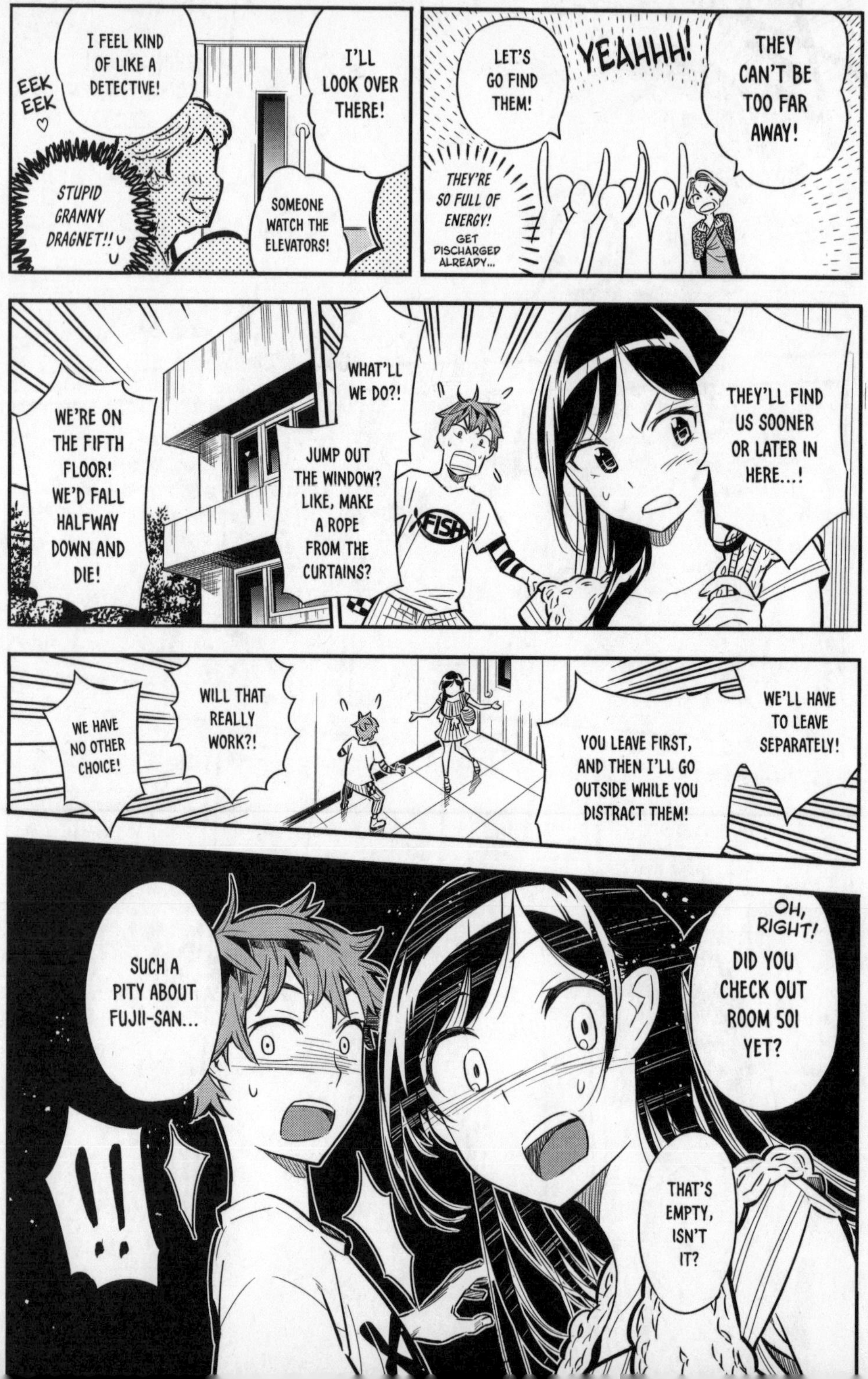
THEY CAN'T BE TOO FAR AWAY!
LET'S GO FIND THEM!
YEAHHH!
THEY'RE SO FULL OF ENERGY!
GET DISCHARGED ALREADY...
I'LL LOOK OVER THERE!
SOMEONE WATCH THE ELEVATORS!
I FEEL KIND OF LIKE A DETECTIVE!
EEK EEK ♡
STUPID GRANNY DRAGNET!!
THEY'LL FIND US SOONER OR LATER IN HERE...!
WHAT'LL WE DO?!
JUMP OUT THE WINDOW? LIKE, MAKE A ROPE FROM THE CURTAINS?
WE'RE ON THE FIFTH FLOOR! WE'D FALL HALFWAY DOWN AND DIE!
WE'LL HAVE TO LEAVE SEPARATELY!
YOU LEAVE FIRST, AND THEN I'LL GO OUTSIDE WHILE YOU DISTRACT THEM!
WILL THAT REALLY WORK?!
WE HAVE NO OTHER CHOICE!
OH, RIGHT!
DID YOU CHECK OUT ROOM 501 YET?
THAT'S EMPTY, ISN'T IT?
SUCH A PITY ABOUT FUJII-SAN...
!!

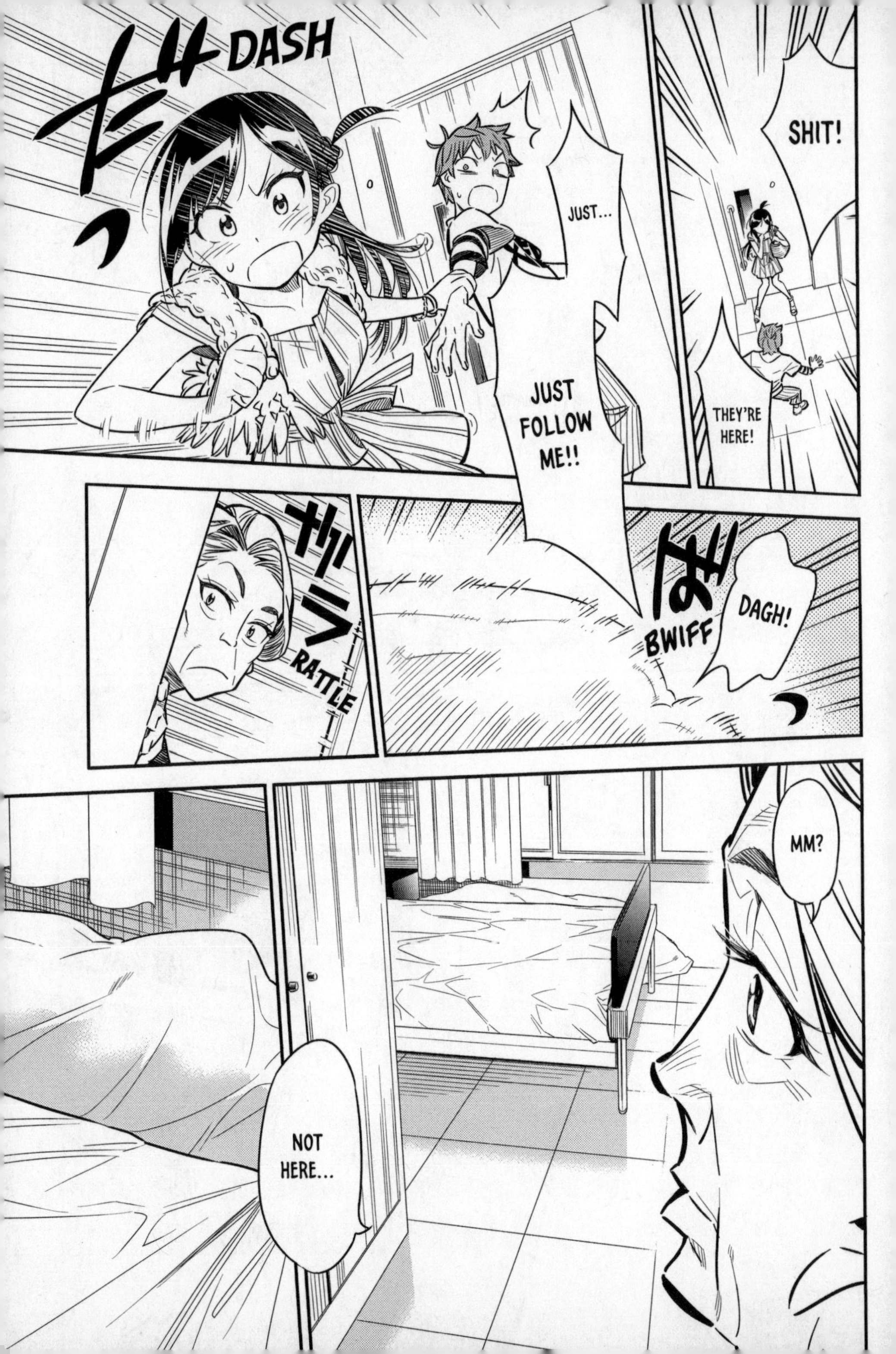
SHIT!
THEY'RE HERE!
DASH
JUST...
JUST FOLLOW ME!!
BWIFF
DAGH!
RATTLE
MM?
NOT HERE...

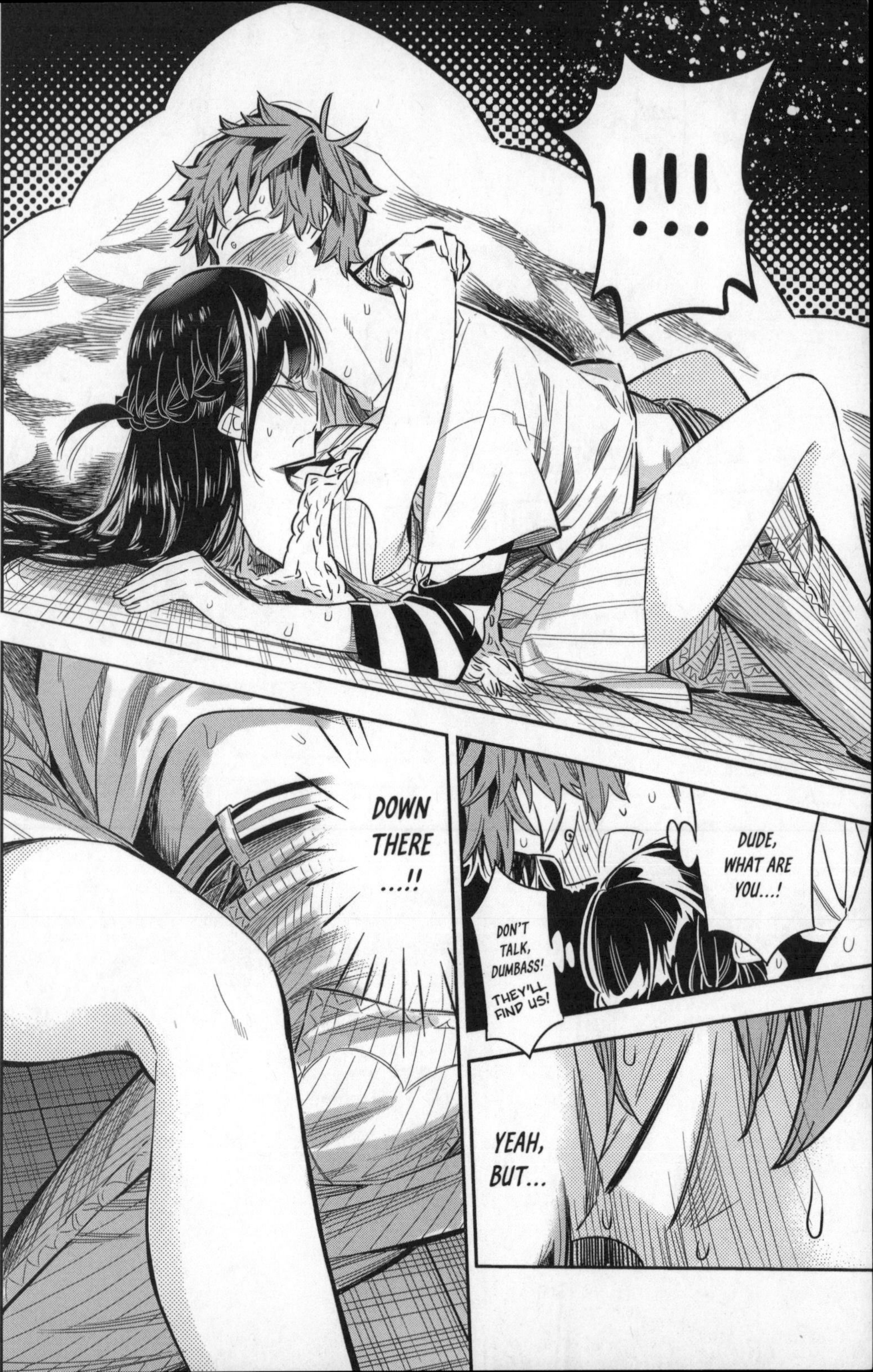
!!!
DUDE, WHAT ARE YOU...!
DON'T TALK, DUMBASS!
THEY'LL FIND US!
YEAH, BUT...
DOWN THERE ...!!

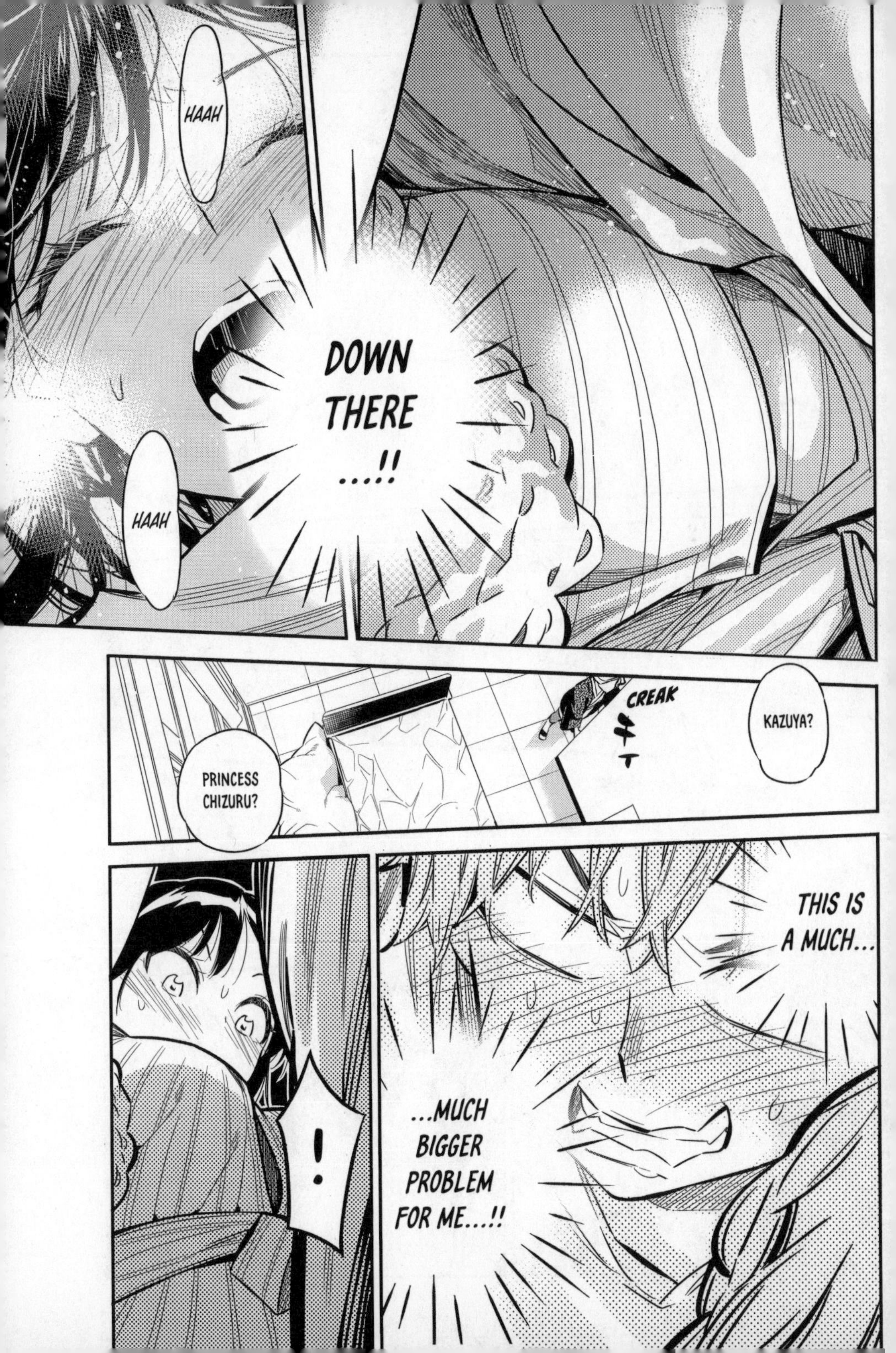
HAAH
DOWN THERE ...!!
HAAH
KAZUYA?
CREAK
PRINCESS CHIZURU?
THIS IS A MUCH...
...MUCH BIGGER PROBLEM FOR ME...!!
!

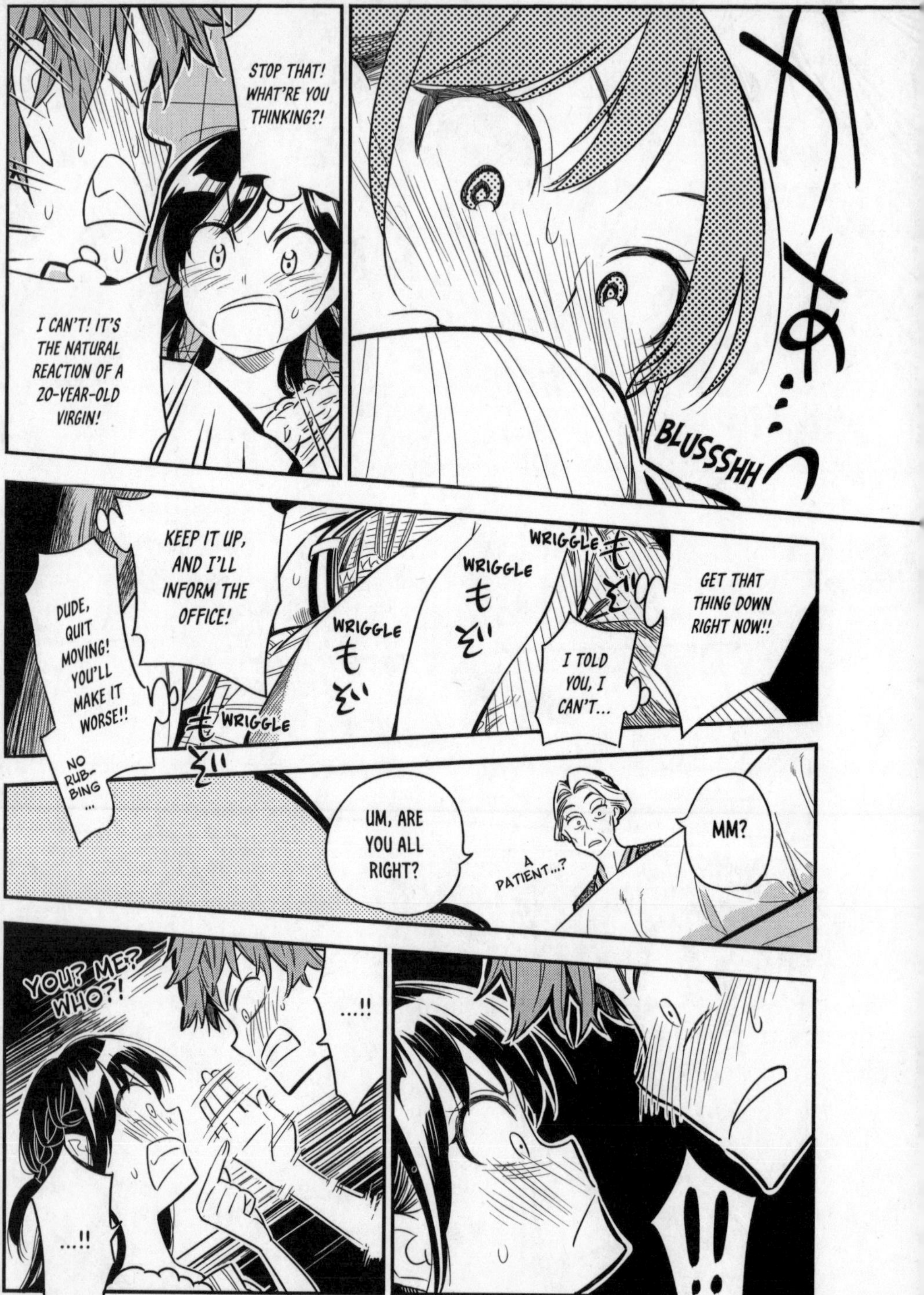
BLUSSSHH
STOP THAT! WHAT'RE YOU THINKING?!
I CAN'T! IT'S THE NATURAL REACTION OF A 20-YEAR-OLD VIRGIN!
GET THAT THING DOWN RIGHT NOW!!
I TOLD YOU, I CAN'T...
WRIGGLE もぞ
WRIGGLE もぞ
WRIGGLE もぞ
KEEP IT UP, AND I'LL INFORM THE OFFICE!
WRIGGLE もぞ
DUDE, QUIT MOVING! YOU'LL MAKE IT WORSE!!
NO RUBBING ...
MM?
A PATIENT...?
UM, ARE YOU ALL RIGHT?
!!
...!!
YOU? ME? WHO?!
...!!

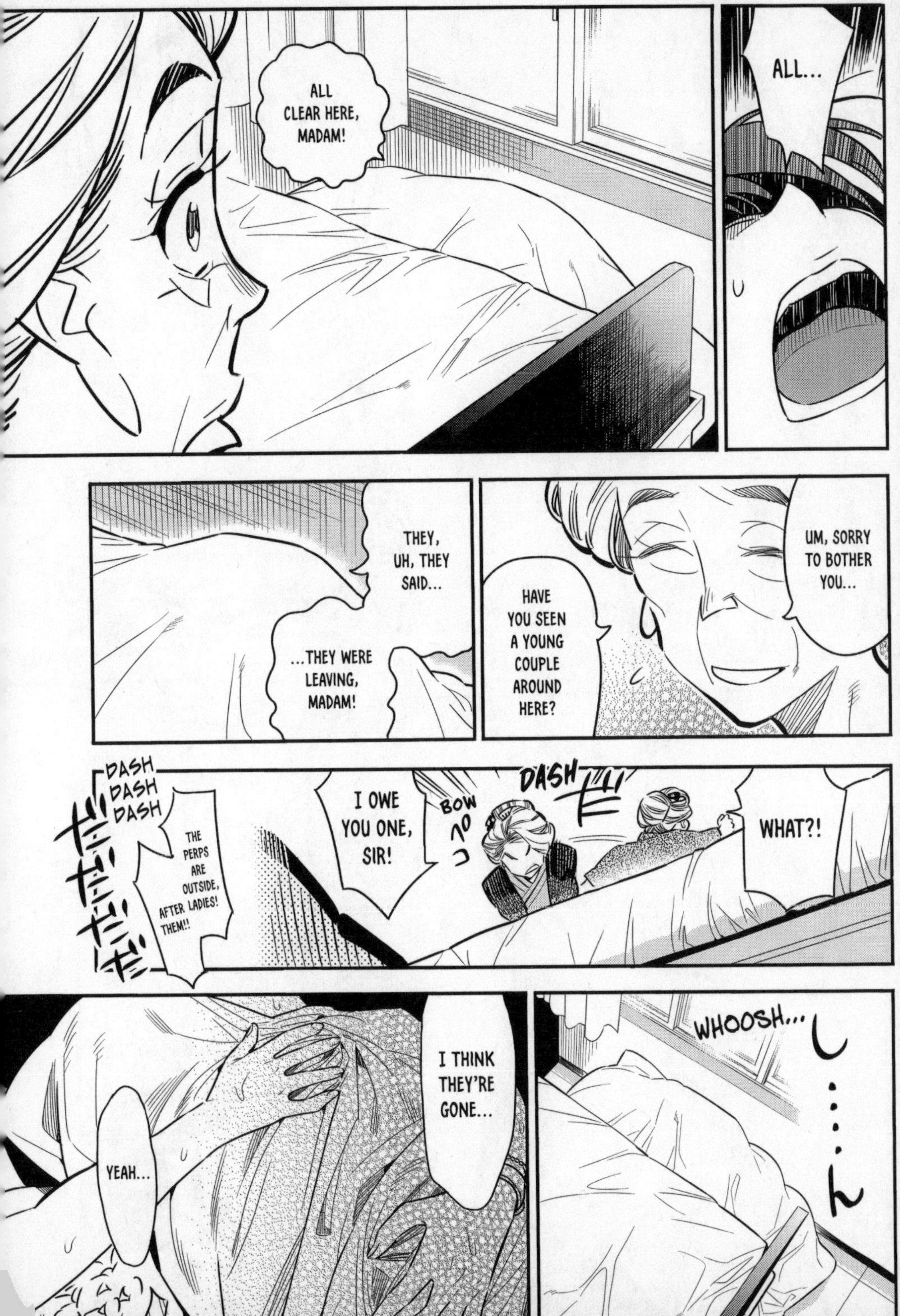
ALL...
ALL CLEAR HERE, MADAM!
UM, SORRY TO BOTHER YOU...
HAVE YOU SEEN A YOUNG COUPLE AROUND HERE?
THEY, UH, THEY SAID...
...THEY WERE LEAVING, MADAM!
WHAT?!
DASH
BOW
I OWE YOU ONE, SIR!
DASH DASH DASH
THE PERPS ARE OUTSIDE, LADIES! AFTER THEM!!
WHOOSH...
I THINK THEY'RE GONE...
YEAH...

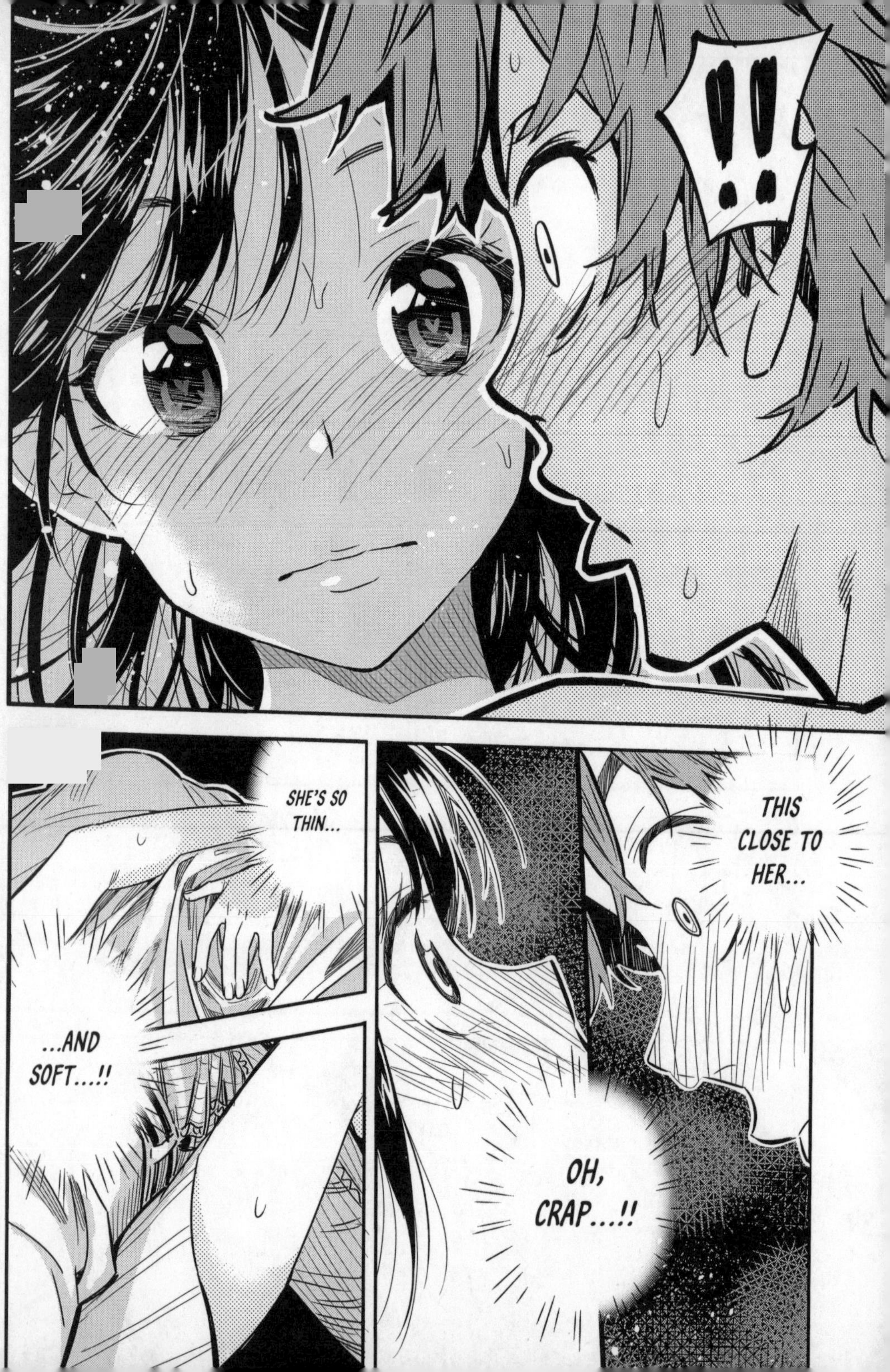
!!
THIS CLOSE TO HER...
OH, CRAP...!!
SHE'S SO THIN...
...AND SOFT...!!

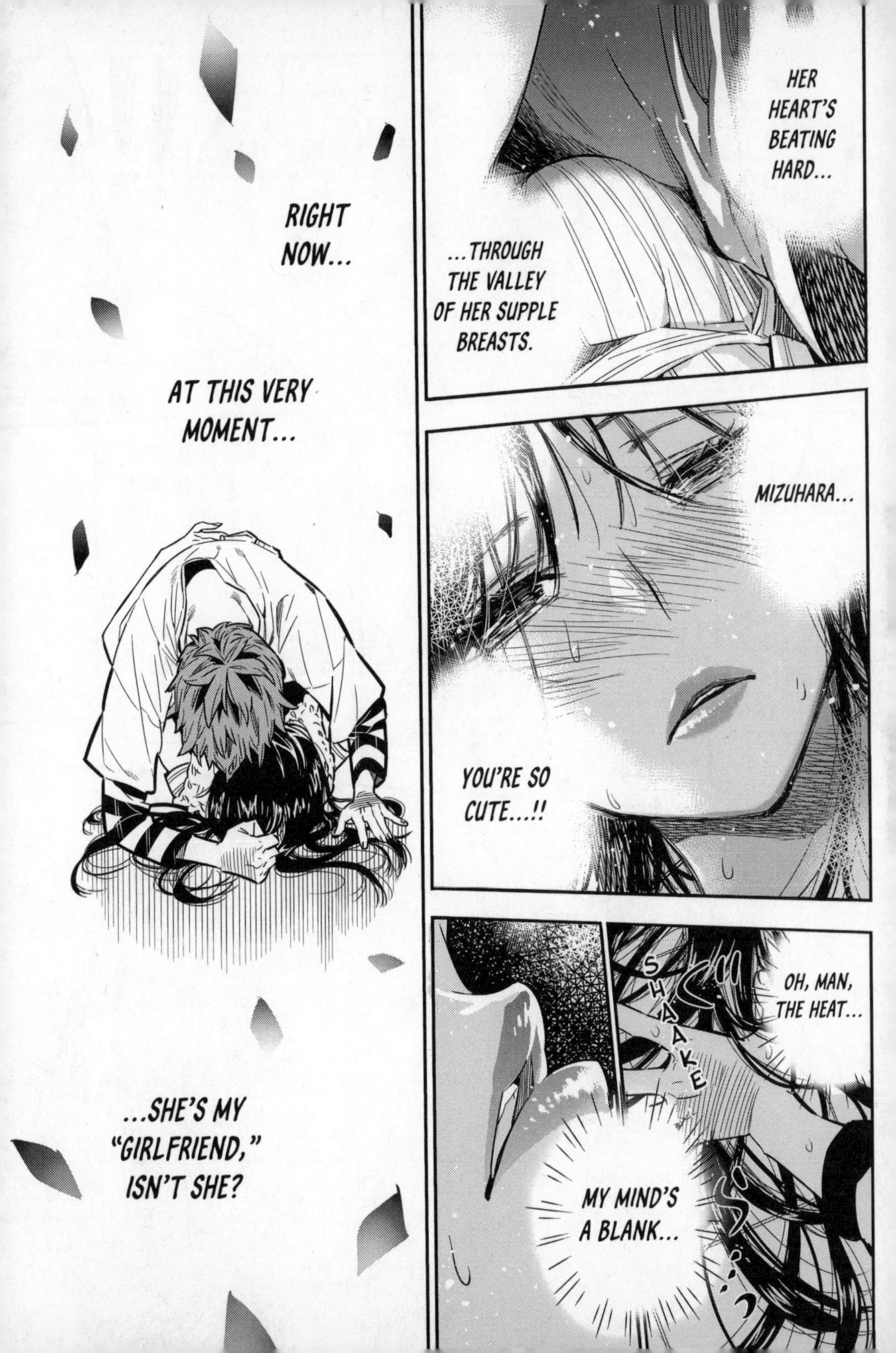
HER HEART'S BEATING HARD...
...THROUGH THE VALLEY OF HER SUPPLE BREASTS.
MIZUHARA...
YOU'RE SO CUTE...!!
OH, MAN, THE HEAT...
SHAKE
MY MIND'S A BLANK...
RIGHT NOW...
AT THIS VERY MOMENT...
...SHE'S MY "GIRLFRIEND," ISN'T SHE?

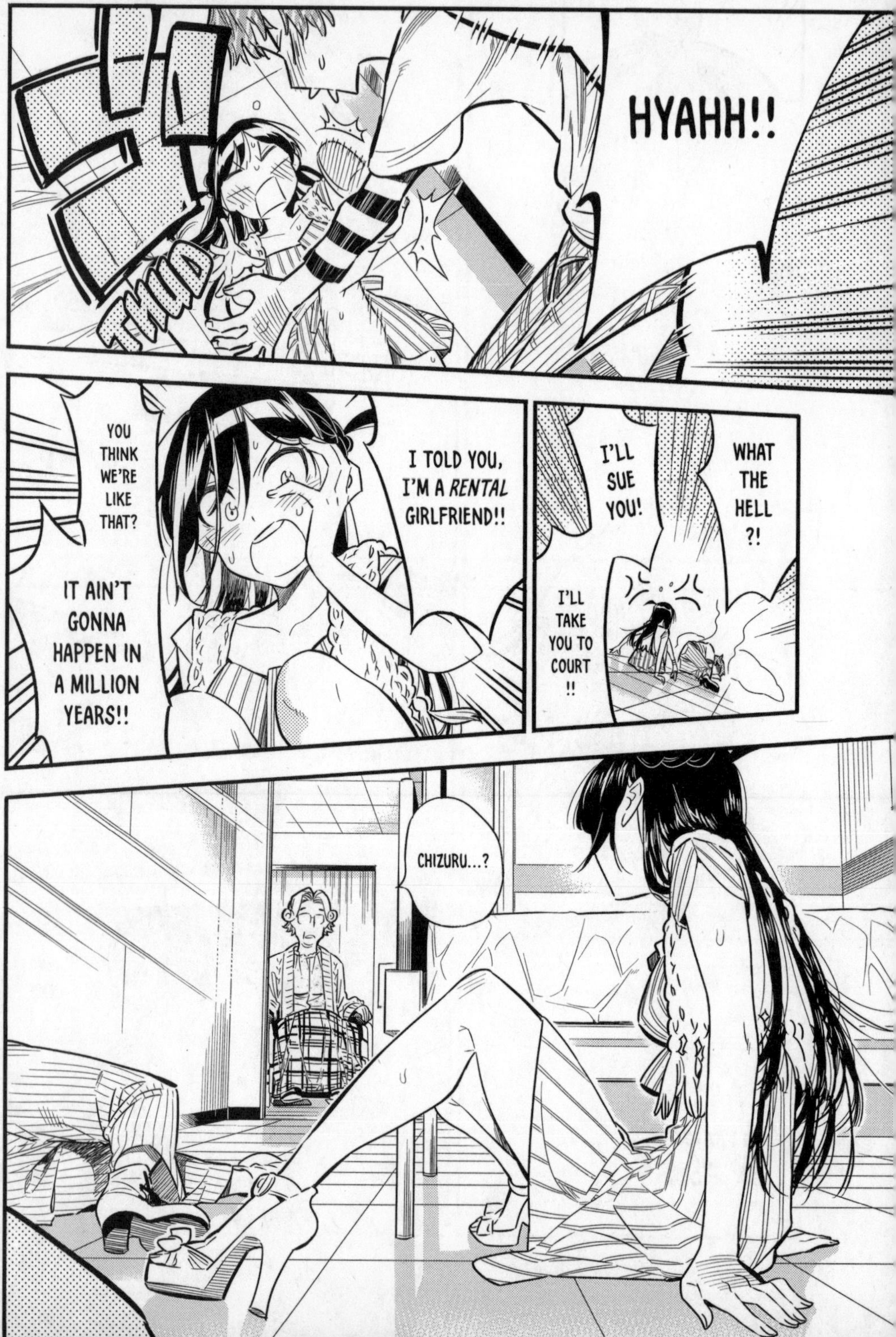
HYAHH!!
THUD
WHAT THE HELL ?!
I'LL SUE YOU!
I'LL TAKE YOU TO COURT !!
I TOLD YOU, I'M A *RENTAL* GIRLFRIEND!!
YOU THINK WE'RE LIKE THAT?
IT AIN'T GONNA HAPPEN IN A MILLION YEARS!!
CHIZURU...?

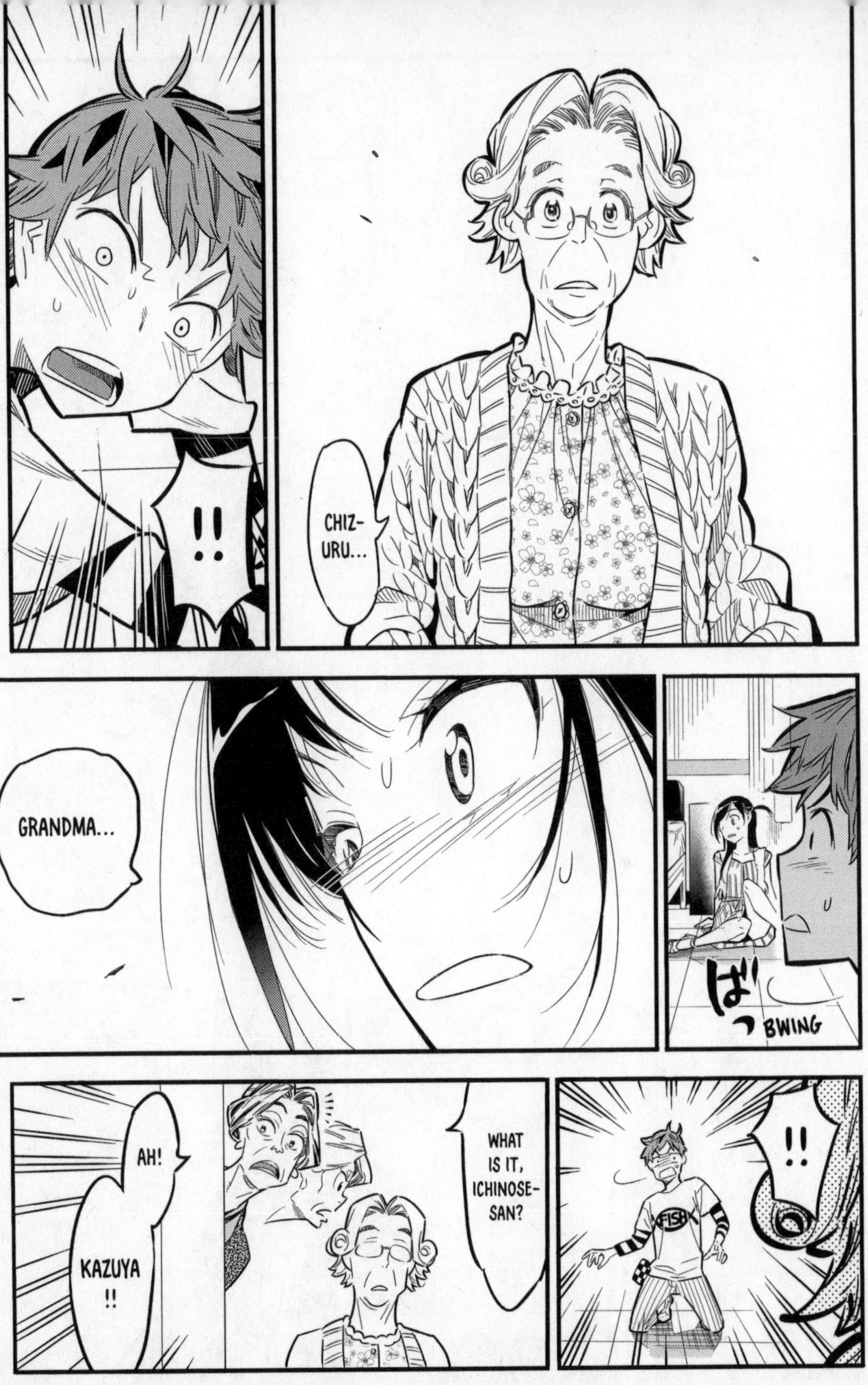
CHIZ-
URU...
!!
ぱっ
BWING
GRANDMA...
!!
WHAT IS IT, ICHINOSE-SAN?
AH!
KAZUYA !!

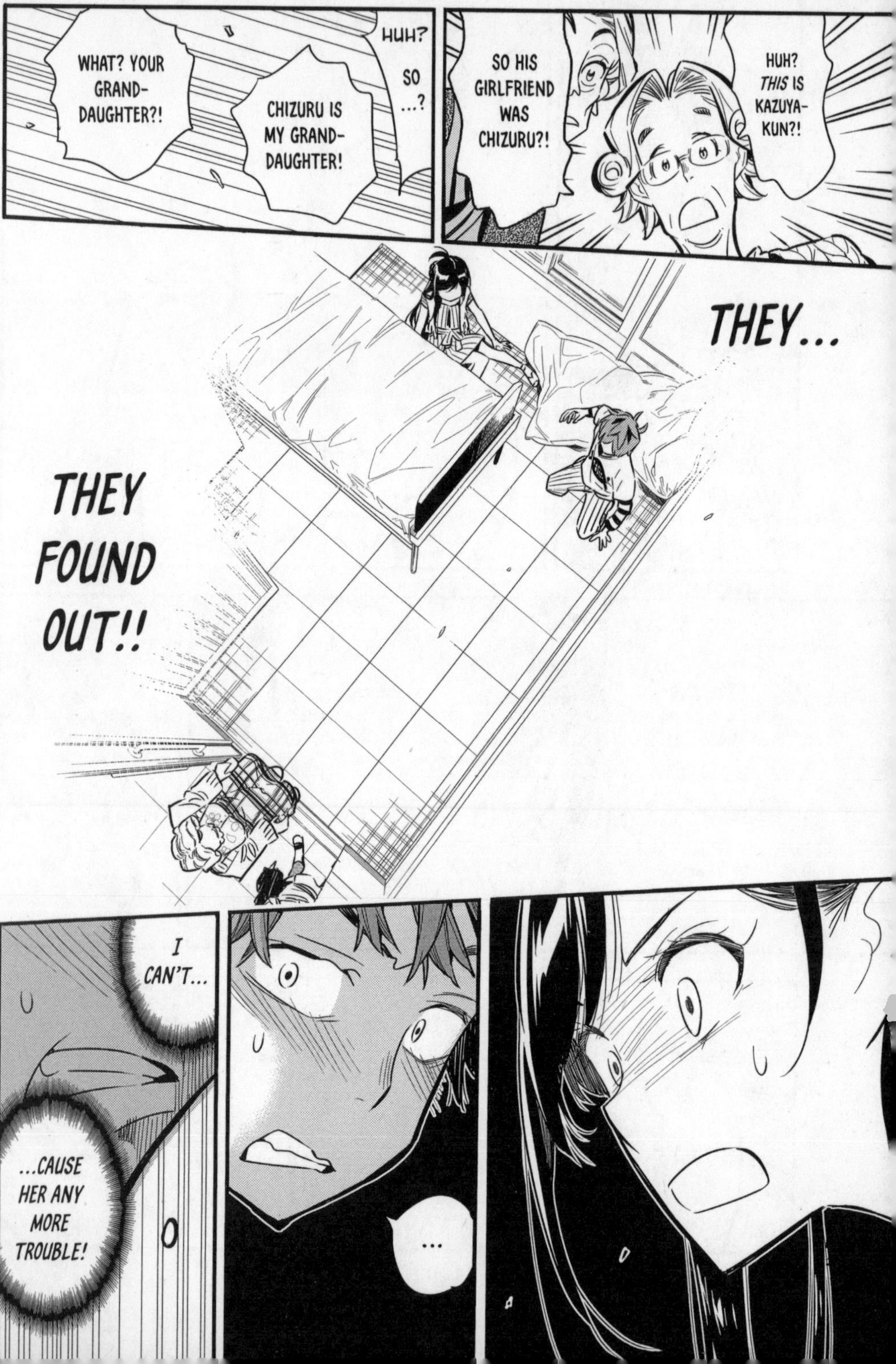
HUH? *THIS* IS KAZUYA-KUN?!
SO HIS GIRLFRIEND WAS CHIZURU?!
HUH? SO ...?
CHIZURU IS MY GRAND-DAUGHTER!
WHAT? YOUR GRAND-DAUGHTER?!
THEY...
THEY FOUND OUT!!
...
I CAN'T...
...CAUSE HER ANY MORE TROUBLE!

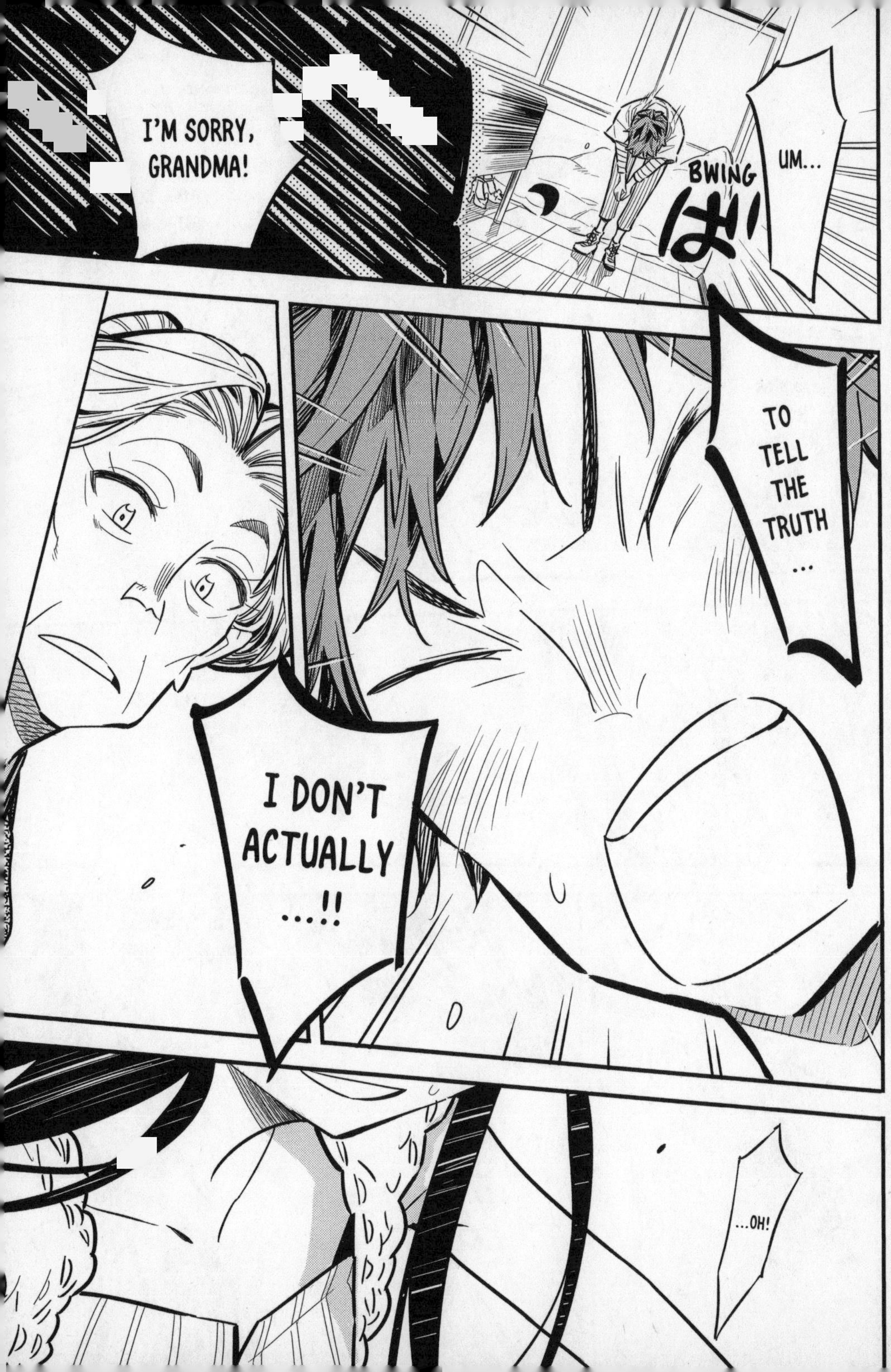
UM...
BWING
I'M SORRY, GRANDMA!
TO TELL THE TRUTH ...
I DON'T ACTUALLY ...!!
...OH!

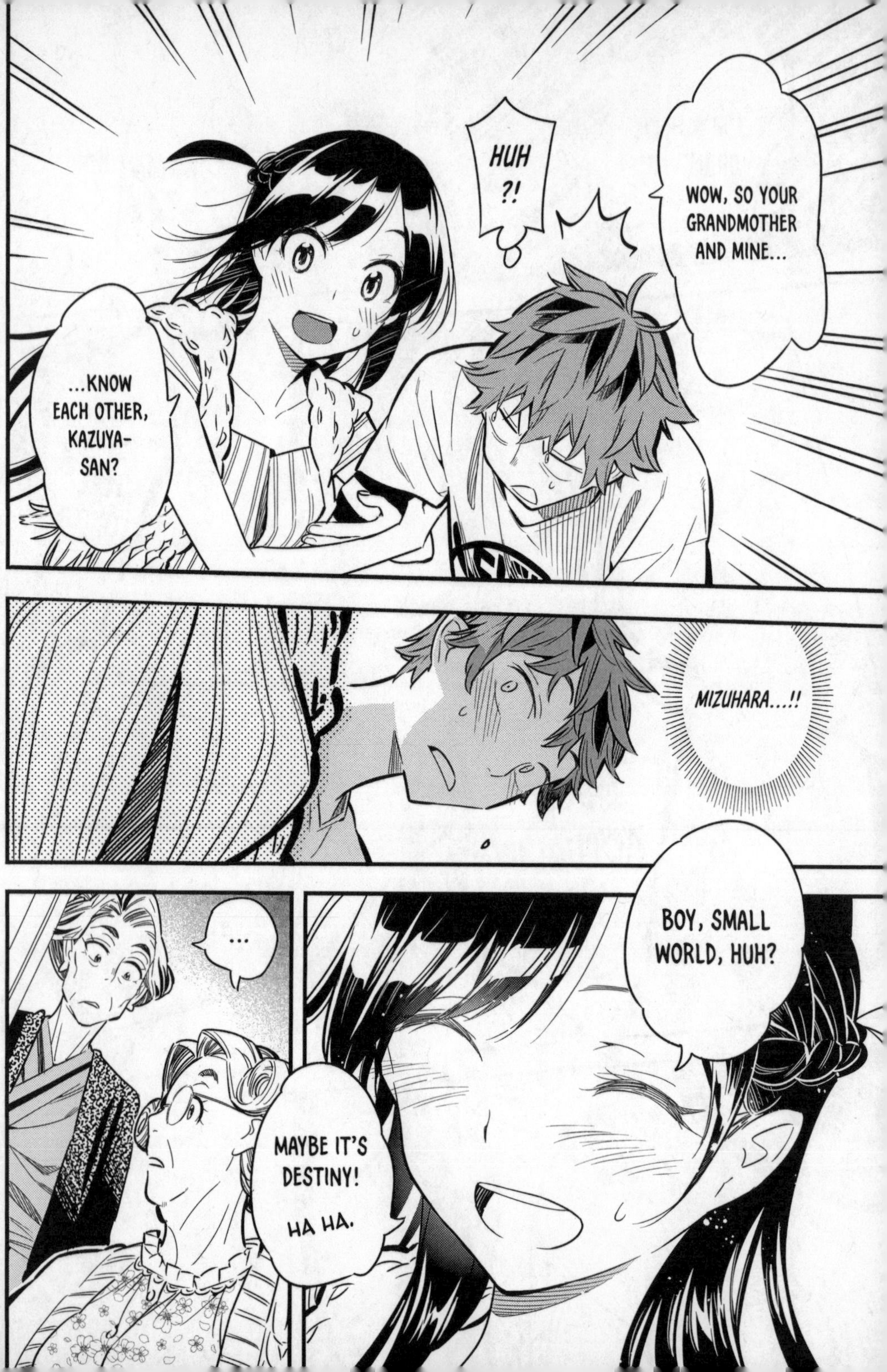

WOW, SO YOUR GRANDMOTHER AND MINE...
HUH ?!
...KNOW EACH OTHER, KAZUYA-SAN?
MIZUHARA...!!
BOY, SMALL WORLD, HUH?
MAYBE IT'S DESTINY! HA HA.
...

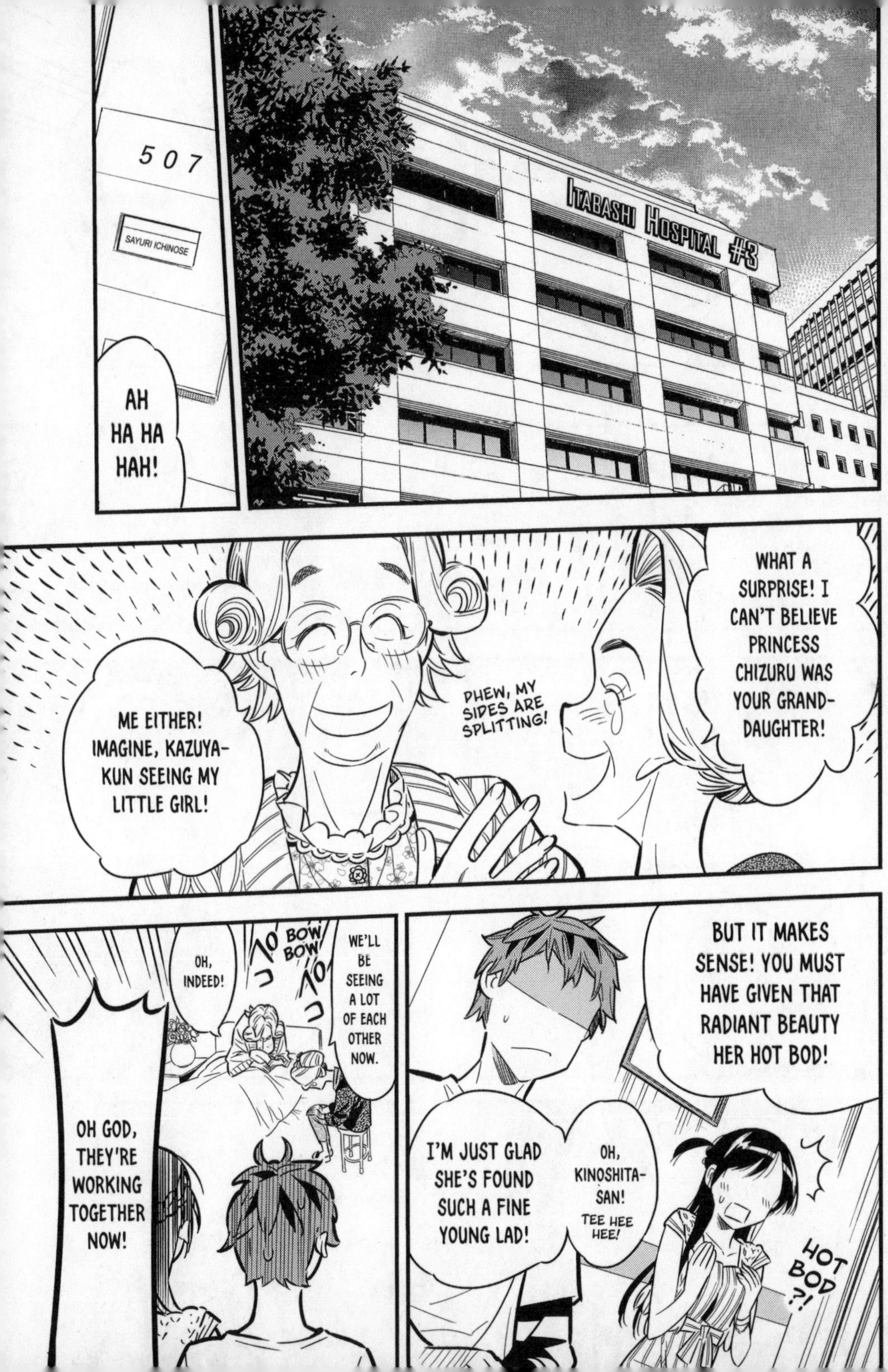
ITABASHI HOSPITAL #3
507
SAYURI ICHINOSE
AH HA HA HAH!
WHAT A SURPRISE! I CAN'T BELIEVE PRINCESS CHIZURU WAS YOUR GRAND-DAUGHTER!
PHEW, MY SIDES ARE SPLITTING!
ME EITHER! IMAGINE, KAZUYA-KUN SEEING MY LITTLE GIRL!
BUT IT MAKES SENSE! YOU MUST HAVE GIVEN THAT RADIANT BEAUTY HER HOT BOD!
I'M JUST GLAD SHE'S FOUND SUCH A FINE YOUNG LAD!
OH, KINOSHITA-SAN!
TEE HEE HEE!
HOT BOD?!
WE'LL BE SEEING A LOT OF EACH OTHER NOW.
BOW BOW
OH, INDEED!
OH GOD, THEY'RE WORKING TOGETHER NOW!

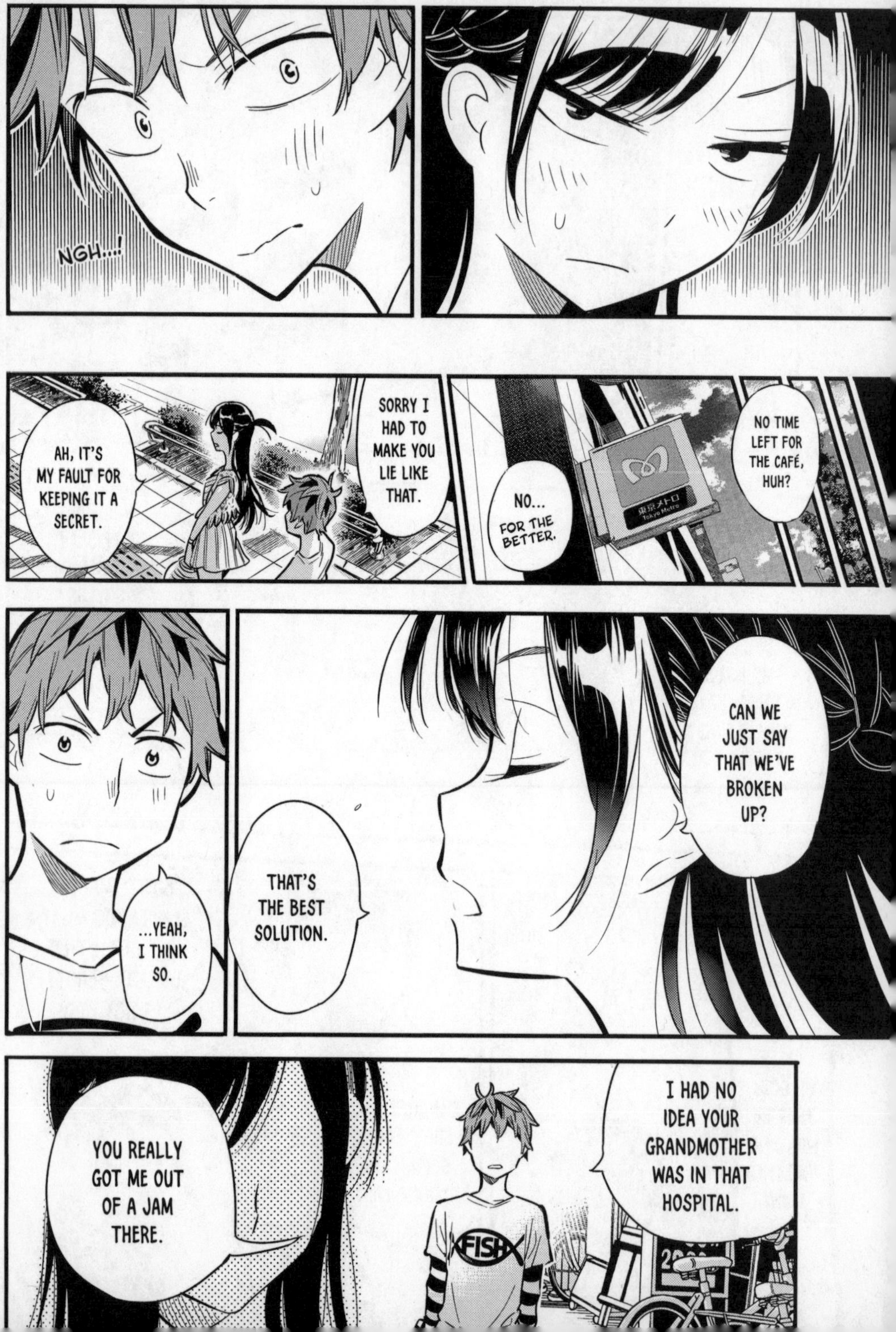
NGH...!
NO TIME LEFT FOR THE CAFÉ, HUH?
東京メトロ
NO... FOR THE BETTER.
SORRY I HAD TO MAKE YOU LIE LIKE THAT.
AH, IT'S MY FAULT FOR KEEPING IT A SECRET.
CAN WE JUST SAY THAT WE'VE BROKEN UP?
THAT'S THE BEST SOLUTION.
...YEAH, I THINK SO.
I HAD NO IDEA YOUR GRANDMOTHER WAS IN THAT HOSPITAL.
FISH
YOU REALLY GOT ME OUT OF A JAM THERE.

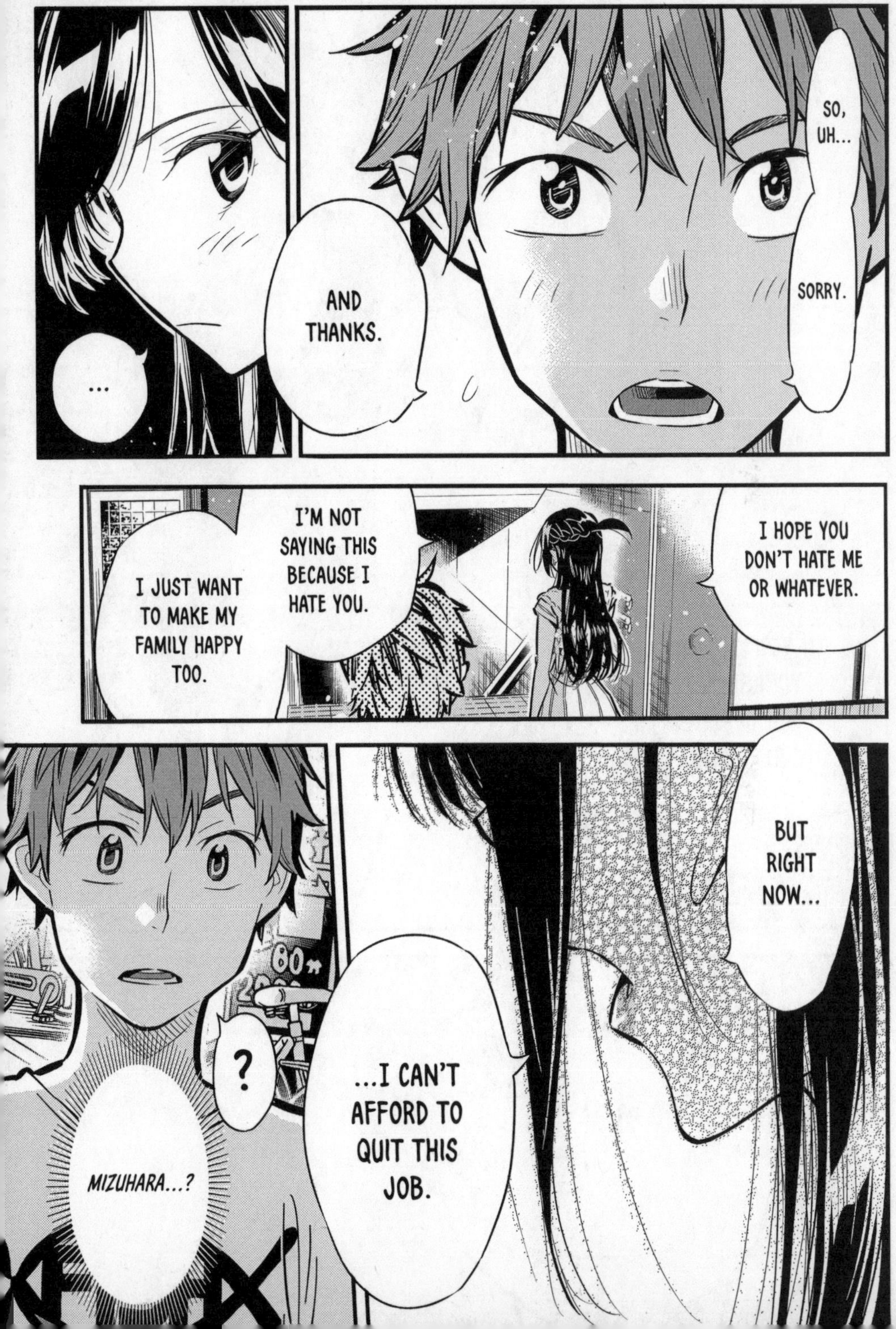
SO, UH...
SORRY.
AND THANKS.
...
I HOPE YOU DON'T HATE ME OR WHATEVER.
I'M NOT SAYING THIS BECAUSE I HATE YOU.
I JUST WANT TO MAKE MY FAMILY HAPPY TOO.
BUT RIGHT NOW...
...I CAN'T AFFORD TO QUIT THIS JOB.
?
MIZUHARA...?

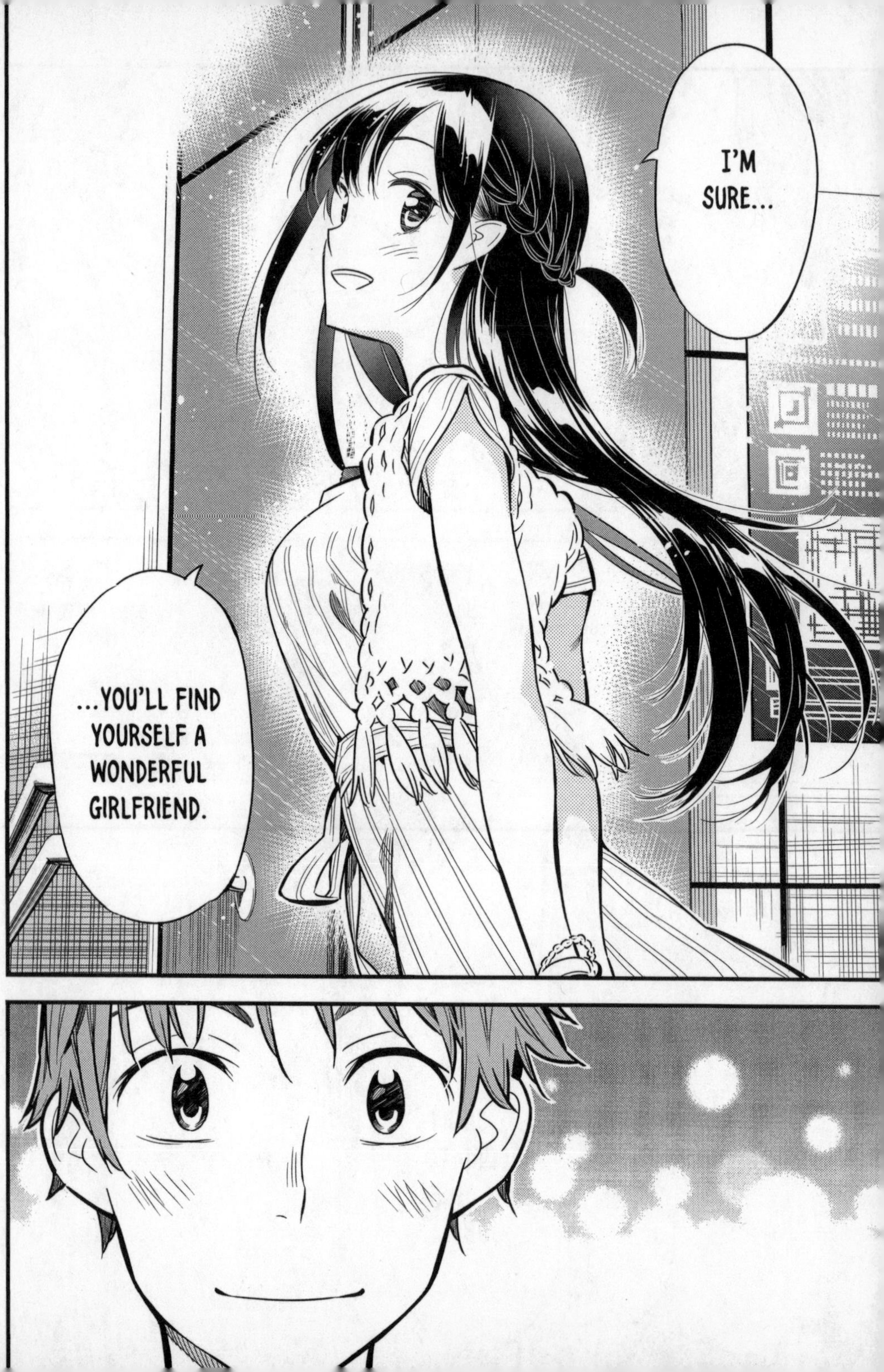
I'M SURE...
...YOU'LL FIND YOURSELF A WONDERFUL GIRLFRIEND.

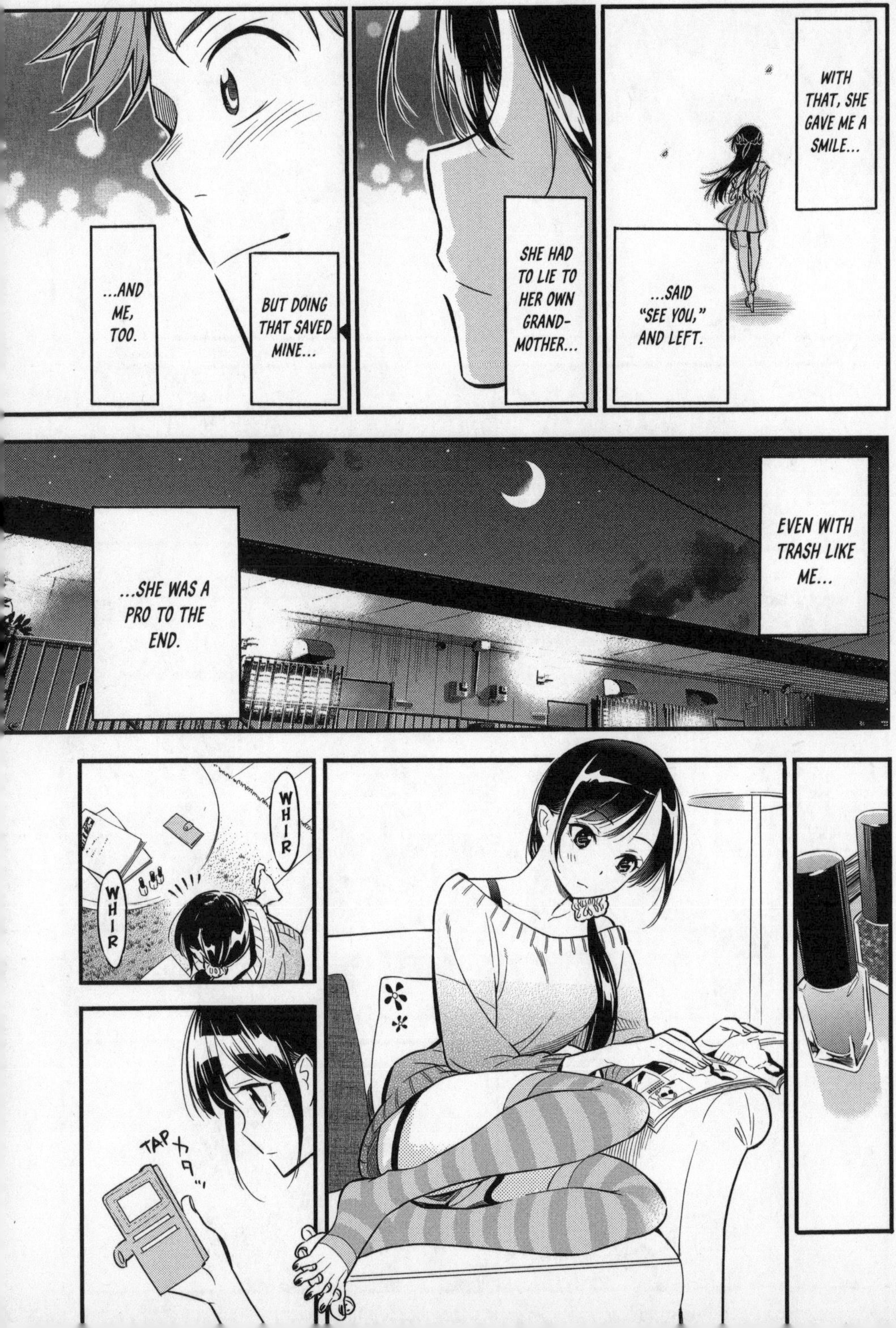
WITH THAT, SHE GAVE ME A SMILE...
...SAID "SEE YOU," AND LEFT.
SHE HAD TO LIE TO HER OWN GRAND-MOTHER...
BUT DOING THAT SAVED MINE...
...AND ME, TOO.
EVEN WITH TRASH LIKE ME...
...SHE WAS A PRO TO THE END.
WHIR
WHIR
TAP

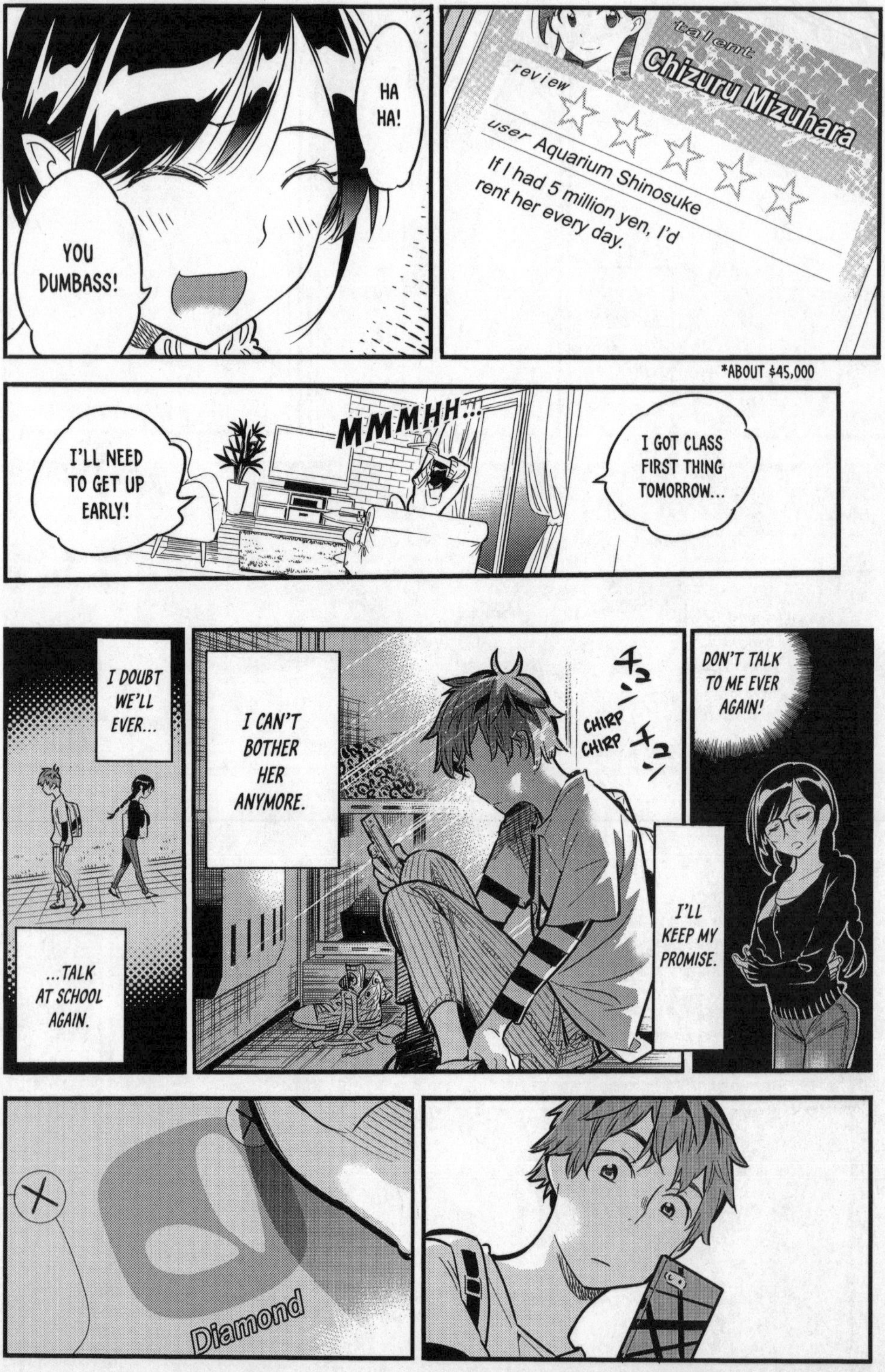
talent
Chizuru Mizuhara
review
user Aquarium Shinosuke
If I had 5 million yen, I'd rent her every day.
HA HA!
YOU DUMBASS!
*ABOUT $45,000
I GOT CLASS FIRST THING TOMORROW...
MMMHH..!!
I'LL NEED TO GET UP EARLY!
DON'T TALK TO ME EVER AGAIN!
CHIRP CHIRP
I'LL KEEP MY PROMISE.
I CAN'T BOTHER HER ANYMORE.
I DOUBT WE'LL EVER...
...TALK AT SCHOOL AGAIN.
Diamond

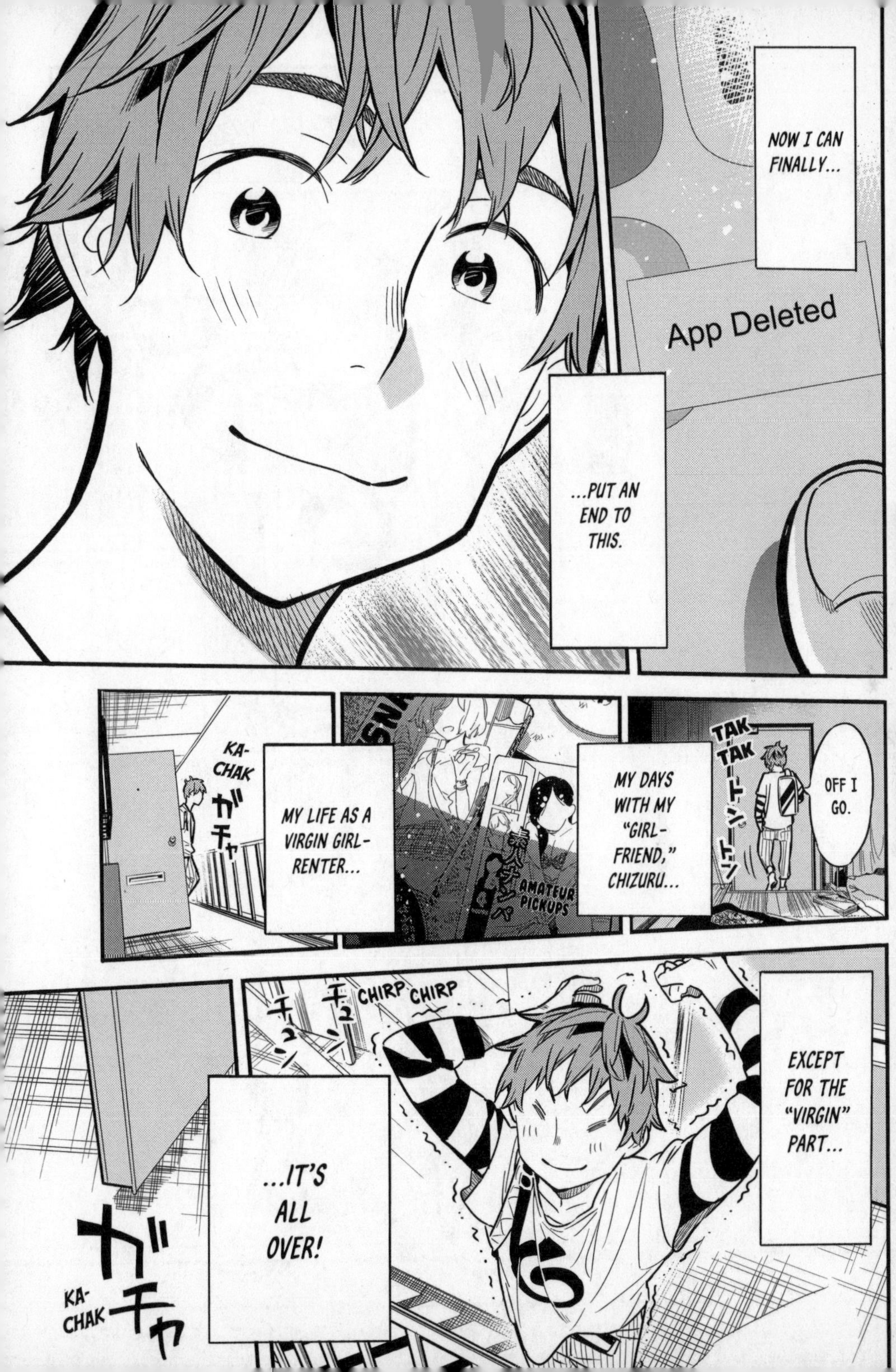
NOW I CAN FINALLY...
App Deleted
...PUT AN END TO THIS.
OFF I GO.
TAK TAK
トントン
MY DAYS WITH MY "GIRL-FRIEND," CHIZURU...
MY LIFE AS A VIRGIN GIRL-RENTER...
AMATEUR PICKUPS
KA-CHAK
ガチャ
EXCEPT FOR THE "VIRGIN" PART...
CHIRP CHIRP
チュンチュン
...IT'S ALL OVER!
ガチャ
KA-CHAK

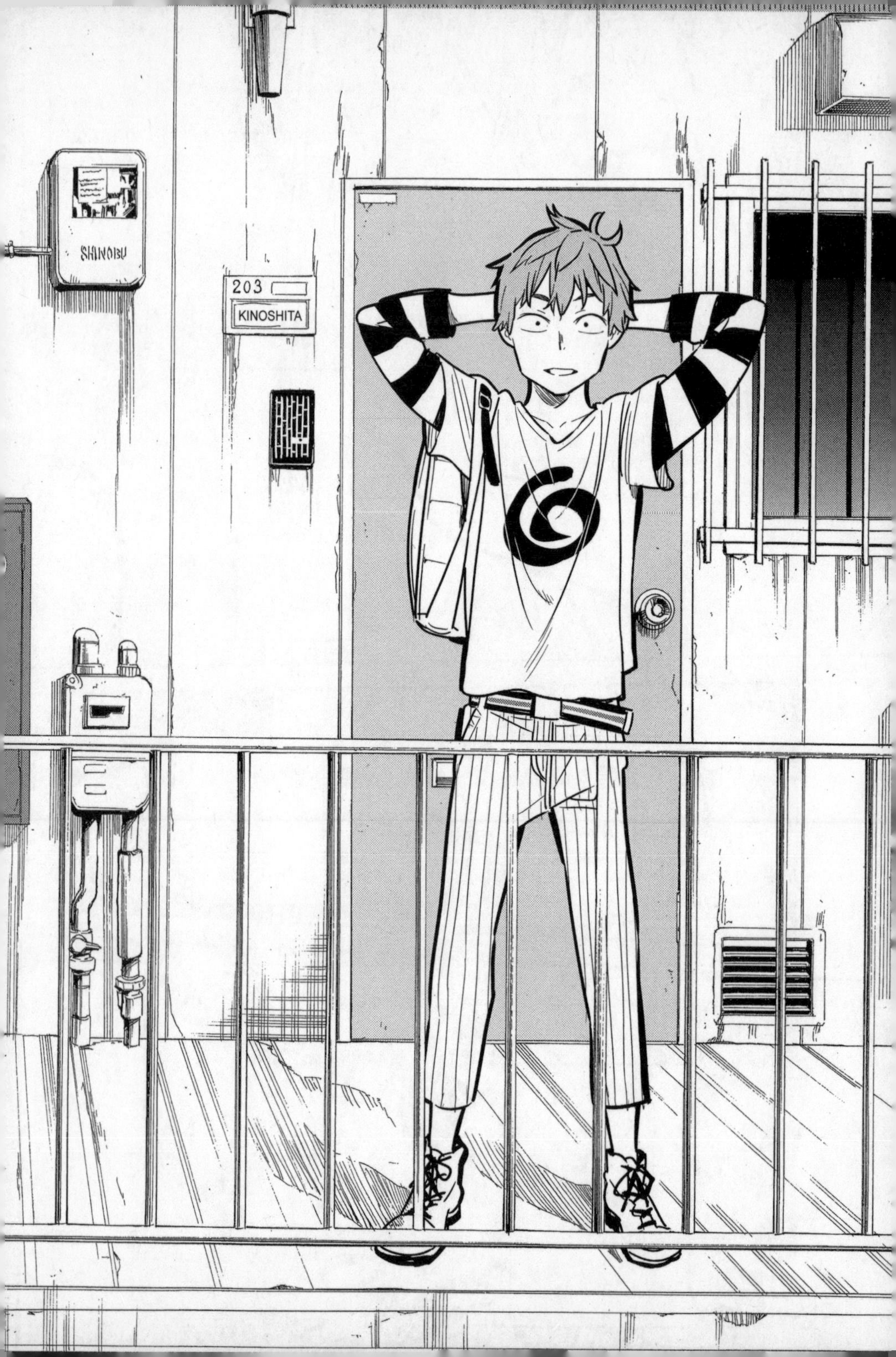
SHINOBU
203
KINOSHITA

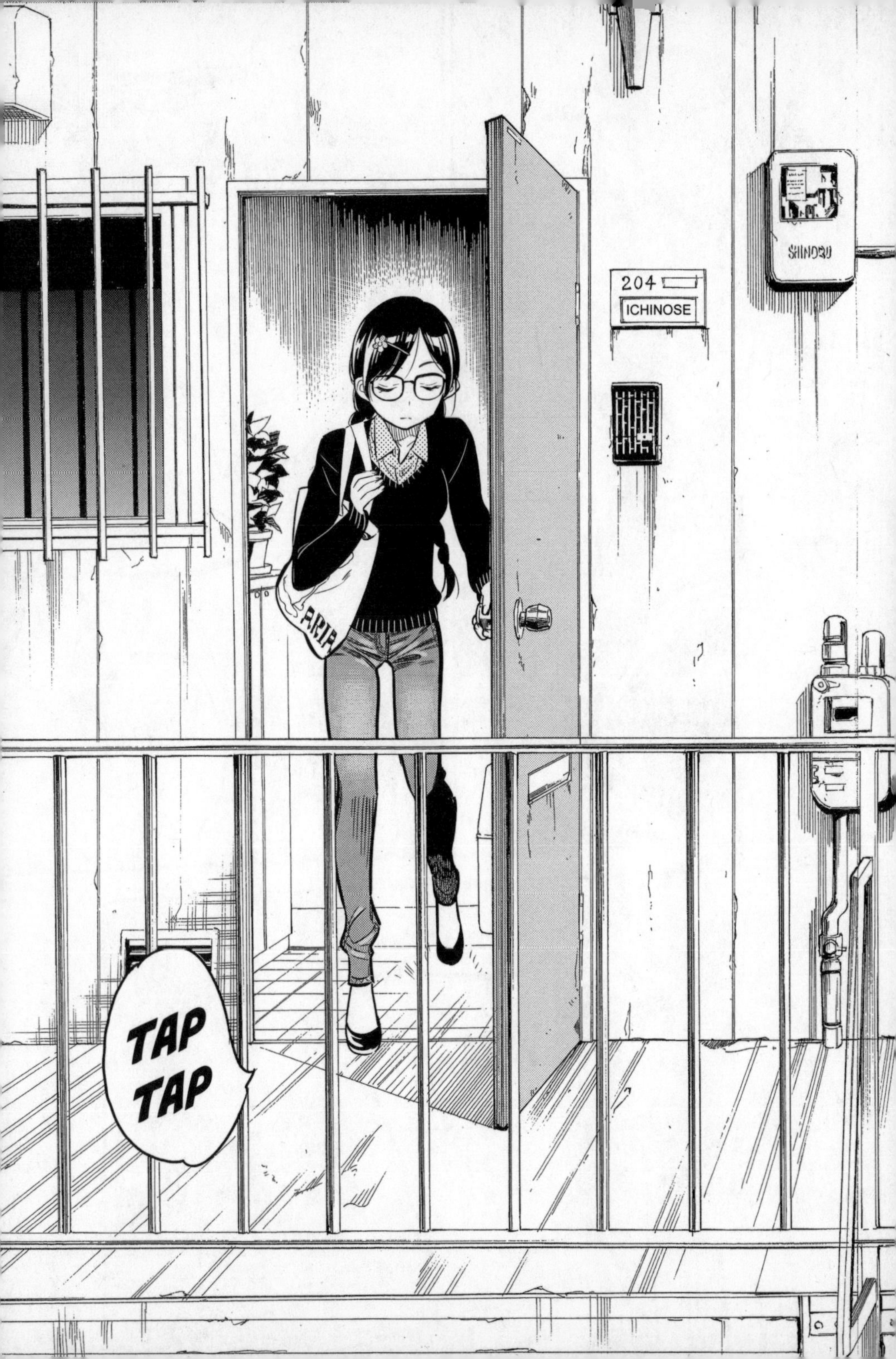
204
ICHINOSE
ARIA
TAP
TAP

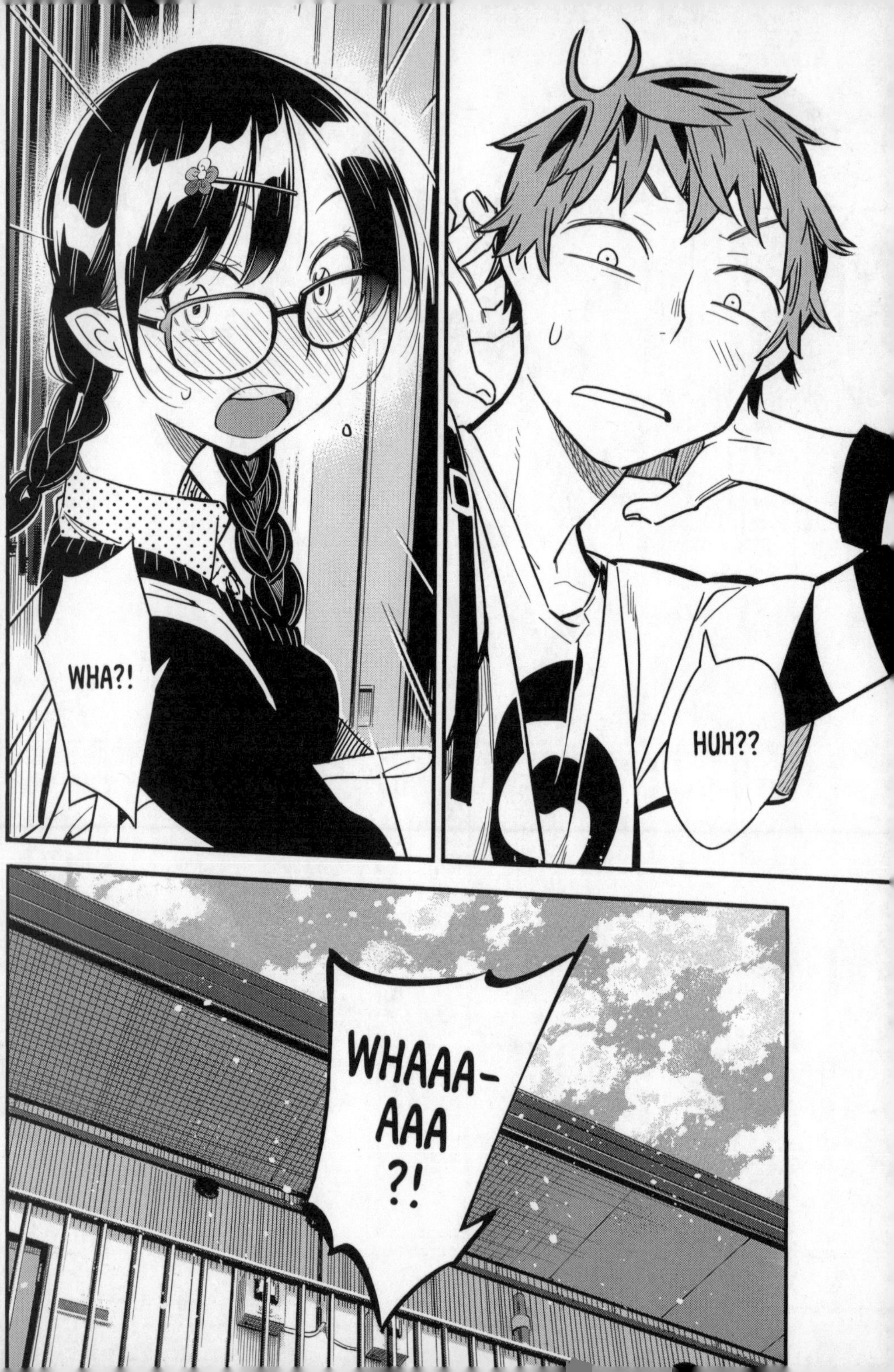
HUH??
WHA?!
WHAAA-AAA?!

RATING 3
THE GIRL NEXT DOOR

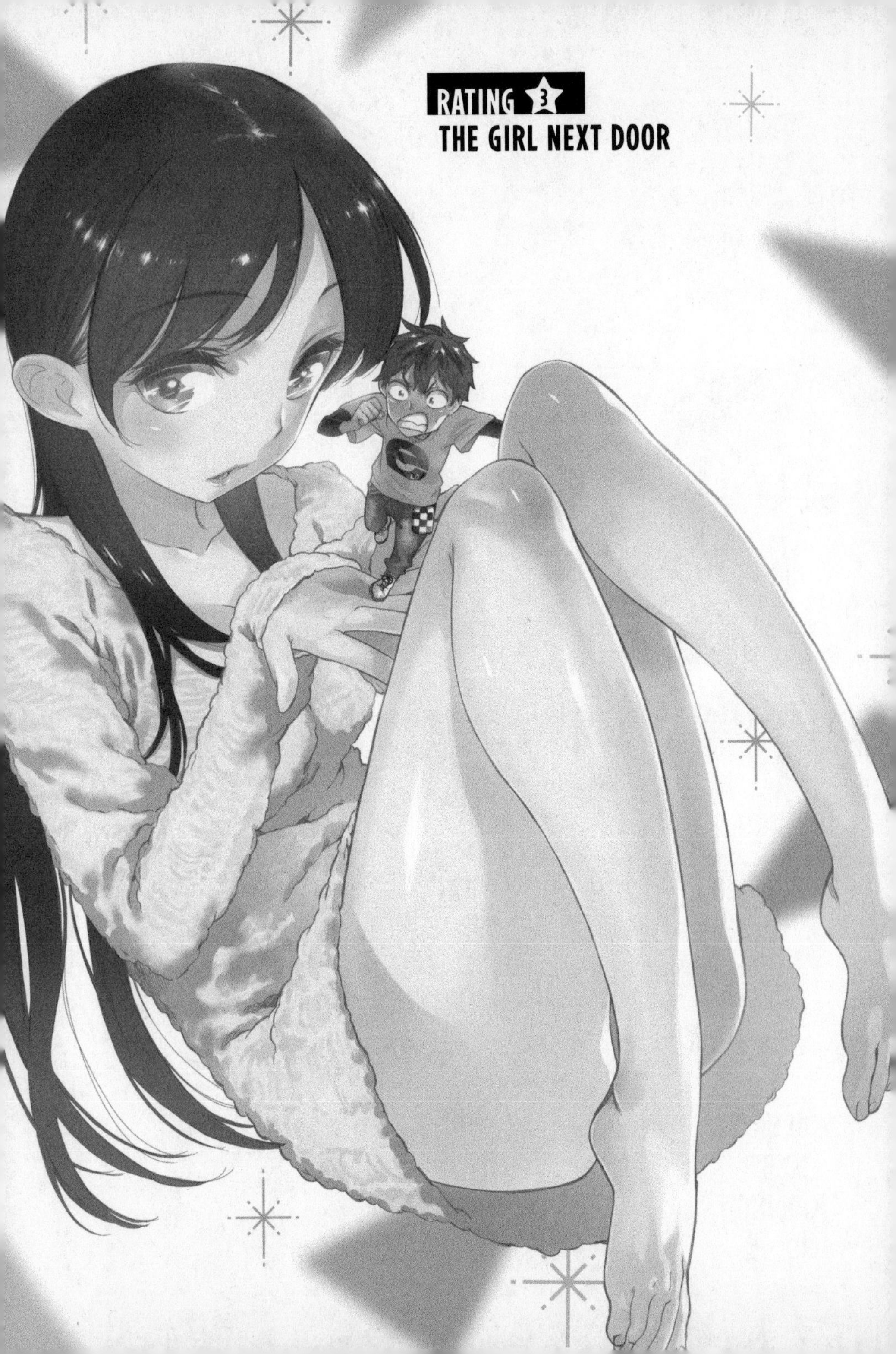

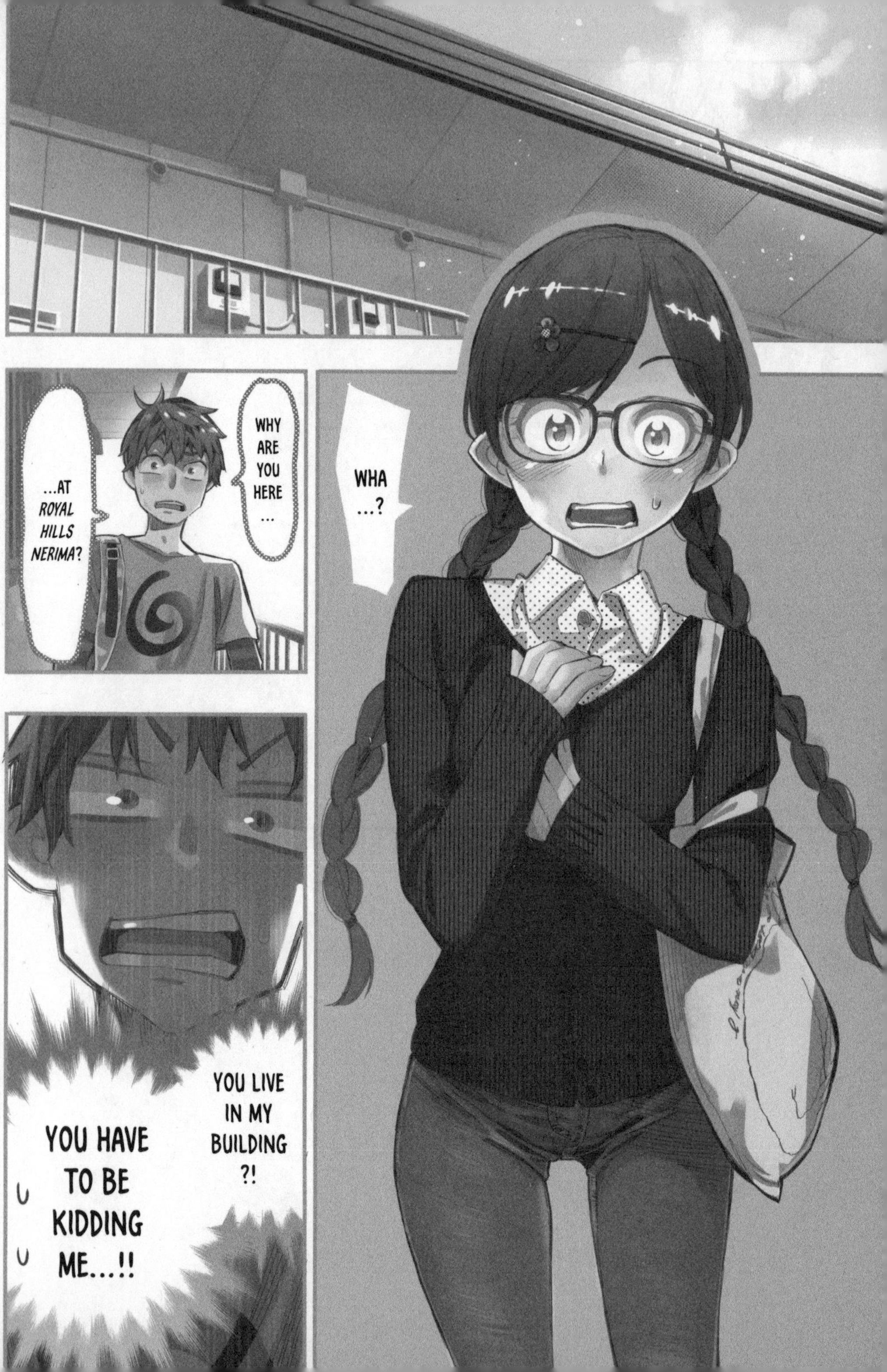
WHA ...?
WHY ARE YOU HERE ...
...AT ROYAL HILLS NERIMA?
YOU LIVE IN MY BUILDING ?!
YOU HAVE TO BE KIDDING ME...!!

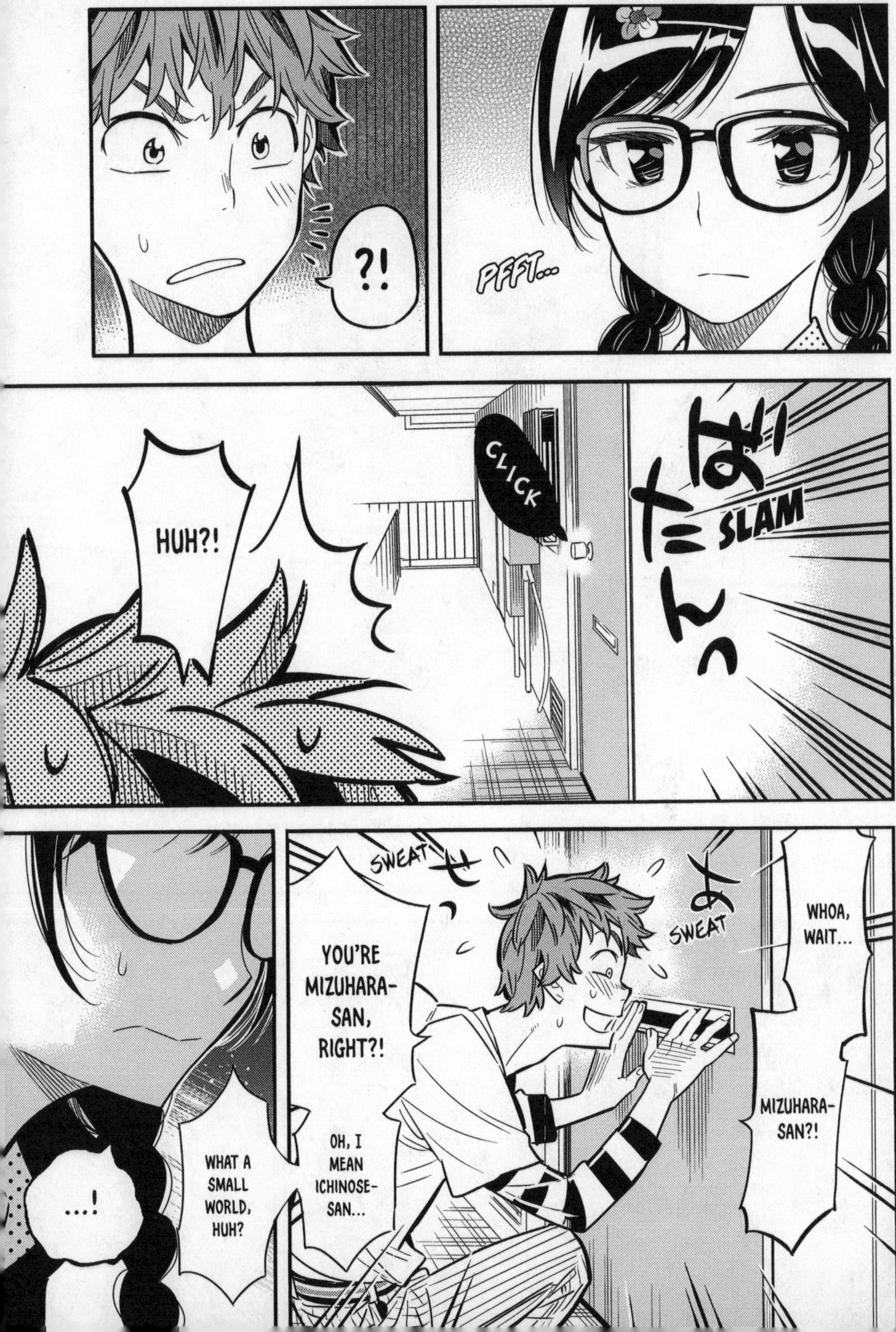
PFFT...
?!
ばたん
SLAM
CLICK
HUH?!
WHOA, WAIT...
MIZUHARA-SAN?!
SWEAT
あ
SWEAT
せ
YOU'RE MIZUHARA-SAN, RIGHT?!
OH, I MEAN ICHINOSE-SAN...
WHAT A SMALL WORLD, HUH?
...!

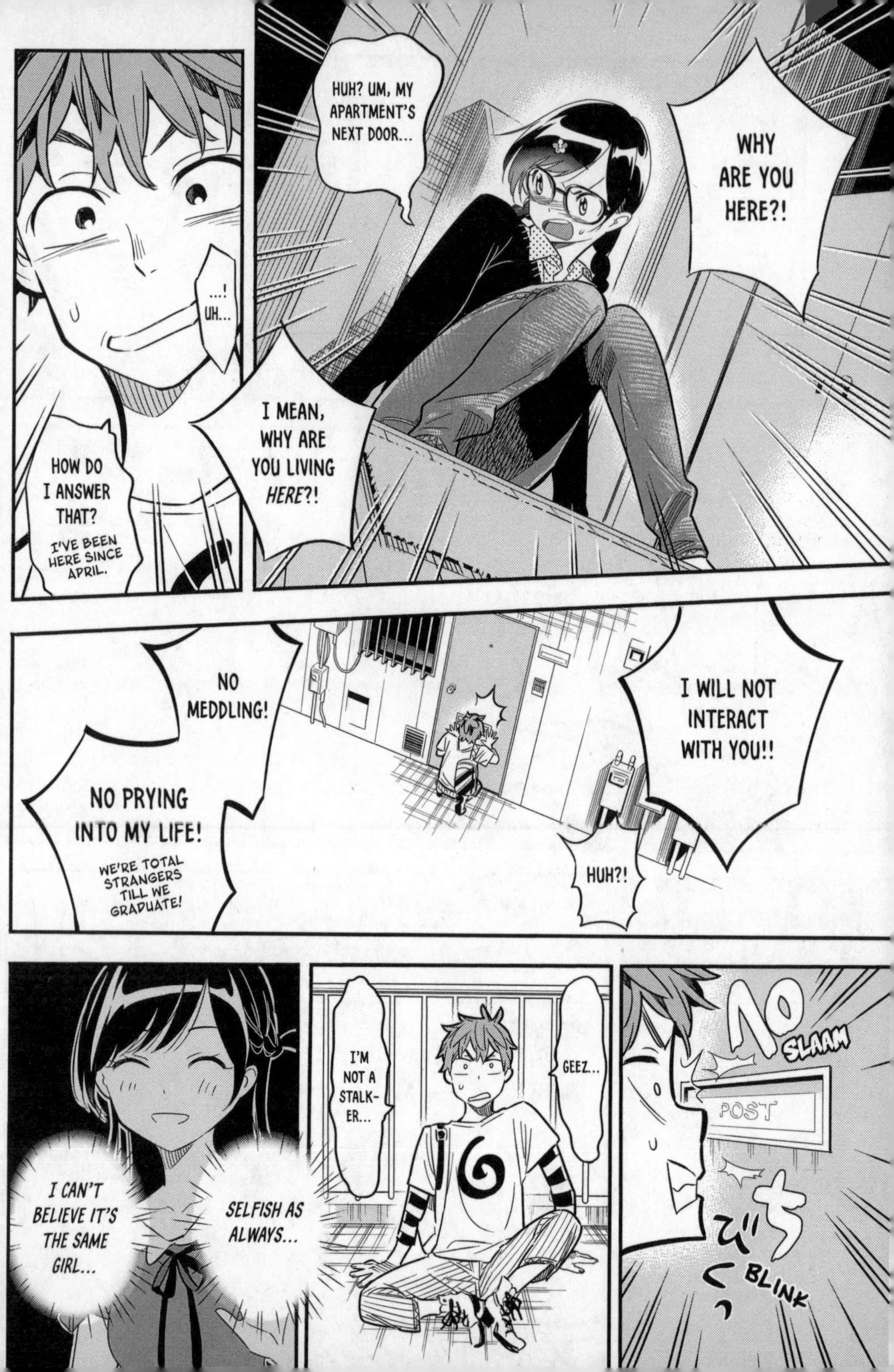
WHY ARE YOU HERE?!
HUH? UM, MY APARTMENT'S NEXT DOOR...
I MEAN, WHY ARE YOU LIVING *HERE*?!
...! UH...
HOW DO I ANSWER THAT?
I'VE BEEN HERE SINCE APRIL.
I WILL NOT INTERACT WITH YOU!!
HUH?!
NO MEDDLING!
NO PRYING INTO MY LIFE!
WE'RE TOTAL STRANGERS TILL WE GRADUATE!
NO
SLAAM
POST
BLINK
GEEZ...
I'M NOT A STALK-ER...
SELFISH AS ALWAYS...
I CAN'T BELIEVE IT'S THE SAME GIRL...

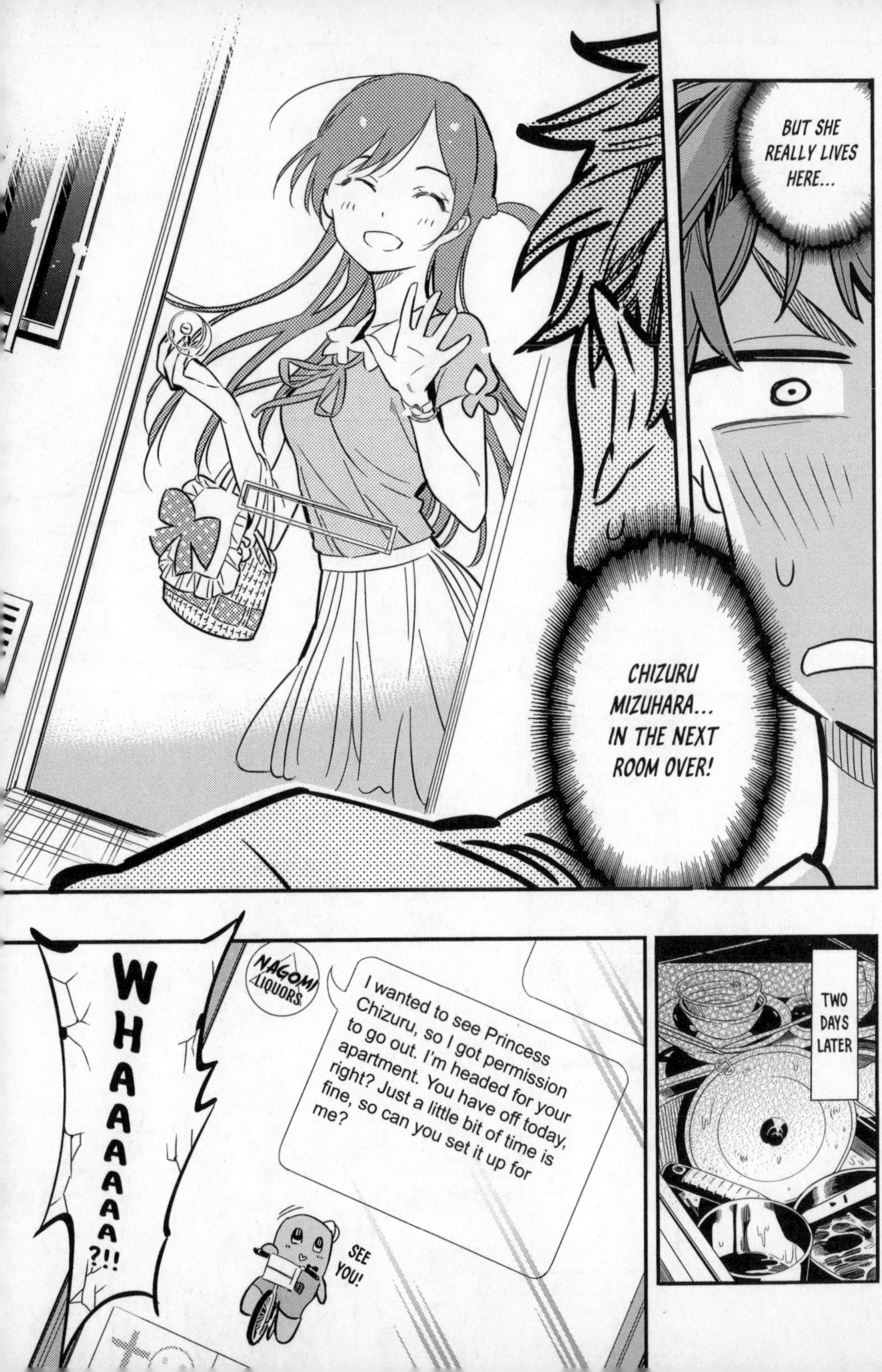
BUT SHE REALLY LIVES HERE...
CHIZURU MIZUHARA... IN THE NEXT ROOM OVER!
TWO DAYS LATER
NAGOMI LIQUORS
I wanted to see Princess Chizuru, so I got permission to go out. I'm headed for your apartment. You have off today, right? Just a little bit of time is fine, so can you set it up for me?
SEE YOU!
WHAAAAAAA?!!

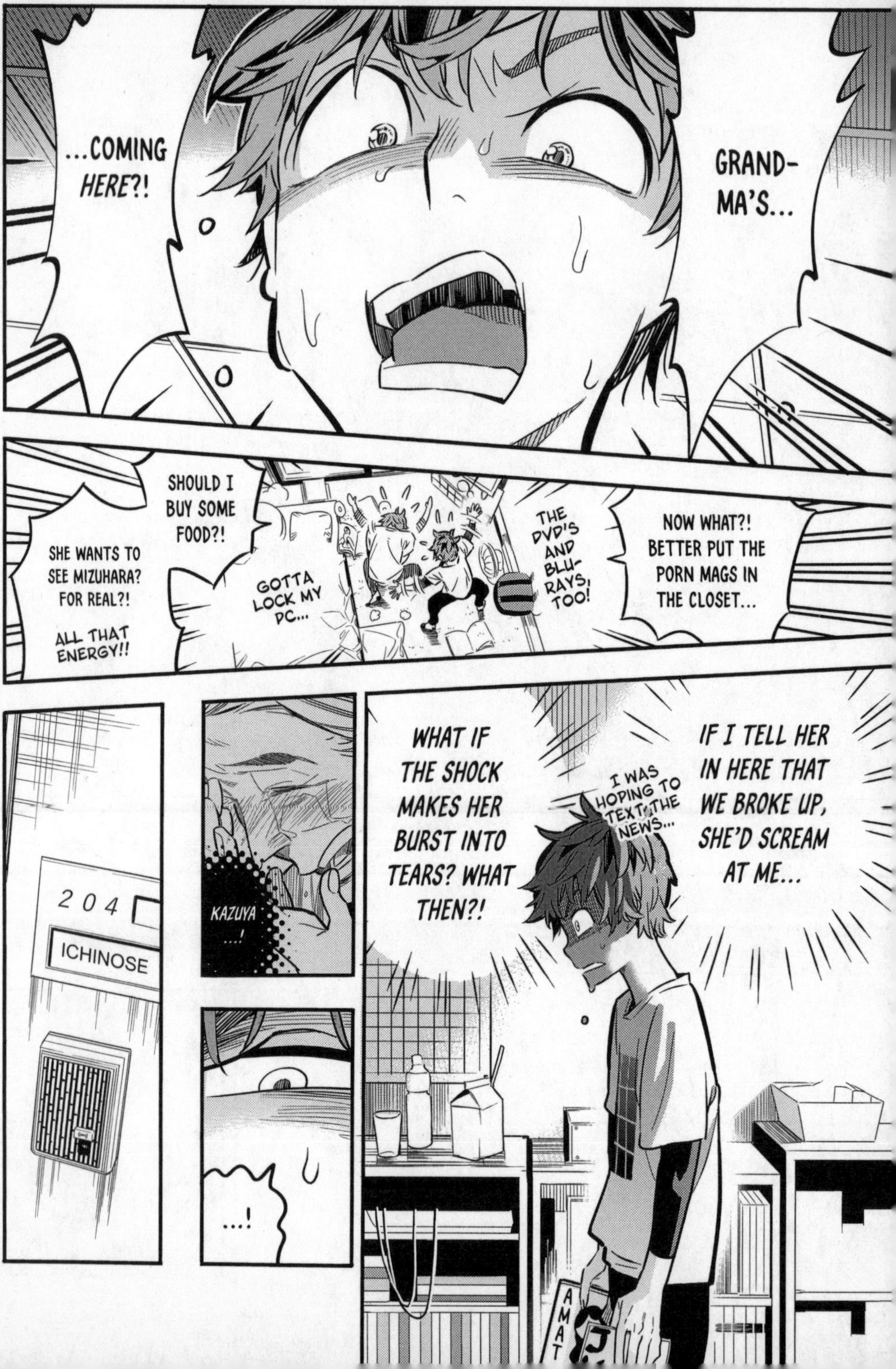
GRAND-MA'S...
...COMING HERE?!
NOW WHAT?! BETTER PUT THE PORN MAGS IN THE CLOSET...
THE DVD'S AND BLU-RAYS, TOO!
GOTTA LOCK MY PC...
SHOULD I BUY SOME FOOD?!
SHE WANTS TO SEE MIZUHARA? FOR REAL?!
ALL THAT ENERGY!!
IF I TELL HER IN HERE THAT WE BROKE UP, SHE'D SCREAM AT ME...
I WAS HOPING TO TEXT THE NEWS...
WHAT IF THE SHOCK MAKES HER BURST INTO TEARS? WHAT THEN?!
KAZUYA...!
...!
204
ICHINOSE

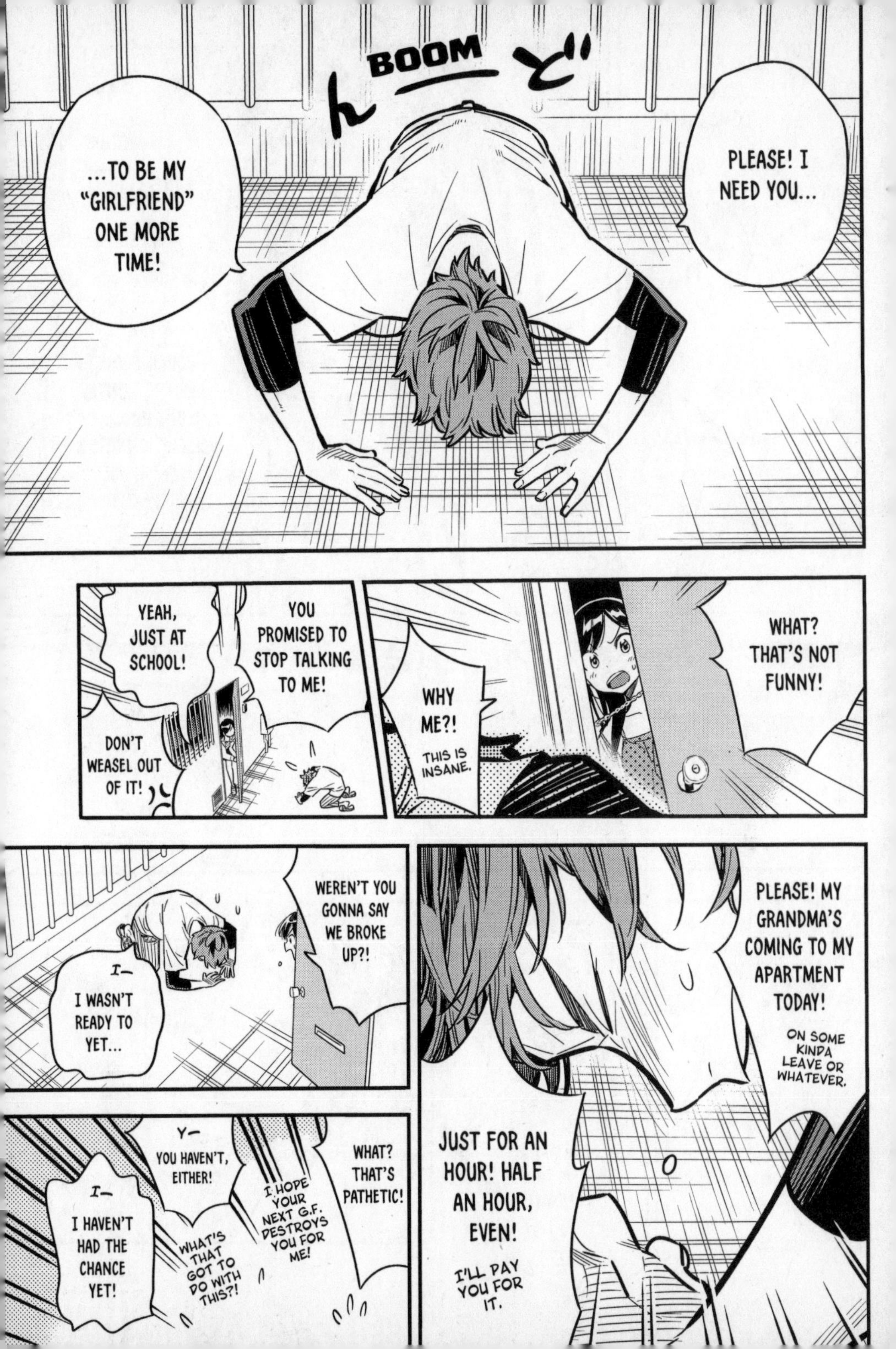

BOOM
どん
PLEASE! I NEED YOU...
...TO BE MY "GIRLFRIEND" ONE MORE TIME!
WHAT? THAT'S NOT FUNNY!
WHY ME?!
THIS IS INSANE.
YOU PROMISED TO STOP TALKING TO ME!
YEAH, JUST AT SCHOOL!
DON'T WEASEL OUT OF IT!
PLEASE! MY GRANDMA'S COMING TO MY APARTMENT TODAY!
ON SOME KINDA LEAVE OR WHATEVER.
JUST FOR AN HOUR! HALF AN HOUR, EVEN!
I'LL PAY YOU FOR IT.
WEREN'T YOU GONNA SAY WE BROKE UP?!
I— I WASN'T READY TO YET...
WHAT? THAT'S PATHETIC!
I HOPE YOUR NEXT G.F. DESTROYS YOU FOR ME!
Y— YOU HAVEN'T, EITHER!
WHAT'S THAT GOT TO DO WITH THIS?!
I— I HAVEN'T HAD THE CHANCE YET!

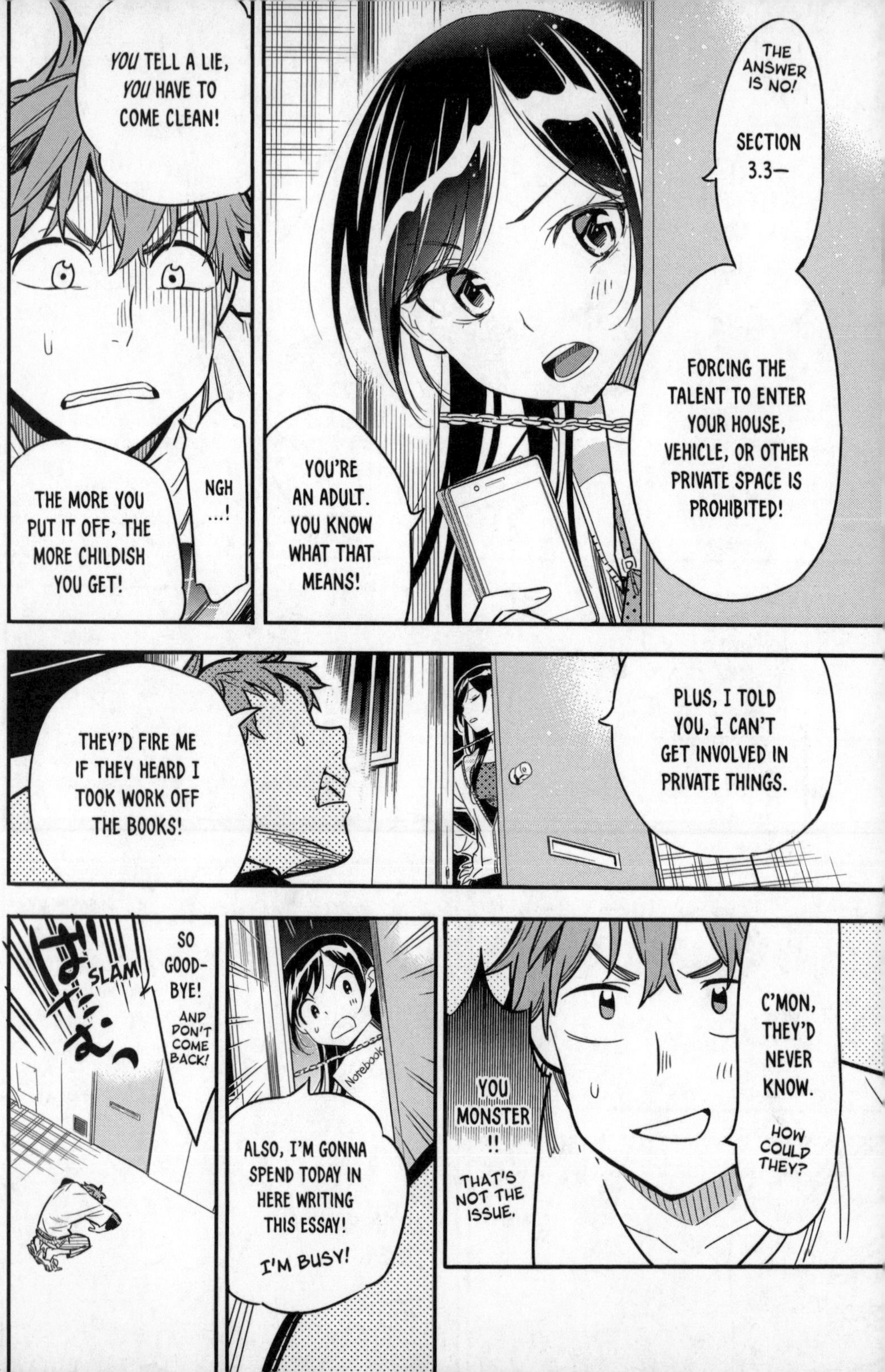
THE ANSWER IS NO!
SECTION 3.3—
FORCING THE TALENT TO ENTER YOUR HOUSE, VEHICLE, OR OTHER PRIVATE SPACE IS PROHIBITED!
YOU'RE AN ADULT. YOU KNOW WHAT THAT MEANS!
YOU TELL A LIE, YOU HAVE TO COME CLEAN!
NGH ...!
THE MORE YOU PUT IT OFF, THE MORE CHILDISH YOU GET!
PLUS, I TOLD YOU, I CAN'T GET INVOLVED IN PRIVATE THINGS.
THEY'D FIRE ME IF THEY HEARD I TOOK WORK OFF THE BOOKS!
C'MON, THEY'D NEVER KNOW.
HOW COULD THEY?
YOU MONSTER!!
THAT'S NOT THE ISSUE.
Notebook
ALSO, I'M GONNA SPEND TODAY IN HERE WRITING THIS ESSAY!
I'M BUSY!
SO GOOD-BYE!
AND DON'T COME BACK!
SLAM

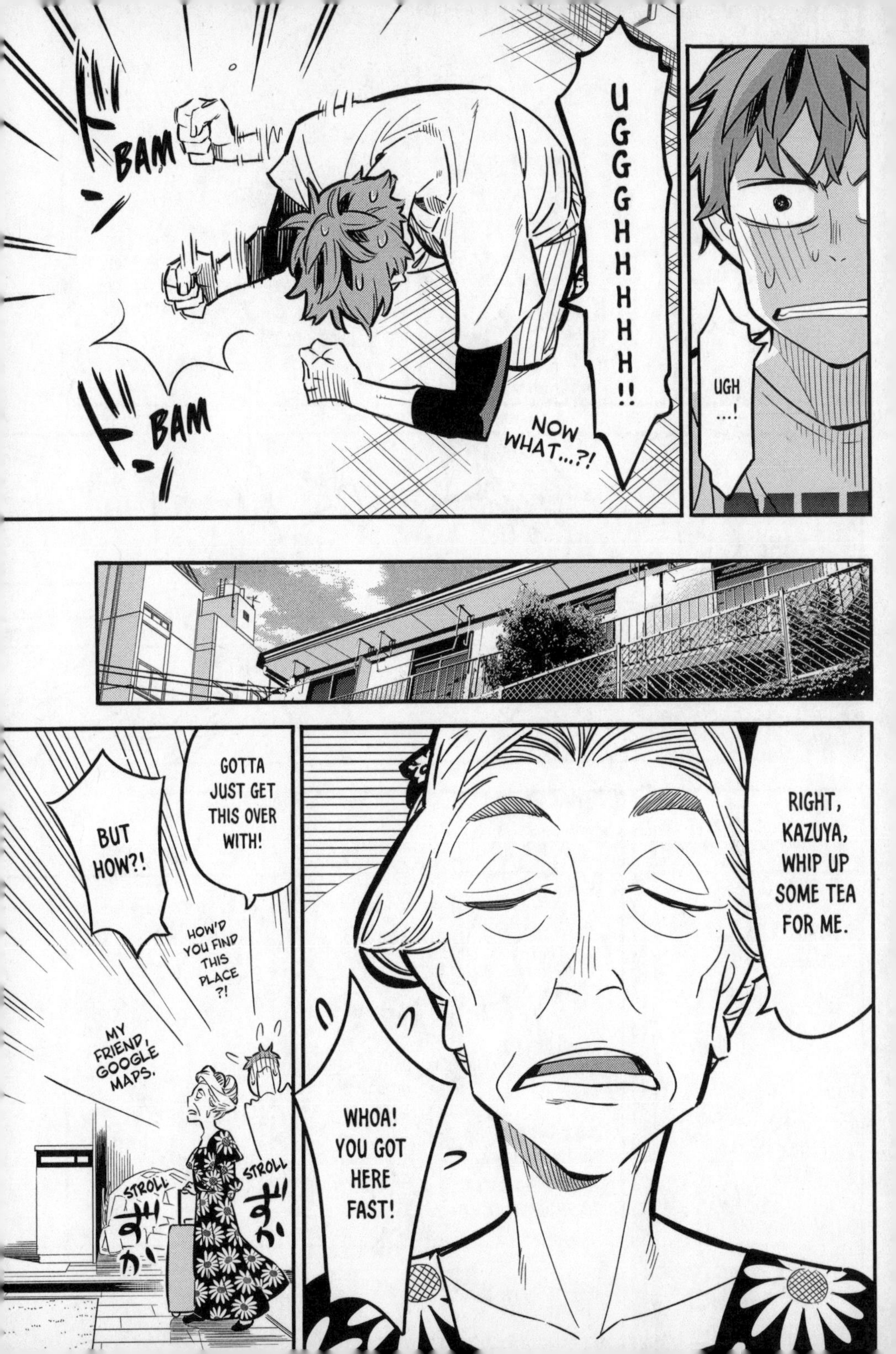
UGH ...!
UGGGHHHHHH!!
NOW WHAT...?!
BAM
BAM
RIGHT, KAZUYA, WHIP UP SOME TEA FOR ME.
WHOA! YOU GOT HERE FAST!
GOTTA JUST GET THIS OVER WITH!
BUT HOW?!
HOW'D YOU FIND THIS PLACE?!
MY FRIEND, GOOGLE MAPS.
STROLL
STROLL

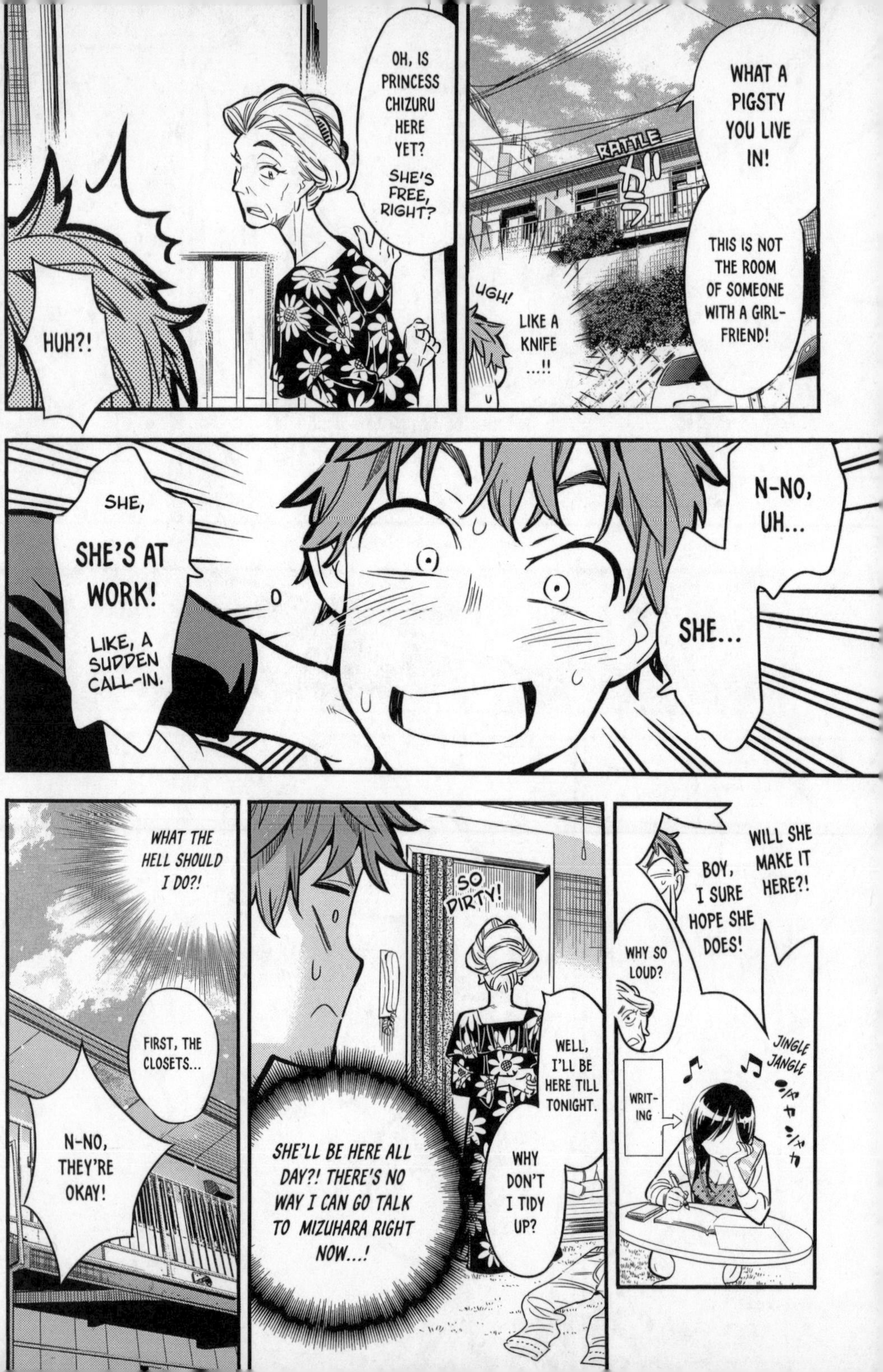
WHAT A PIGSTY YOU LIVE IN!
RATTLE
THIS IS NOT THE ROOM OF SOMEONE WITH A GIRL-FRIEND!
UGH!
LIKE A KNIFE ...!!
OH, IS PRINCESS CHIZURU HERE YET?
SHE'S FREE, RIGHT?
HUH?!
N-NO, UH...
SHE...
SHE,
SHE'S AT WORK!
LIKE, A SUDDEN CALL-IN.
WILL SHE MAKE IT HERE?!
BOY, I SURE HOPE SHE DOES!
WHY SO LOUD?
JINGLE JANGLE
WRITING
SO DIRTY!
WELL, I'LL BE HERE TILL TONIGHT.
WHY DON'T I TIDY UP?
SHE'LL BE HERE ALL DAY?! THERE'S NO WAY I CAN GO TALK TO MIZUHARA RIGHT NOW...!
WHAT THE HELL SHOULD I DO?!
FIRST, THE CLOSETS...
N-NO, THEY'RE OKAY!

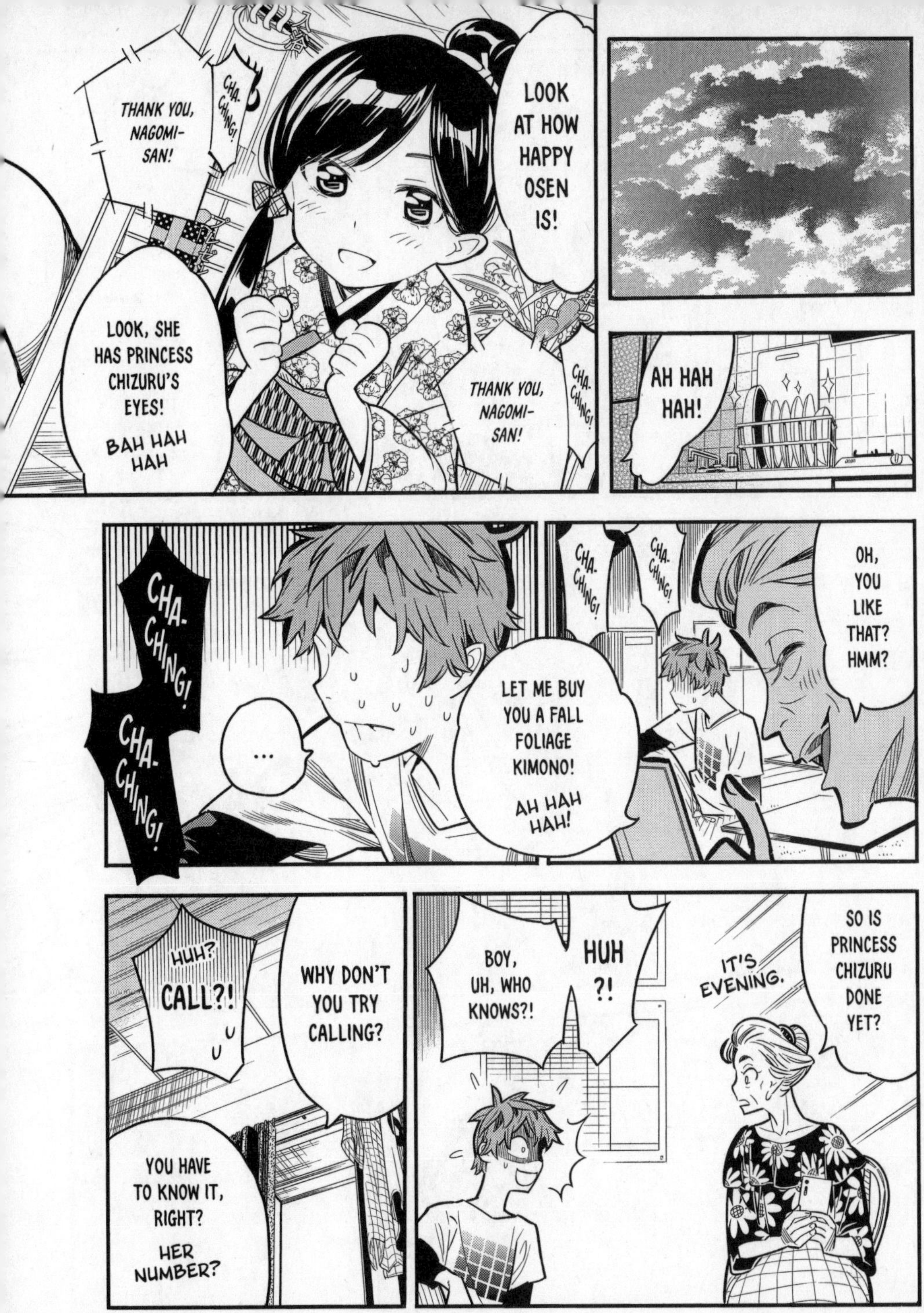
AH HAH HAH!
LOOK AT HOW HAPPY OSEN IS!
CHA-CHING!
THANK YOU, NAGOMI-SAN!
CHA-CHING!
THANK YOU, NAGOMI-SAN!
LOOK, SHE HAS PRINCESS CHIZURU'S EYES!
BAH HAH HAH
OH, YOU LIKE THAT? HMM?
CHA-CHING!
CHA-CHING!
LET ME BUY YOU A FALL FOLIAGE KIMONO!
AH HAH HAH!
CHA-CHING!
CHA-CHING!
...
SO IS PRINCESS CHIZURU DONE YET?
IT'S EVENING.
HUH?!
BOY, UH, WHO KNOWS?!
WHY DON'T YOU TRY CALLING?
HUH? CALL?!
YOU HAVE TO KNOW IT, RIGHT?
HER NUMBER?

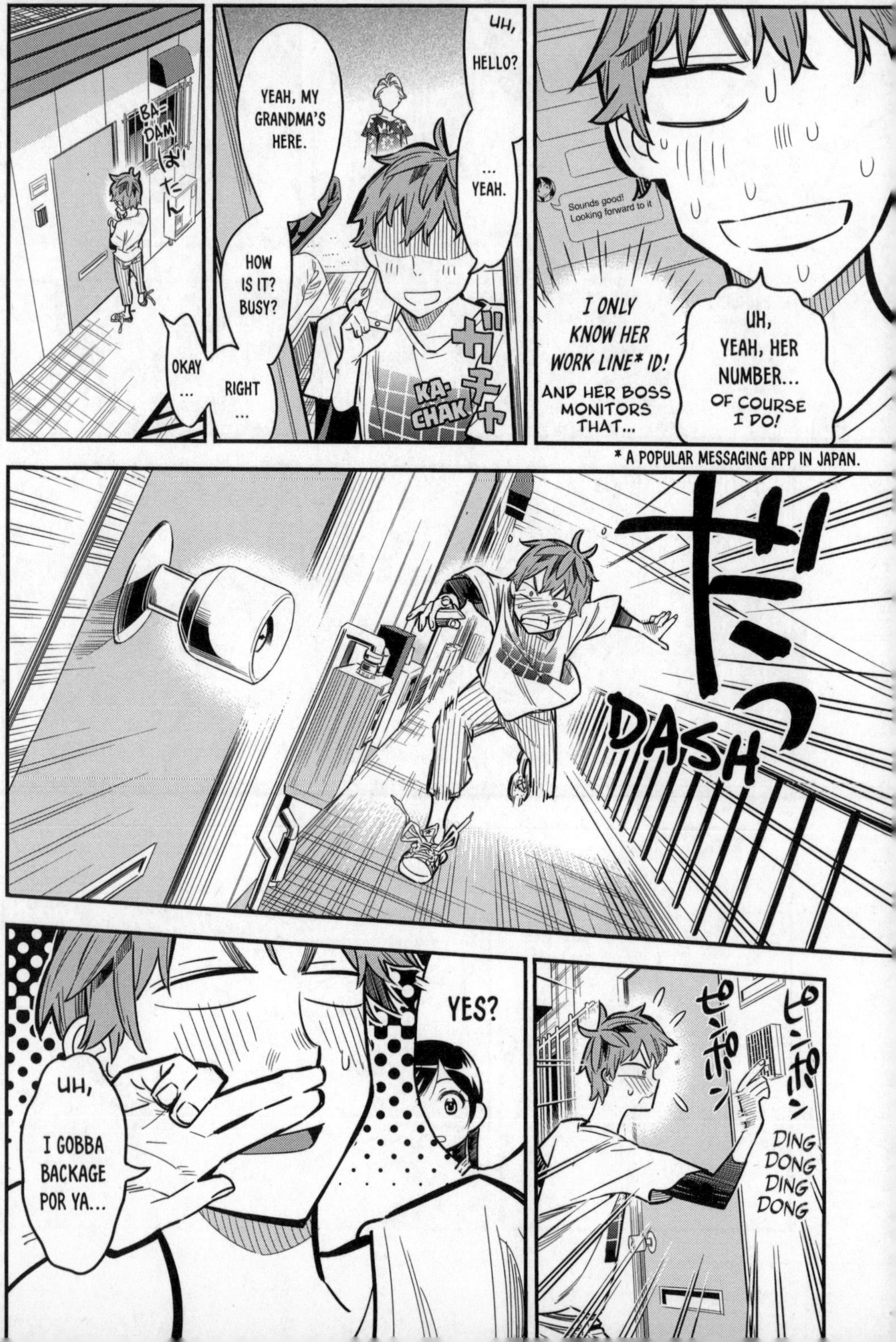
UH, YEAH, HER NUMBER... OF COURSE I DO!
I ONLY KNOW HER WORK LINE* ID! AND HER BOSS MONITORS THAT...
Sounds good! Looking forward to it
UH, HELLO?
... YEAH.
YEAH, MY GRANDMA'S HERE.
HOW IS IT? BUSY?
ガチャ KA-CHAK
RIGHT ...
OKAY ...
BA-DAM ばたん
* A POPULAR MESSAGING APP IN JAPAN.
だっ DASH
ピンポンピンポン DING DONG DING DONG
YES?
UH,
I GOBBA BACKAGE POR YA...

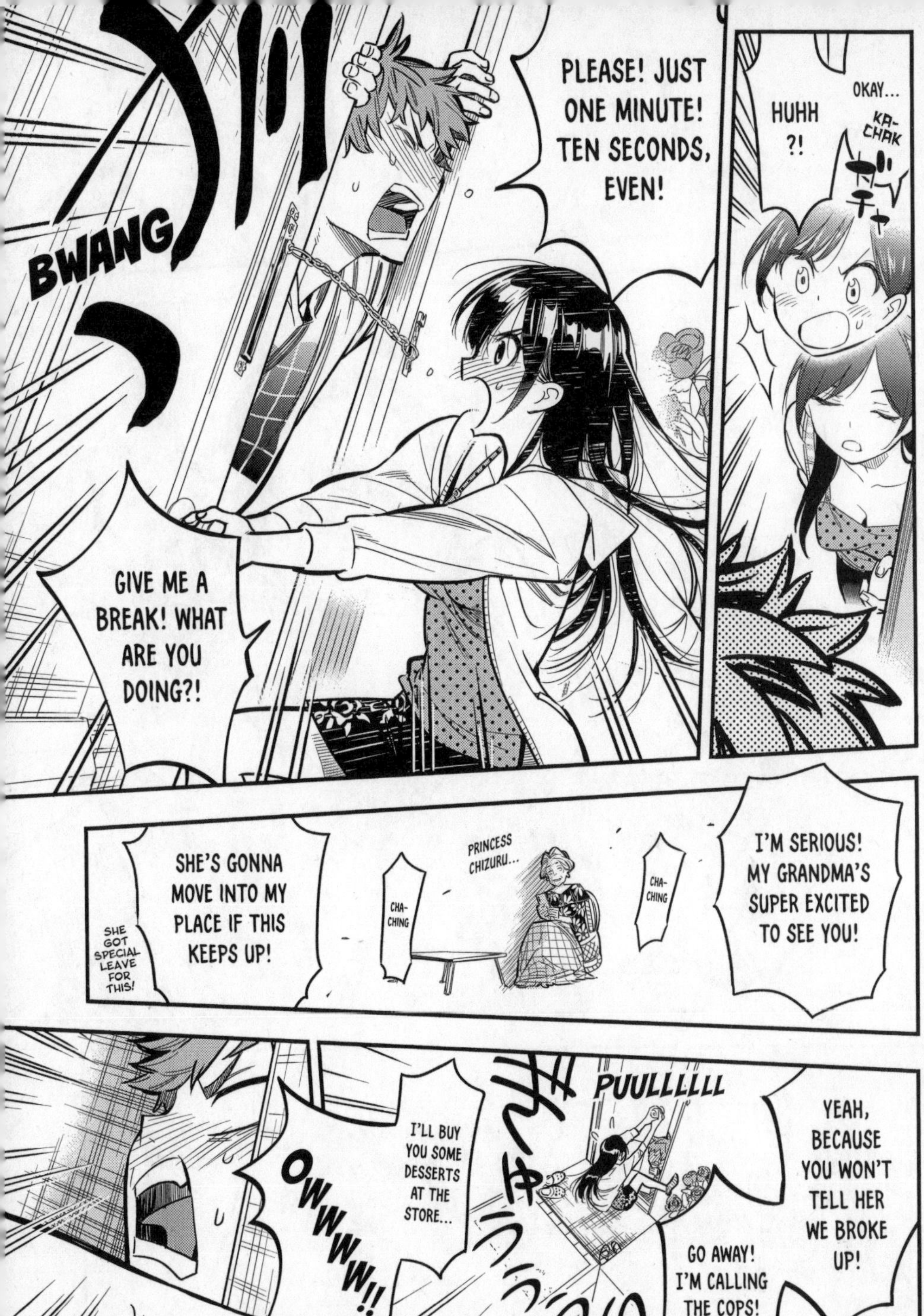
OKAY...
KA-CHAK
HUHH ?!
PLEASE! JUST ONE MINUTE! TEN SECONDS, EVEN!
BWANG
GIVE ME A BREAK! WHAT ARE YOU DOING?!
I'M SERIOUS! MY GRANDMA'S SUPER EXCITED TO SEE YOU!
CHA-CHING
PRINCESS CHIZURU...
CHA-CHING
SHE'S GONNA MOVE INTO MY PLACE IF THIS KEEPS UP!
SHE GOT SPECIAL LEAVE FOR THIS!
YEAH, BECAUSE YOU WON'T TELL HER WE BROKE UP!
GO AWAY! I'M CALLING THE COPS!
PUULLLLLL
I'LL BUY YOU SOME DESSERTS AT THE STORE...
OWWWW!!

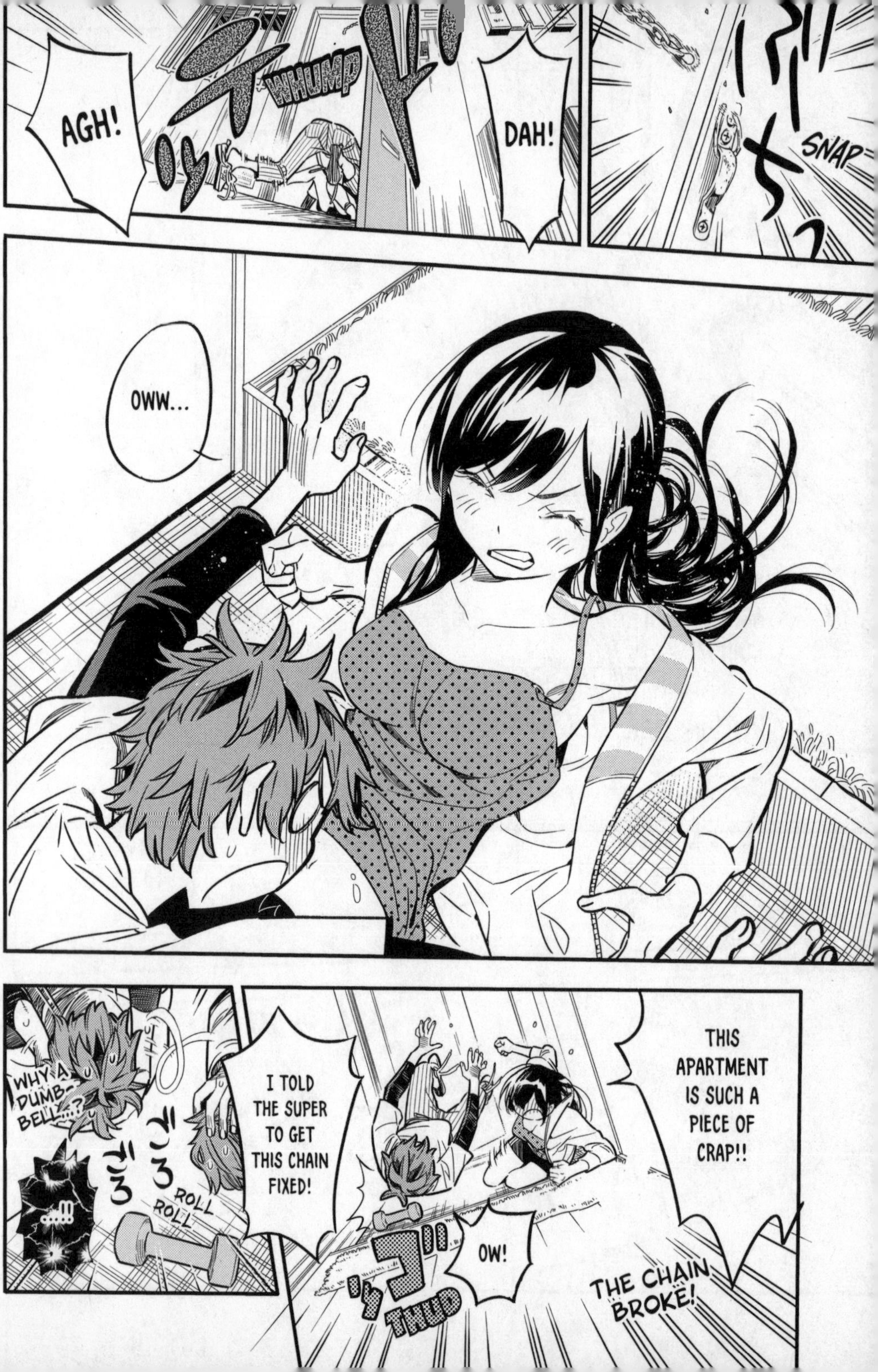

SNAP
DAH!
WHUMP
AGH!
OWW...
THIS APARTMENT IS SUCH A PIECE OF CRAP!!
I TOLD THE SUPER TO GET THIS CHAIN FIXED!
THE CHAIN BROKE!
OW!
THUD
WHY A DUMBBELL...?
ROLL ROLL
...!!

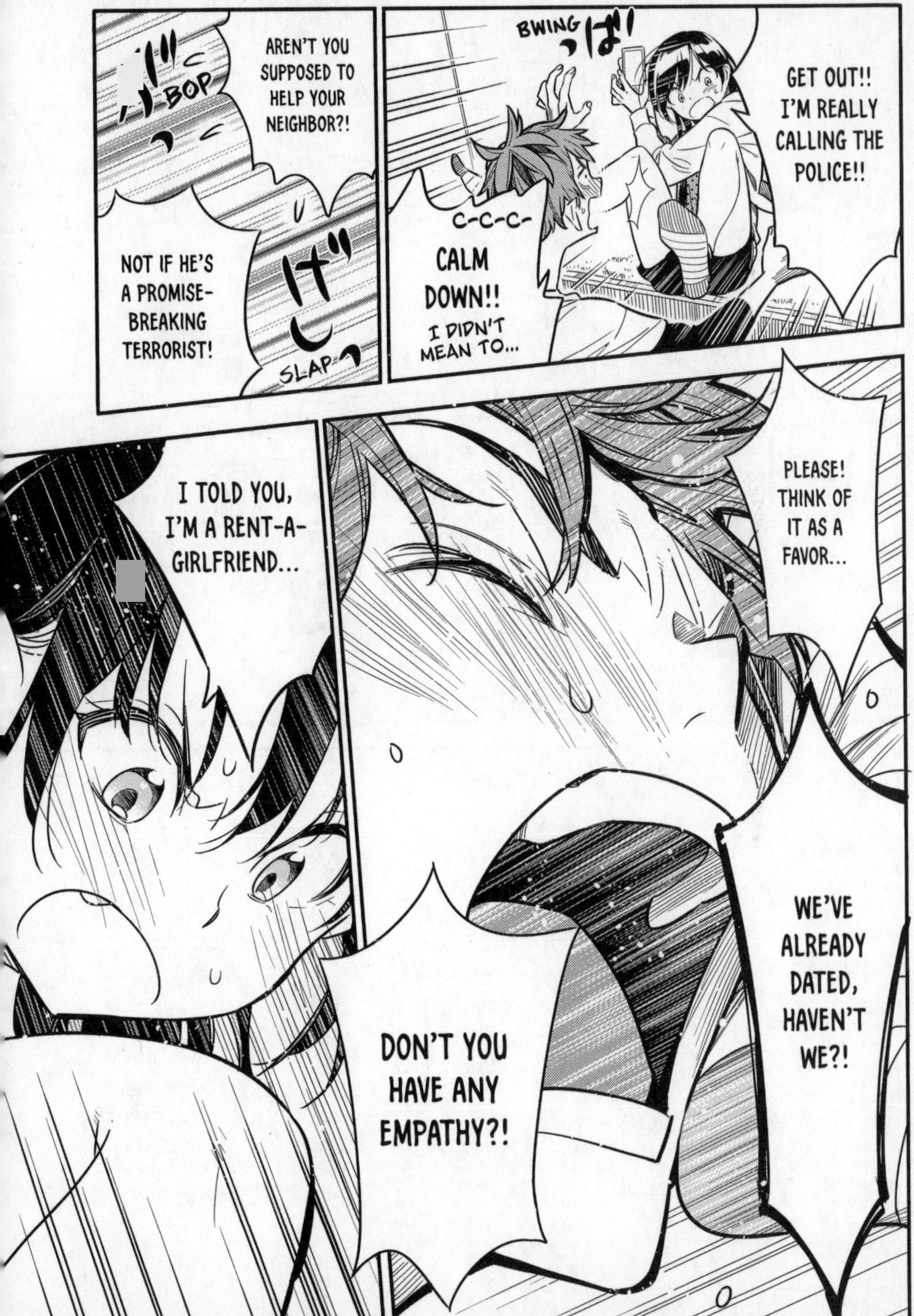
BWING
GET OUT!! I'M REALLY CALLING THE POLICE!!
C-C-C-
CALM DOWN!!
I DIDN'T MEAN TO...
AREN'T YOU SUPPOSED TO HELP YOUR NEIGHBOR?!
BOP
NOT IF HE'S A PROMISE-BREAKING TERRORIST!
SLAP
PLEASE! THINK OF IT AS A FAVOR...
WE'VE ALREADY DATED, HAVEN'T WE?!
DON'T YOU HAVE ANY EMPATHY?!
I TOLD YOU, I'M A RENT-A-GIRLFRIEND...

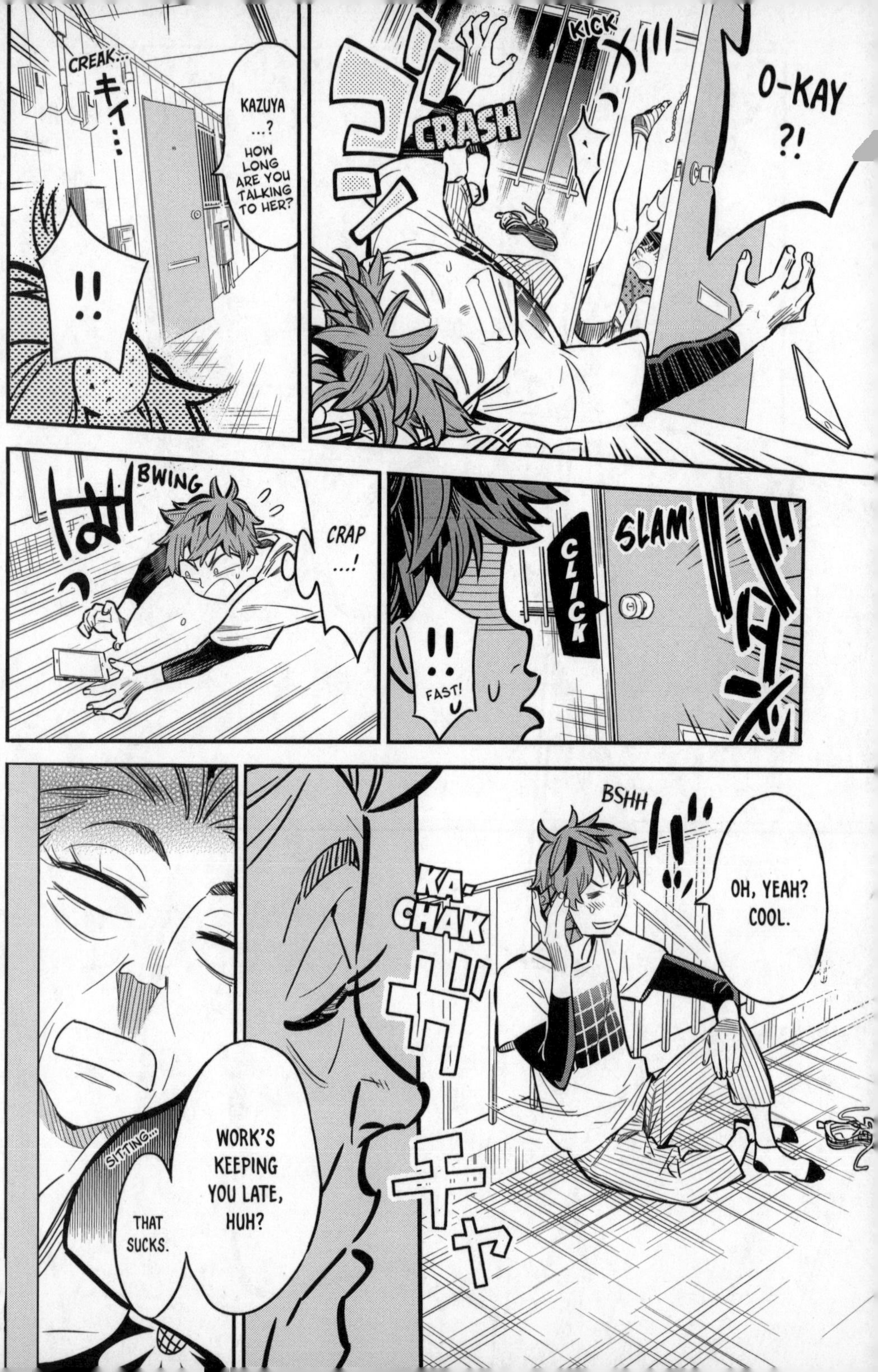
O-KAY ?!
KICK
CRASH
CREAK...
キイ…
KAZUYA ...? HOW LONG ARE YOU TALKING TO HER?
!!
SLAM
CLICK
!!
FAST!
BWING
CRAP ...!
BSHH
OH, YEAH? COOL.
KA-CHAK
WORK'S KEEPING YOU LATE, HUH?
SITTING...
THAT SUCKS.

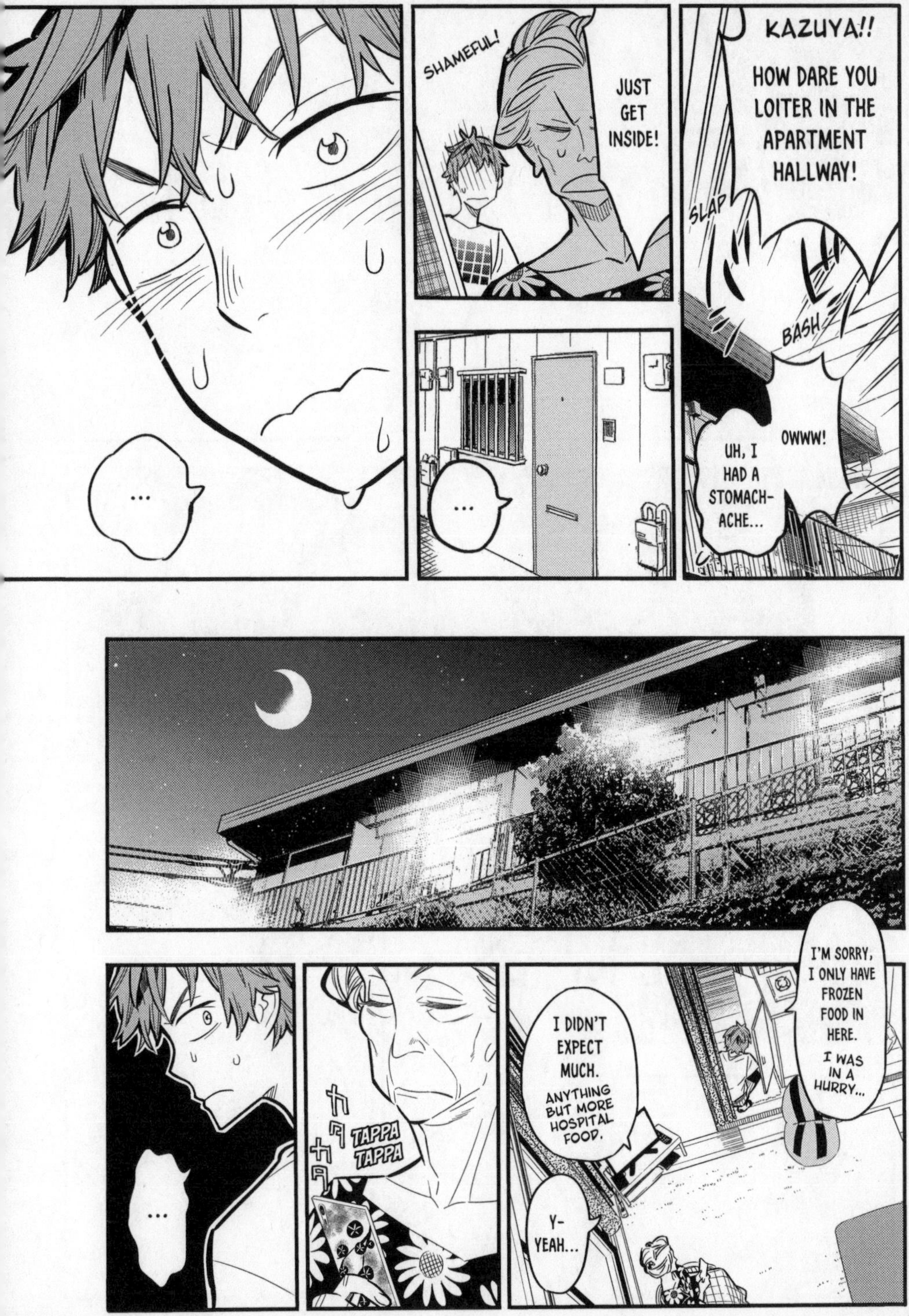
KAZUYA!!
HOW DARE YOU LOITER IN THE APARTMENT HALLWAY!
SLAP
BASH
OWWW!
UH, I HAD A STOMACH-ACHE...
SHAMEFUL!
JUST GET INSIDE!
...
...
I'M SORRY, I ONLY HAVE FROZEN FOOD IN HERE.
I WAS IN A HURRY...
I DIDN'T EXPECT MUCH.
ANYTHING BUT MORE HOSPITAL FOOD.
Y-YEAH...
カタカタ
TAPPA TAPPA
...

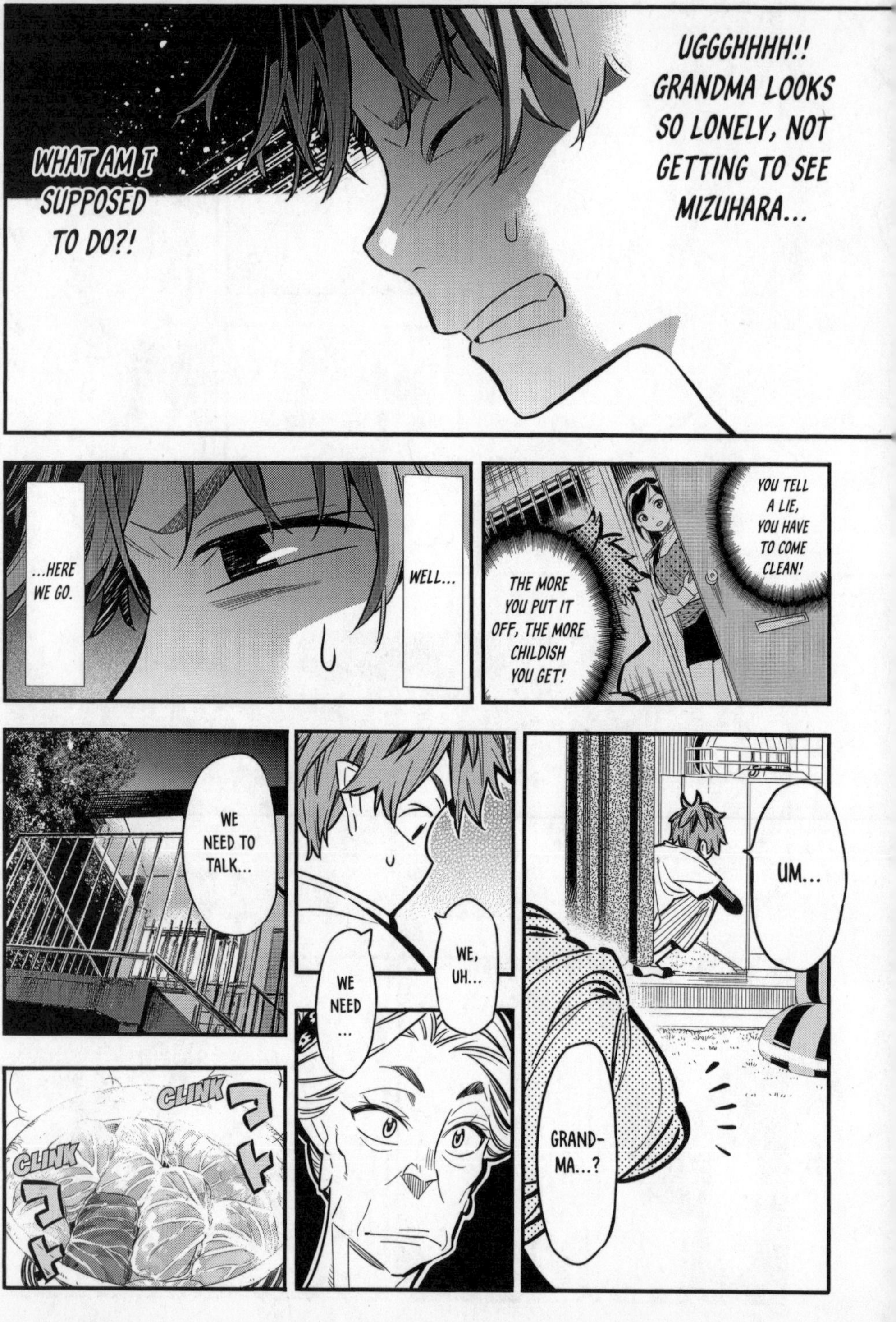
UGGGHHHH!! GRANDMA LOOKS SO LONELY, NOT GETTING TO SEE MIZUHARA...
WHAT AM I SUPPOSED TO DO?!
YOU TELL A LIE, YOU HAVE TO COME CLEAN!
THE MORE YOU PUT IT OFF, THE MORE CHILDISH YOU GET!
WELL...
...HERE WE GO.
UM...
GRAND-MA...?
WE, UH...
WE NEED ...
WE NEED TO TALK...
CLINK
コト
CLINK
コト

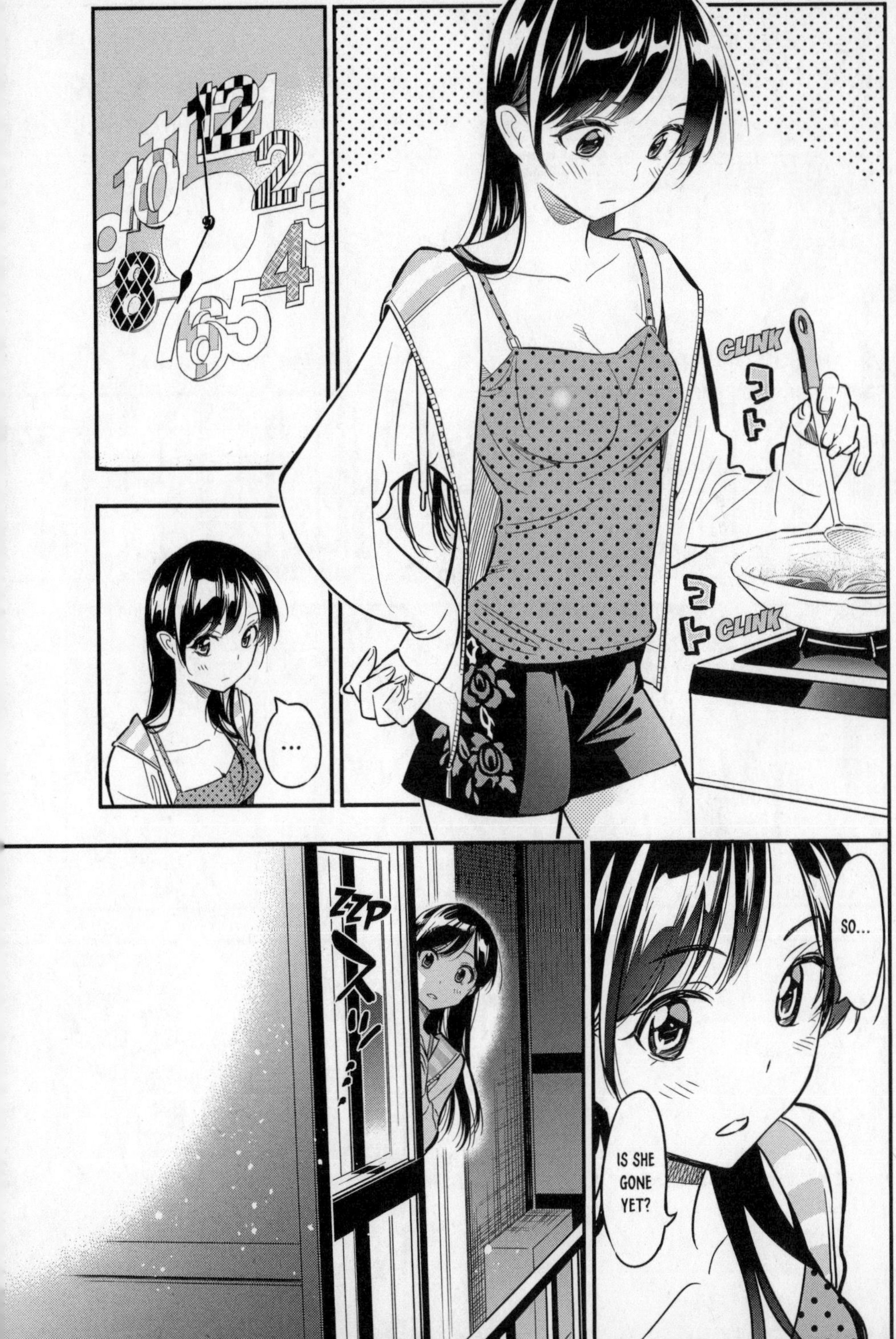

CLINK
コト
コト
CLINK
...
SO...
IS SHE GONE YET?
ZZZP
スッ

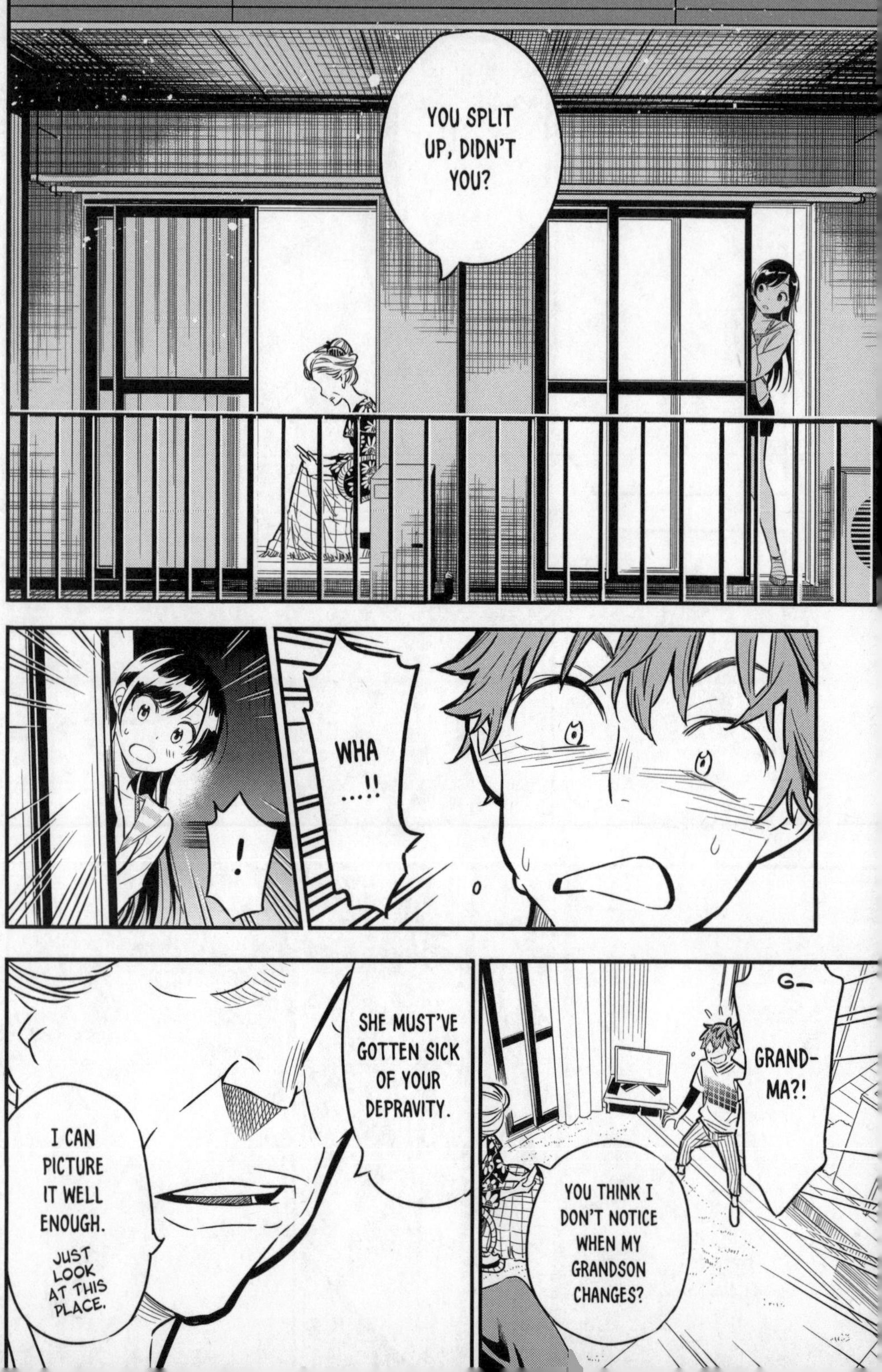
YOU SPLIT UP, DIDN'T YOU?
WHA ...!!
!
G—
GRAND-MA?!
YOU THINK I DON'T NOTICE WHEN MY GRANDSON CHANGES?
SHE MUST'VE GOTTEN SICK OF YOUR DEPRAVITY.
I CAN PICTURE IT WELL ENOUGH.
JUST LOOK AT THIS PLACE.

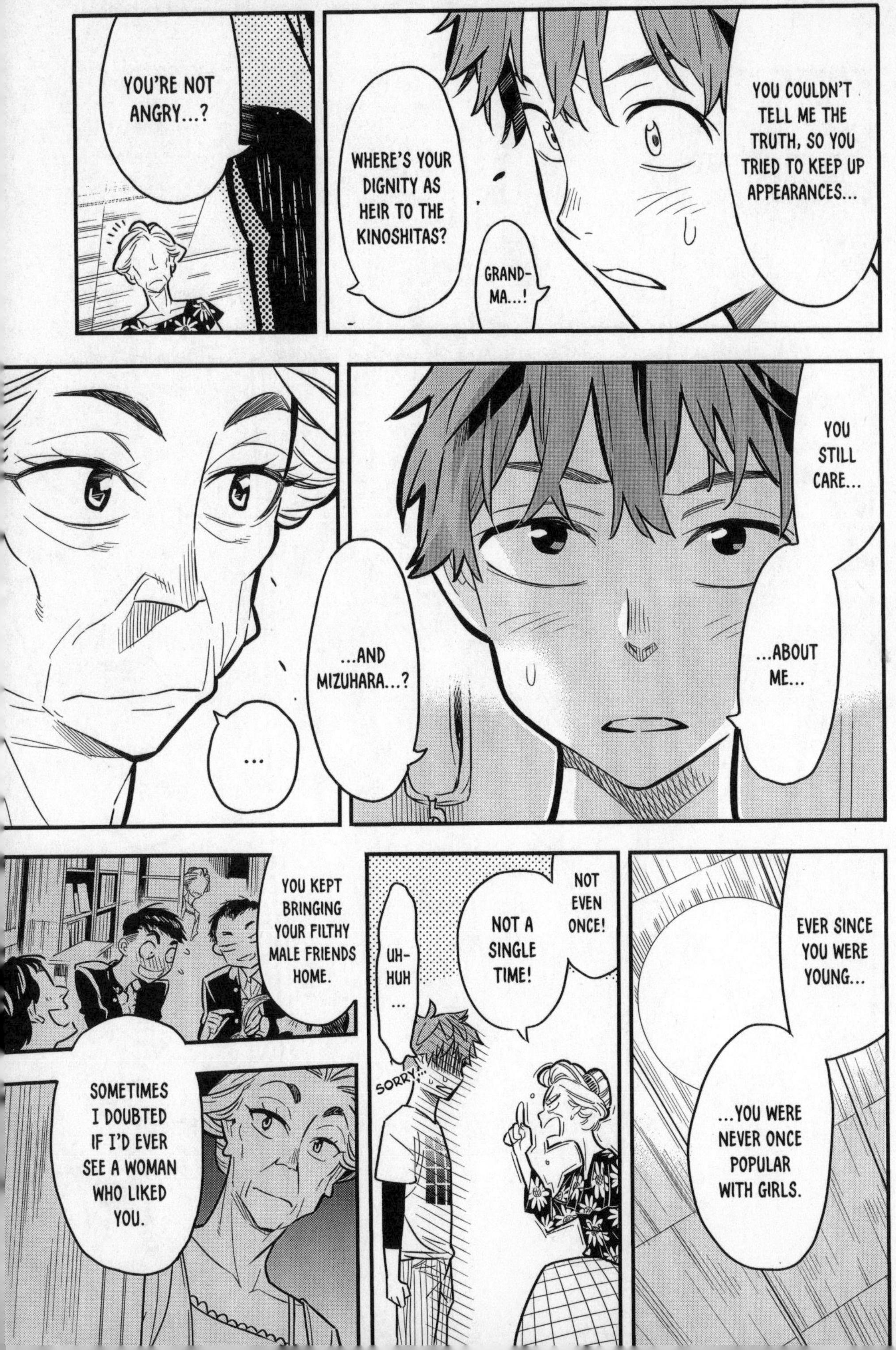
YOU COULDN'T TELL ME THE TRUTH, SO YOU TRIED TO KEEP UP APPEARANCES...
WHERE'S YOUR DIGNITY AS HEIR TO THE KINOSHITAS?
GRAND-MA...!
YOU'RE NOT ANGRY...?
YOU STILL CARE...
...ABOUT ME...
...AND MIZUHARA...?
...
EVER SINCE YOU WERE YOUNG...
...YOU WERE NEVER ONCE POPULAR WITH GIRLS.
NOT EVEN ONCE!
NOT A SINGLE TIME!
UH-HUH...
SORRY...
YOU KEPT BRINGING YOUR FILTHY MALE FRIENDS HOME.
SOMETIMES I DOUBTED IF I'D EVER SEE A WOMAN WHO LIKED YOU.

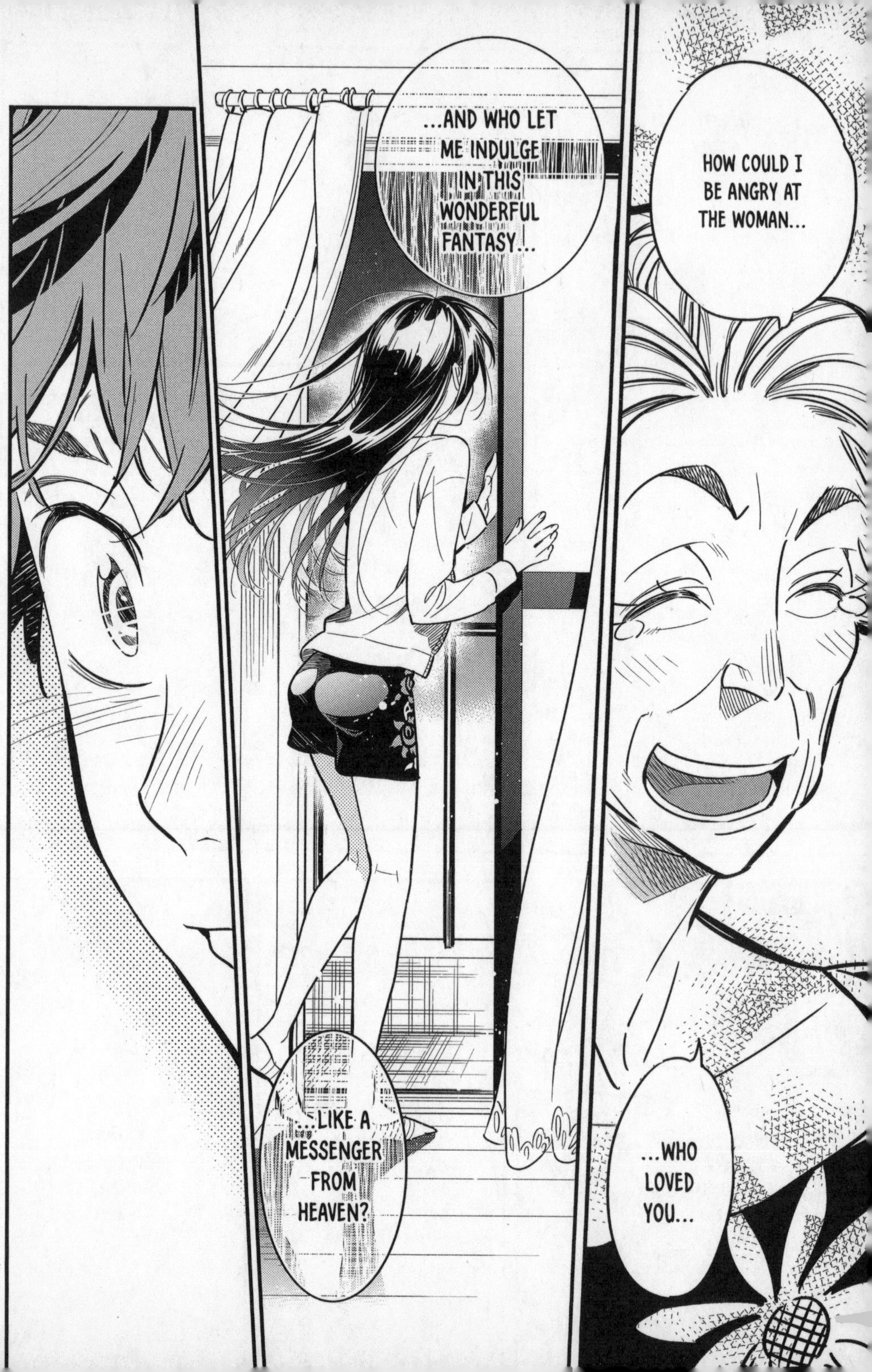
HOW COULD I BE ANGRY AT THE WOMAN...
...WHO LOVED YOU...
...AND WHO LET ME INDULGE IN THIS WONDERFUL FANTASY...
...LIKE A MESSENGER FROM HEAVEN?

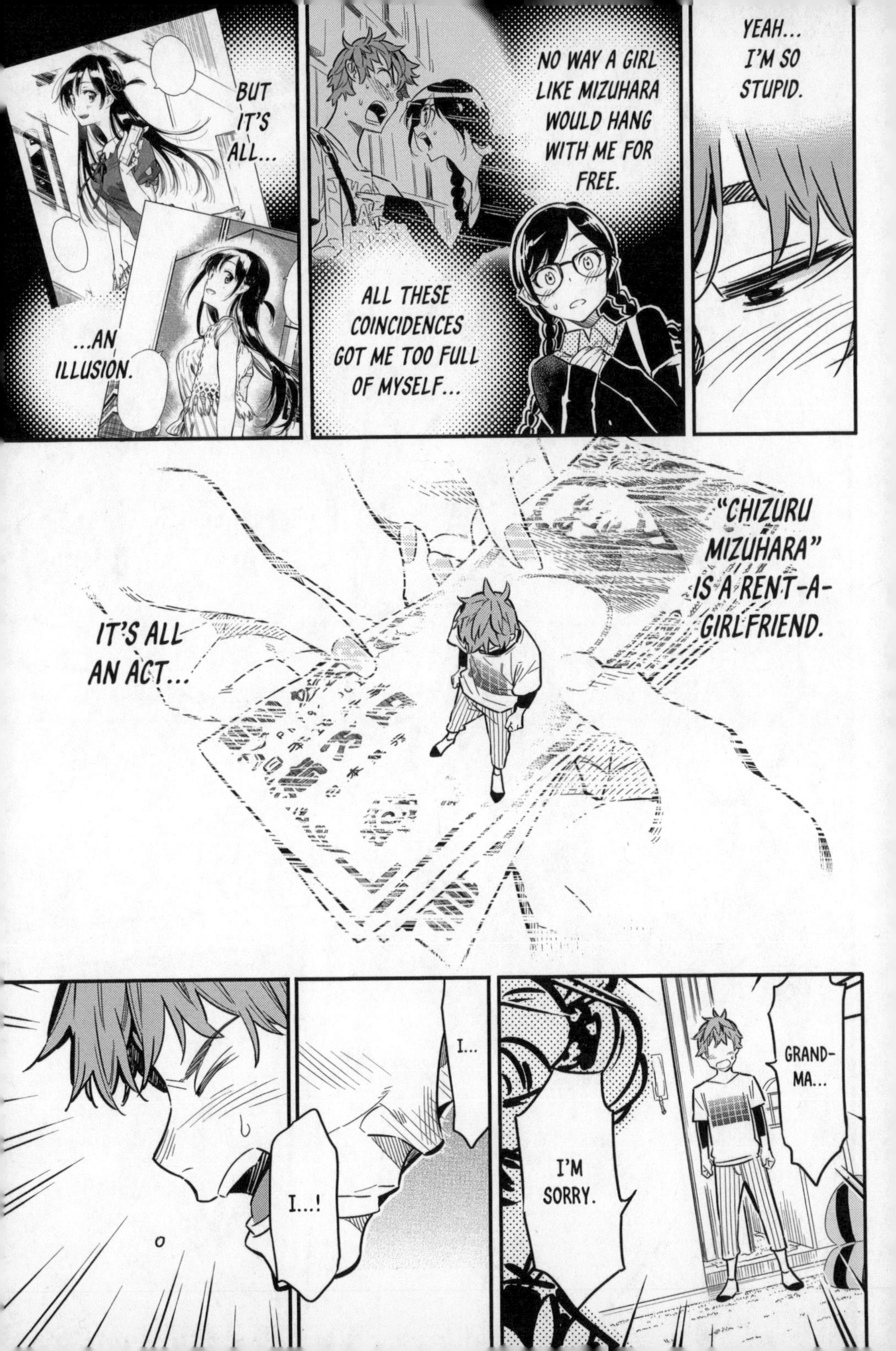
YEAH... I'M SO STUPID.
NO WAY A GIRL LIKE MIZUHARA WOULD HANG WITH ME FOR FREE.
ALL THESE COINCIDENCES GOT ME TOO FULL OF MYSELF...
BUT IT'S ALL...
...AN ILLUSION.
"CHIZURU MIZUHARA" IS A RENT-A-GIRLFRIEND.
IT'S ALL AN ACT...
GRAND-MA...
I'M SORRY.
I...
I...!

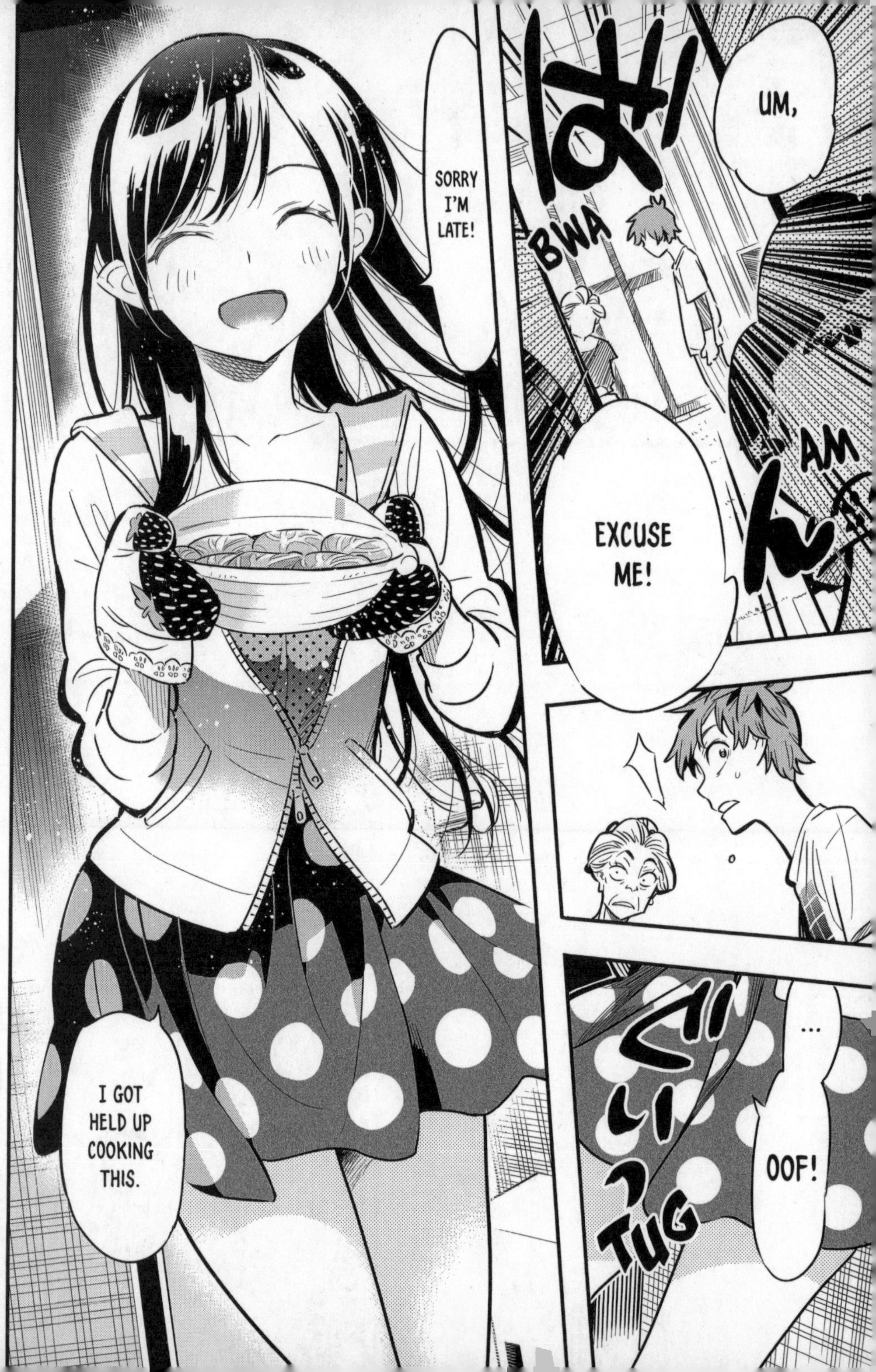
UM,
BWA
AM
EXCUSE ME!
...
OOF!
TUG
SORRY I'M LATE!
I GOT HELD UP COOKING THIS.

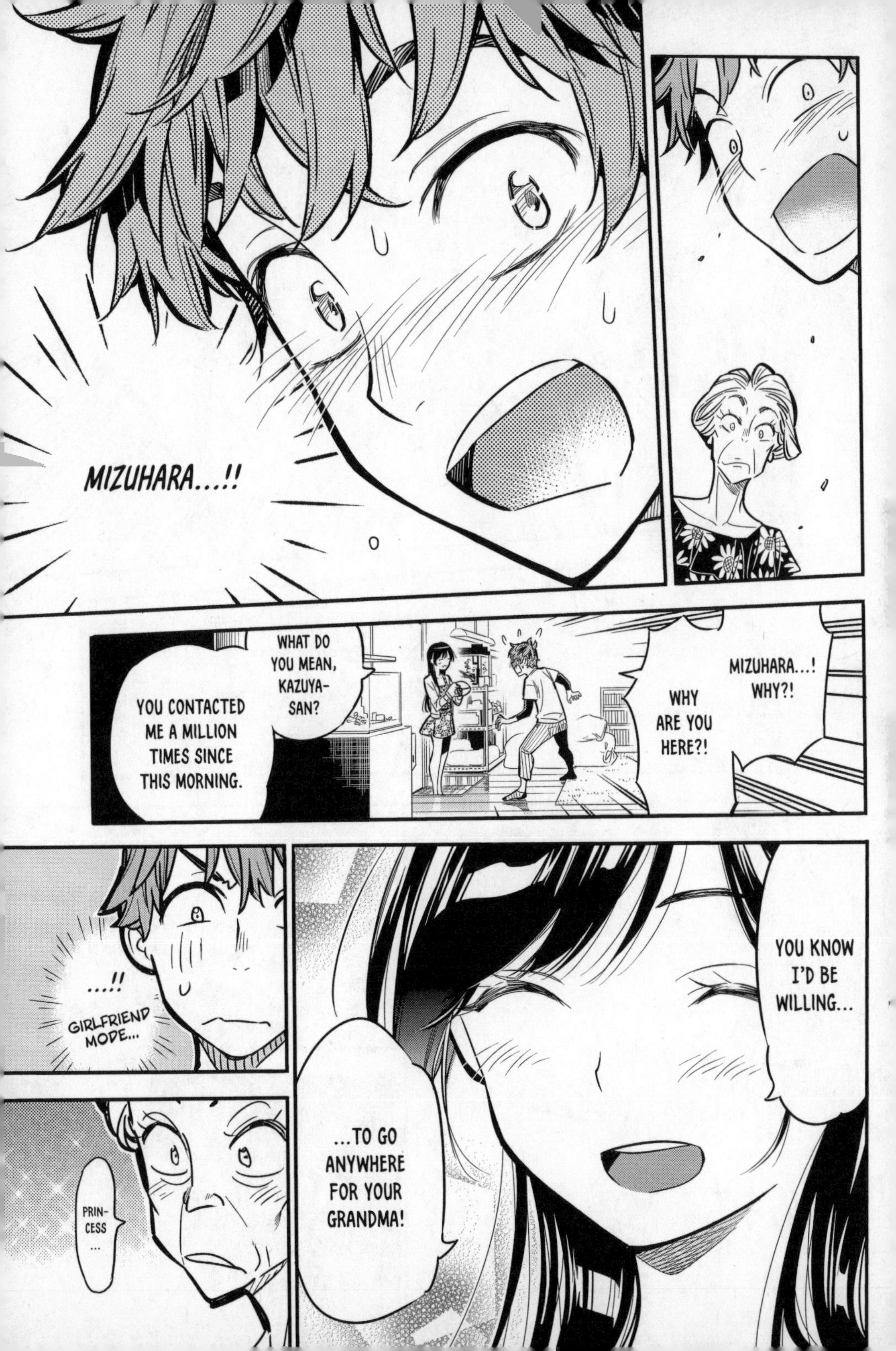
MIZUHARA...!!
MIZUHARA...! WHY?!
WHY ARE YOU HERE?!
WHAT DO YOU MEAN, KAZUYA-SAN?
YOU CONTACTED ME A MILLION TIMES SINCE THIS MORNING.
YOU KNOW I'D BE WILLING...
...TO GO ANYWHERE FOR YOUR GRANDMA!
...!!
GIRLFRIEND MODE...
PRIN-CESS ...

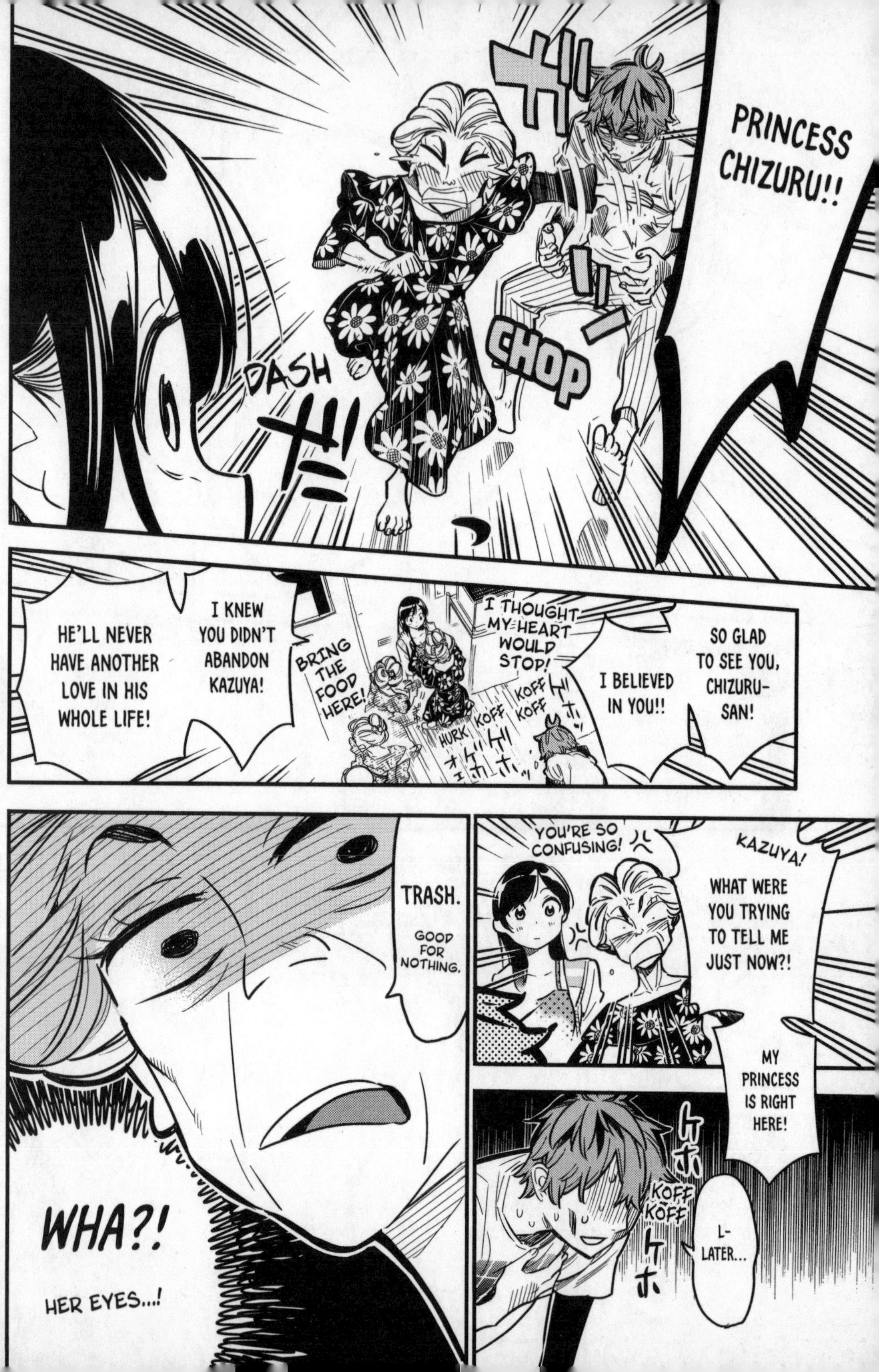
PRINCESS CHIZURU!!
CHOP
DASH
SO GLAD TO SEE YOU, CHIZURU-SAN!
I BELIEVED IN YOU!!
I THOUGHT MY HEART WOULD STOP!
KOFF KOFF
KOFF
HURK
BRING THE FOOD HERE!
I KNEW YOU DIDN'T ABANDON KAZUYA!
HE'LL NEVER HAVE ANOTHER LOVE IN HIS WHOLE LIFE!
KAZUYA!
WHAT WERE YOU TRYING TO TELL ME JUST NOW?!
YOU'RE SO CONFUSING!
MY PRINCESS IS RIGHT HERE!
KOFF KOFF
L- LATER...
TRASH.
GOOD FOR NOTHING.
WHA?!
HER EYES...!

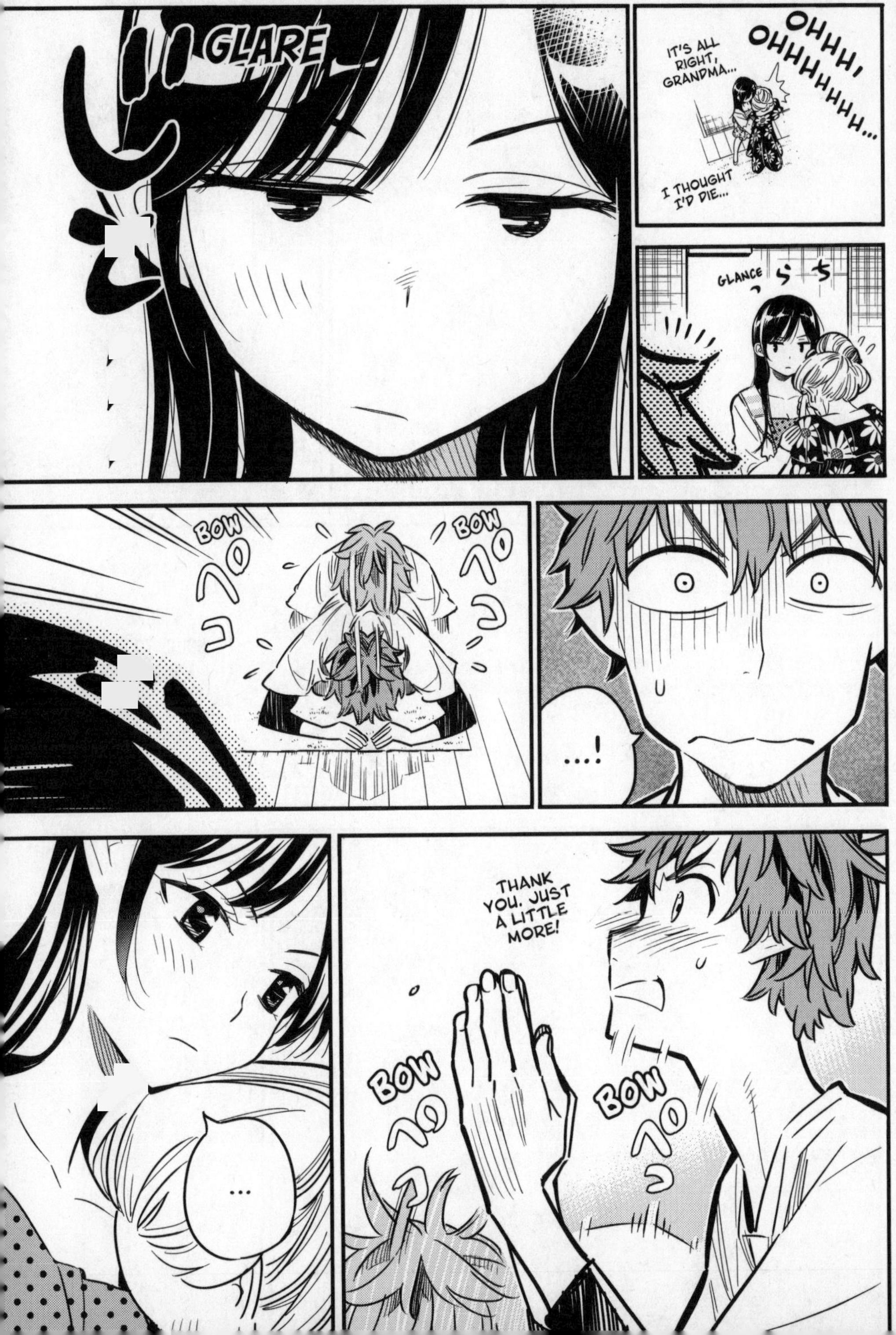
OHHHH, OHHHHHHHH...
IT'S ALL RIGHT, GRANDMA...
I THOUGHT I'D DIE...
GLANCE
GLARE
...!
BOW
BOW
THANK YOU. JUST A LITTLE MORE!
BOW
BOW
...

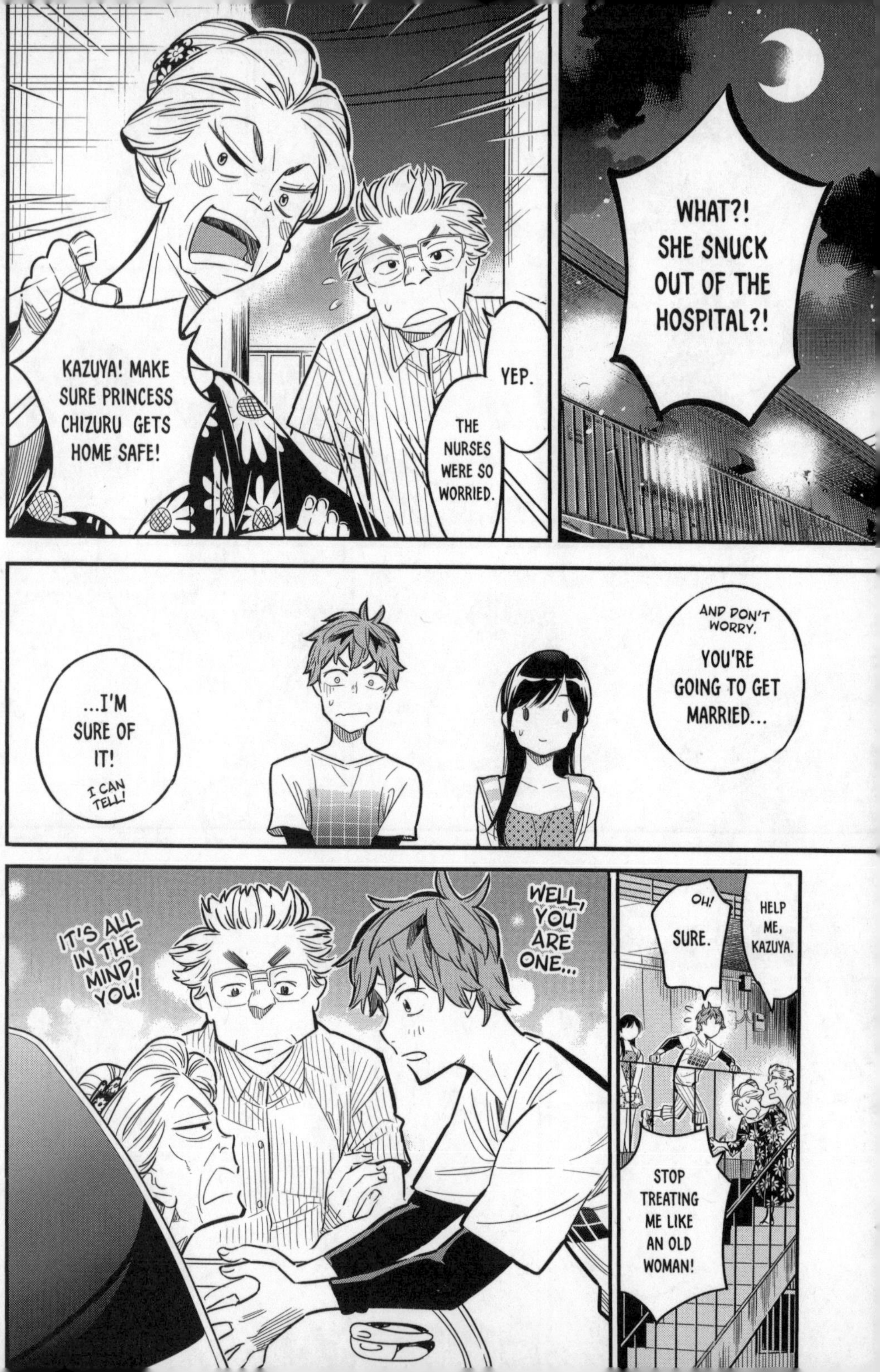
WHAT?! SHE SNUCK OUT OF THE HOSPITAL?!
YEP.
THE NURSES WERE SO WORRIED.
KAZUYA! MAKE SURE PRINCESS CHIZURU GETS HOME SAFE!
AND DON'T WORRY.
YOU'RE GOING TO GET MARRIED...
...I'M SURE OF IT!
I CAN TELL!
HELP ME, KAZUYA.
OH!
SURE.
STOP TREATING ME LIKE AN OLD WOMAN!
WELL, YOU ARE ONE...
IT'S ALL IN THE MIND YOU!

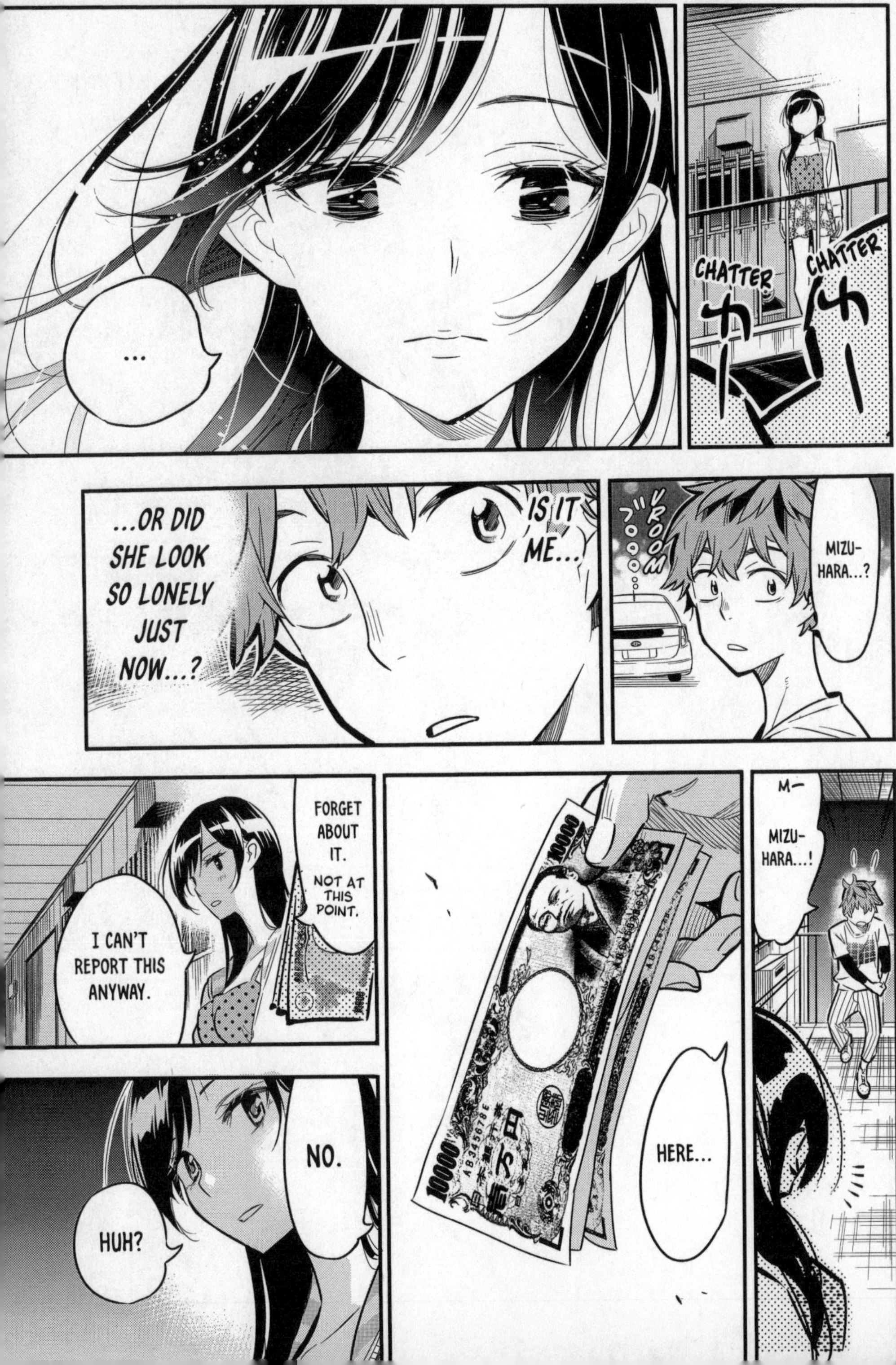
CHATTER
CHATTER
...
MIZU-HARA...?
VROOM
IS IT ME...
...OR DID SHE LOOK SO LONELY JUST NOW...?
M—
MIZU-HARA...!
HERE...
FORGET ABOUT IT.
NOT AT THIS POINT.
I CAN'T REPORT THIS ANYWAY.
NO.
HUH?

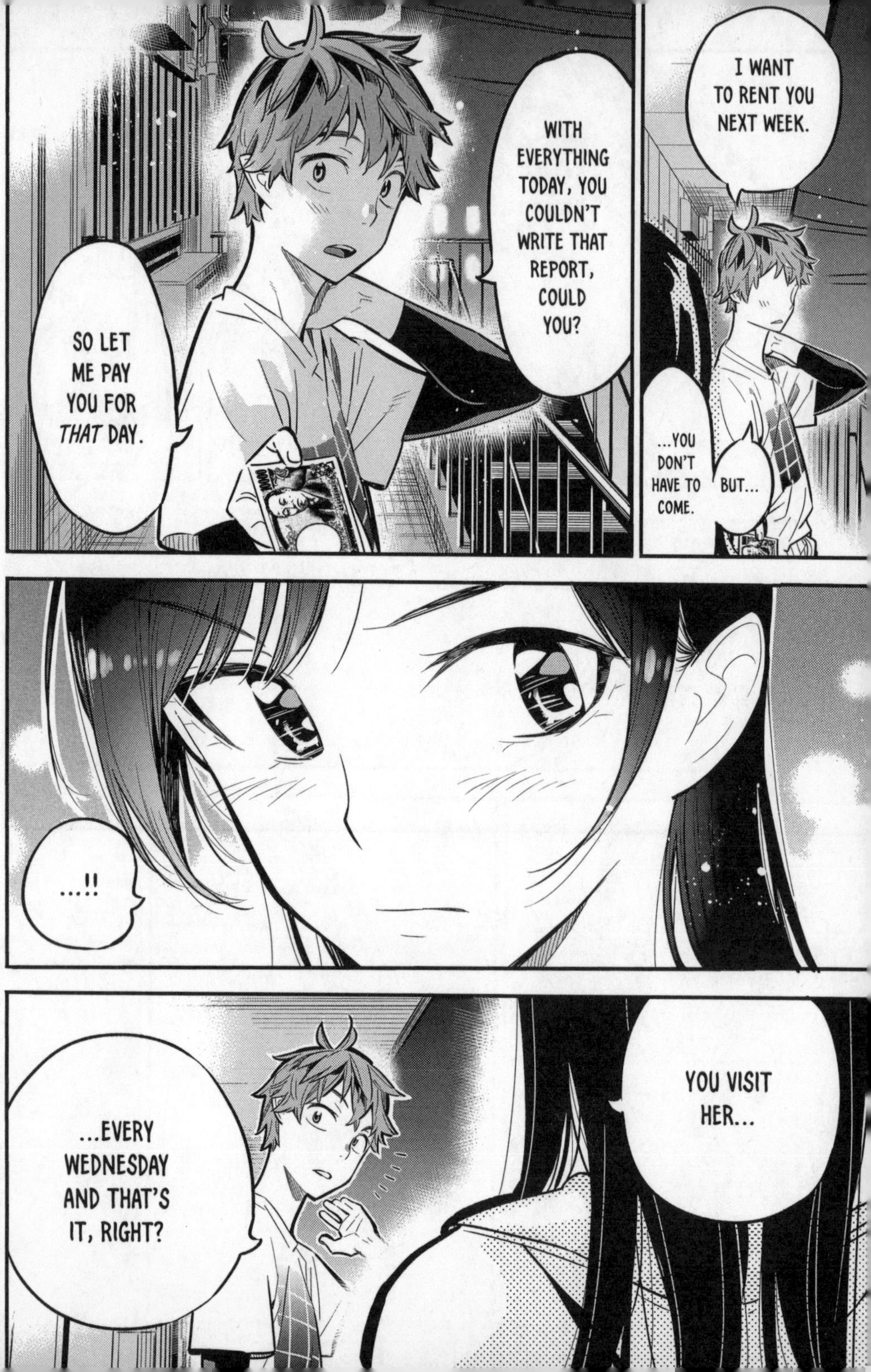
I WANT TO RENT YOU NEXT WEEK.
BUT...
...YOU DON'T HAVE TO COME.
WITH EVERYTHING TODAY, YOU COULDN'T WRITE THAT REPORT, COULD YOU?
SO LET ME PAY YOU FOR *THAT* DAY.
...!!
YOU VISIT HER...
...EVERY WEDNESDAY AND THAT'S IT, RIGHT?

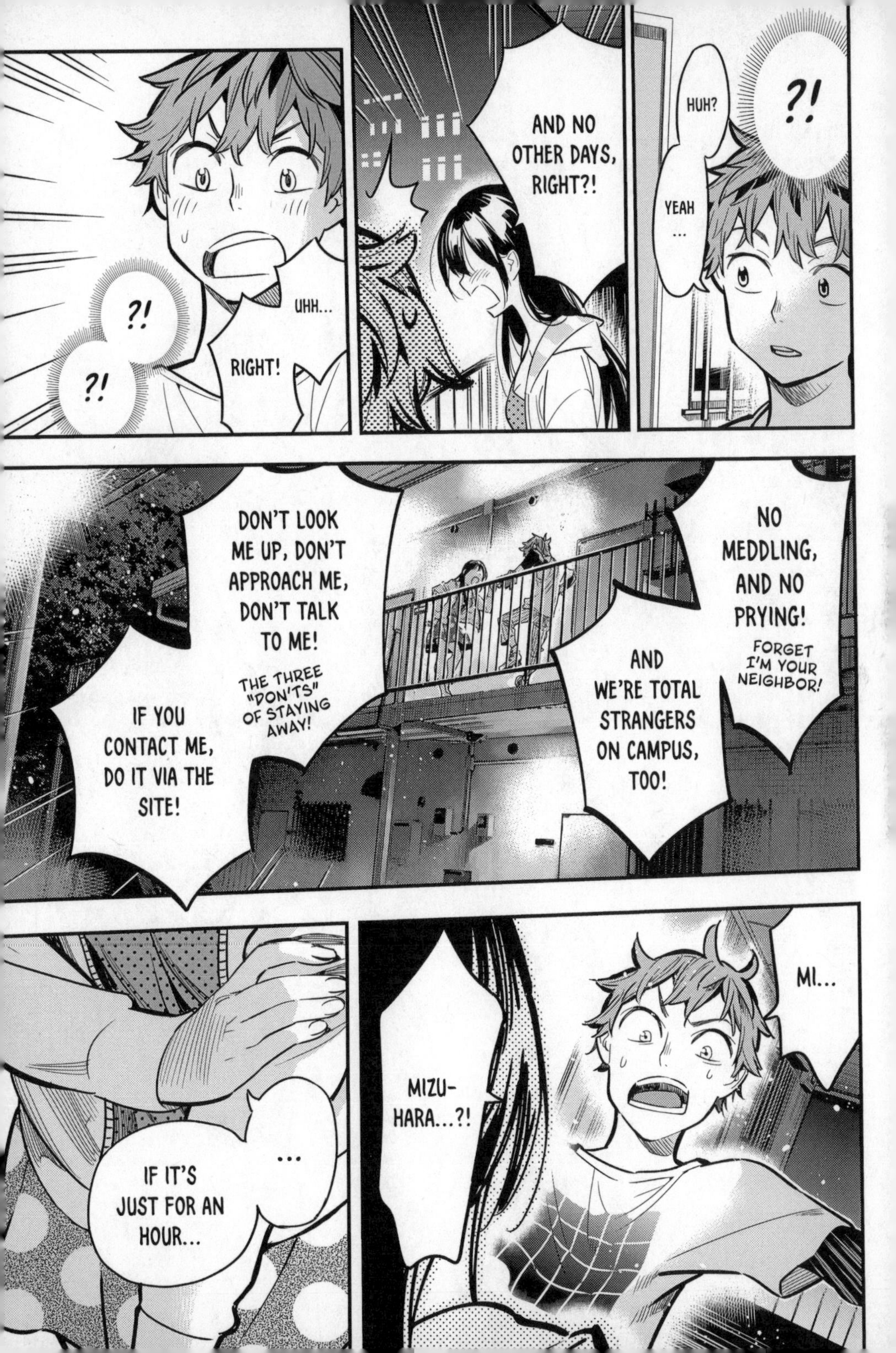
?!
HUH?
YEAH …
AND NO OTHER DAYS, RIGHT?!
UHH…
RIGHT!
?!
?!
NO MEDDLING, AND NO PRYING!
FORGET I'M YOUR NEIGHBOR!
AND WE'RE TOTAL STRANGERS ON CAMPUS, TOO!
DON'T LOOK ME UP, DON'T APPROACH ME, DON'T TALK TO ME!
THE THREE "DON'TS" OF STAYING AWAY!
IF YOU CONTACT ME, DO IT VIA THE SITE!
MI…
MIZU-HARA…?!
…
IF IT'S JUST FOR AN HOUR…

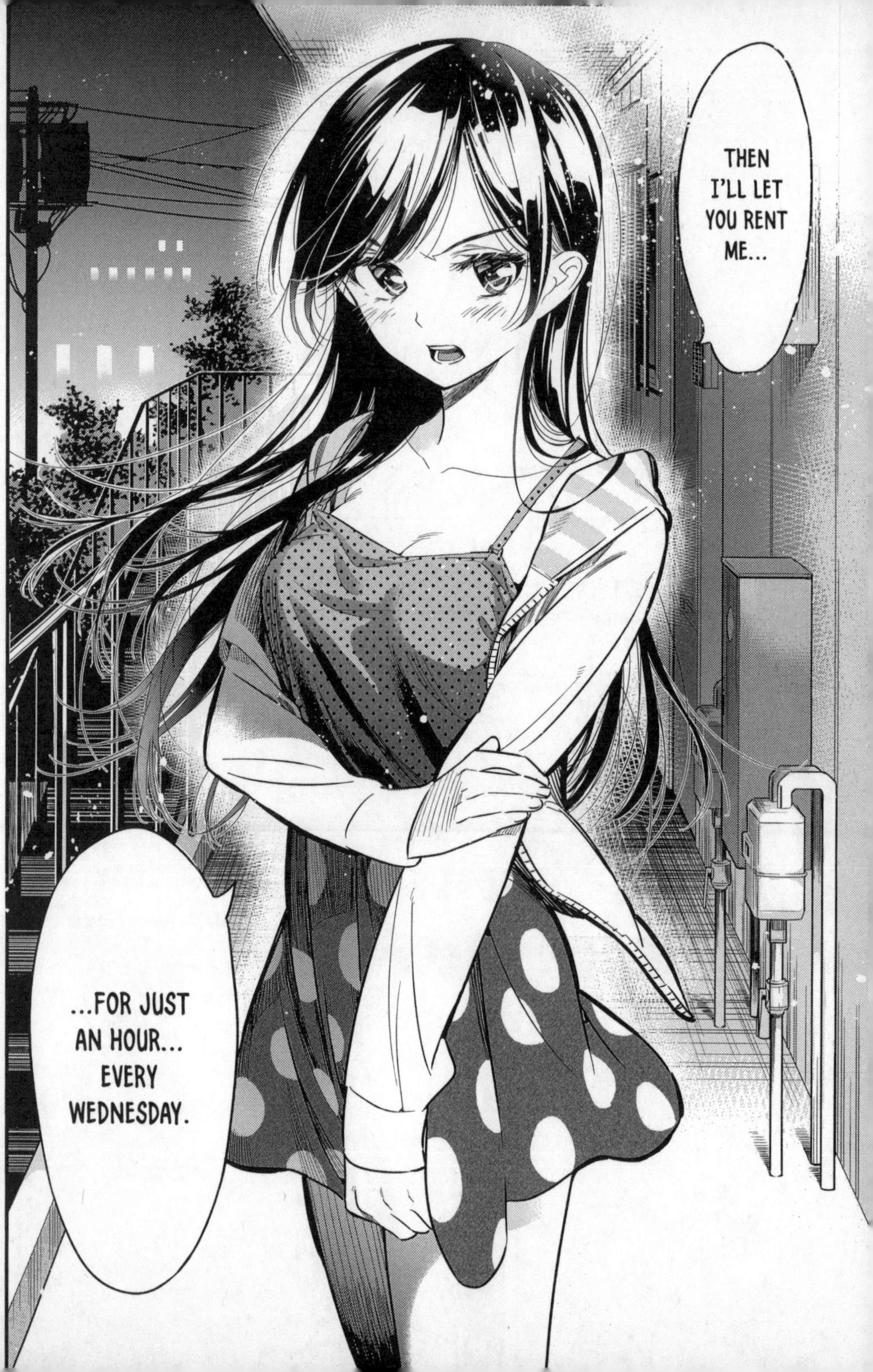
THEN I'LL LET YOU RENT ME...
...FOR JUST AN HOUR... EVERY WEDNESDAY.

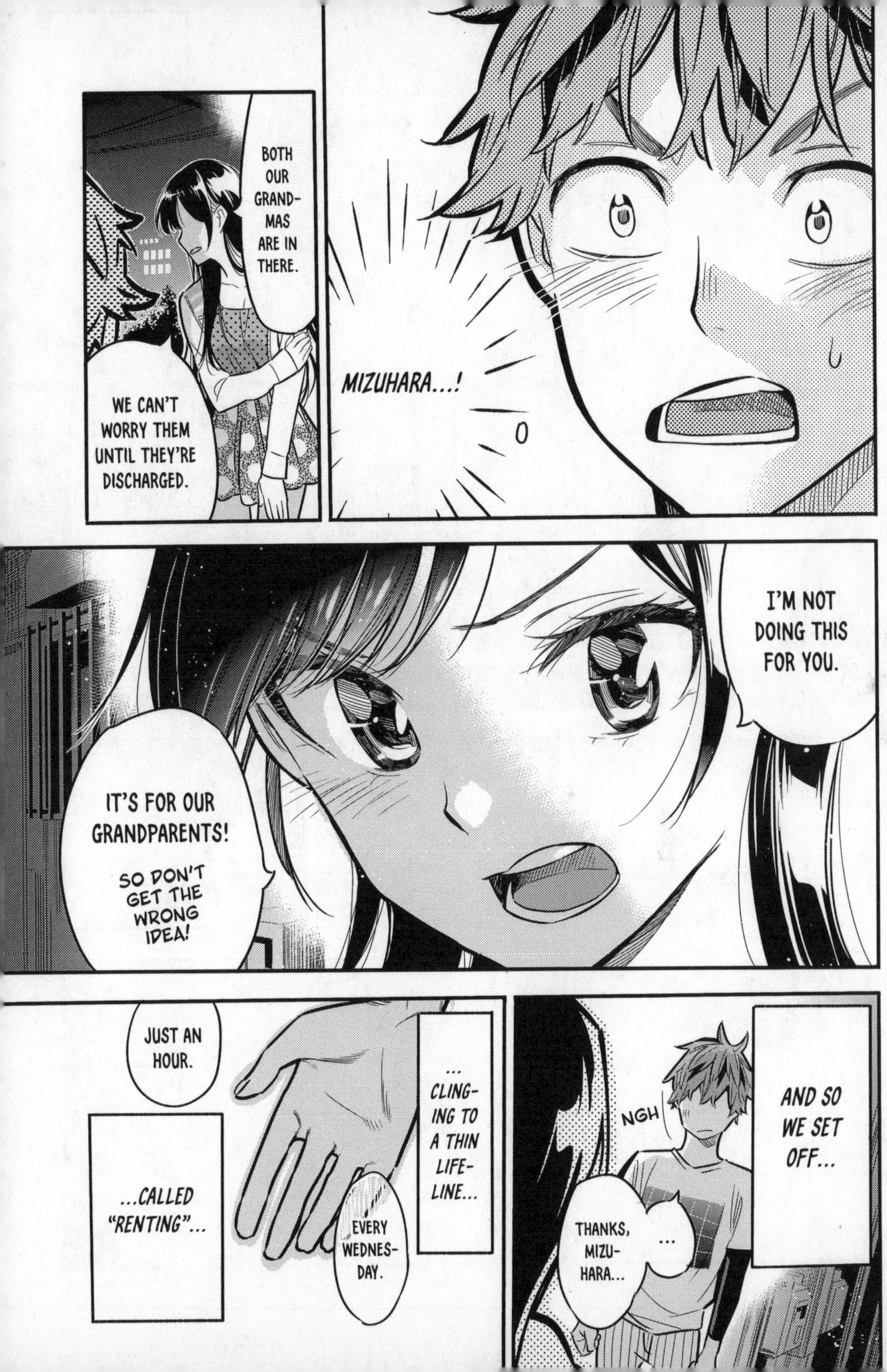
MIZUHARA...!
BOTH OUR GRAND-MAS ARE IN THERE.
WE CAN'T WORRY THEM UNTIL THEY'RE DISCHARGED.
I'M NOT DOING THIS FOR YOU.
IT'S FOR OUR GRANDPARENTS!
SO DON'T GET THE WRONG IDEA!
AND SO WE SET OFF...
NGH
...
THANKS, MIZU-HARA...
...CLING-ING TO A THIN LIFE-LINE...
JUST AN HOUR.
EVERY WEDNES-DAY.
...CALLED "RENTING"...

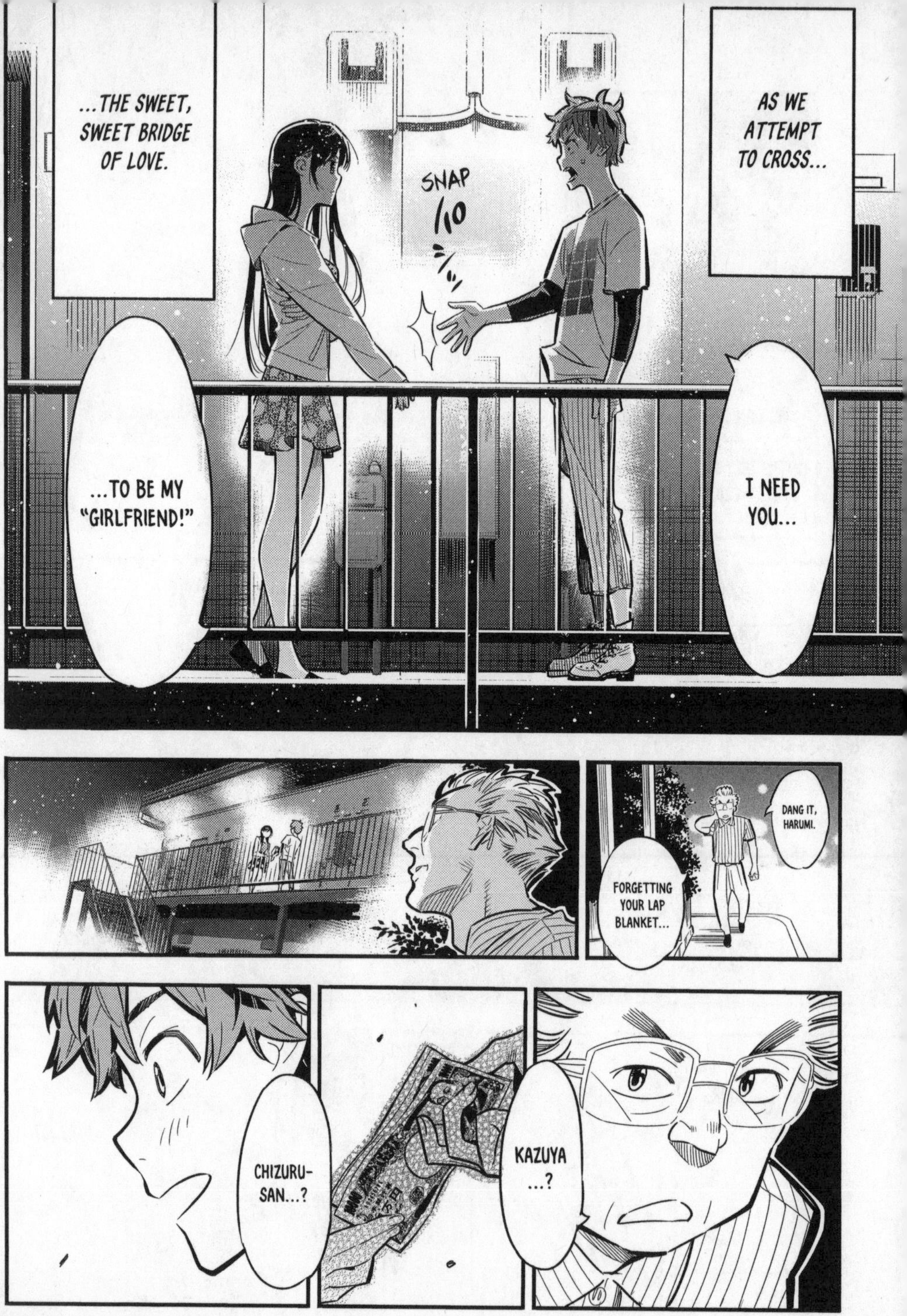
AS WE ATTEMPT TO CROSS...
...THE SWEET, SWEET BRIDGE OF LOVE.
SNAP
I NEED YOU...
...TO BE MY "GIRLFRIEND!"
DANG IT, HARUMI.
FORGETTING YOUR LAP BLANKET...
KAZUYA ...?
CHIZURU-SAN...?

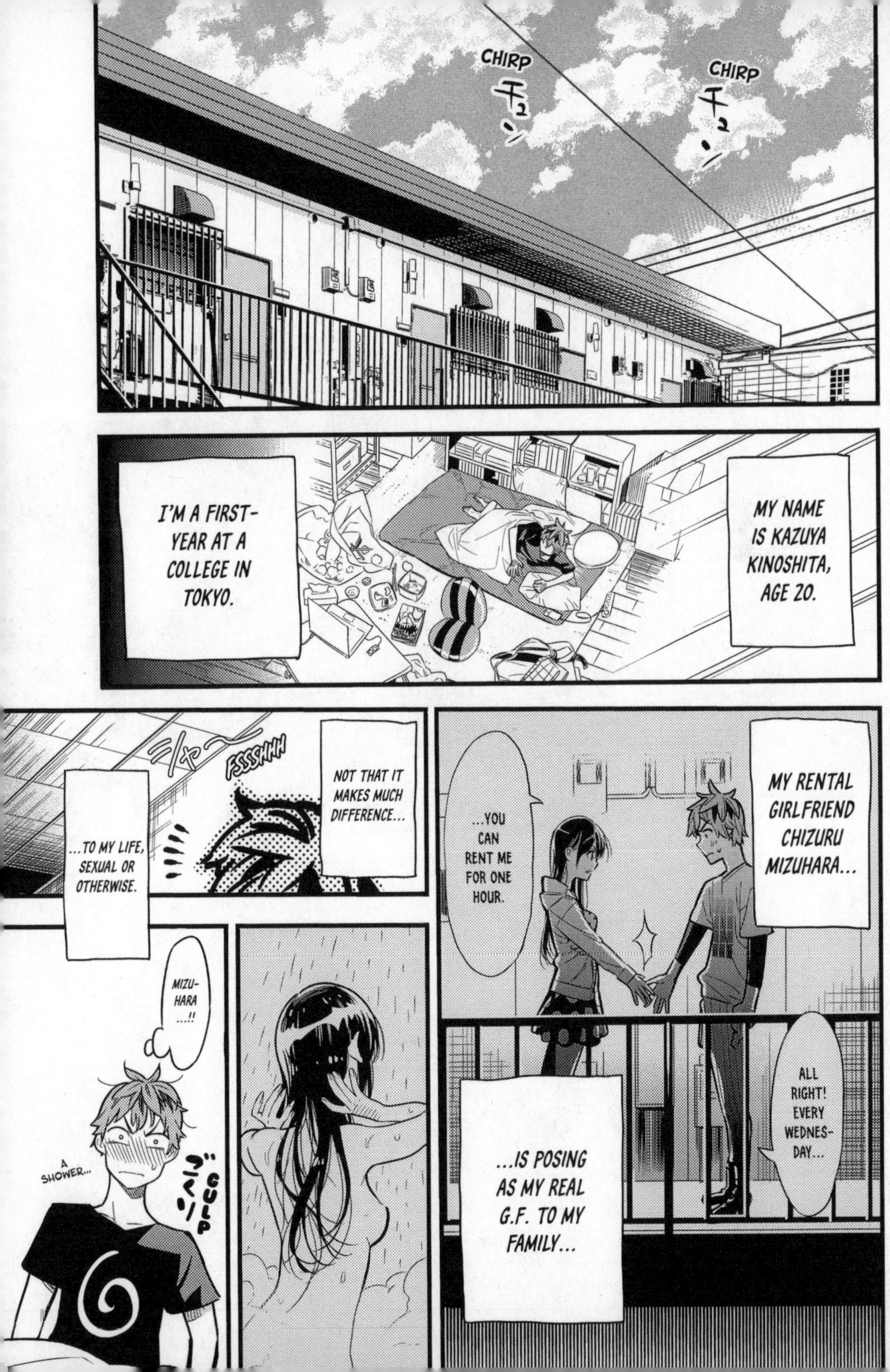
CHIRP
チュン
CHIRP
チュン
MY NAME IS KAZUYA KINOSHITA, AGE 20.
I'M A FIRST-YEAR AT A COLLEGE IN TOKYO.
MY RENTAL GIRLFRIEND CHIZURU MIZUHARA...
...YOU CAN RENT ME FOR ONE HOUR.
ALL RIGHT! EVERY WEDNES-DAY...
...IS POSING AS MY REAL G.F. TO MY FAMILY...
NOT THAT IT MAKES MUCH DIFFERENCE...
FSSSHHH
シャー
...TO MY LIFE, SEXUAL OR OTHERWISE.
MIZU-HARA ...!!
A SHOWER...
ごくり
GULP

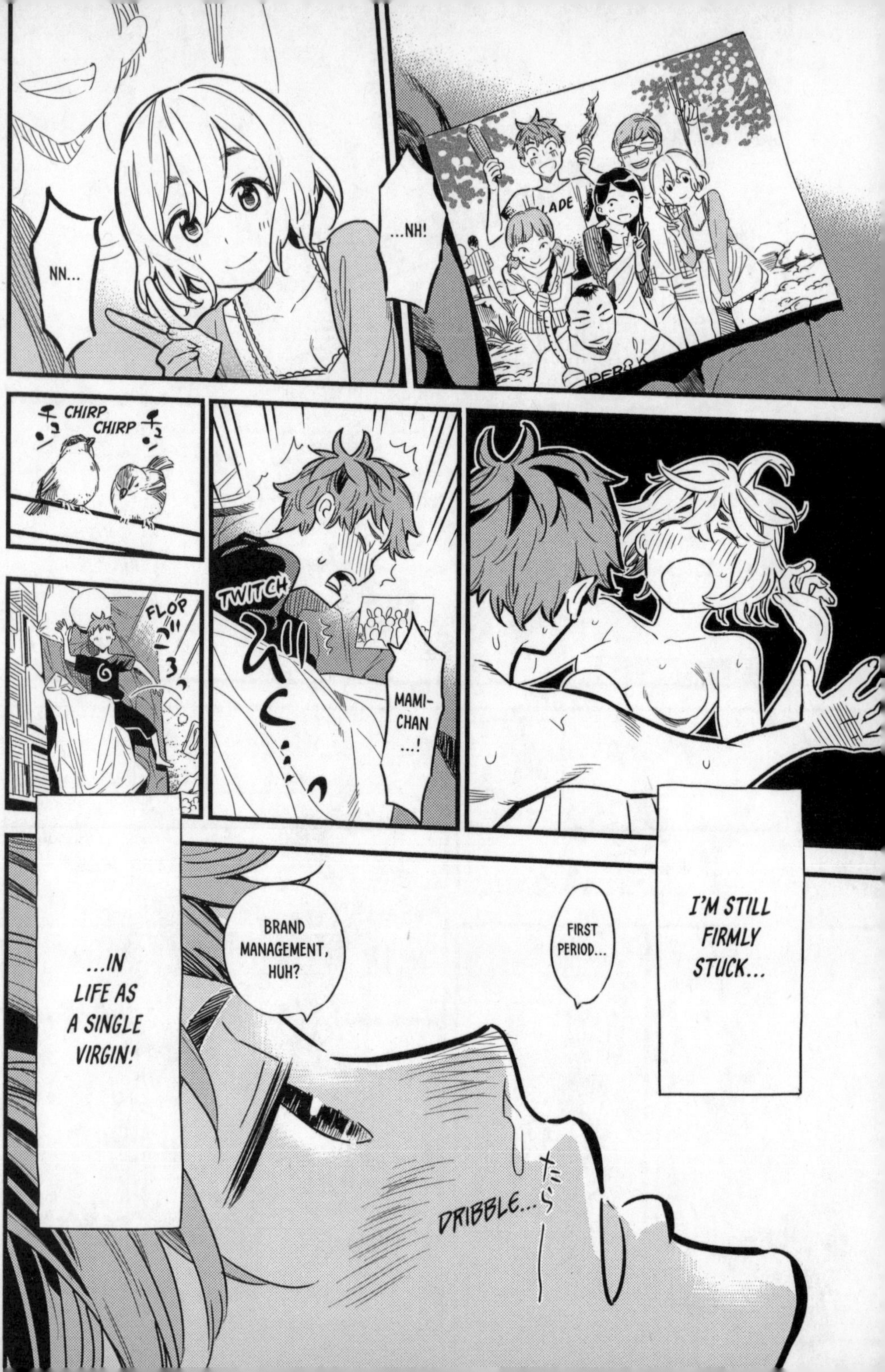
...NH!
NN...
TWITCH
MAMI-CHAN ...!
CHIRP CHIRP
FLOP
I'M STILL FIRMLY STUCK...
FIRST PERIOD...
BRAND MANAGEMENT, HUH?
...IN LIFE AS A SINGLE VIRGIN!
DRIBBLE...

RATING 4
MY EX, MAMI NANAMI

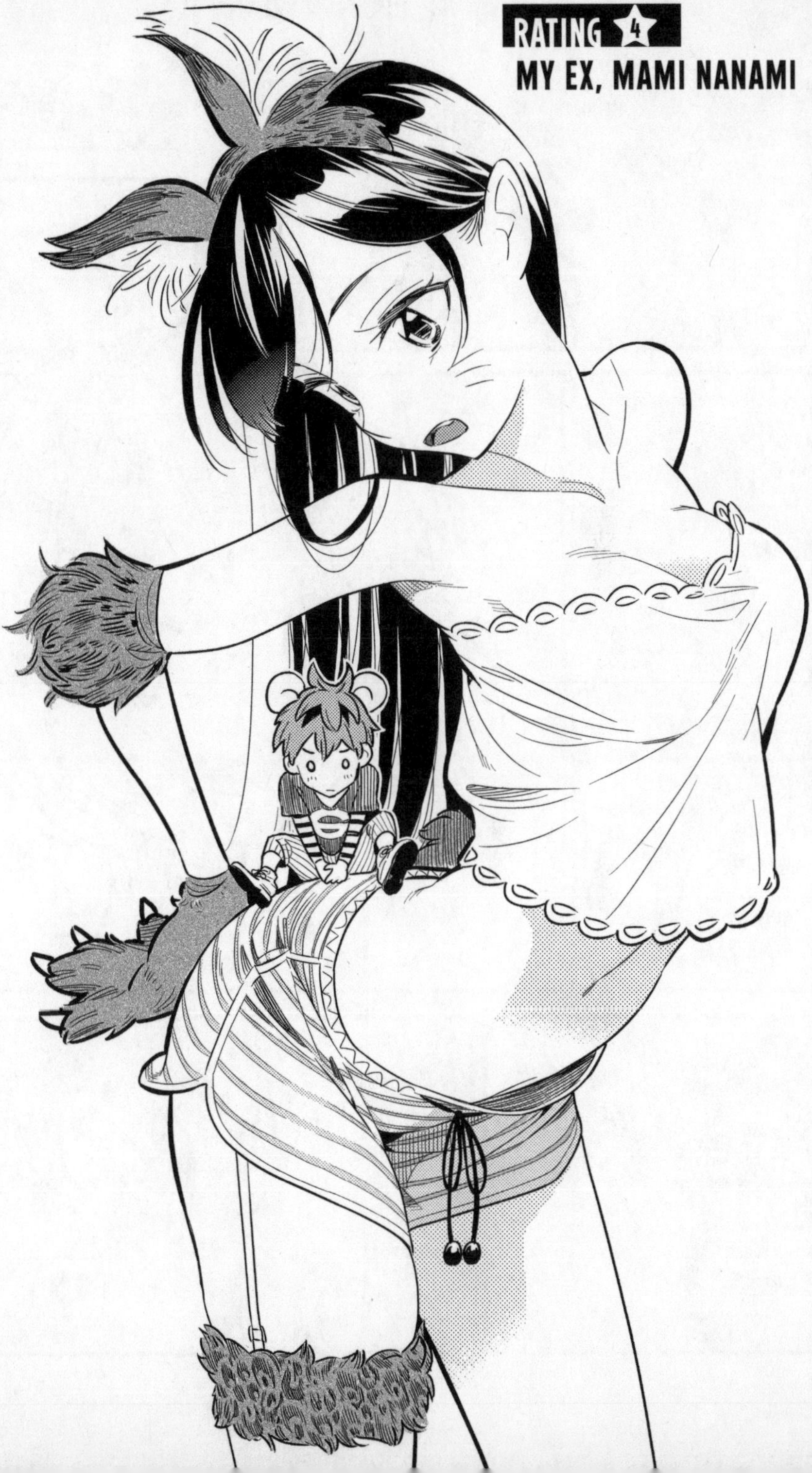

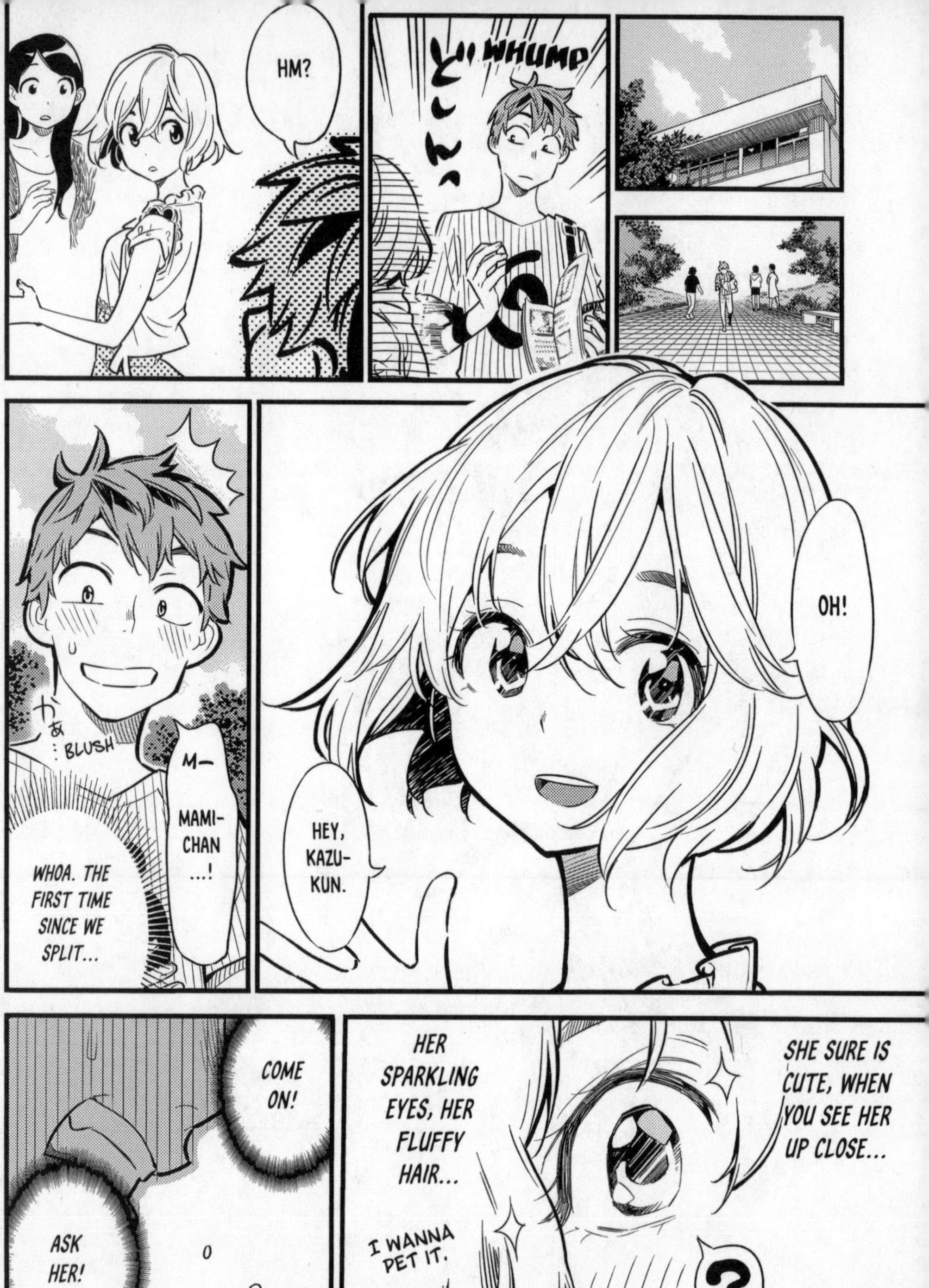
どしんっ
WHUMP
HM?
OH!
HEY, KAZU-KUN.
M— MAMI-CHAN ...!
かぁ BLUSH
WHOA. THE FIRST TIME SINCE WE SPLIT...
SHE SURE IS CUTE, WHEN YOU SEE HER UP CLOSE...
HER SPARKLING EYES, HER FLUFFY HAIR...
I WANNA PET IT.
?
COME ON!
ASK HER!

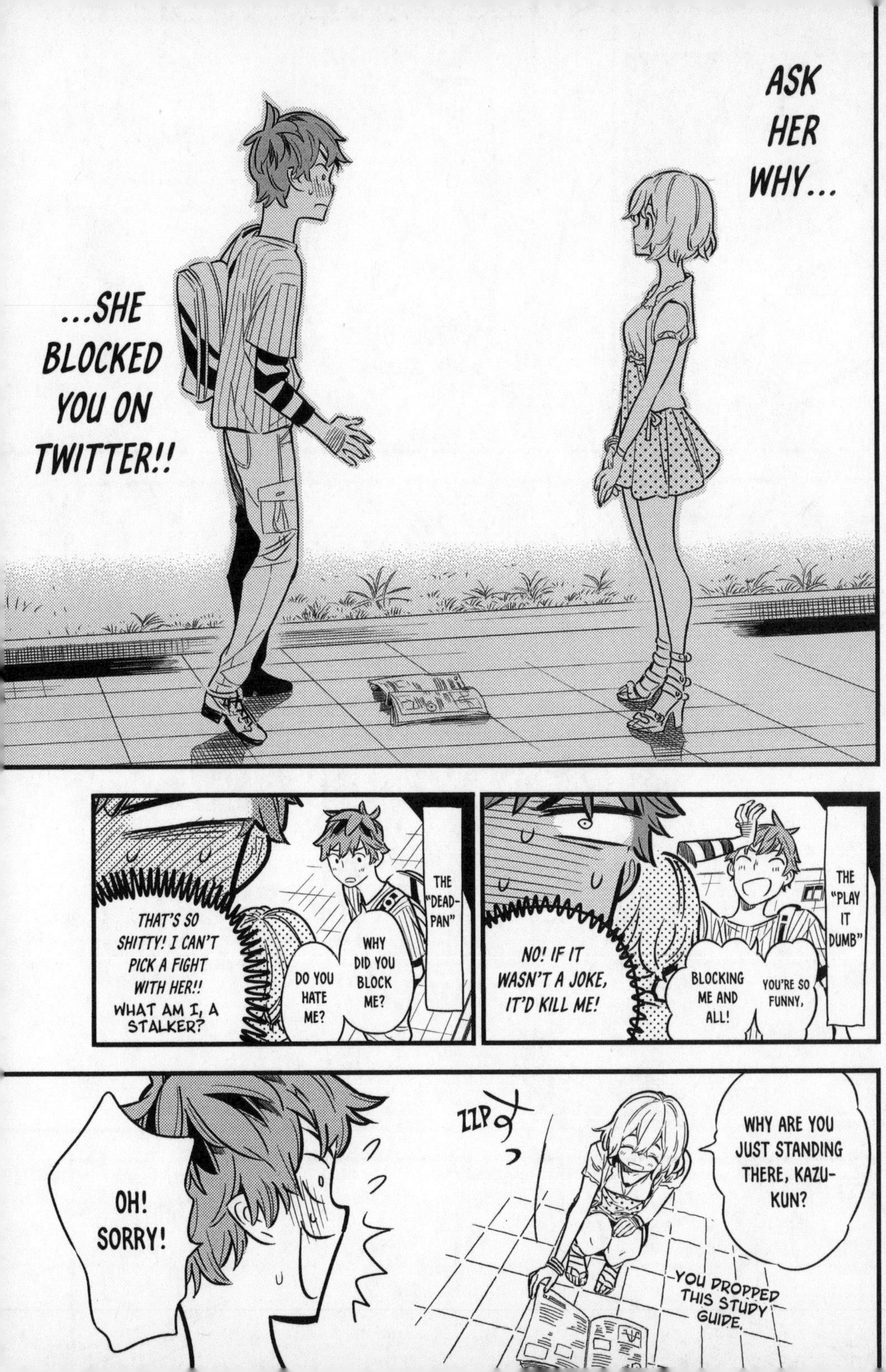
ASK HER WHY...
...SHE BLOCKED YOU ON TWITTER!!
THE "PLAY IT DUMB"
YOU'RE SO FUNNY,
BLOCKING ME AND ALL!
NO! IF IT WASN'T A JOKE, IT'D KILL ME!
THE "DEAD-PAN"
WHY DID YOU BLOCK ME?
DO YOU HATE ME?
THAT'S SO SHITTY! I CAN'T PICK A FIGHT WITH HER!!
WHAT AM I, A STALKER?
ZZIP
WHY ARE YOU JUST STANDING THERE, KAZU-KUN?
YOU DROPPED THIS STUDY GUIDE.
OH! SORRY!

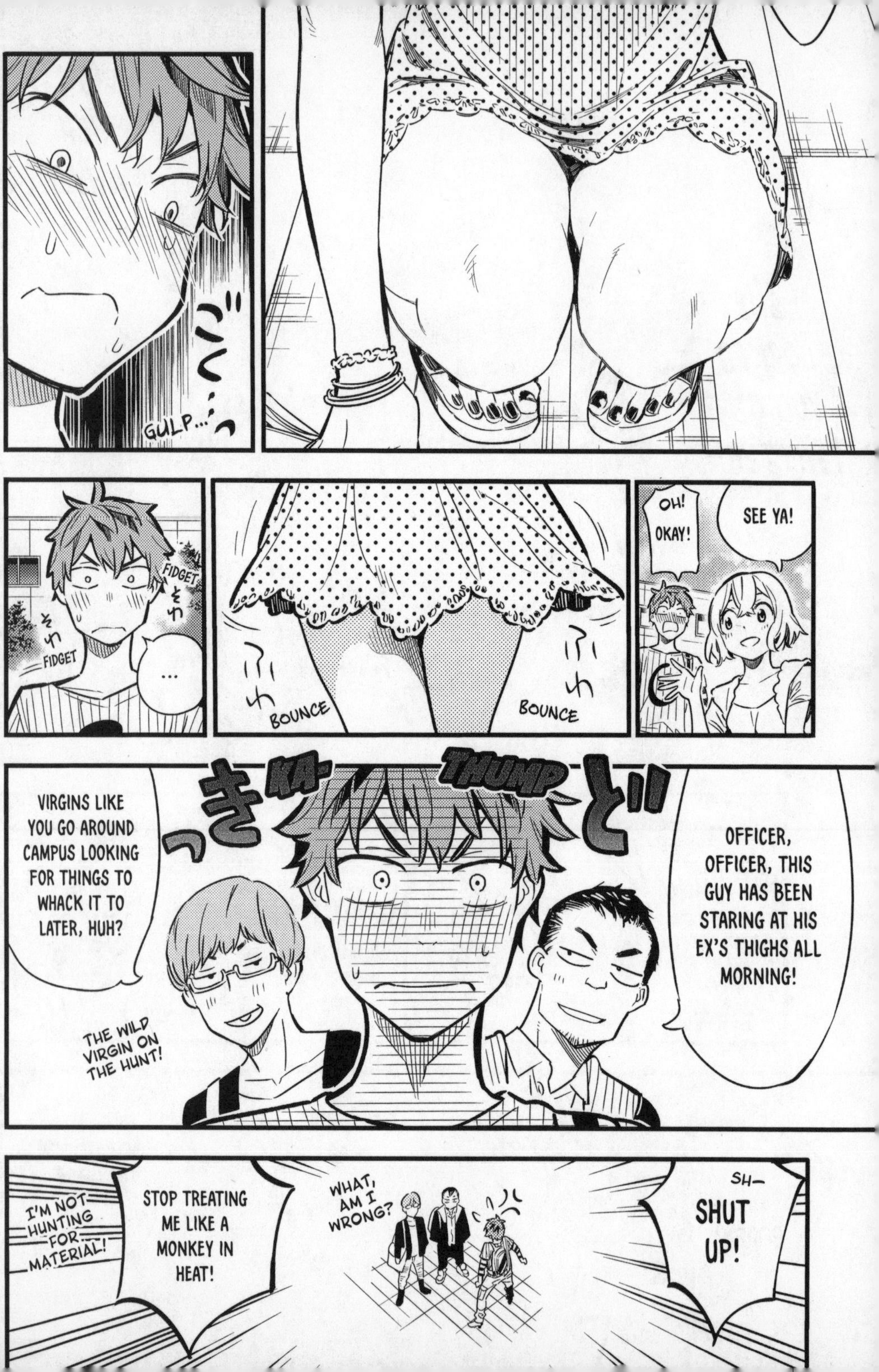

ごく…っ
GULP…
SEE YA!
OH! OKAY!
ふわ
BOUNCE
ふわ
BOUNCE
そわ
FIDGET
そわ
FIDGET
…
OFFICER, OFFICER, THIS GUY HAS BEEN STARING AT HIS EX'S THIGHS ALL MORNING!
どっ
THUMP
っき
KA-
THE WILD VIRGIN ON THE HUNT!
VIRGINS LIKE YOU GO AROUND CAMPUS LOOKING FOR THINGS TO WHACK IT TO LATER, HUH?
SH— SHUT UP!
WHAT, AM I WRONG?
STOP TREATING ME LIKE A MONKEY IN HEAT!
I'M NOT HUNTING FOR MATERIAL!

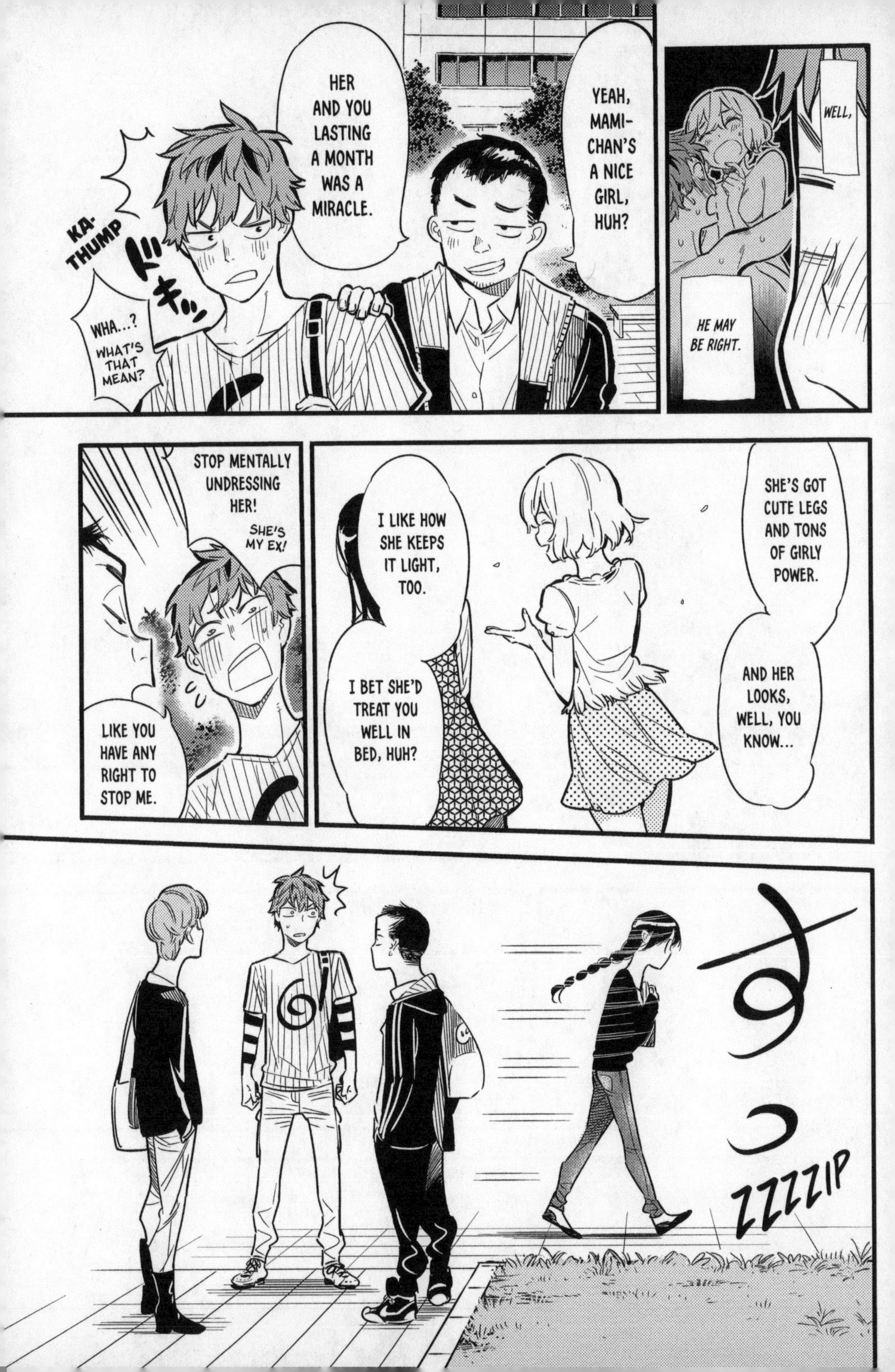
WELL,
HE MAY BE RIGHT.
YEAH, MAMI-CHAN'S A NICE GIRL, HUH?
HER AND YOU LASTING A MONTH WAS A MIRACLE.
KA-THUMP
ドキッ
WHA...? WHAT'S THAT MEAN?
SHE'S GOT CUTE LEGS AND TONS OF GIRLY POWER.
AND HER LOOKS, WELL, YOU KNOW...
I LIKE HOW SHE KEEPS IT LIGHT, TOO.
I BET SHE'D TREAT YOU WELL IN BED, HUH?
STOP MENTALLY UNDRESSING HER!
SHE'S MY EX!
LIKE YOU HAVE ANY RIGHT TO STOP ME.
すっ
ZZZZIP

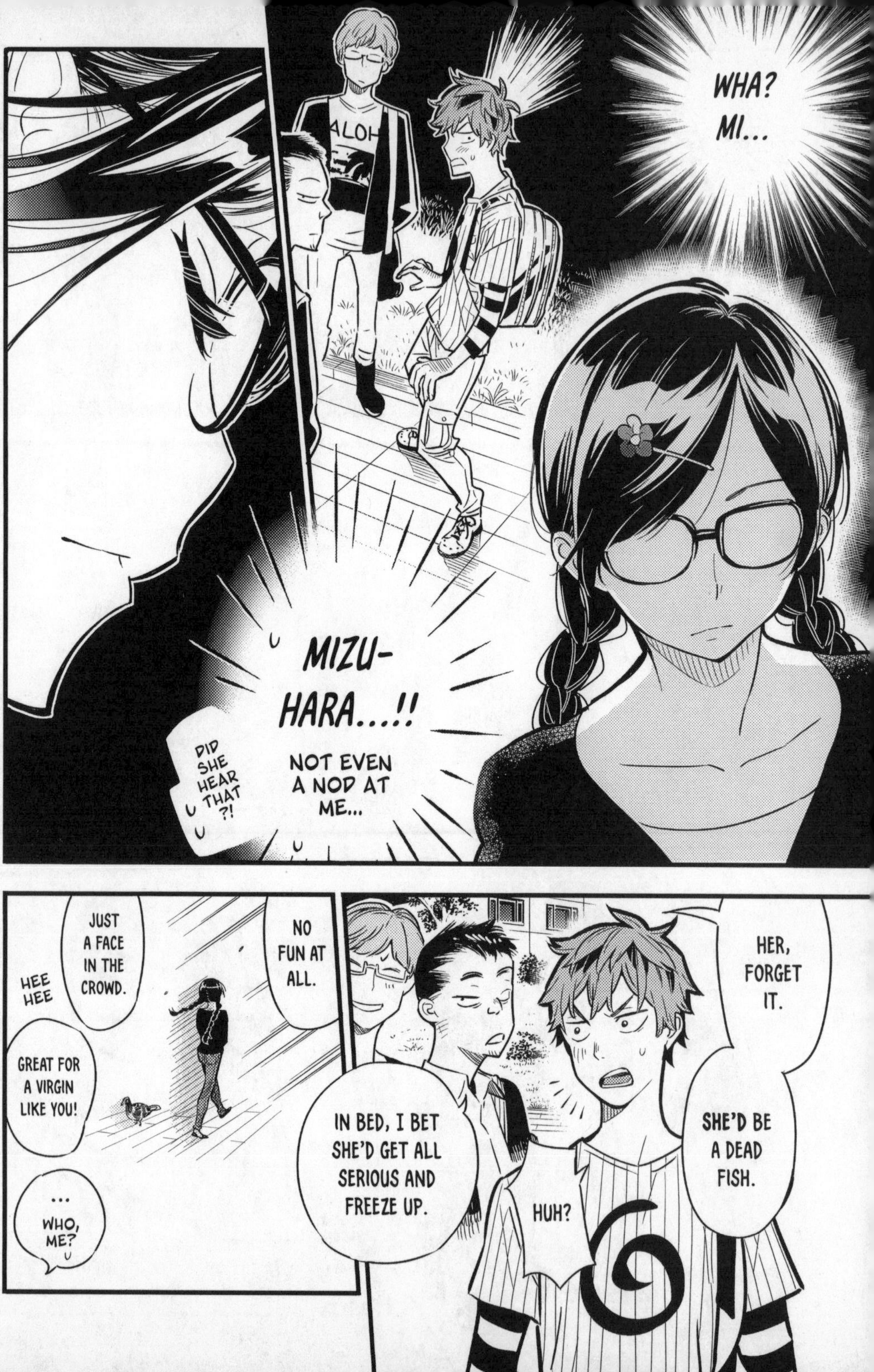
WHA? MI...
MIZU-HARA...!!
NOT EVEN A NOD AT ME...
DID SHE HEAR THAT?!
HER, FORGET IT.
SHE'D BE A DEAD FISH.
HUH?
IN BED, I BET SHE'D GET ALL SERIOUS AND FREEZE UP.
NO FUN AT ALL.
JUST A FACE IN THE CROWD.
HEE HEE
GREAT FOR A VIRGIN LIKE YOU!
... WHO, ME?

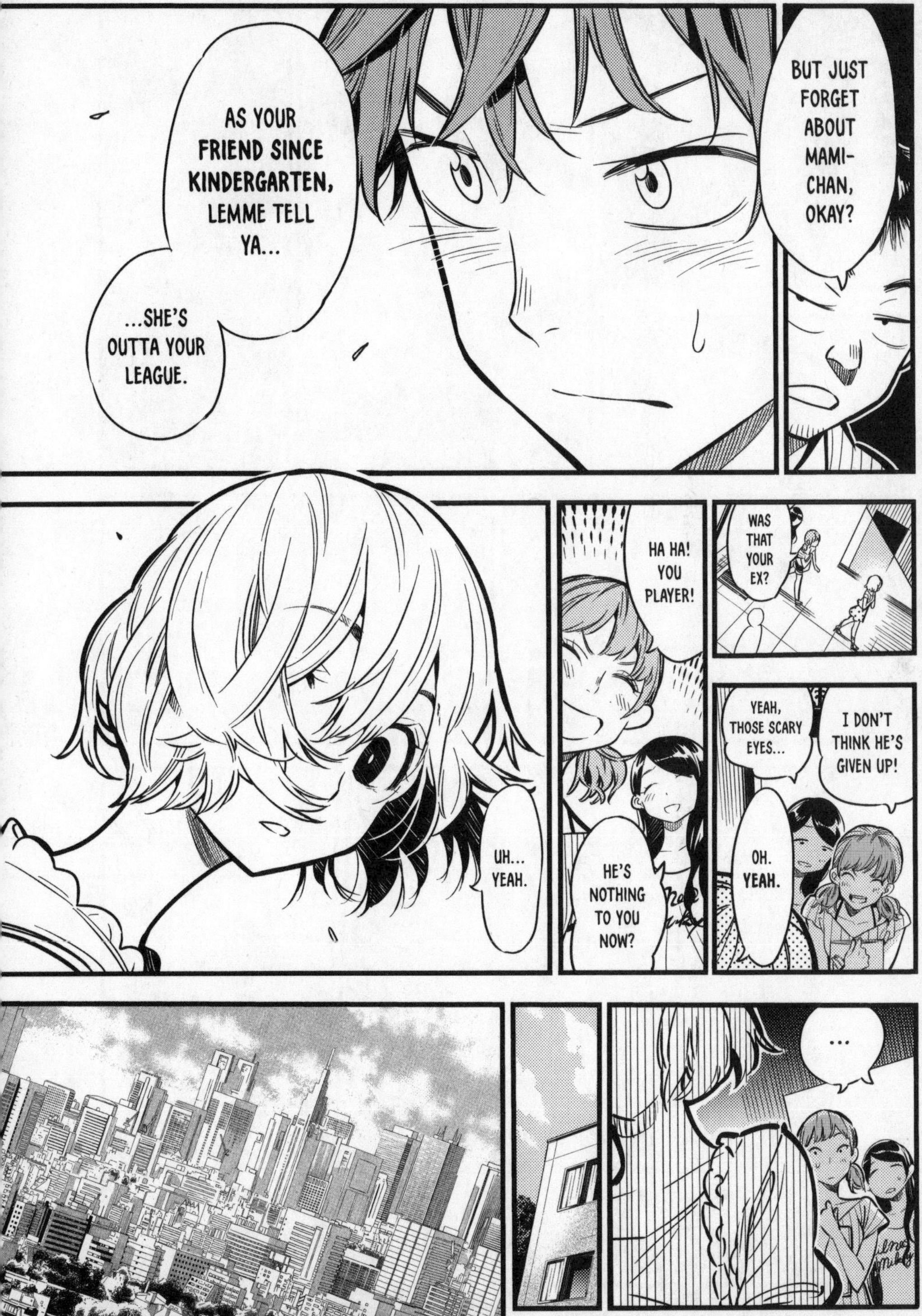
BUT JUST FORGET ABOUT MAMI-CHAN, OKAY?
AS YOUR FRIEND SINCE KINDERGARTEN, LEMME TELL YA...
...SHE'S OUTTA YOUR LEAGUE.
WAS THAT YOUR EX?
I DON'T THINK HE'S GIVEN UP!
YEAH, THOSE SCARY EYES...
OH. YEAH.
HA HA! YOU PLAYER!
HE'S NOTHING TO YOU NOW?
UH... YEAH.
...

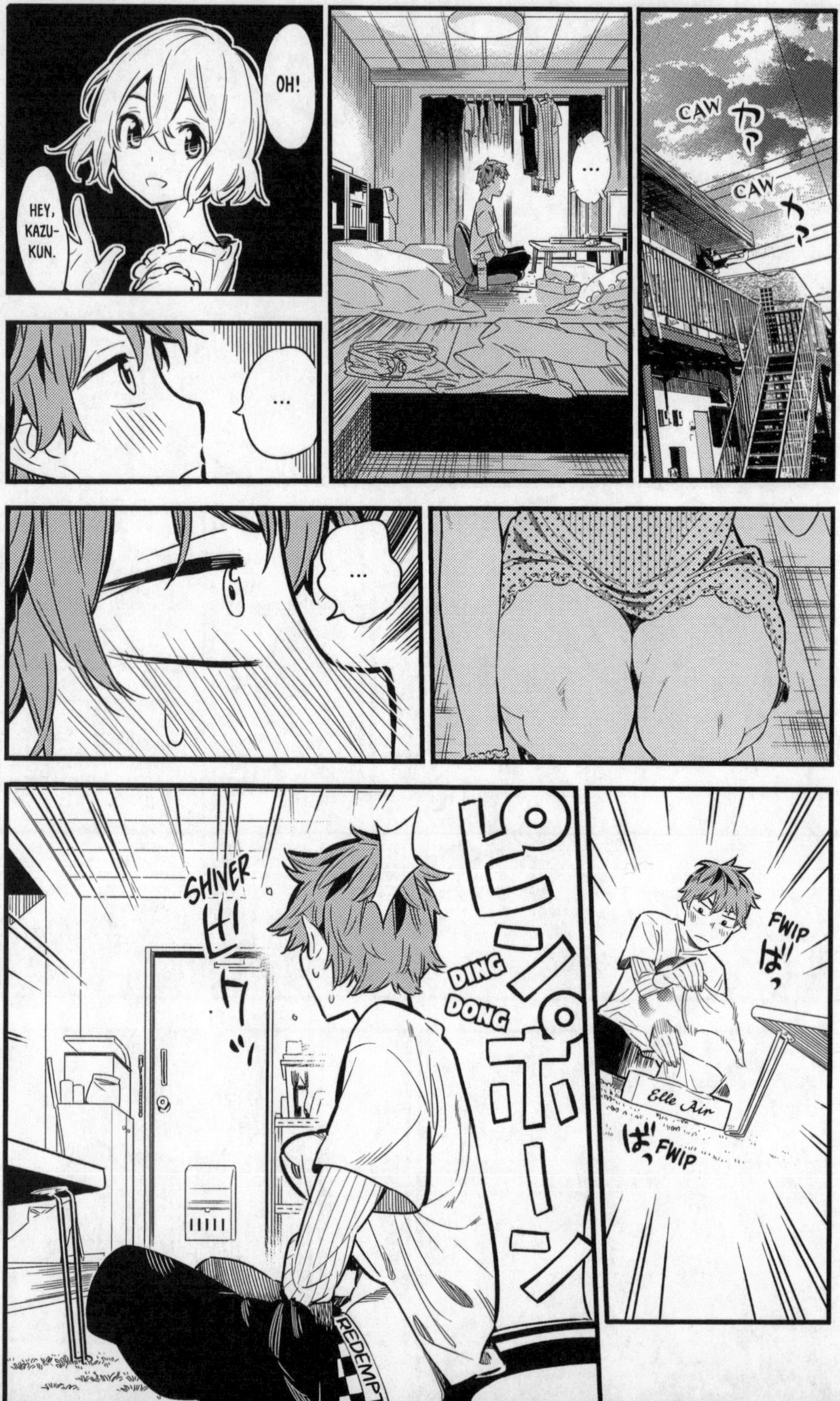
CAW ヤァ
CAW ヤァ
...
OH!
HEY, KAZU-KUN.
...
...
FWIP ばっ
Elle Air
ばっ FWIP
ピンポーン
DING DONG
SHIVER ビクッ
REDEMPT

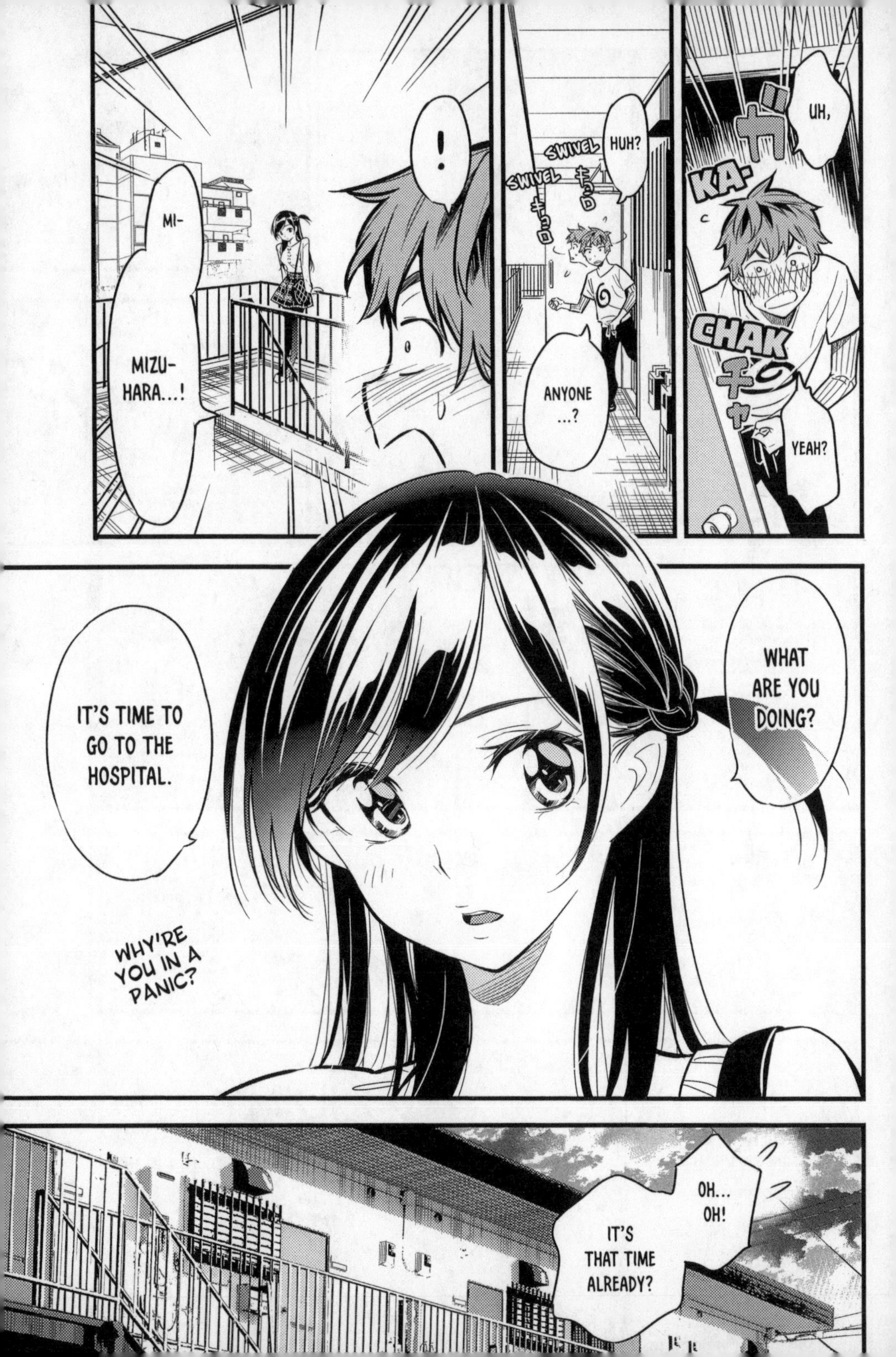
UH,
KA-
ガ
CHAK
チャ
YEAH?
HUH?
SWIVEL
キョロ
SWIVEL
キョロ
ANYONE ...?
!
MI-
MIZUHARA...!
WHAT ARE YOU DOING?
IT'S TIME TO GO TO THE HOSPITAL.
WHY'RE YOU IN A PANIC?
OH... OH!
IT'S THAT TIME ALREADY?

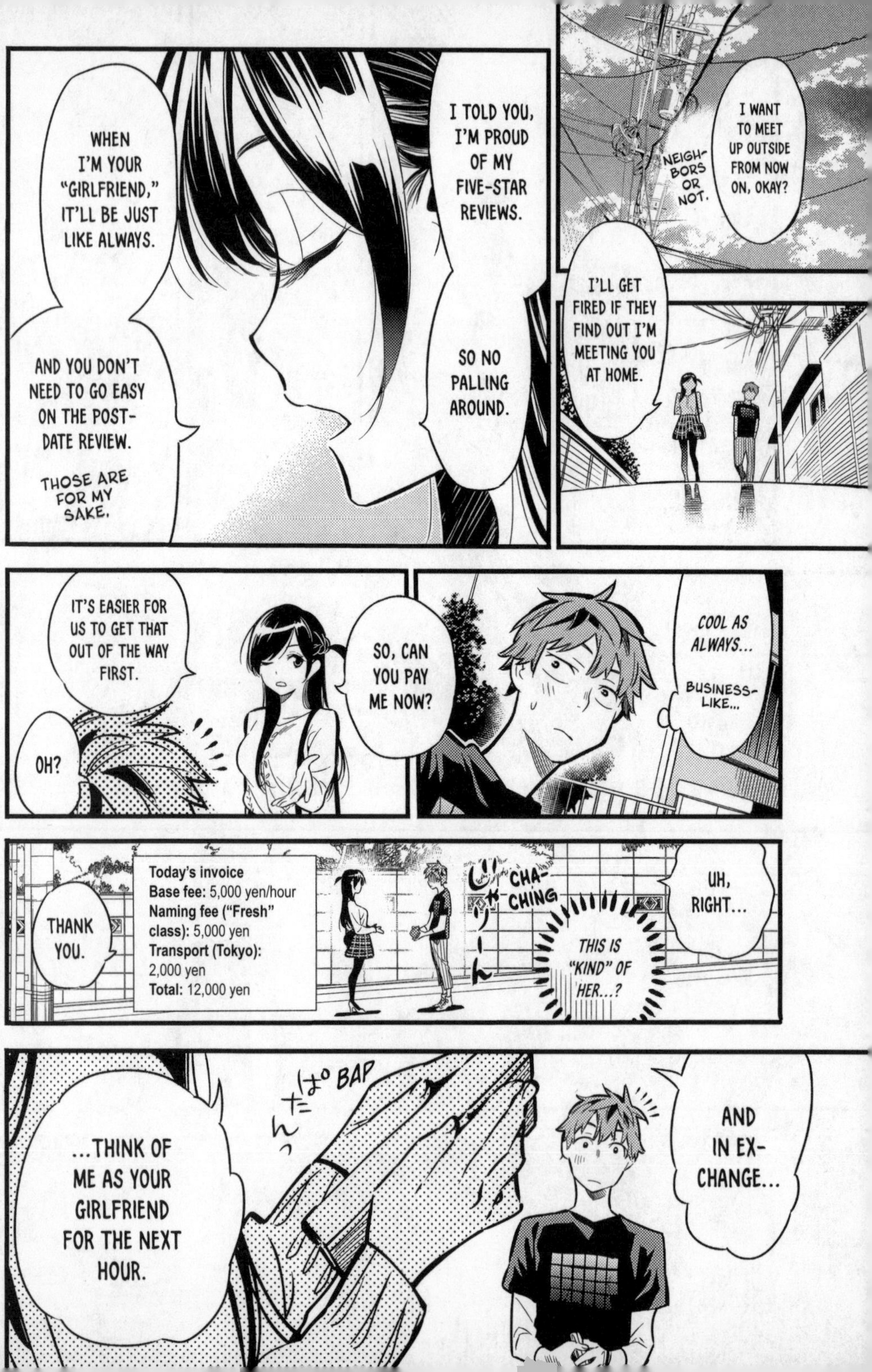
I WANT TO MEET UP OUTSIDE FROM NOW ON, OKAY?
NEIGHBORS OR NOT.
I'LL GET FIRED IF THEY FIND OUT I'M MEETING YOU AT HOME.
I TOLD YOU, I'M PROUD OF MY FIVE-STAR REVIEWS.
SO NO PALLING AROUND.
WHEN I'M YOUR "GIRLFRIEND," IT'LL BE JUST LIKE ALWAYS.
AND YOU DON'T NEED TO GO EASY ON THE POST-DATE REVIEW.
THOSE ARE FOR MY SAKE.
COOL AS ALWAYS...
BUSINESS-LIKE...
SO, CAN YOU PAY ME NOW?
IT'S EASIER FOR US TO GET THAT OUT OF THE WAY FIRST.
OH?
UH, RIGHT...
THIS IS "KIND" OF HER...?
CHA-CHING
THANK YOU.
Today's invoice
Base fee: 5,000 yen/hour
Naming fee ("Fresh" class): 5,000 yen
Transport (Tokyo): 2,000 yen
Total: 12,000 yen
AND IN EX-CHANGE...
BAP
...THINK OF ME AS YOUR GIRLFRIEND FOR THE NEXT HOUR.

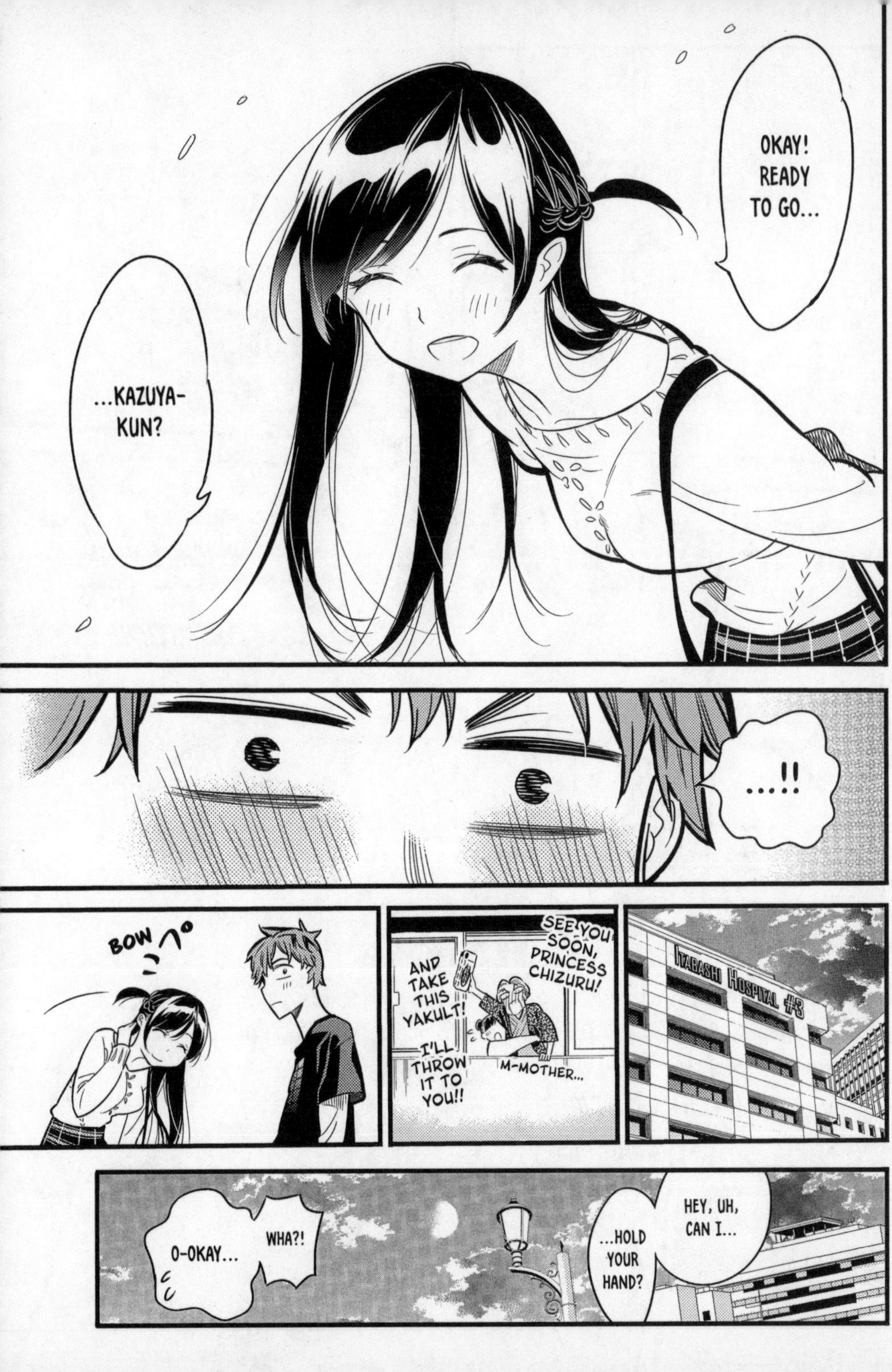
OKAY! READY TO GO...
...KAZUYA-KUN?
...!!
ITABASHI HOSPITAL #3
SEE YOU SOON, PRINCESS CHIZURU!
AND TAKE THIS YAKULT!
I'LL THROW IT TO YOU!!
M-MOTHER...
BOW
HEY, UH, CAN I...
...HOLD YOUR HAND?
WHA?!
O-OKAY...

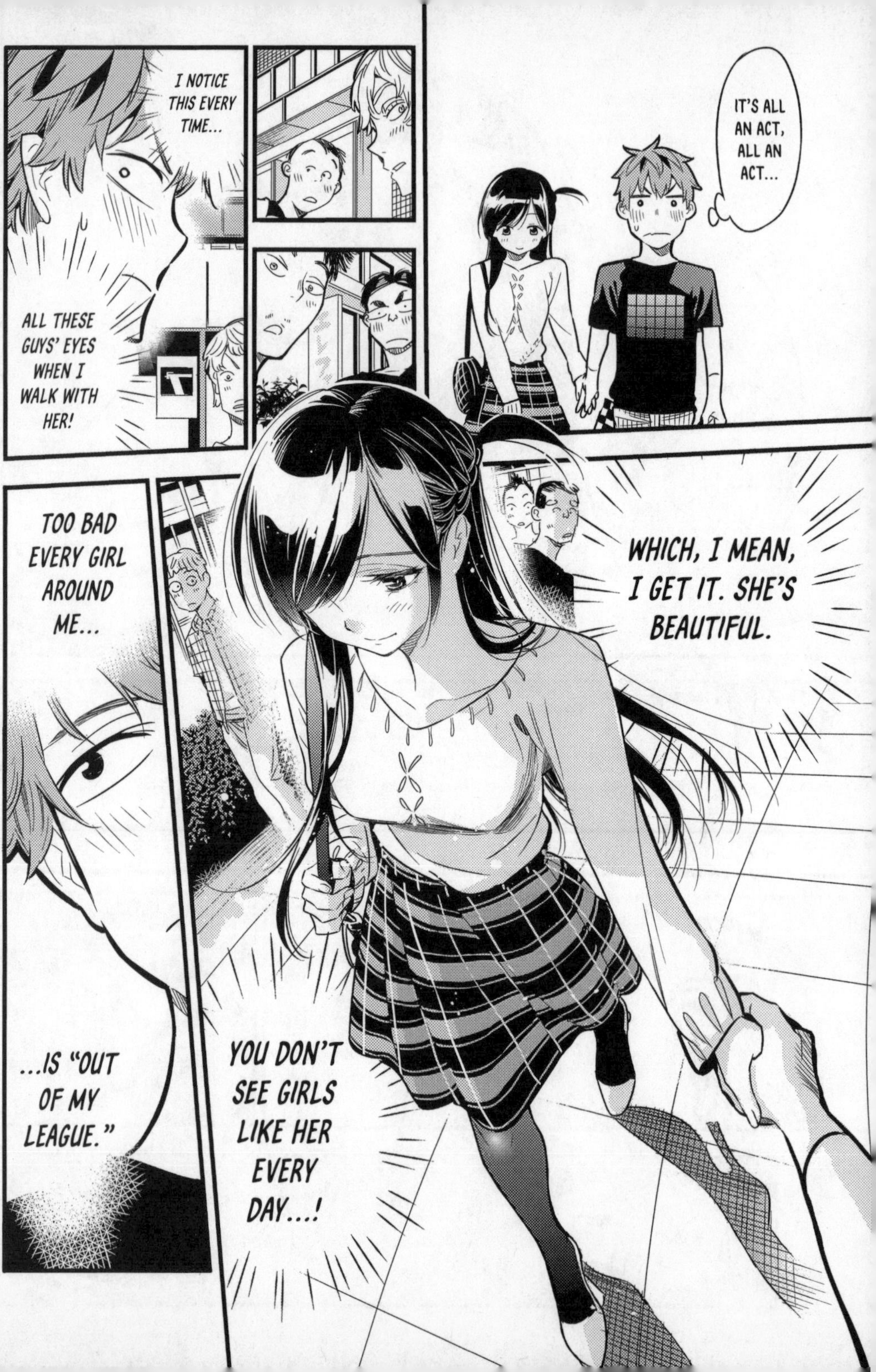
IT'S ALL AN ACT, ALL AN ACT...
I NOTICE THIS EVERY TIME...
ALL THESE GUYS' EYES WHEN I WALK WITH HER!
WHICH, I MEAN, I GET IT. SHE'S BEAUTIFUL.
YOU DON'T SEE GIRLS LIKE HER EVERY DAY...!
TOO BAD EVERY GIRL AROUND ME...
...IS "OUT OF MY LEAGUE."

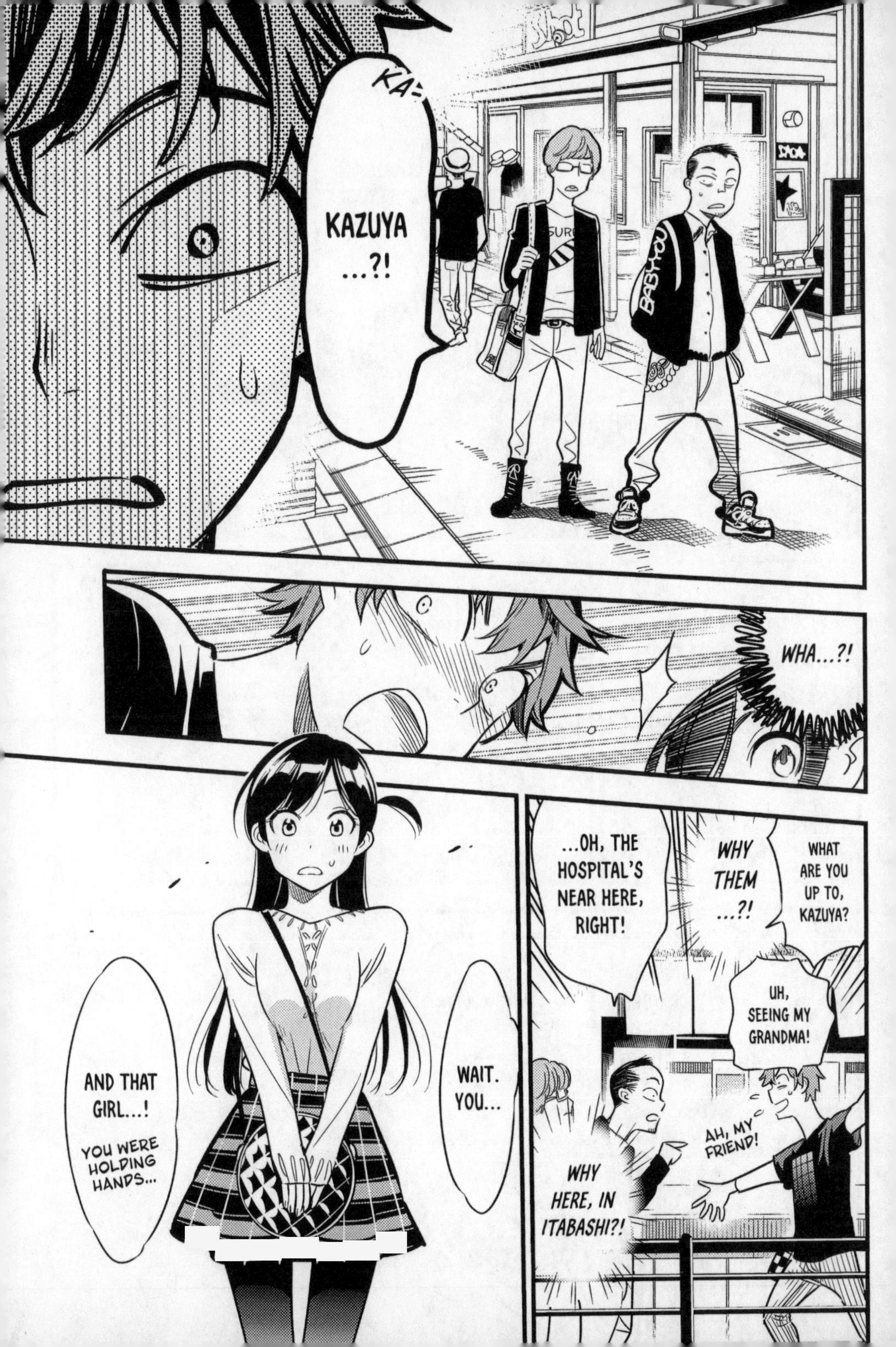
KA-
KAZUYA ...?!
WHA...?!
WHAT ARE YOU UP TO, KAZUYA?
WHY THEM ...?!
...OH, THE HOSPITAL'S NEAR HERE, RIGHT!
UH, SEEING MY GRANDMA!
AH, MY FRIEND!
WHY HERE, IN ITABASHI?!
WAIT. YOU...
AND THAT GIRL...!
YOU WERE HOLDING HANDS...

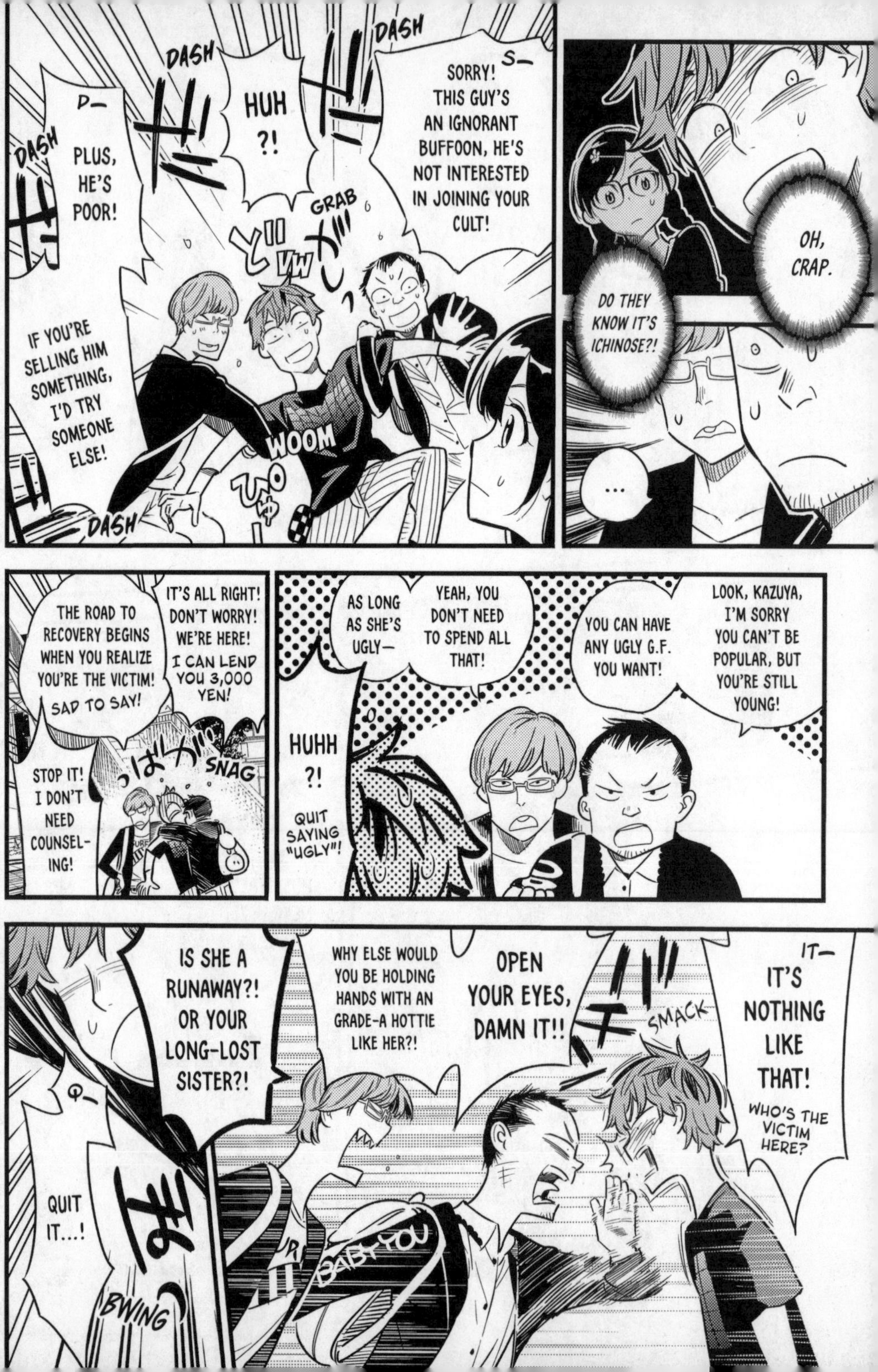
OH, CRAP.
DO THEY KNOW IT'S ICHINOSE?!
...
S— SORRY! THIS GUY'S AN IGNORANT BUFFOON, HE'S NOT INTERESTED IN JOINING YOUR CULT!
DASH
HUH ?!
DASH
D— PLUS, HE'S POOR!
DASH
GRAB
IF YOU'RE SELLING HIM SOMETHING, I'D TRY SOMEONE ELSE!
WOOM
DASH
LOOK, KAZUYA, I'M SORRY YOU CAN'T BE POPULAR, BUT YOU'RE STILL YOUNG!
YOU CAN HAVE ANY UGLY G.F. YOU WANT!
YEAH, YOU DON'T NEED TO SPEND ALL THAT!
AS LONG AS SHE'S UGLY—
HUHH ?!
QUIT SAYING "UGLY"!
IT'S ALL RIGHT! DON'T WORRY! WE'RE HERE! I CAN LEND YOU 3,000 YEN!
THE ROAD TO RECOVERY BEGINS WHEN YOU REALIZE YOU'RE THE VICTIM! SAD TO SAY!
SNAG
STOP IT! I DON'T NEED COUNSEL-ING!
IT— IT'S NOTHING LIKE THAT!
WHO'S THE VICTIM HERE?
SMACK
OPEN YOUR EYES, DAMN IT!!
WHY ELSE WOULD YOU BE HOLDING HANDS WITH AN GRADE-A HOTTIE LIKE HER?!
IS SHE A RUNAWAY?! OR YOUR LONG-LOST SISTER?!
Q— QUIT IT...!
BWING

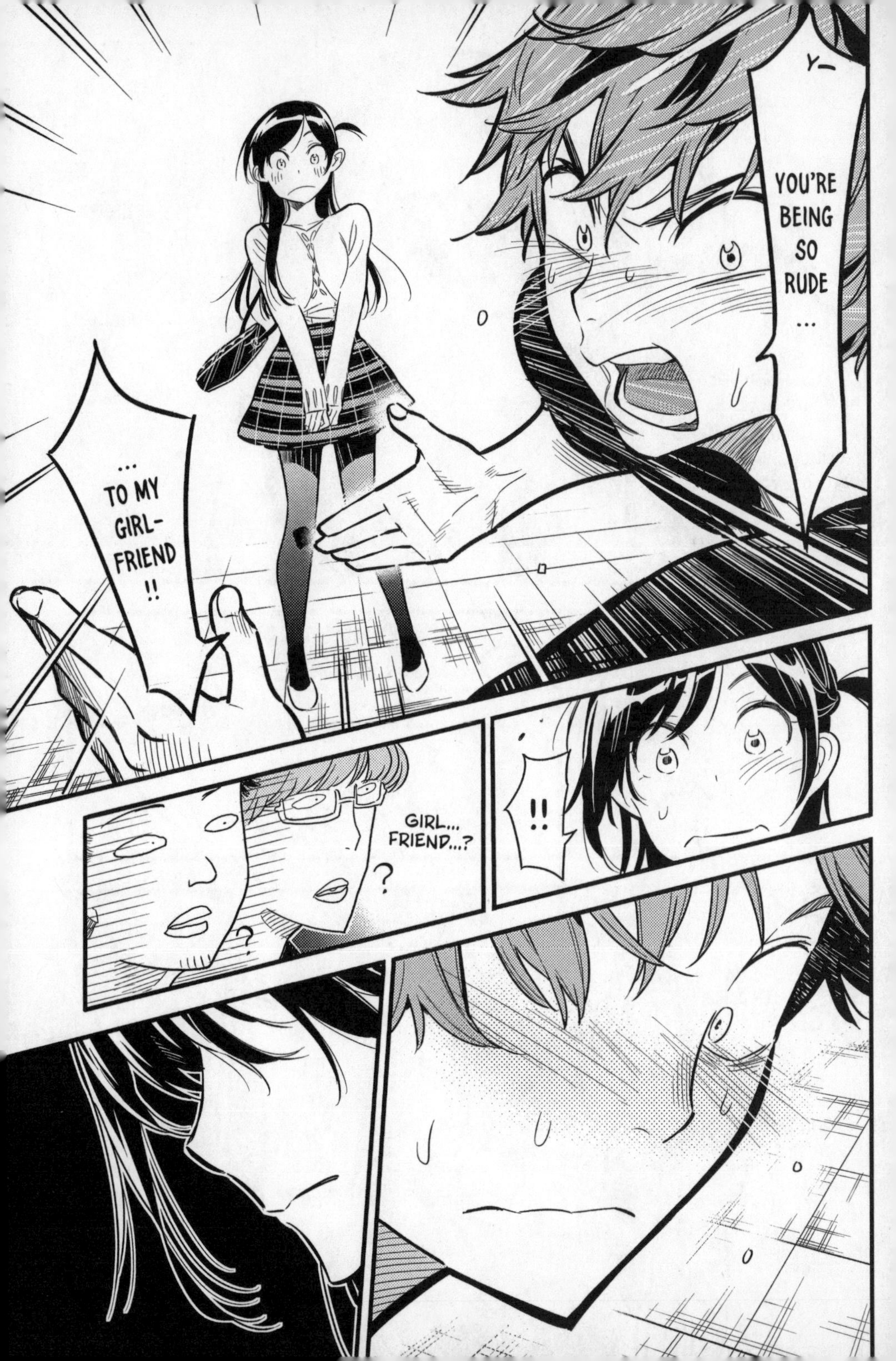
Y—
YOU'RE BEING SO RUDE ...
... TO MY GIRL-FRIEND !!
!!
GIRL... FRIEND...?

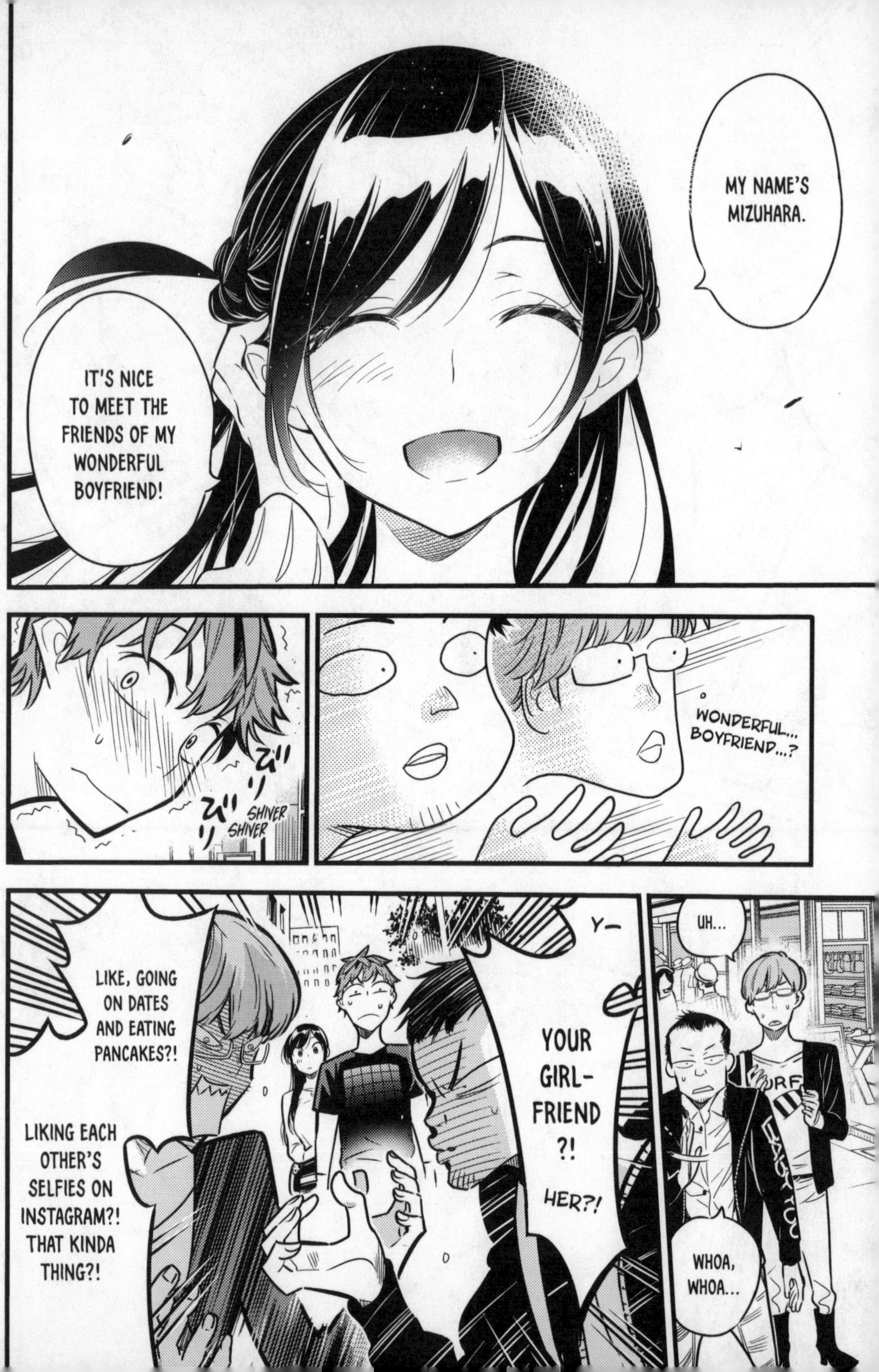
MY NAME'S MIZUHARA.
IT'S NICE TO MEET THE FRIENDS OF MY WONDERFUL BOYFRIEND!
WONDERFUL... BOYFRIEND...?
びり びり
SHIVER SHIVER
UH...
WHOA, WHOA...
Y—
YOUR GIRL-FRIEND?!
HER?!
LIKE, GOING ON DATES AND EATING PANCAKES?!
LIKING EACH OTHER'S SELFIES ON INSTAGRAM?! THAT KINDA THING?!

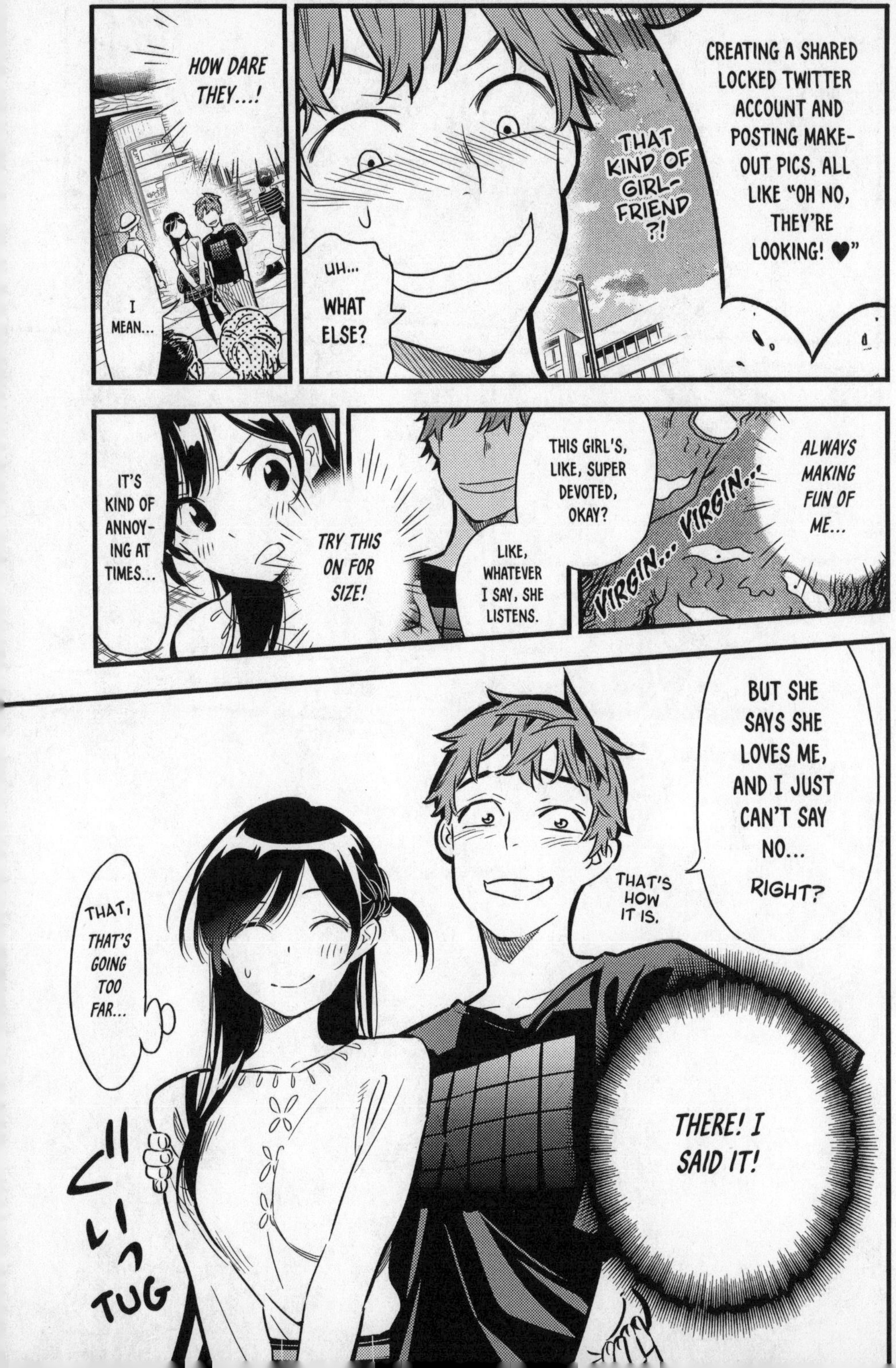
CREATING A SHARED LOCKED TWITTER ACCOUNT AND POSTING MAKE-OUT PICS, ALL LIKE "OH NO, THEY'RE LOOKING! ♥"
THAT KIND OF GIRL-FRIEND?!
UH... WHAT ELSE?
HOW DARE THEY...!
I MEAN...
ALWAYS MAKING FUN OF ME...
VIRGIN... VIRGIN...
THIS GIRL'S, LIKE, SUPER DEVOTED, OKAY?
LIKE, WHATEVER I SAY, SHE LISTENS.
TRY THIS ON FOR SIZE!
IT'S KIND OF ANNOY-ING AT TIMES...
BUT SHE SAYS SHE LOVES ME, AND I JUST CAN'T SAY NO... RIGHT?
THAT'S HOW IT IS.
THERE! I SAID IT!
THAT, THAT'S GOING TOO FAR...
TUG

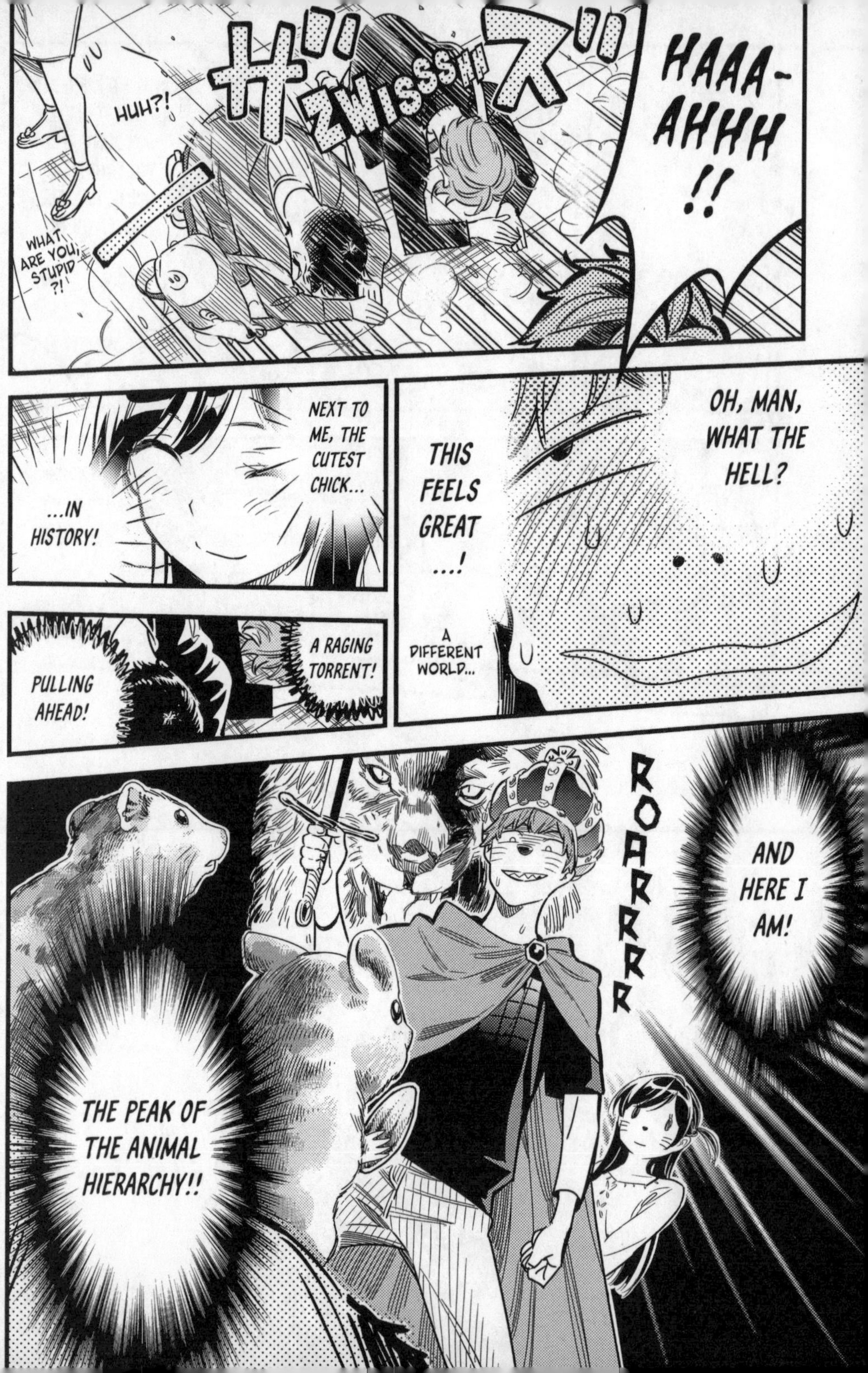
HAAAA-AHHH!!
ZWISSSH
HUH?!
WHAT ARE YOU, STUPID?!
OH, MAN, WHAT THE HELL?
THIS FEELS GREAT...!
A DIFFERENT WORLD...
NEXT TO ME, THE CUTEST CHICK...
...IN HISTORY!
A RAGING TORRENT!
PULLING AHEAD!
ROARRRR
AND HERE I AM!
THE PEAK OF THE ANIMAL HIERARCHY!!

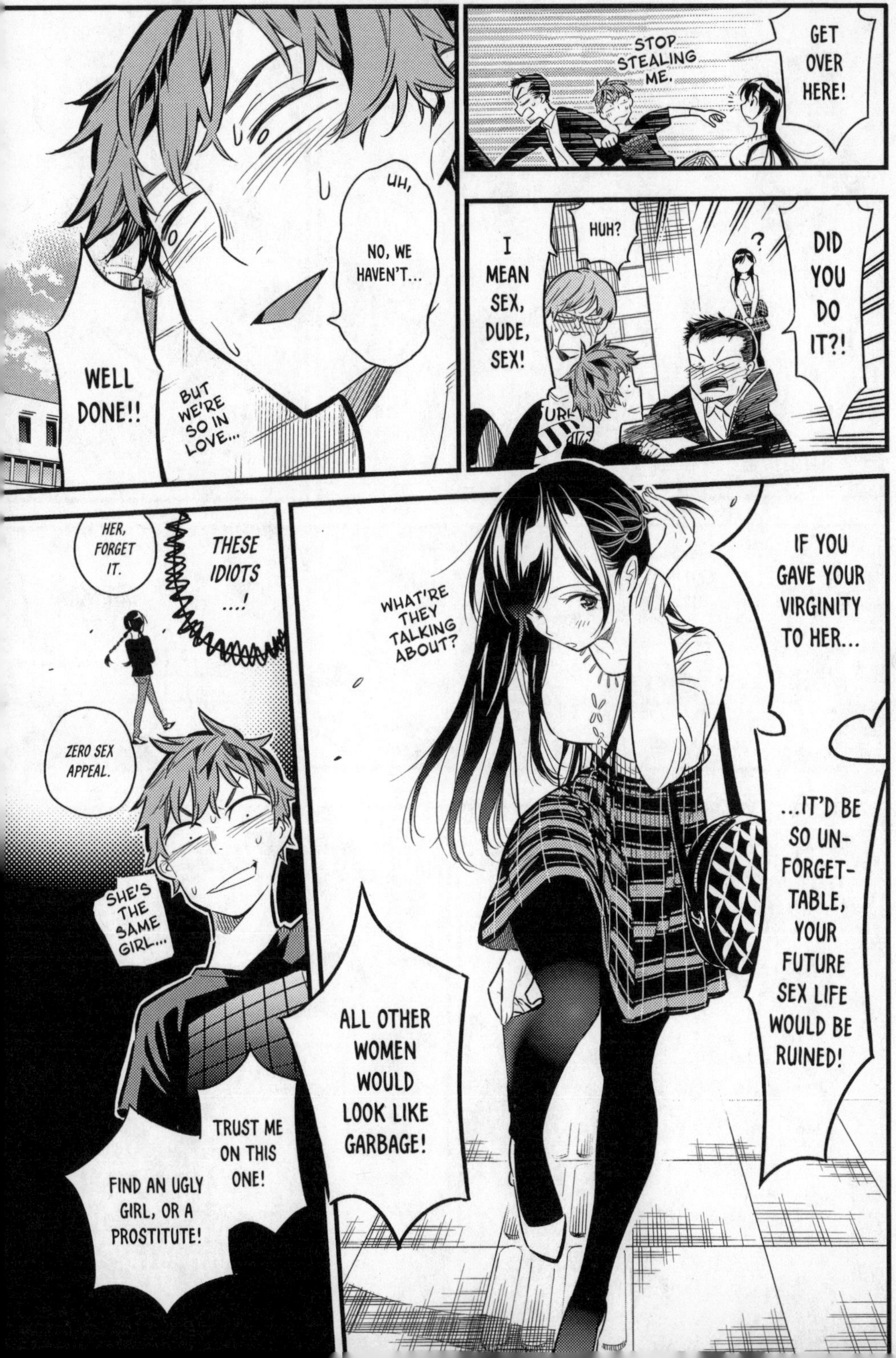
GET OVER HERE!
STOP STEALING ME.
DID YOU DO IT?!
HUH?
I MEAN SEX, DUDE, SEX!
UH,
NO, WE HAVEN'T...
BUT WE'RE SO IN LOVE...
WELL DONE!!
IF YOU GAVE YOUR VIRGINITY TO HER...
...IT'D BE SO UN-FORGET-TABLE, YOUR FUTURE SEX LIFE WOULD BE RUINED!
WHAT'RE THEY TALKING ABOUT?
ALL OTHER WOMEN WOULD LOOK LIKE GARBAGE!
THESE IDIOTS ...!
HER, FORGET IT.
ZERO SEX APPEAL.
SHE'S THE SAME GIRL...
TRUST ME ON THIS ONE!
FIND AN UGLY GIRL, OR A PROSTITUTE!

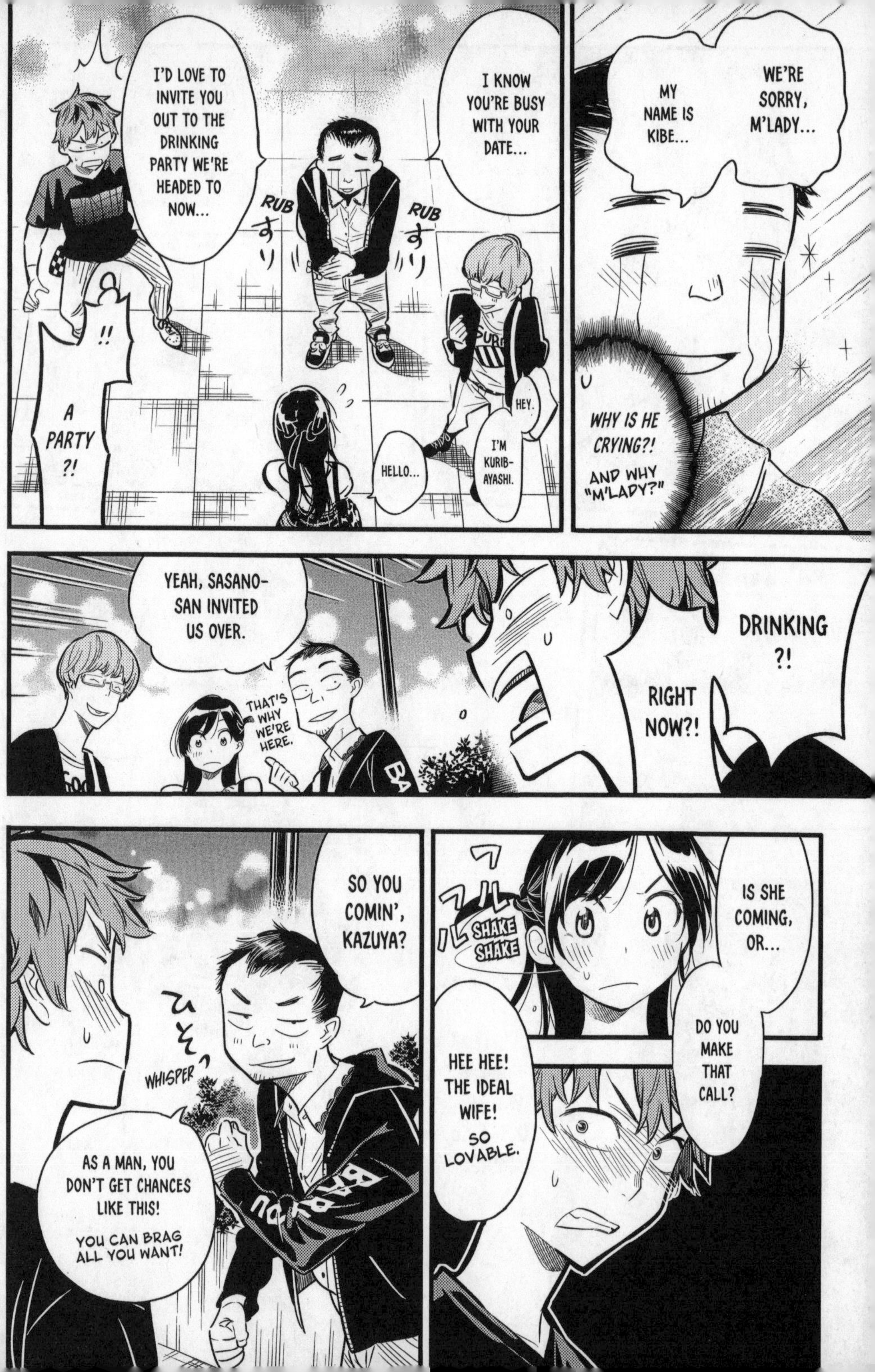
WE'RE SORRY, M'LADY...
MY NAME IS KIBE...
WHY IS HE CRYING?!
AND WHY "M'LADY?"
I KNOW YOU'RE BUSY WITH YOUR DATE...
RUB すり
RUB すり
I'D LOVE TO INVITE YOU OUT TO THE DRINKING PARTY WE'RE HEADED TO NOW...
HEY.
I'M KURIB-AYASHI.
HELLO...
!!
A PARTY ?!
DRINKING ?!
RIGHT NOW?!
YEAH, SASANO-SAN INVITED US OVER.
THAT'S WHY WE'RE HERE.
IS SHE COMING, OR...
DO YOU MAKE THAT CALL?
SHAKE SHAKE
HEE HEE! THE IDEAL WIFE!
SO LOVABLE.
SO YOU COMIN', KAZUYA?
ひそ
WHISPER
AS A MAN, YOU DON'T GET CHANCES LIKE THIS!
YOU CAN BRAG ALL YOU WANT!

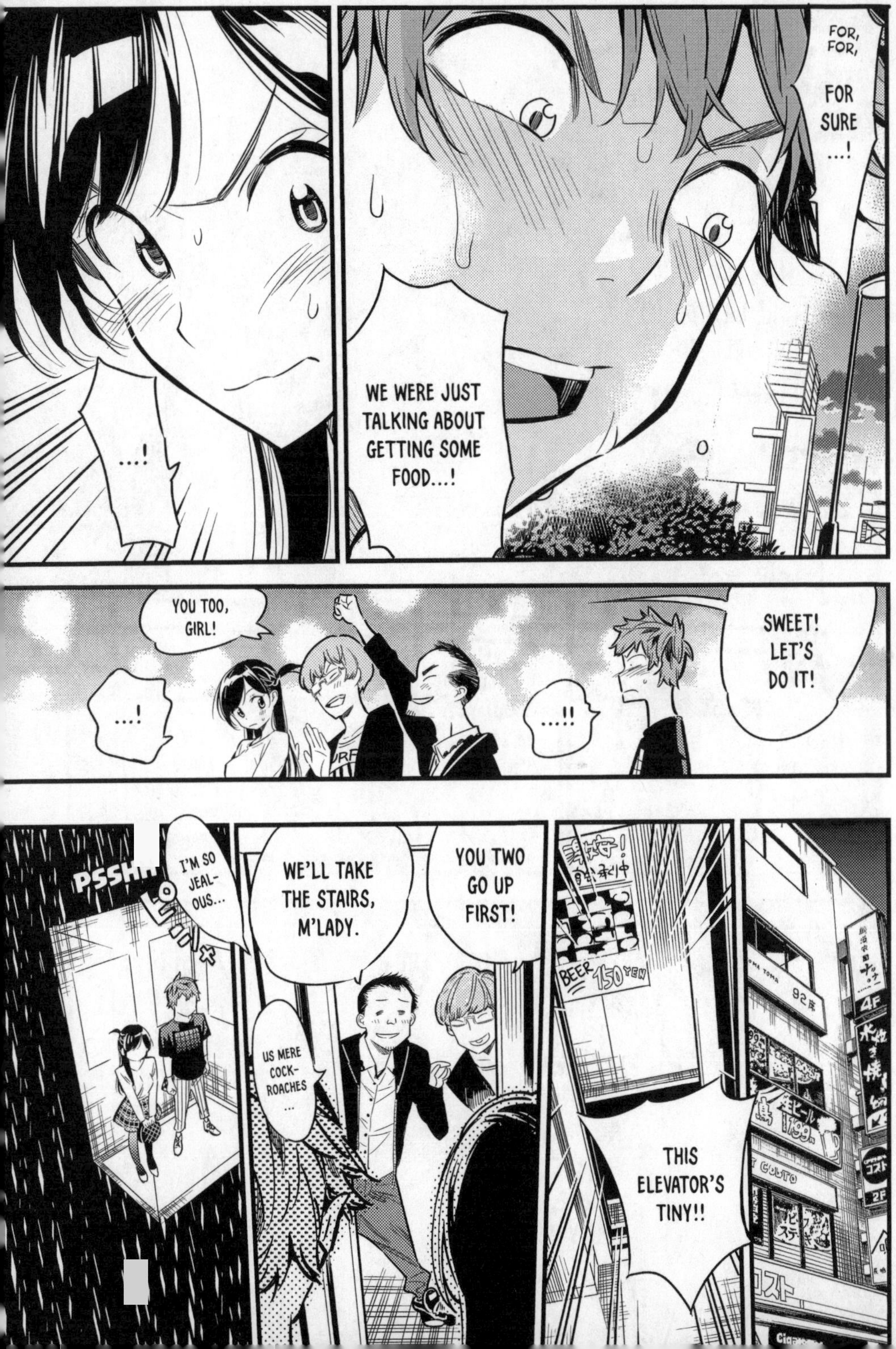
FOR, FOR,
FOR SURE ...!
WE WERE JUST TALKING ABOUT GETTING SOME FOOD...!
...!
SWEET! LET'S DO IT!
...!!
YOU TOO, GIRL!
...!
THIS ELEVATOR'S TINY!!
BEER 150 YEN
YOU TWO GO UP FIRST!
WE'LL TAKE THE STAIRS, M'LADY.
US MERE COCK-ROACHES ...
I'M SO JEAL-OUS...
PSSHH

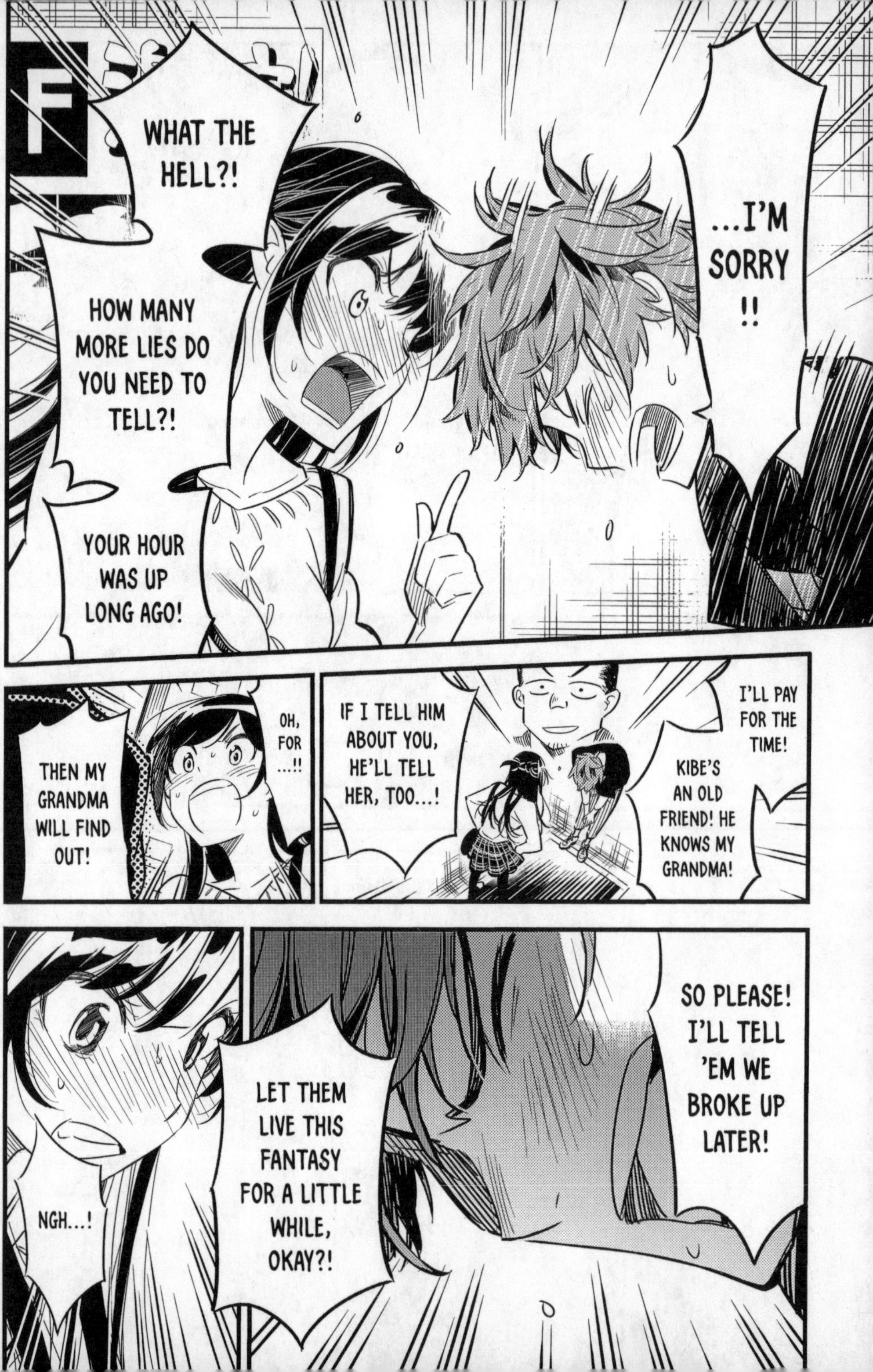
...I'M SORRY !!
WHAT THE HELL?!
HOW MANY MORE LIES DO YOU NEED TO TELL?!
YOUR HOUR WAS UP LONG AGO!
I'LL PAY FOR THE TIME!
KIBE'S AN OLD FRIEND! HE KNOWS MY GRANDMA!
IF I TELL HIM ABOUT YOU, HE'LL TELL HER, TOO...!
OH, FOR ...!!
THEN MY GRANDMA WILL FIND OUT!
SO PLEASE! I'LL TELL 'EM WE BROKE UP LATER!
LET THEM LIVE THIS FANTASY FOR A LITTLE WHILE, OKAY?!
NGH...!

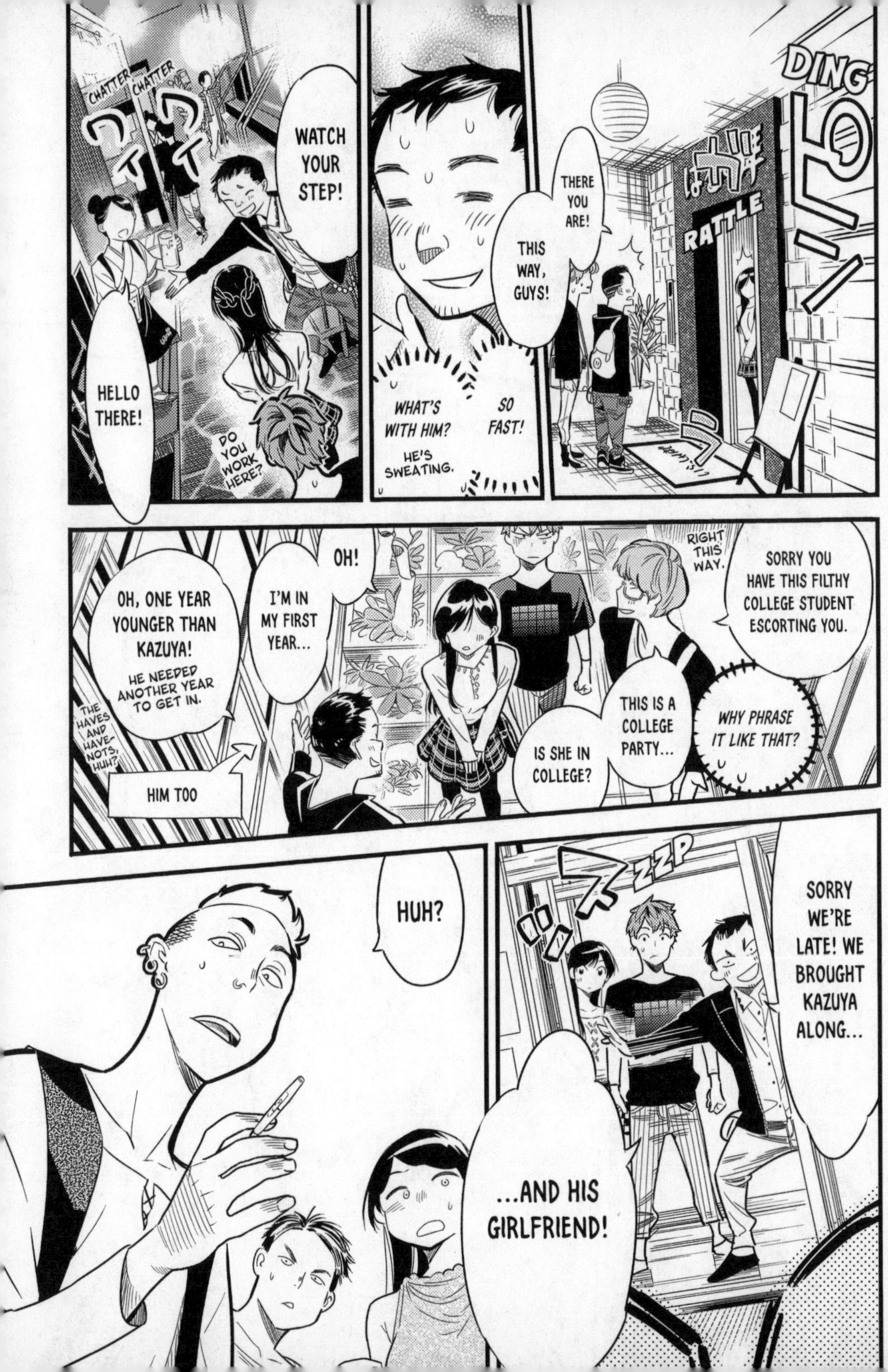
DING-
RATTLE
THERE YOU ARE!
THIS WAY, GUYS!
SO FAST!
WHAT'S WITH HIM?
HE'S SWEATING.
WATCH YOUR STEP!
CHATTER CHATTER
HELLO THERE!
DO YOU WORK HERE?
SORRY YOU HAVE THIS FILTHY COLLEGE STUDENT ESCORTING YOU.
RIGHT THIS WAY.
WHY PHRASE IT LIKE THAT?
THIS IS A COLLEGE PARTY...
IS SHE IN COLLEGE?
OH!
I'M IN MY FIRST YEAR...
OH, ONE YEAR YOUNGER THAN KAZUYA!
HE NEEDED ANOTHER YEAR TO GET IN.
THE HAVES AND HAVE-NOTS, HUH?
HIM TOO
ZZZP
SORRY WE'RE LATE! WE BROUGHT KAZUYA ALONG...
...AND HIS GIRLFRIEND!
HUH?

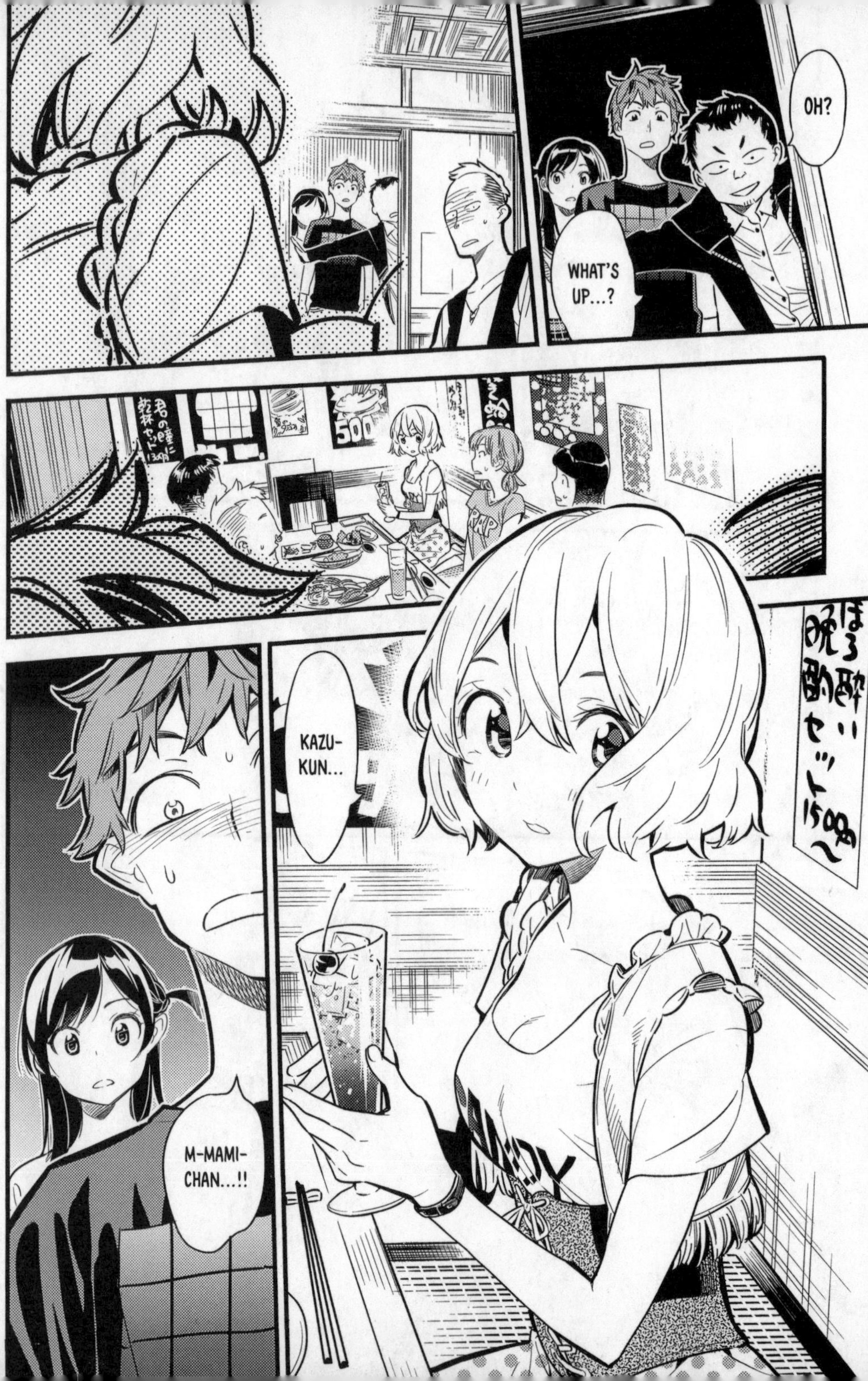
OH?
WHAT'S UP...?
君の瞳に乾杯セット1300円
500
ほろ酔い晩酌セット1500円～
KAZU-KUN...
M-MAMI-CHAN...!!

RATING 5

MY GIRLFRIEND AND MY EX

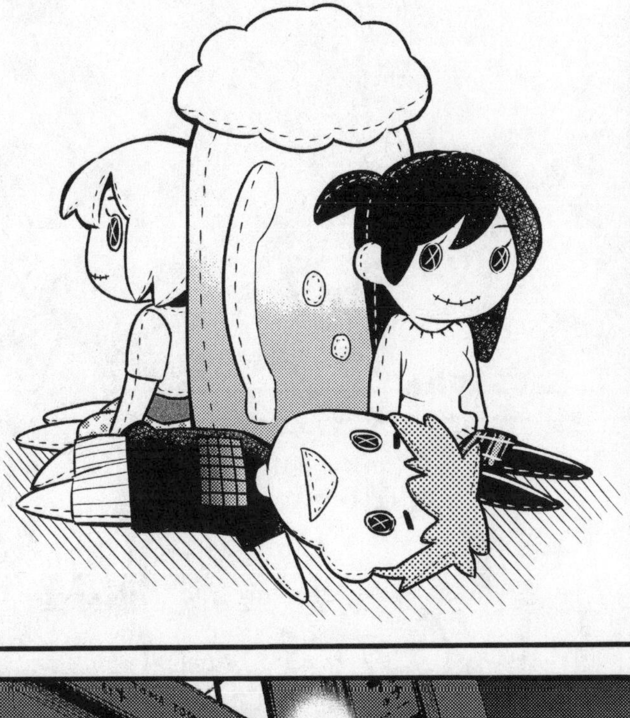

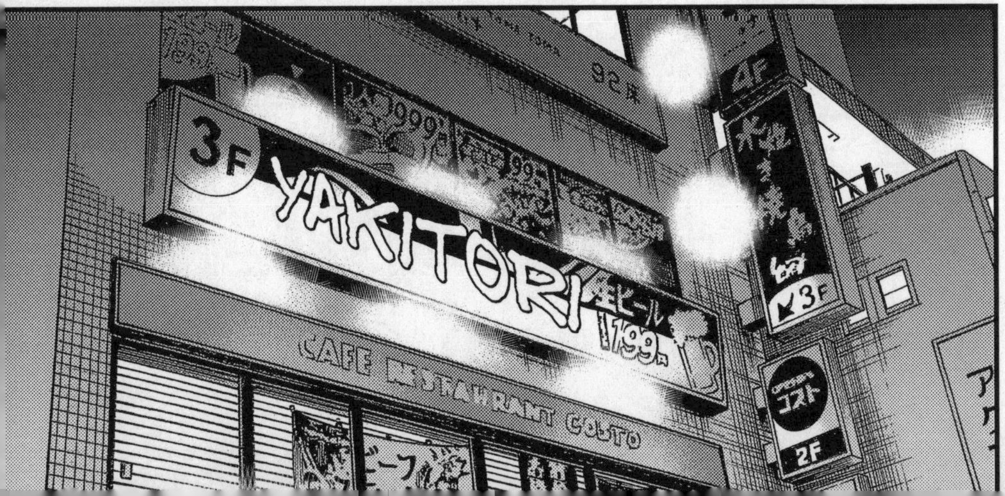
3F
YAKITORI
4F
3F
コスト
2F

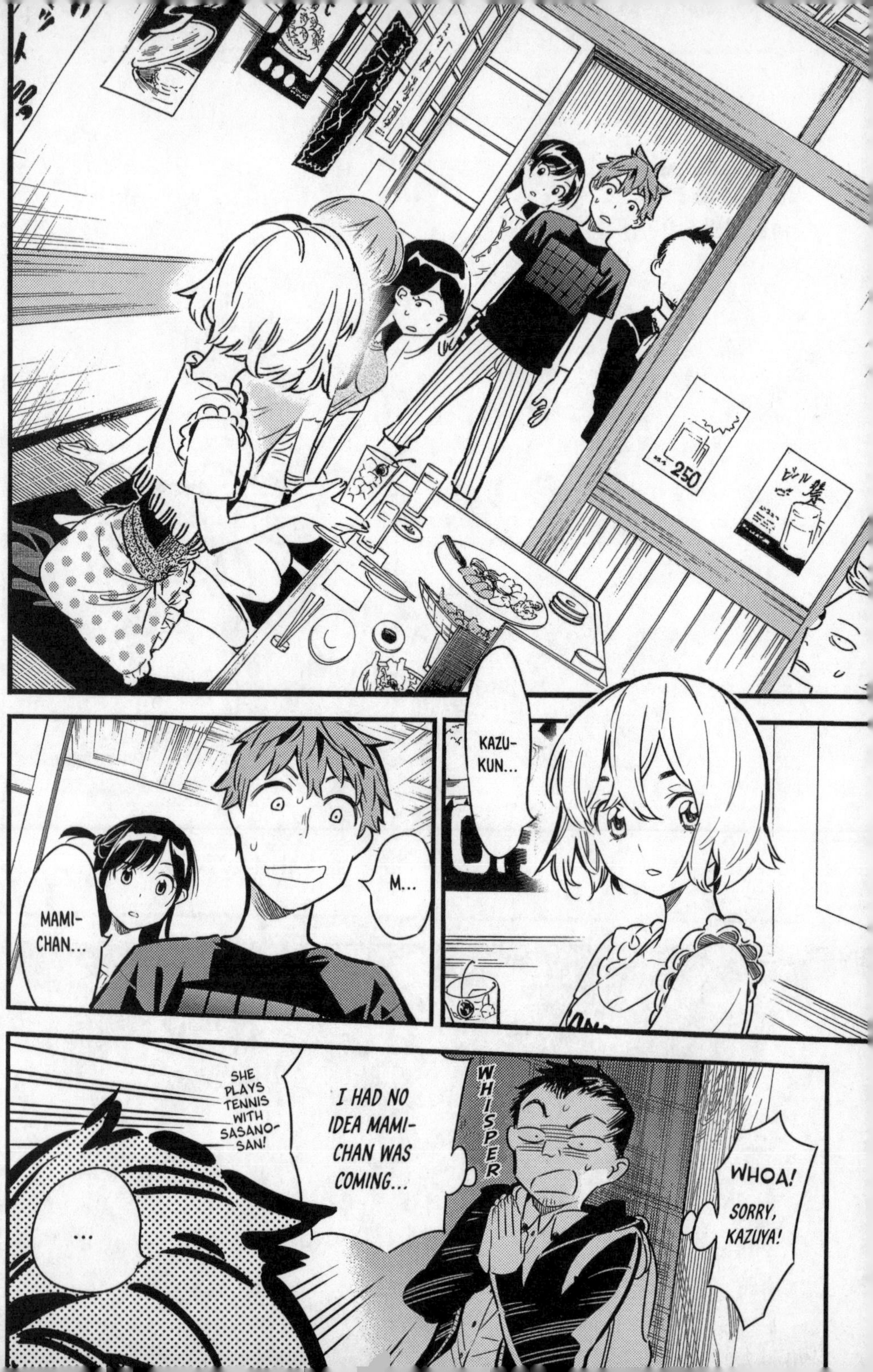
250
KAZU-KUN...
M...
MAMI-CHAN...
WHOA!
SORRY, KAZUYA!
WHISPER
I HAD NO IDEA MAMI-CHAN WAS COMING...
SHE PLAYS TENNIS WITH SASANO-SAN!
...

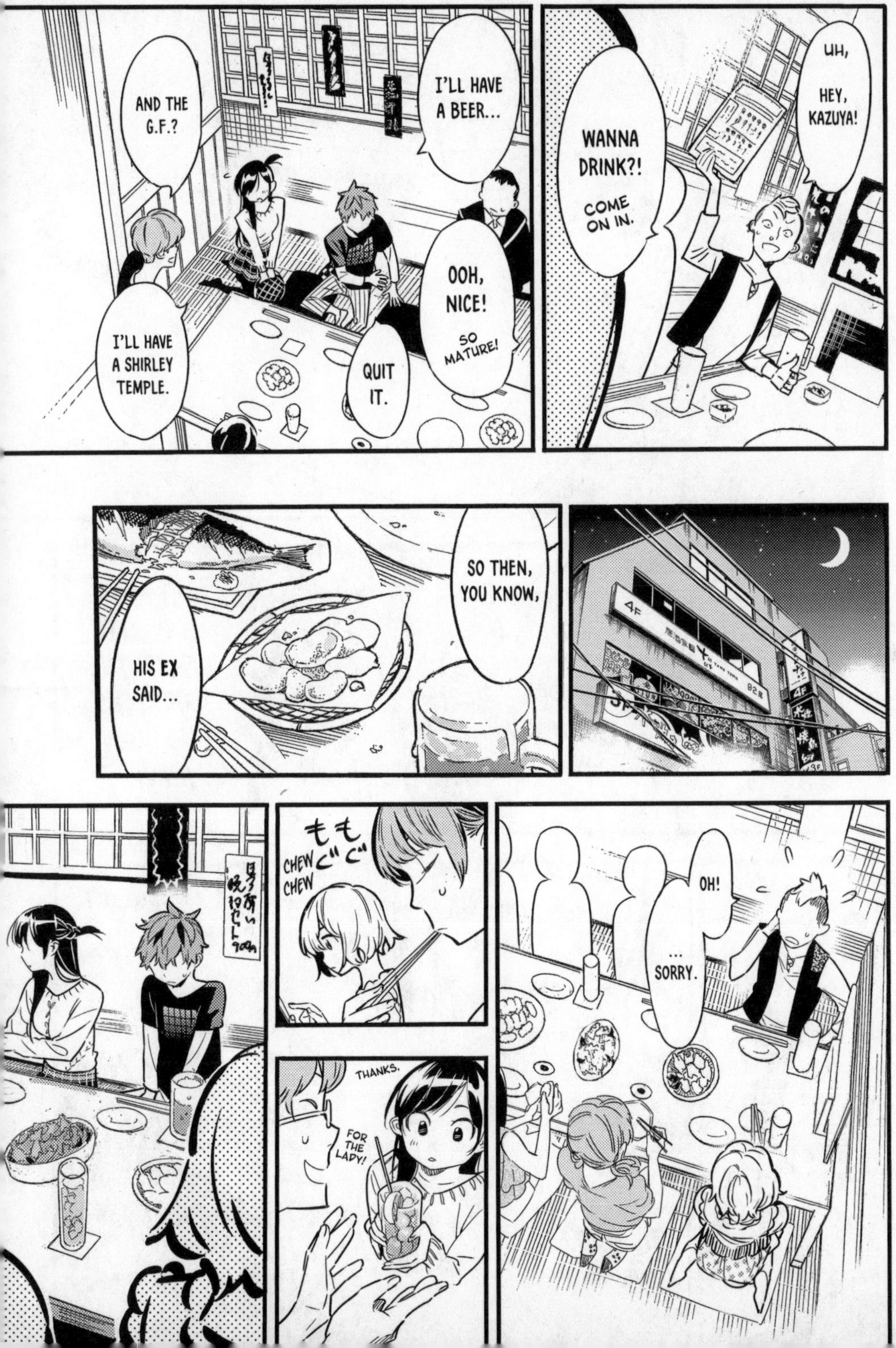
UH,
HEY, KAZUYA!
WANNA DRINK?!
COME ON IN.
I'LL HAVE A BEER...
AND THE G.F.?
OOH, NICE!
SO MATURE!
QUIT IT.
I'LL HAVE A SHIRLEY TEMPLE.
SO THEN, YOU KNOW,
HIS EX SAID...
OH!
...SORRY.
もぐもぐ
CHEW CHEW
THANKS.
FOR THE LADY!

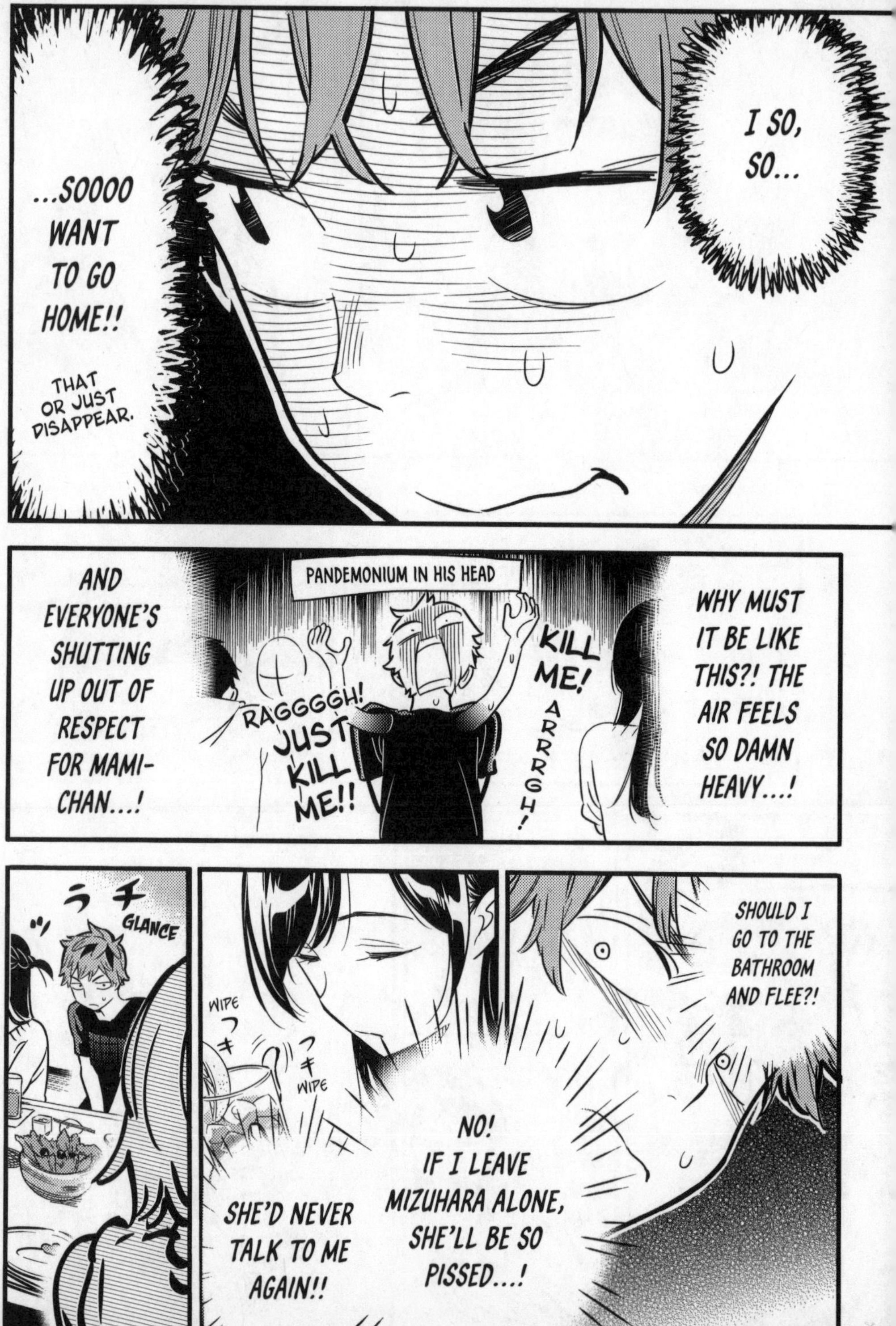
I SO, SO...
...SOOOO WANT TO GO HOME!!
THAT OR JUST DISAPPEAR.
PANDEMONIUM IN HIS HEAD
WHY MUST IT BE LIKE THIS?! THE AIR FEELS SO DAMN HEAVY...!
KILL ME!
ARRRGH!
RAGGGGH! JUST KILL ME!!
AND EVERYONE'S SHUTTING UP OUT OF RESPECT FOR MAMI-CHAN...!
SHOULD I GO TO THE BATHROOM AND FLEE?!
NO! IF I LEAVE MIZUHARA ALONE, SHE'LL BE SO PISSED...!
SHE'D NEVER TALK TO ME AGAIN!!
フキ WIPE
フキ WIPE
チラ GLANCE

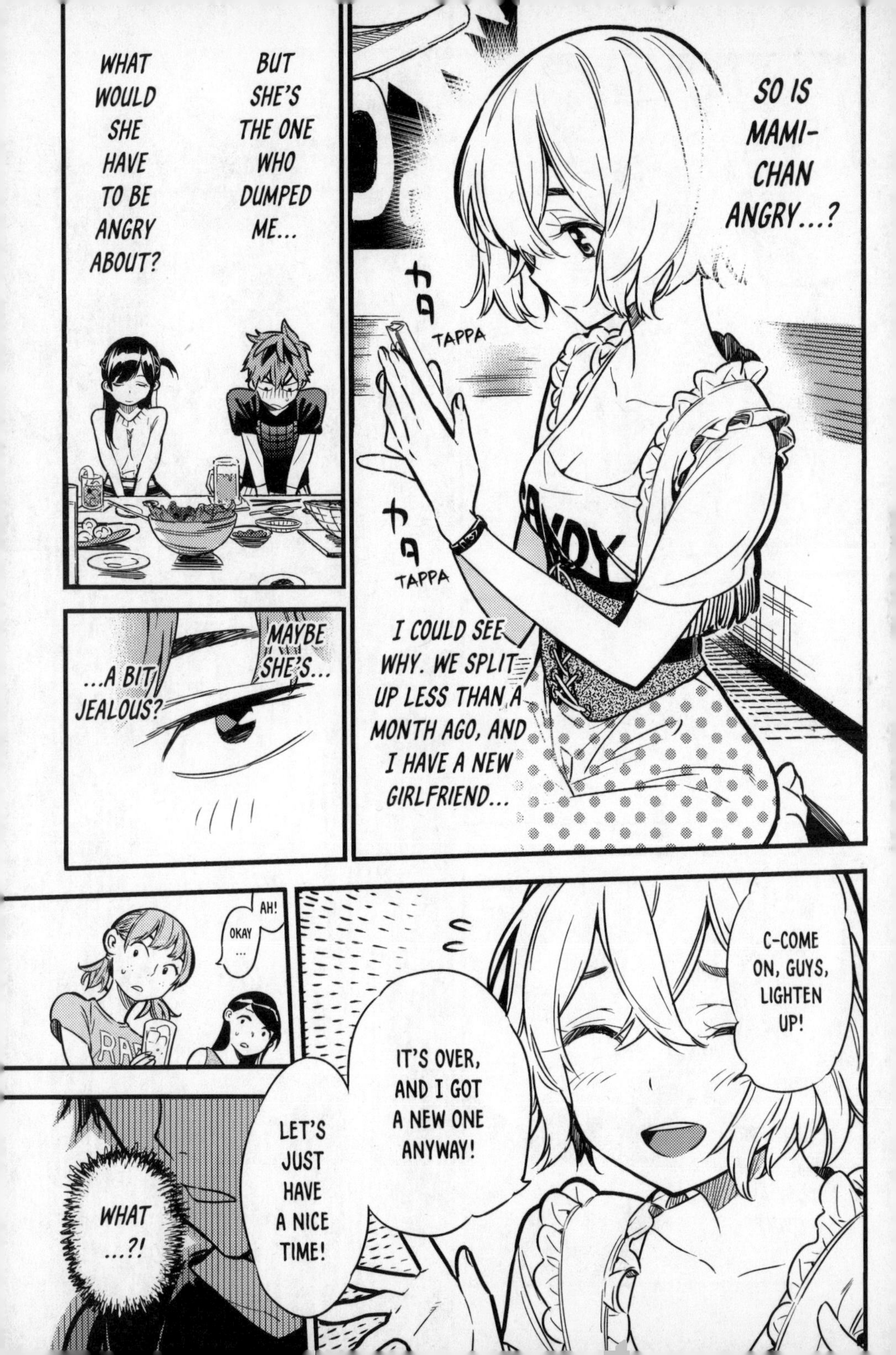
SO IS MAMI-CHAN ANGRY...?
TAPPA
TAPPA
I COULD SEE WHY. WE SPLIT UP LESS THAN A MONTH AGO, AND I HAVE A NEW GIRLFRIEND...
BUT SHE'S THE ONE WHO DUMPED ME...
WHAT WOULD SHE HAVE TO BE ANGRY ABOUT?
MAYBE SHE'S...
...A BIT JEALOUS?
C-COME ON, GUYS, LIGHTEN UP!
IT'S OVER, AND I GOT A NEW ONE ANYWAY!
LET'S JUST HAVE A NICE TIME!
AH!
OKAY...
WHAT...?!

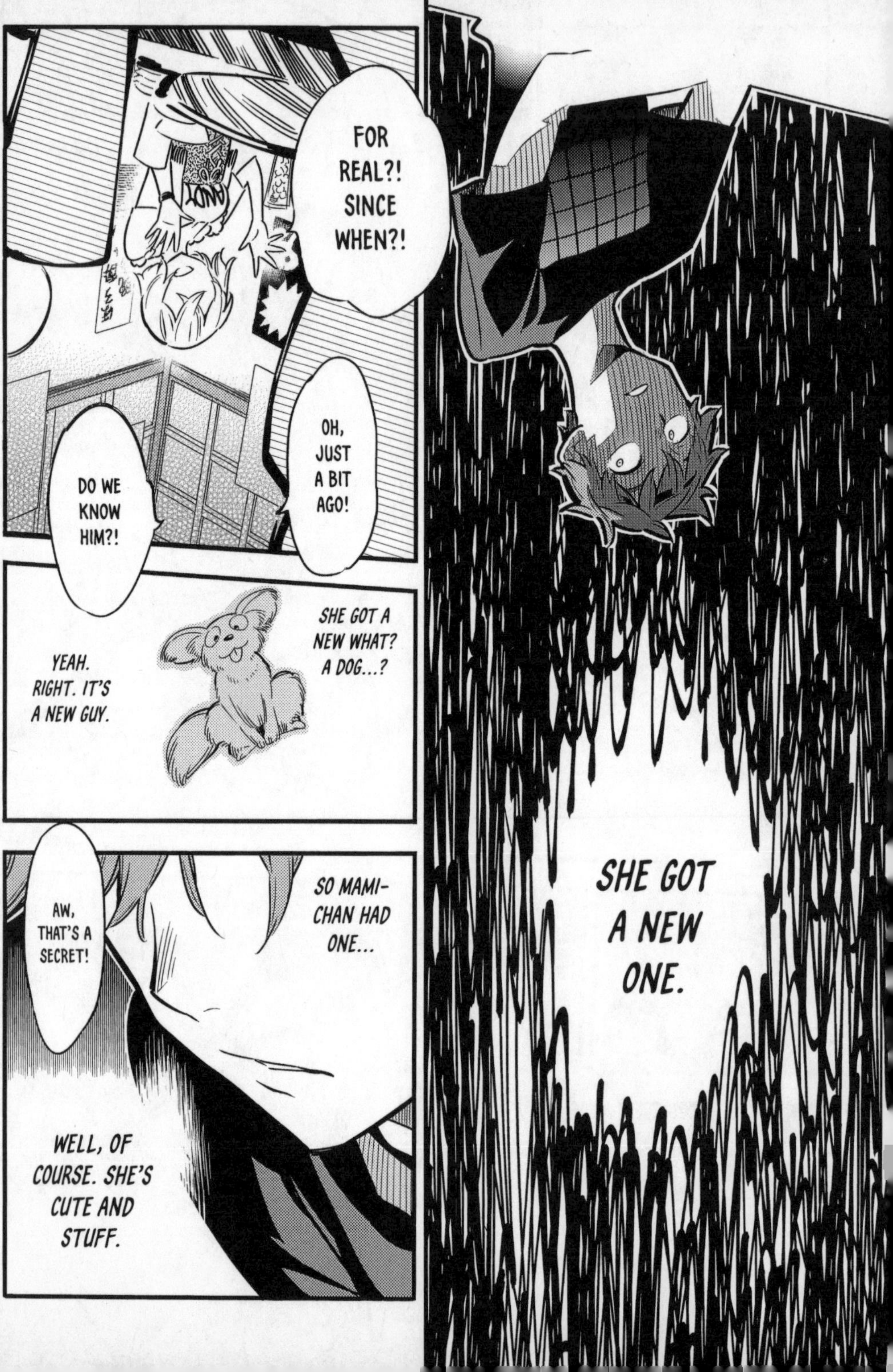
SHE GOT A NEW ONE.
FOR REAL?! SINCE WHEN?!
OH, JUST A BIT AGO!
DO WE KNOW HIM?!
SHE GOT A NEW WHAT? A DOG...?
YEAH. RIGHT. IT'S A NEW GUY.
SO MAMI-CHAN HAD ONE...
AW, THAT'S A SECRET!
WELL, OF COURSE. SHE'S CUTE AND STUFF.

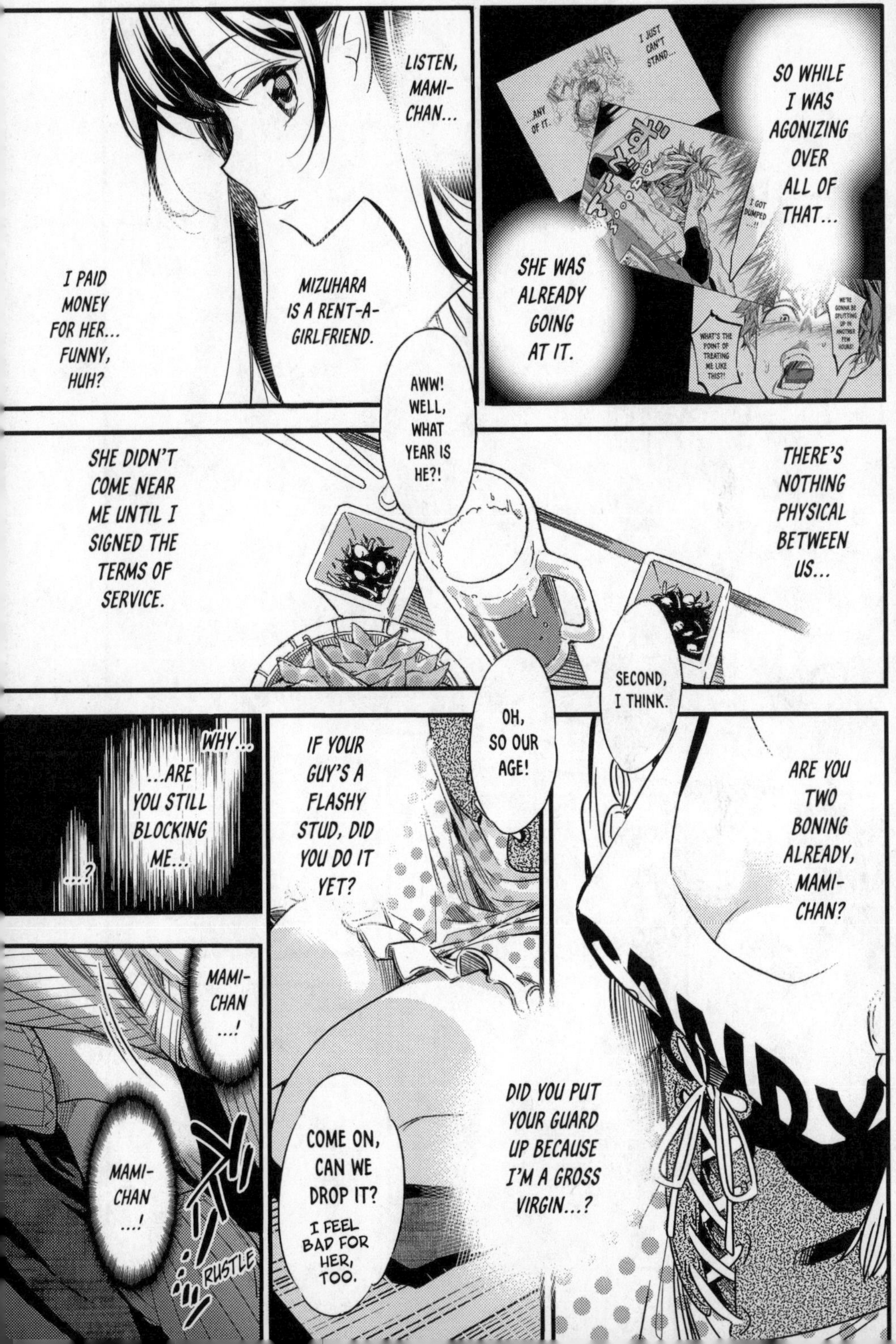

SO WHILE I WAS AGONIZING OVER ALL OF THAT...
I JUST CAN'T STAND...
...ANY OF IT.
I GOT DUMPED...!!
WE'RE GONNA BE SPLITTING UP IN ANOTHER FEW HOURS!
WHAT'S THE POINT OF TREATING ME LIKE THIS?!
SHE WAS ALREADY GOING AT IT.
LISTEN, MAMI-CHAN...
MIZUHARA IS A RENT-A-GIRLFRIEND.
I PAID MONEY FOR HER... FUNNY, HUH?
AWW! WELL, WHAT YEAR IS HE?!
THERE'S NOTHING PHYSICAL BETWEEN US...
SHE DIDN'T COME NEAR ME UNTIL I SIGNED THE TERMS OF SERVICE.
SECOND, I THINK.
OH, SO OUR AGE!
ARE YOU TWO BONING ALREADY, MAMI-CHAN?
CANDY
DID YOU PUT YOUR GUARD UP BECAUSE I'M A GROSS VIRGIN...?
IF YOUR GUY'S A FLASHY STUD, DID YOU DO IT YET?
COME ON, CAN WE DROP IT?
I FEEL BAD FOR HER, TOO.
WHY...
...ARE YOU STILL BLOCKING ME...
...?
MAMI-CHAN...!
MAMI-CHAN...!
RUSTLE

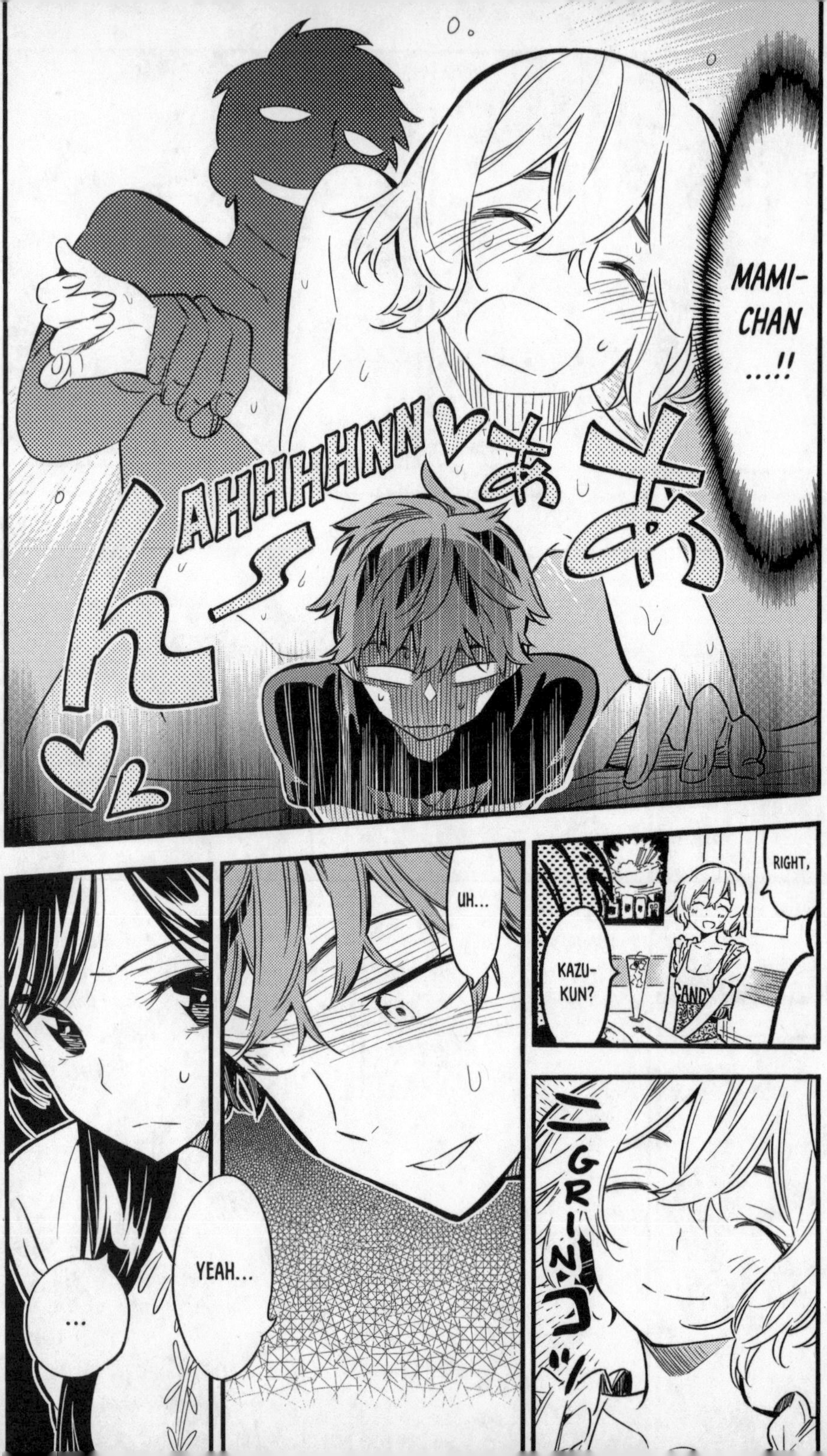
MAMI-CHAN ...!!
AHHHHNN♡
RIGHT,
KAZU-KUN?
GRIN
UH...
YEAH...
...

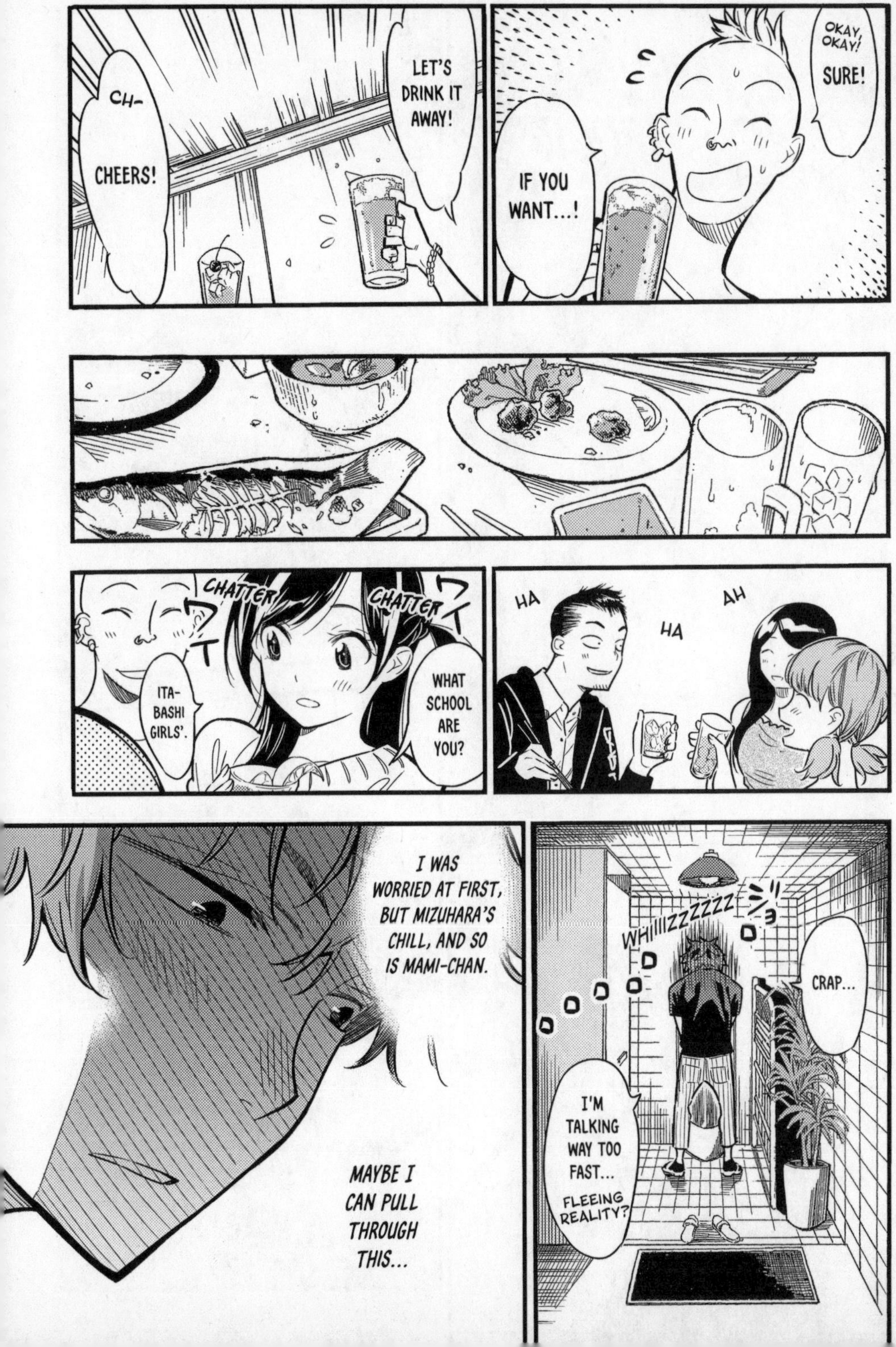
OKAY, OKAY! SURE!
IF YOU WANT...!
LET'S DRINK IT AWAY!
CH- CHEERS!
HA HA AH
CHATTER
CHATTER
WHAT SCHOOL ARE YOU?
ITA-BASHI GIRLS'.
WHIIIZZZZZ
CRAP...
I'M TALKING WAY TOO FAST...
FLEEING REALITY?
I WAS WORRIED AT FIRST, BUT MIZUHARA'S CHILL, AND SO IS MAMI-CHAN.
MAYBE I CAN PULL THROUGH THIS...

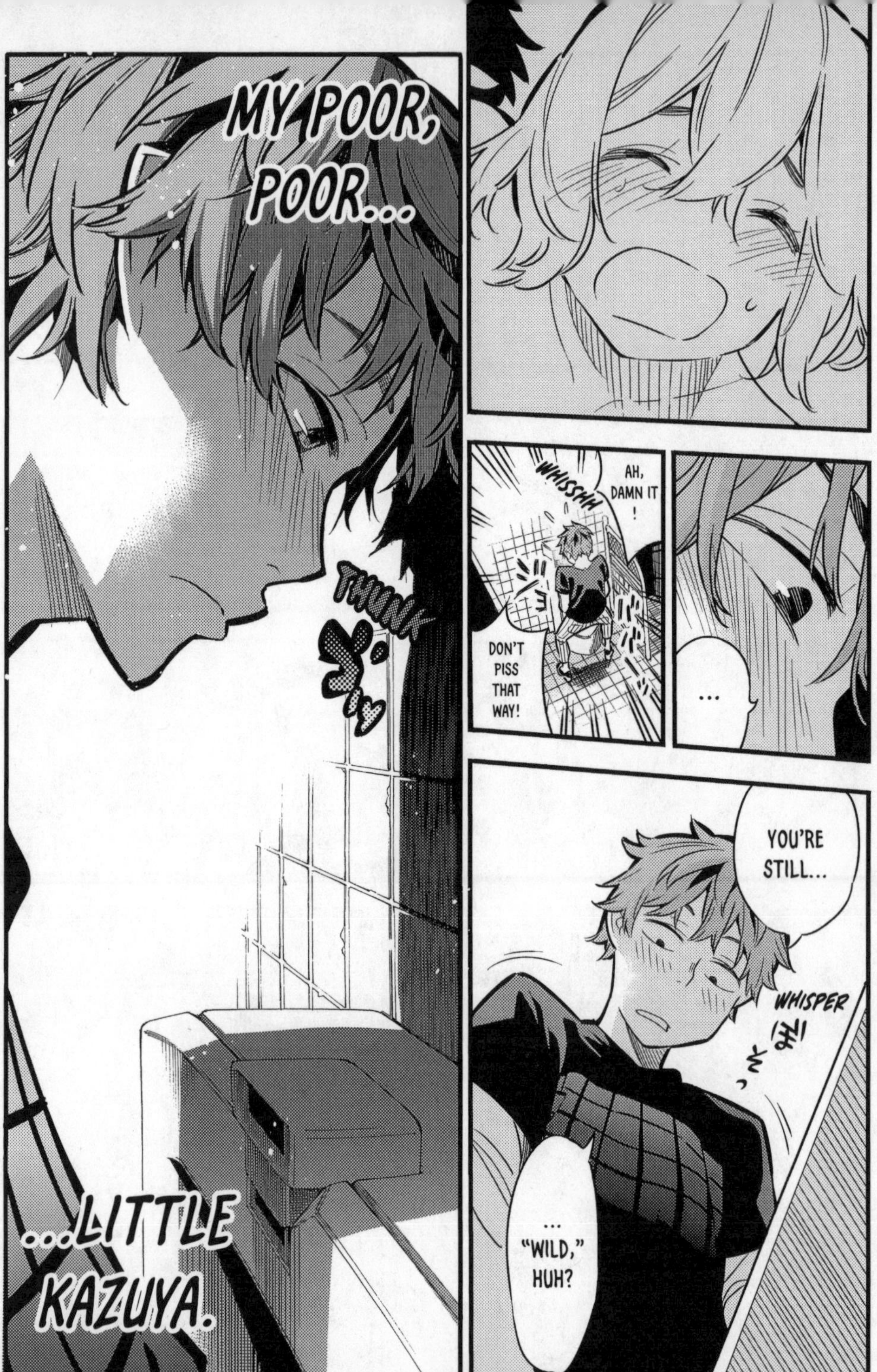
...
AH, DAMN IT!
WHISSHH
DON'T PISS THAT WAY!
YOU'RE STILL...
WHISPER
... "WILD," HUH?
MY POOR, POOR...
THUNK
...LITTLE KAZUYA.

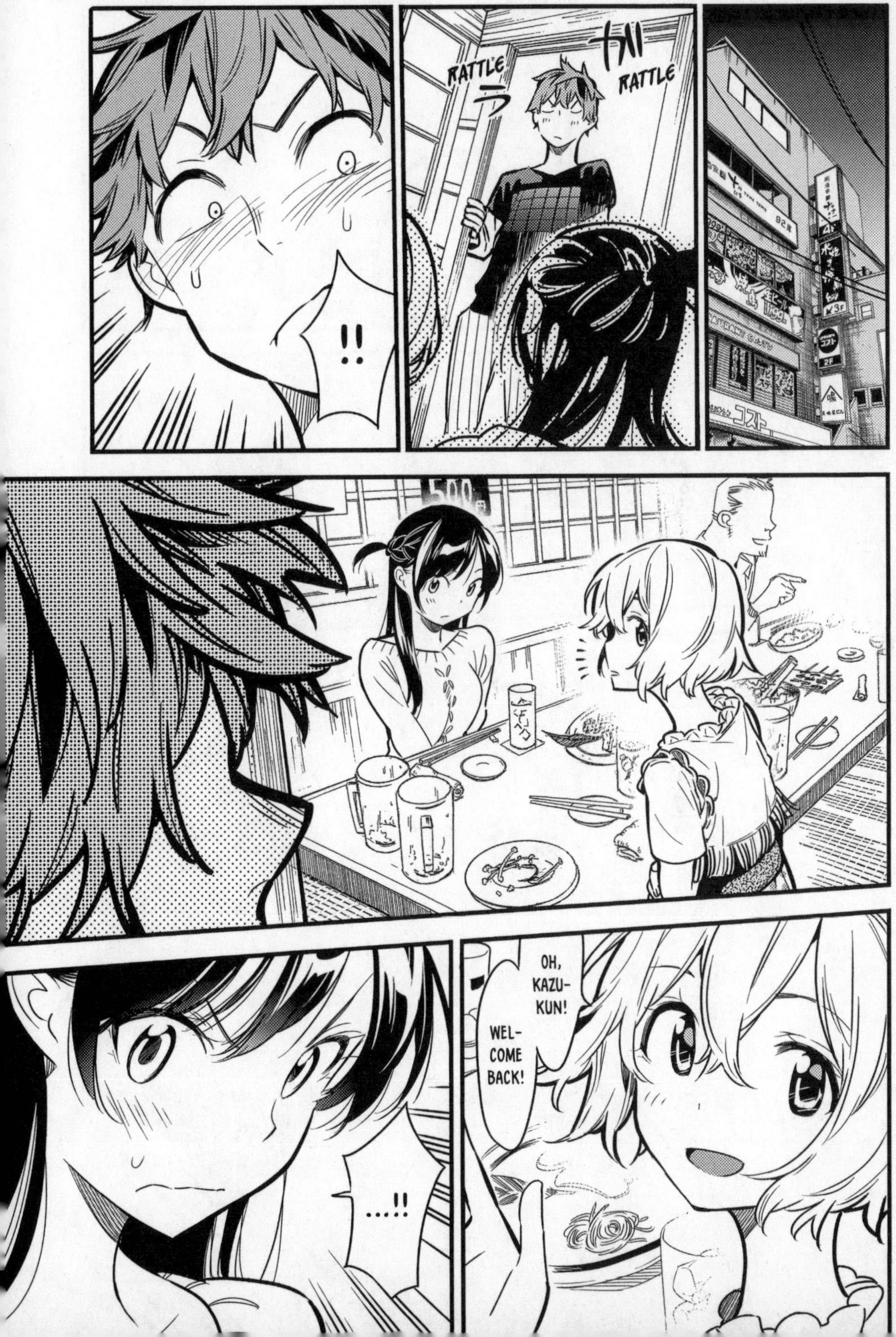
RATTLE
RATTLE
!!
OH, KAZU-KUN!
WEL-COME BACK!
...!!

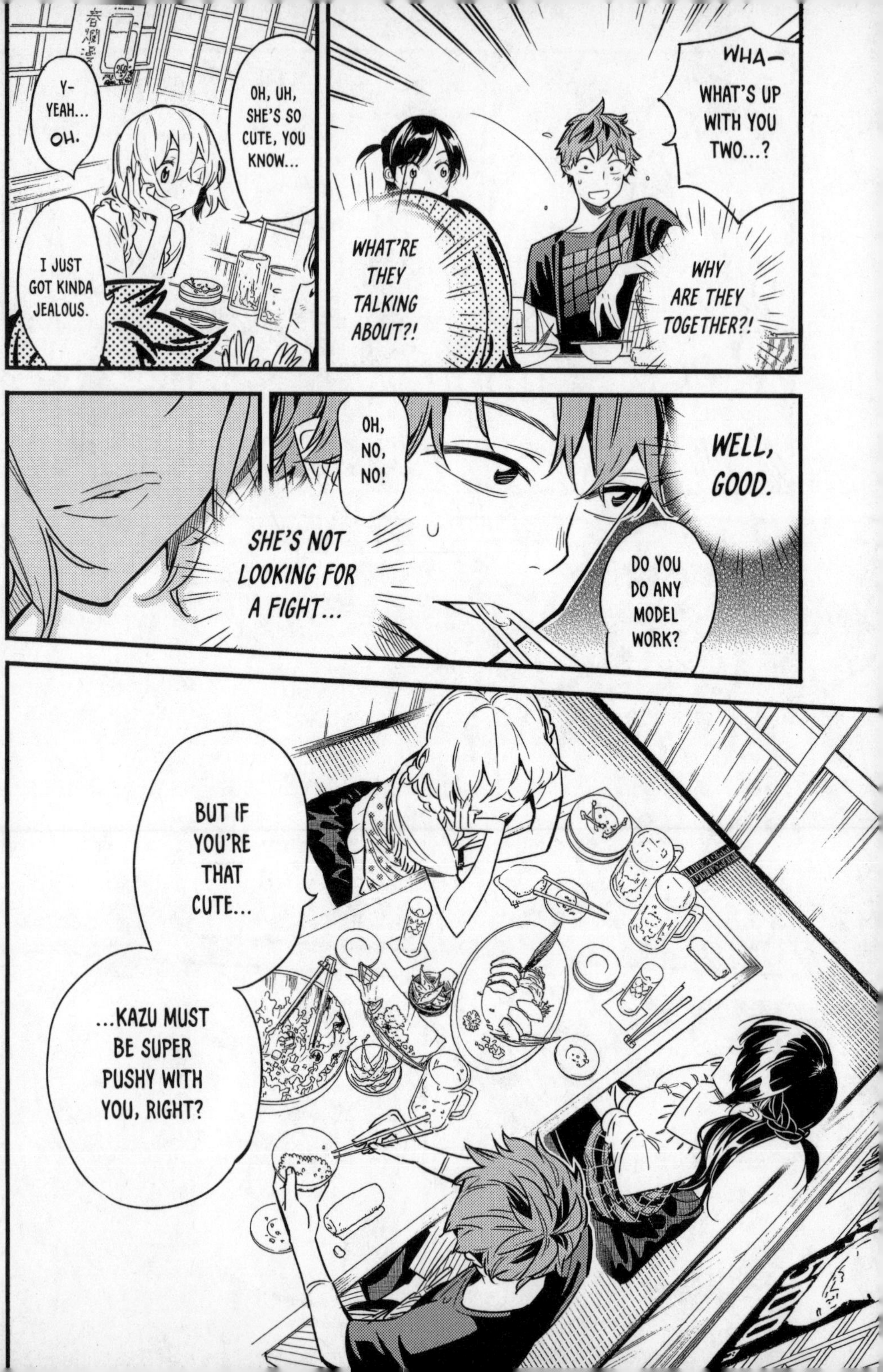
WHA— WHAT'S UP WITH YOU TWO...?
WHY ARE THEY TOGETHER?!
WHAT'RE THEY TALKING ABOUT?!
OH, UH, SHE'S SO CUTE, YOU KNOW...
Y-YEAH... OH.
I JUST GOT KINDA JEALOUS.
WELL, GOOD.
OH, NO, NO!
DO YOU DO ANY MODEL WORK?
SHE'S NOT LOOKING FOR A FIGHT...
BUT IF YOU'RE THAT CUTE...
...KAZU MUST BE SUPER PUSHY WITH YOU, RIGHT?

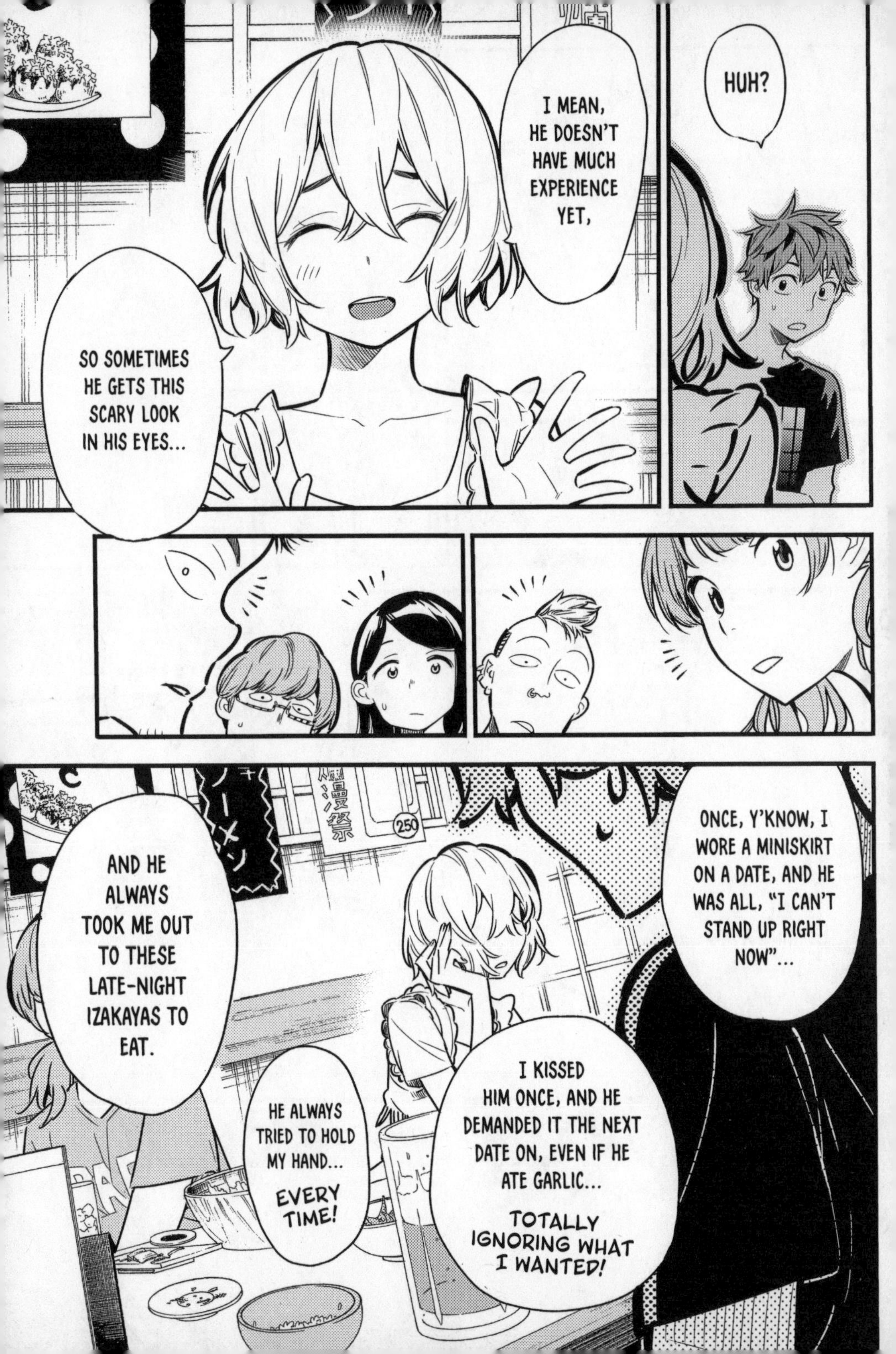
HUH?
I MEAN, HE DOESN'T HAVE MUCH EXPERIENCE YET,
SO SOMETIMES HE GETS THIS SCARY LOOK IN HIS EYES...
250
ONCE, Y'KNOW, I WORE A MINISKIRT ON A DATE, AND HE WAS ALL, "I CAN'T STAND UP RIGHT NOW"...
I KISSED HIM ONCE, AND HE DEMANDED IT THE NEXT DATE ON, EVEN IF HE ATE GARLIC...
TOTALLY IGNORING WHAT I WANTED!
HE ALWAYS TRIED TO HOLD MY HAND...
EVERY TIME!
AND HE ALWAYS TOOK ME OUT TO THESE LATE-NIGHT IZAKAYAS TO EAT.

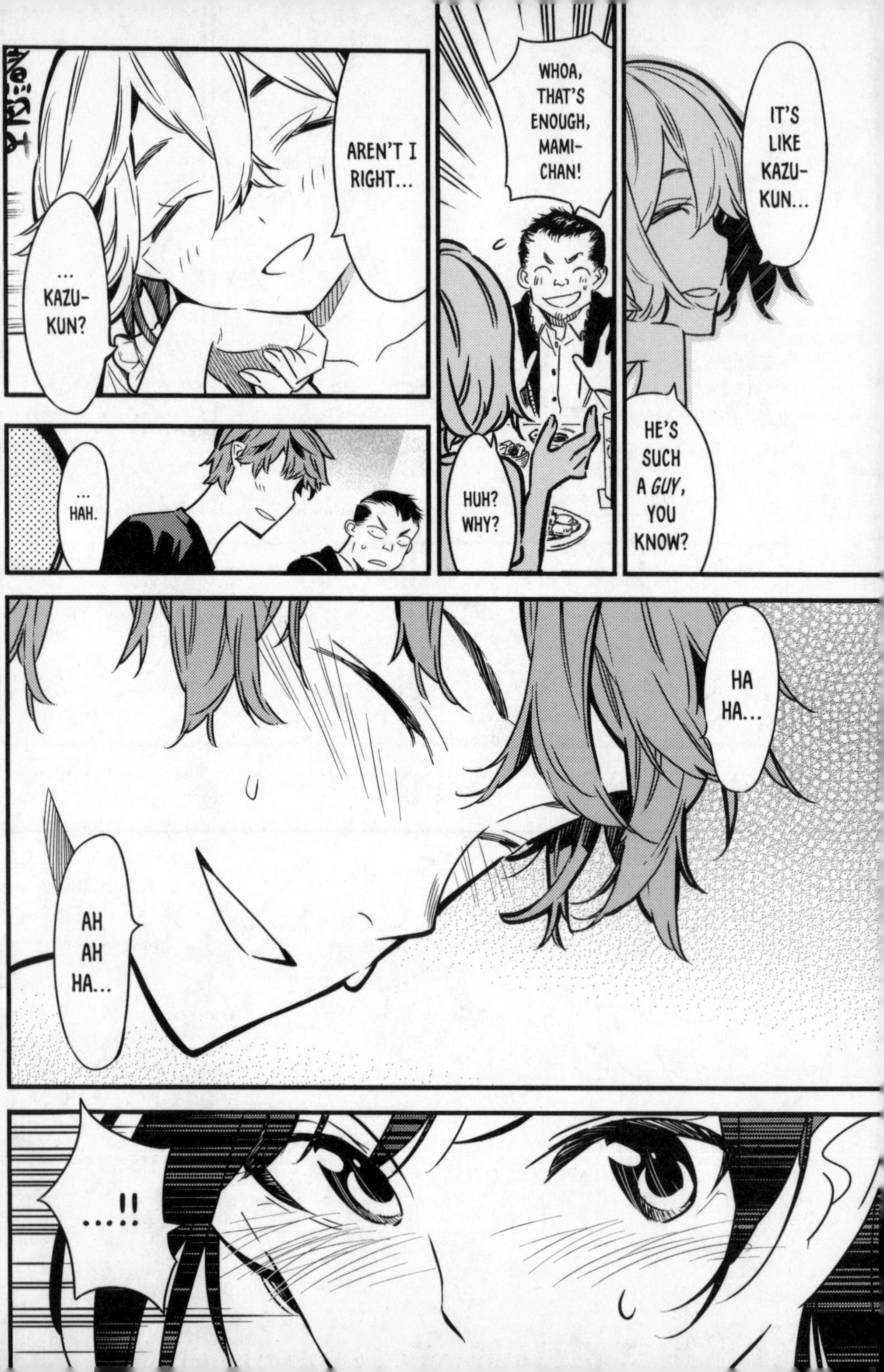
IT'S LIKE KAZU-KUN...
HE'S SUCH A *GUY*, YOU KNOW?
WHOA, THAT'S ENOUGH, MAMI-CHAN!
HUH? WHY?
AREN'T I RIGHT...
... KAZU-KUN?
... HAH.
HA HA...
AH AH HA...
...!!

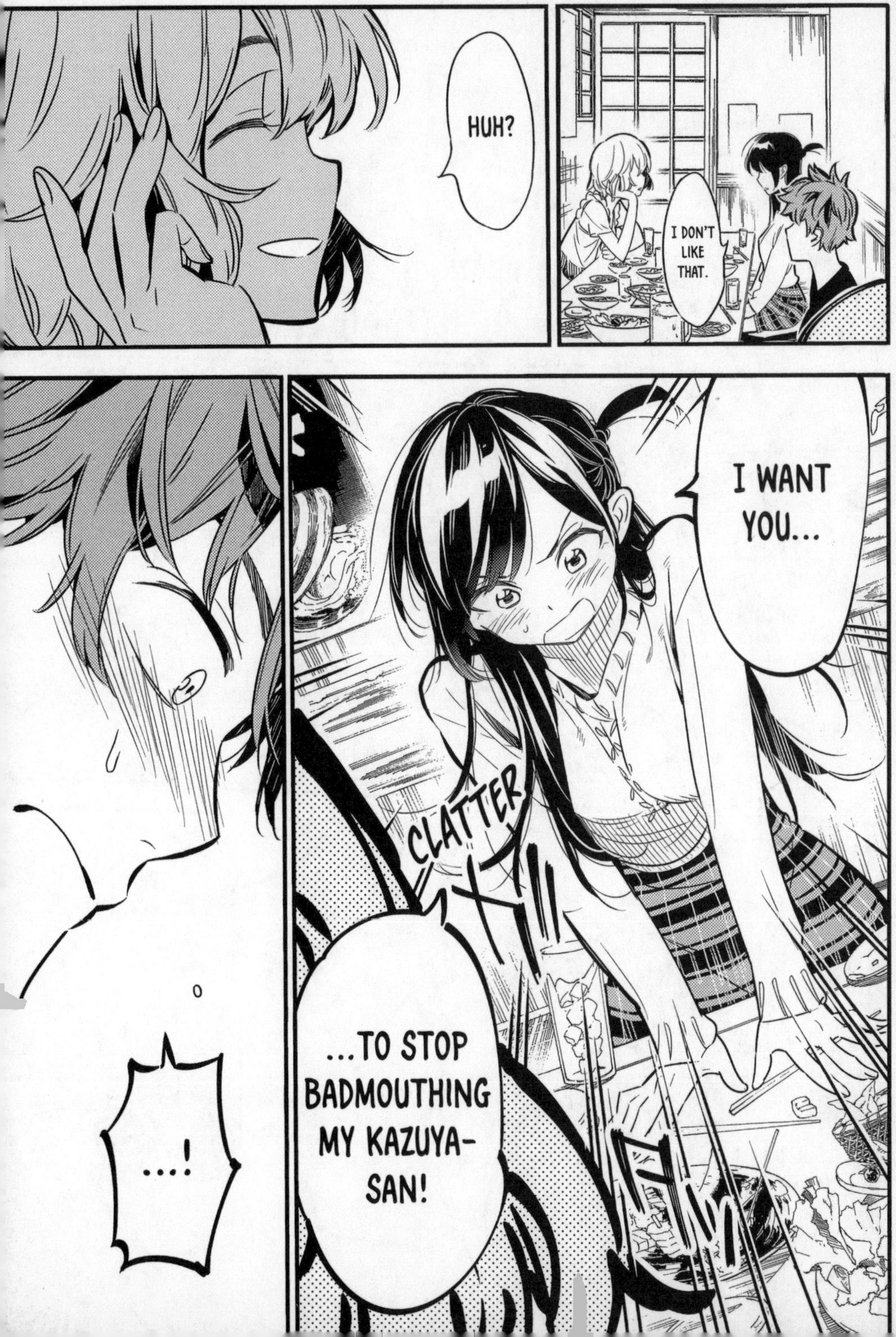
I DON'T LIKE THAT.
HUH?
I WANT YOU...
CLATTER
...TO STOP BADMOUTHING MY KAZUYA-SAN!
...!

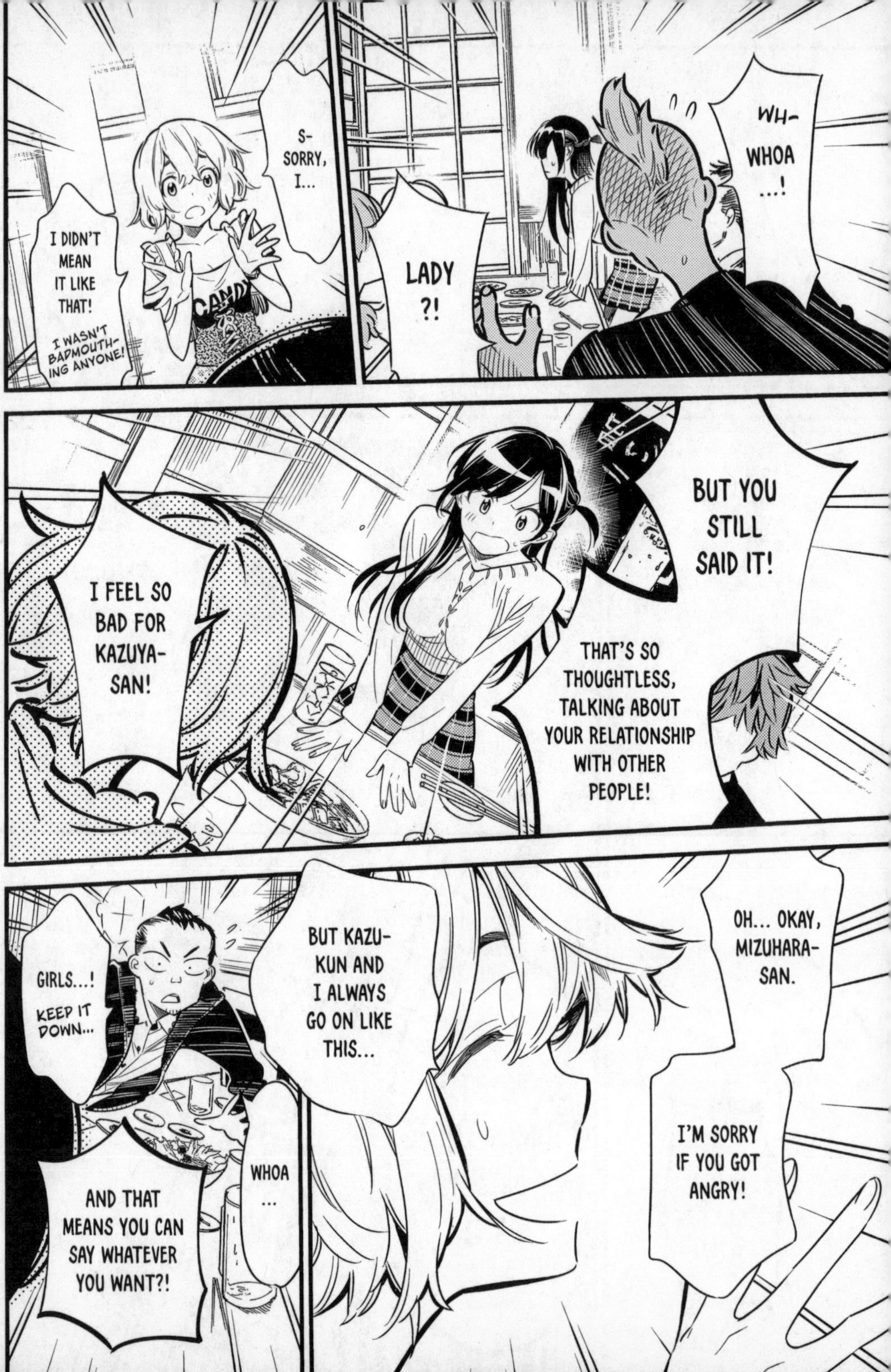
WH- WHOA ...!
LADY ?!
S- SORRY, I...
I DIDN'T MEAN IT LIKE THAT!
I WASN'T BADMOUTHING ANYONE!
BUT YOU STILL SAID IT!
THAT'S SO THOUGHTLESS, TALKING ABOUT YOUR RELATIONSHIP WITH OTHER PEOPLE!
I FEEL SO BAD FOR KAZUYA-SAN!
OH... OKAY, MIZUHARA-SAN.
I'M SORRY IF YOU GOT ANGRY!
BUT KAZU-KUN AND I ALWAYS GO ON LIKE THIS...
GIRLS...!
KEEP IT DOWN...
WHOA ...
AND THAT MEANS YOU CAN SAY WHATEVER YOU WANT?!

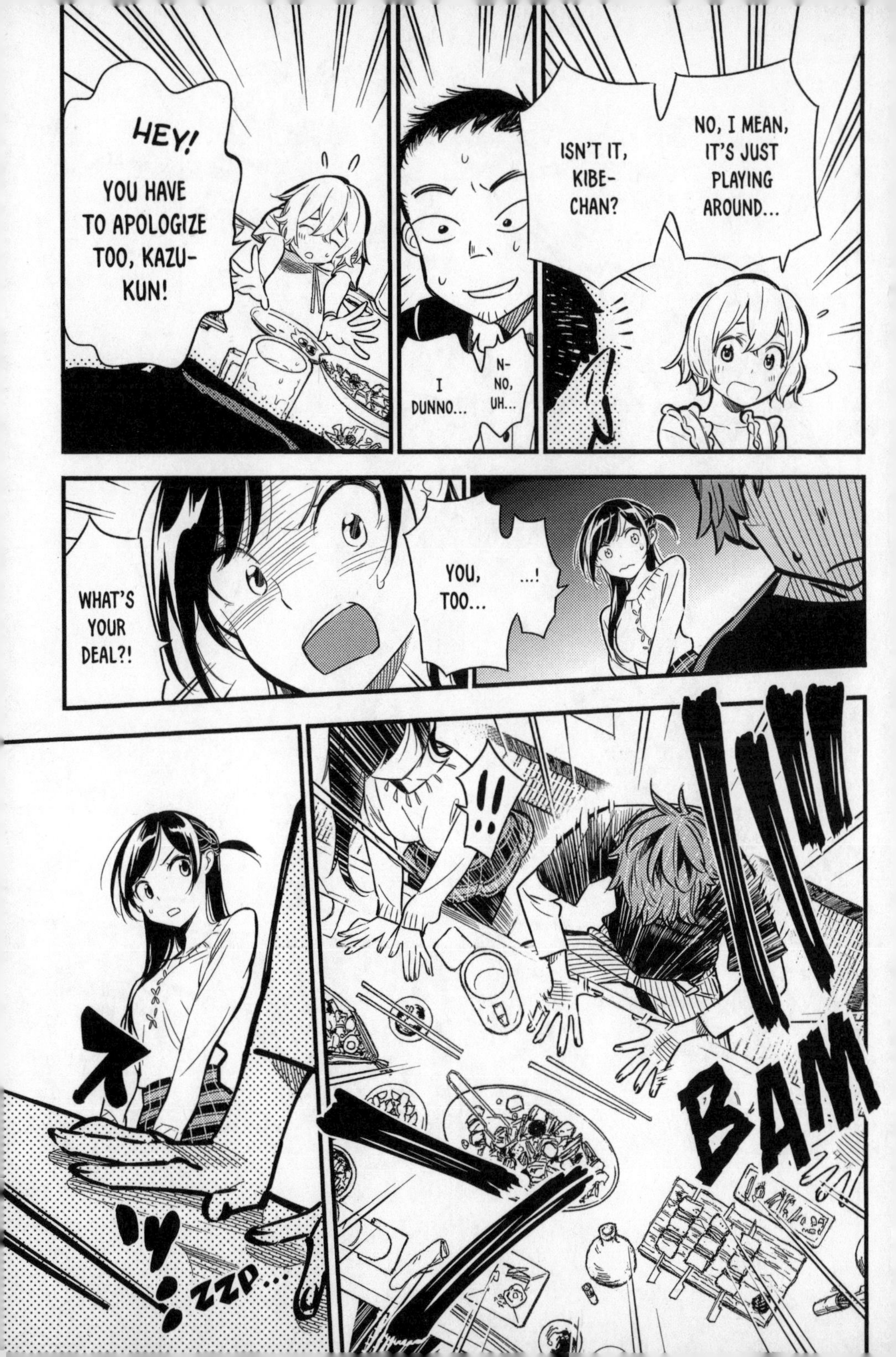

NO, I MEAN, IT'S JUST PLAYING AROUND...
ISN'T IT, KIBE-CHAN?
N-NO, UH...
I DUNNO...
HEY!
YOU HAVE TO APOLOGIZE TOO, KAZU-KUN!
...!
YOU, TOO...
WHAT'S YOUR DEAL?!
!!
BAM
ZZP...

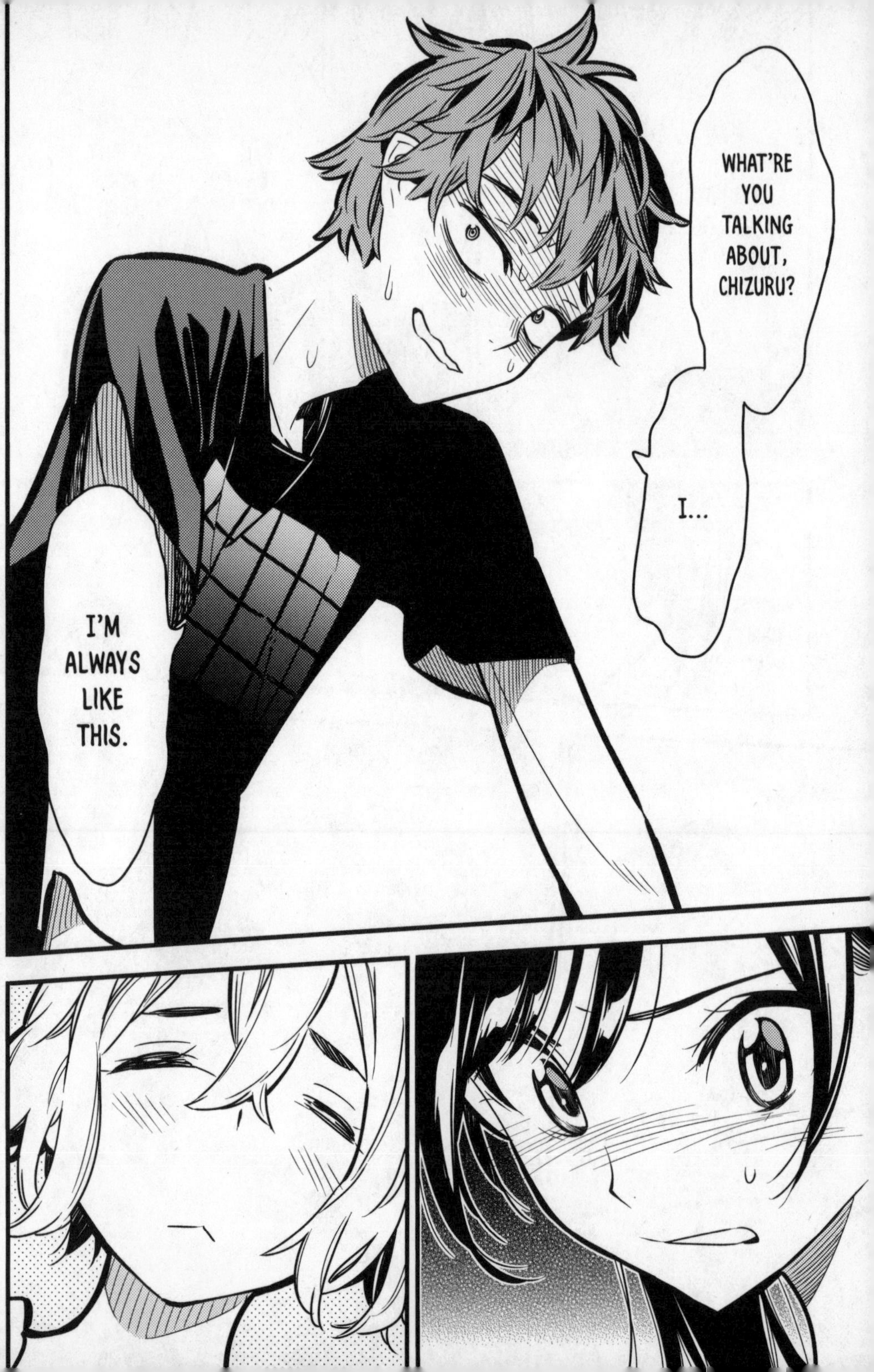
WHAT'RE YOU TALKING ABOUT, CHIZURU?
I...
I'M ALWAYS LIKE THIS.

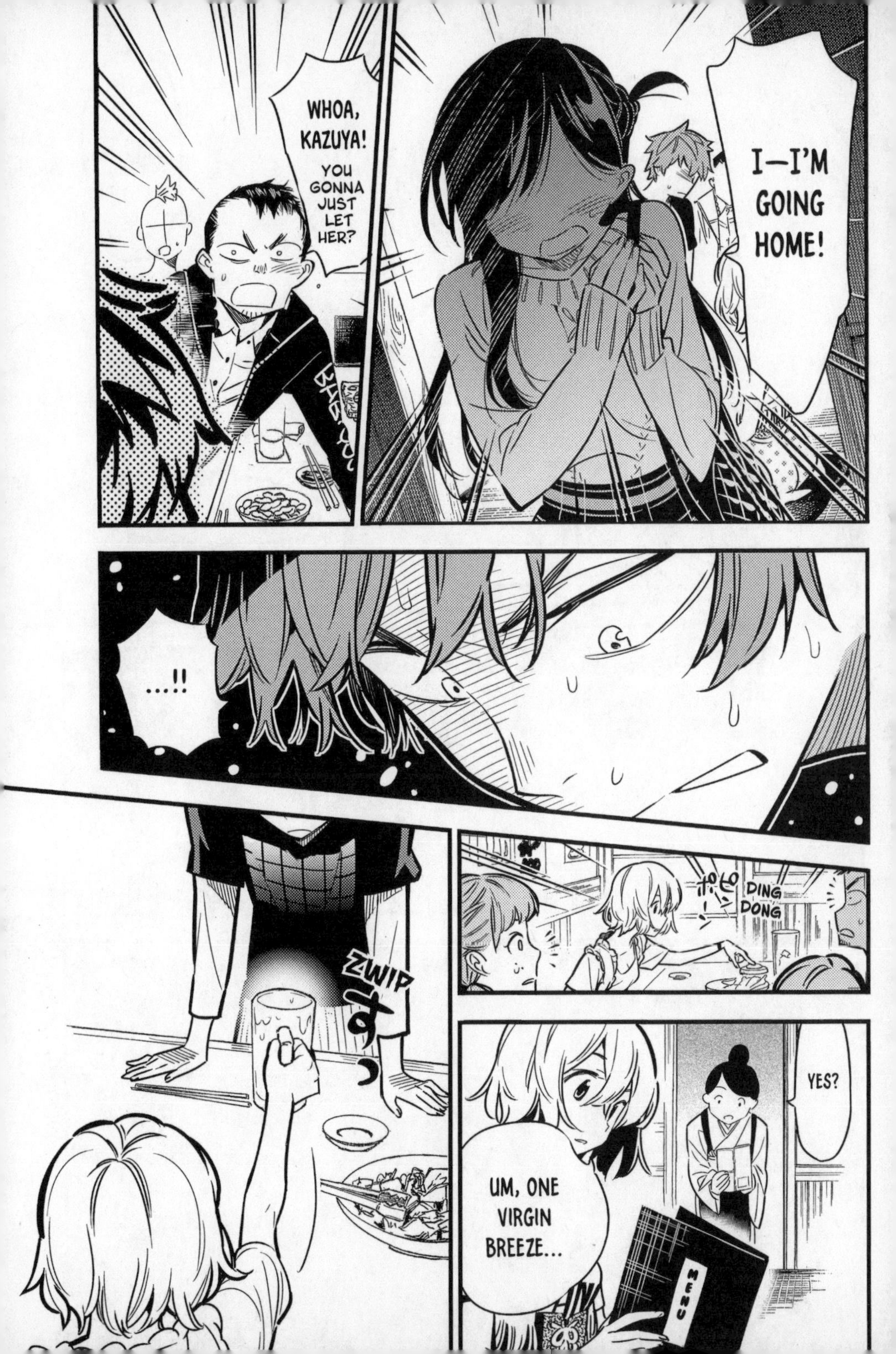
I—I'M GOING HOME!
WHOA, KAZUYA!
YOU GONNA JUST LET HER?
...!!
DING DONG
YES?
UM, ONE VIRGIN BREEZE...
MENU
ZWIP
すっ

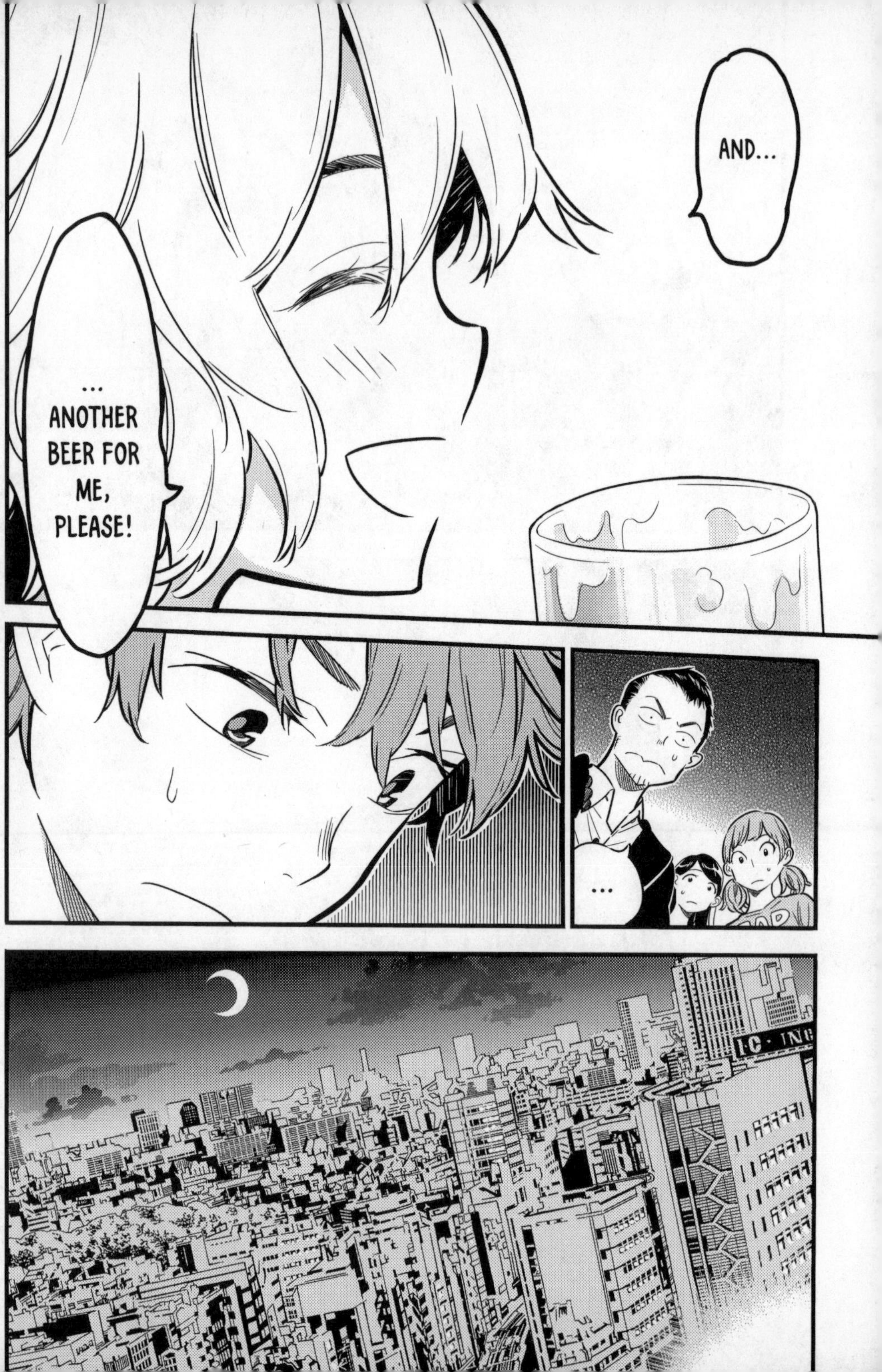
AND...
... ANOTHER BEER FOR ME, PLEASE!
...

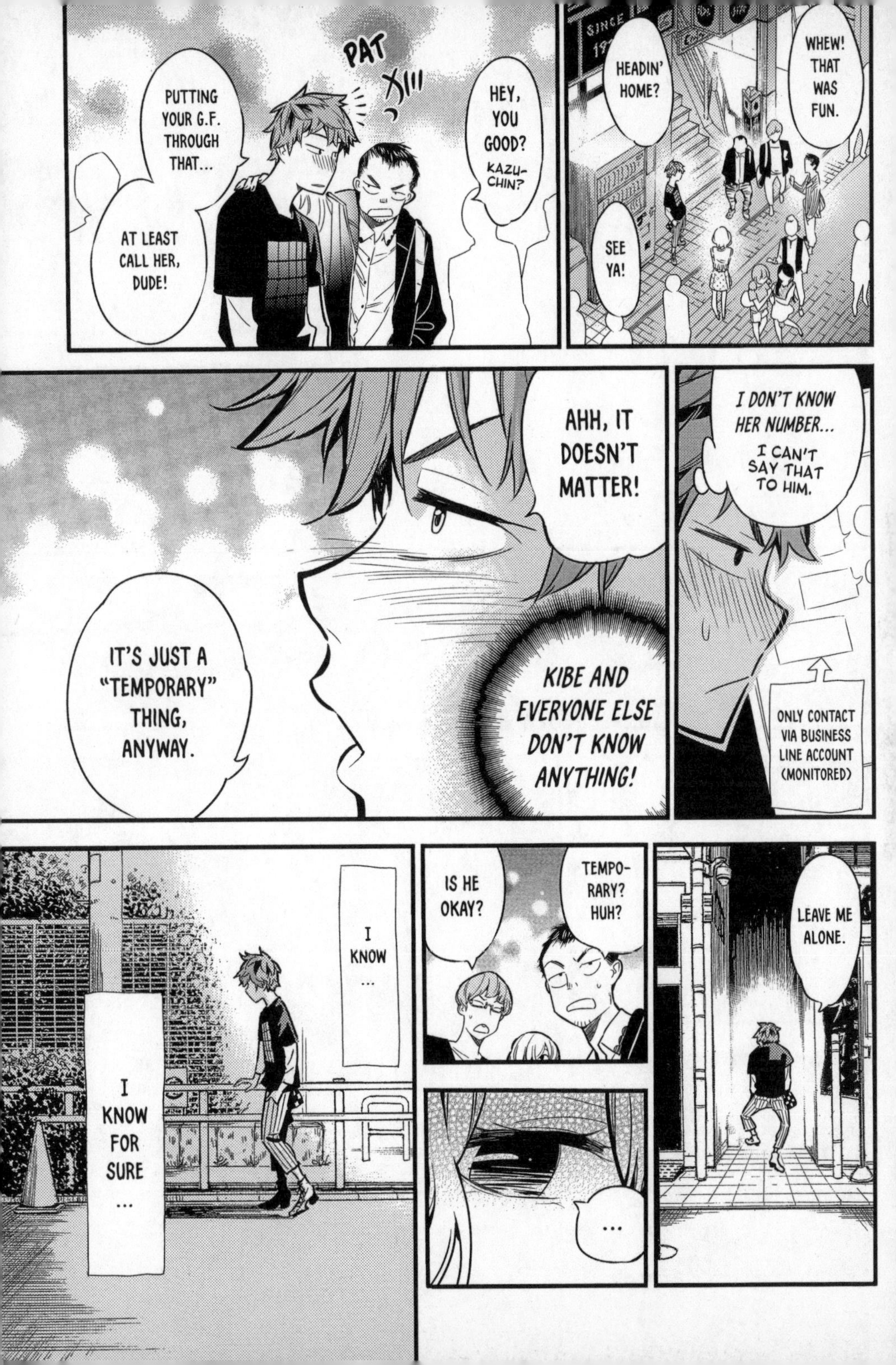
WHEW! THAT WAS FUN.
HEADIN' HOME?
SEE YA!
HEY, YOU GOOD? KAZU-CHIN?
PAT
PUTTING YOUR G.F. THROUGH THAT...
AT LEAST CALL HER, DUDE!
I DON'T KNOW HER NUMBER...
I CAN'T SAY THAT TO HIM.
ONLY CONTACT VIA BUSINESS LINE ACCOUNT (MONITORED)
AHH, IT DOESN'T MATTER!
KIBE AND EVERYONE ELSE DON'T KNOW ANYTHING!
IT'S JUST A "TEMPORARY" THING, ANYWAY.
LEAVE ME ALONE.
TEMPO-RARY? HUH?
IS HE OKAY?
...
I KNOW ...
I KNOW FOR SURE ...

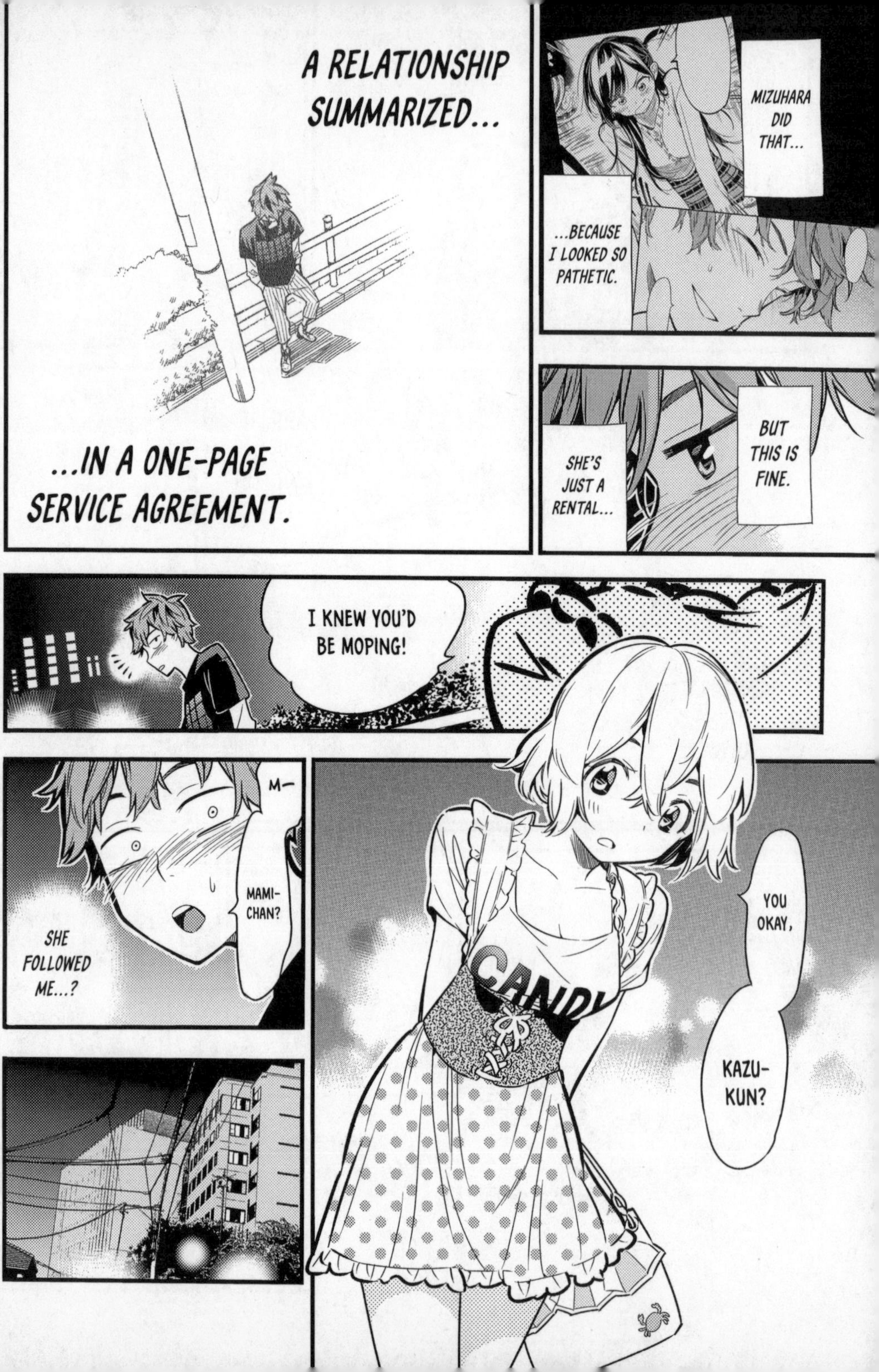
MIZUHARA DID THAT...
...BECAUSE I LOOKED SO PATHETIC.
BUT THIS IS FINE.
SHE'S JUST A RENTAL...
A RELATIONSHIP SUMMARIZED...
...IN A ONE-PAGE SERVICE AGREEMENT.
I KNEW YOU'D BE MOPING!
YOU OKAY,
KAZU-KUN?
M—
MAMI-CHAN?
SHE FOLLOWED ME...?

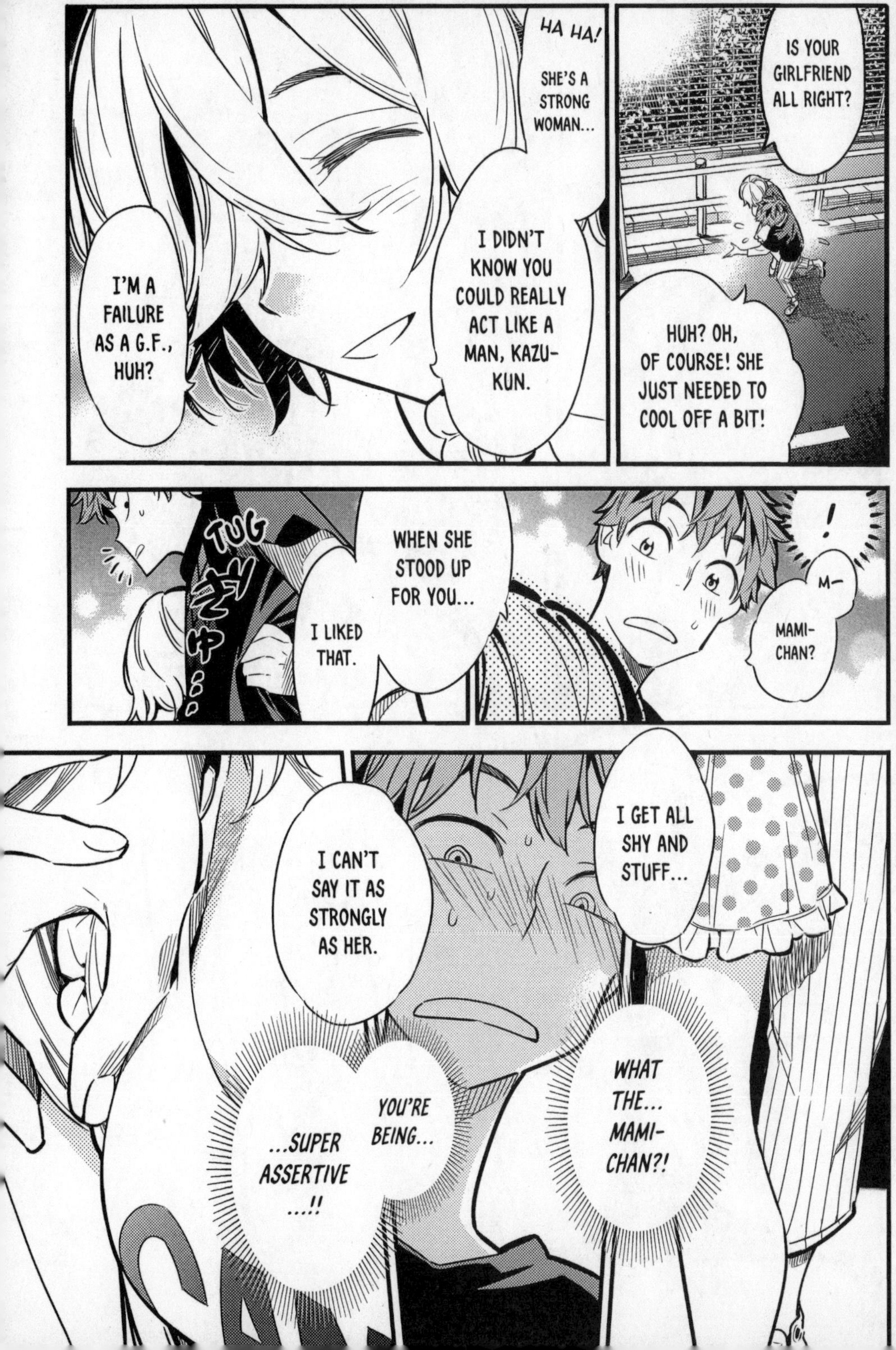
IS YOUR GIRLFRIEND ALL RIGHT?
HUH? OH, OF COURSE! SHE JUST NEEDED TO COOL OFF A BIT!
HA HA!
SHE'S A STRONG WOMAN...
I DIDN'T KNOW YOU COULD REALLY ACT LIKE A MAN, KAZU-KUN.
I'M A FAILURE AS A G.F., HUH?
!
M—
MAMI-CHAN?
WHEN SHE STOOD UP FOR YOU...
I LIKED THAT.
TUG
ぎゅ…
I GET ALL SHY AND STUFF...
I CAN'T SAY IT AS STRONGLY AS HER.
WHAT THE... MAMI-CHAN?!
YOU'RE BEING...
...SUPER ASSERTIVE ...!!

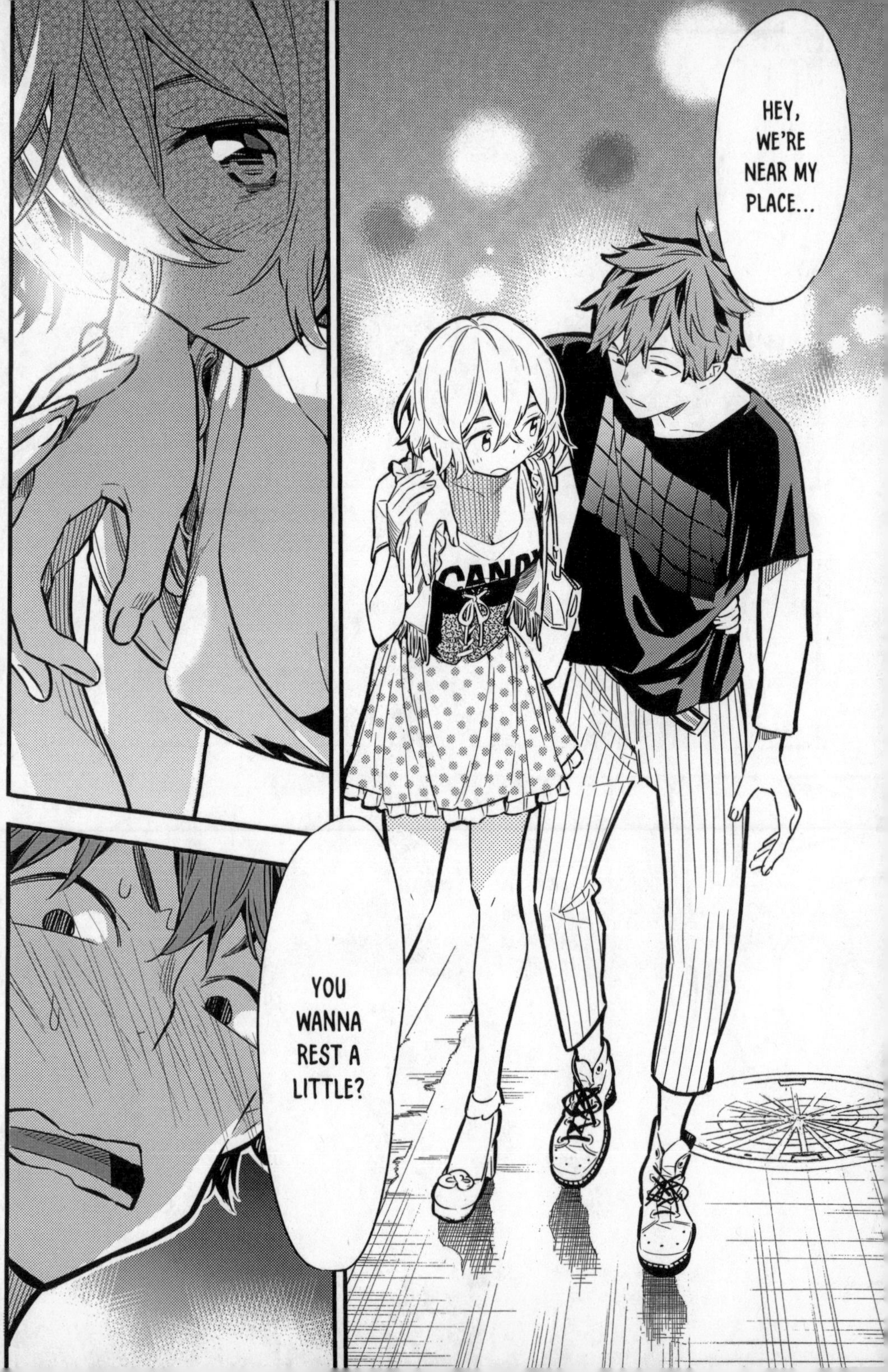
HEY, WE'RE NEAR MY PLACE...
YOU WANNA REST A LITTLE?

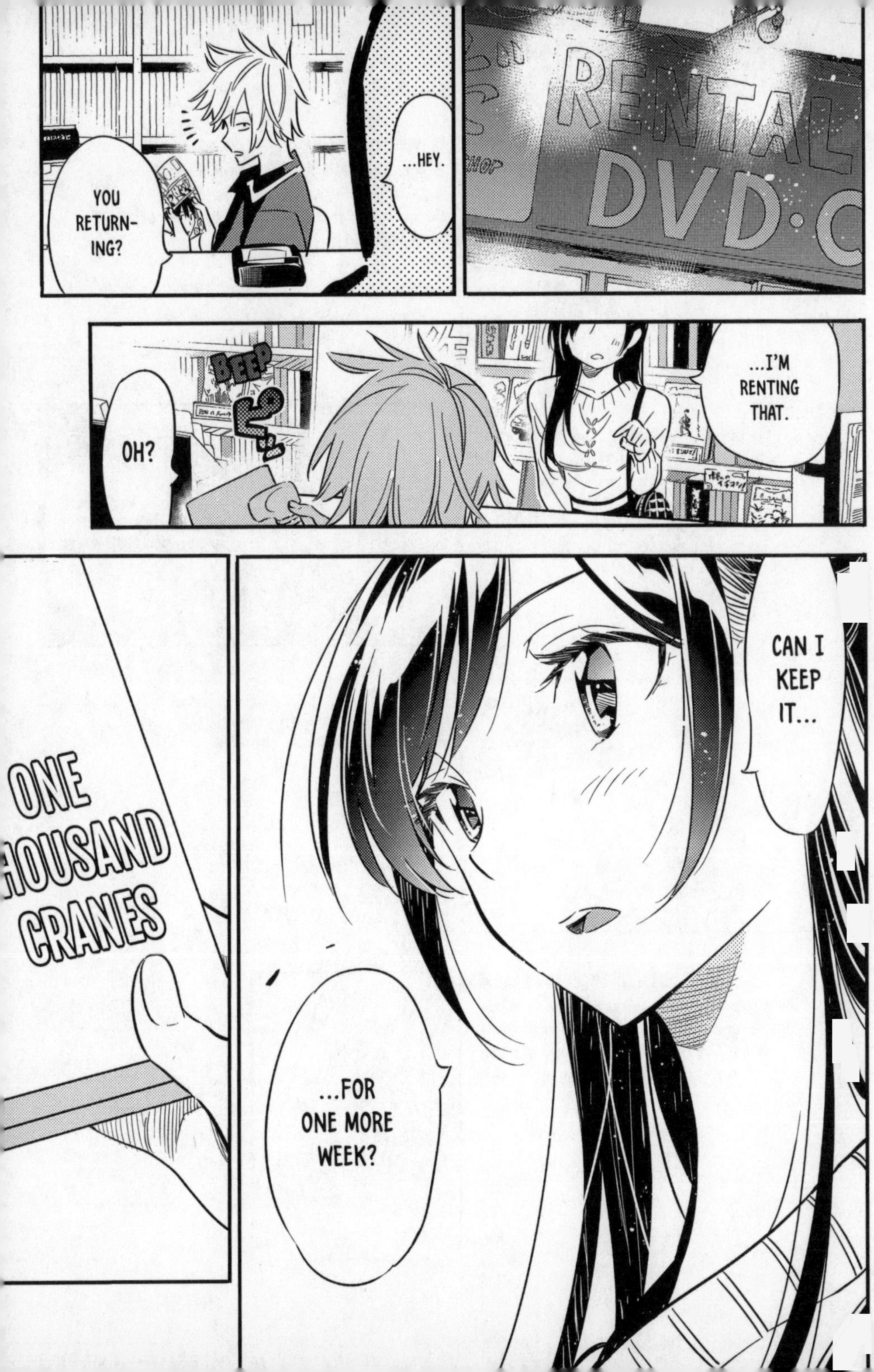
RENTAL
DVD
...HEY.
YOU RETURNING?
...I'M RENTING THAT.
BEEP
OH?
CAN I KEEP IT...
...FOR ONE MORE WEEK?
ONE HOUSAND CRANES

TRANSLATION NOTES:

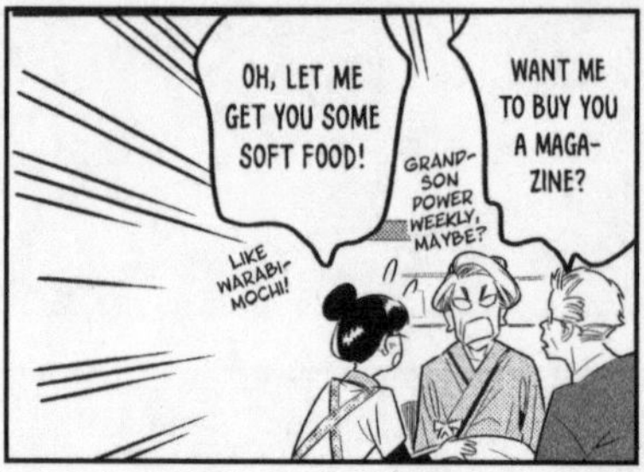
WANT ME TO BUY YOU A MAGA-ZINE?
GRAND-SON POWER WEEKLY, MAYBE?
OH, LET ME GET YOU SOME SOFT FOOD!
LIKE WARABI-MOCHI!

35, WARABI-MOCHI

Warabi-mochi is a sweet popular in the Kansai and Okinawa regions in Japan made from glutinous rice that resembles jelly, covered in a nutty soybean powder or flakes.

36, IDOL

In Japanese, the phoneticized word *aidoru*, or idol, is used to refer to pop stars who are often members of a band.

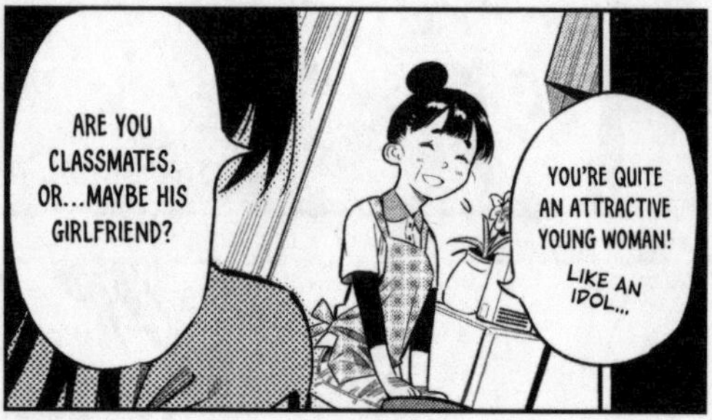
YOU'RE QUITE AN ATTRACTIVE YOUNG WOMAN!
LIKE AN IDOL...
ARE YOU CLASSMATES, OR...MAYBE HIS GIRLFRIEND?

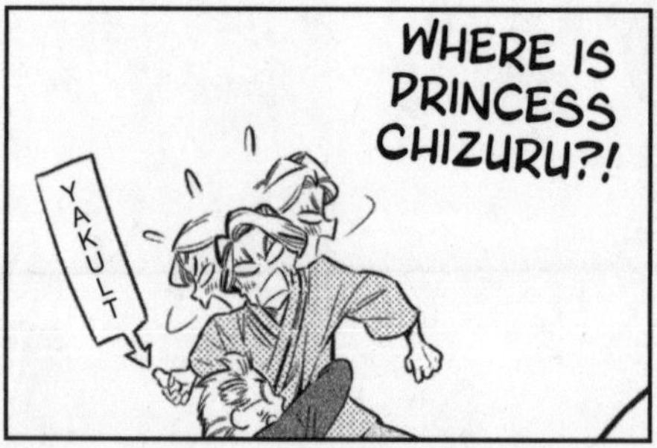
WHERE IS PRINCESS CHIZURU?!
YAKULT

43, YAKULT

Yakult is a sweetened, fermented milk drink popular in Japan, often consumed as a priobiotic.

193, ONE THOUSAND CRANES

This refers to a *senbazuru*, a thousand origami paper cranes tied together in a group with string. Creating this assemblage of paper cranes is traditionally said to bring good luck.

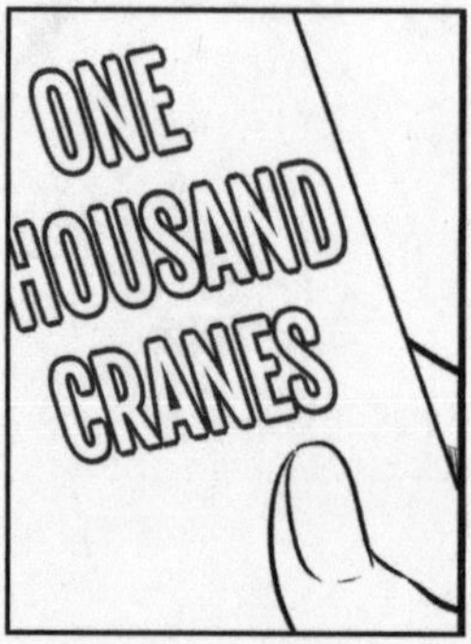
ONE
HOUSAND
CRANES

A SMART, NEW ROMANTIC COMEDY FOR FANS OF *SHORTCAKE CAKE* AND *TERRACE HOUSE*!

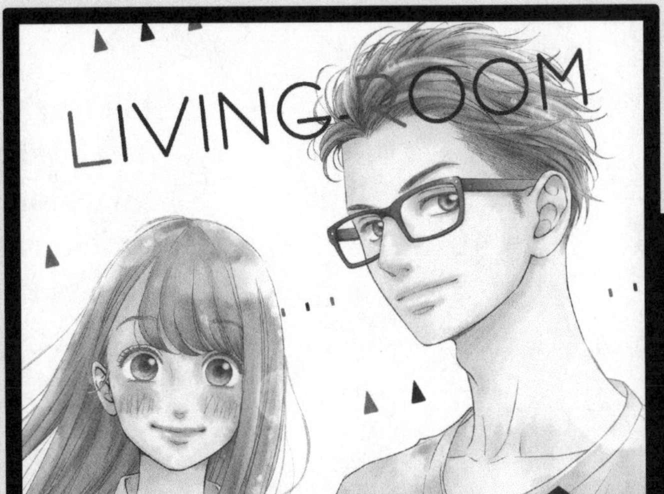
LIVING-ROOM
1
Keiko Iwashita
MATSUNAGA-SAN

KC KODANSHA COMICS

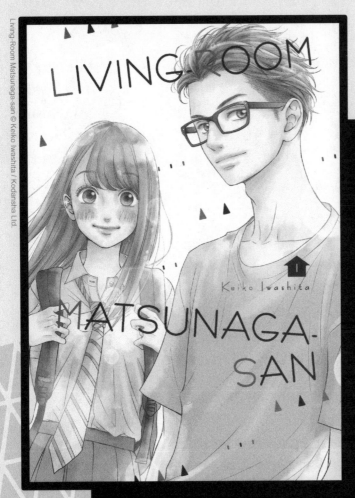

A romance manga starring high school girl Meeko, who learns to live on her own in a boarding house whose living room is home to the odd (but handsome) Matsunaga-san. She begins to adjust to her new life away from her parents, but Meeko soon learns that no matter how far away from home she is, she's still a young girl at heart — especially when she finds herself falling for Matsunaga-san.

Something's Wrong With Us

NATSUMI ANDO

The dark, psychological, sexy shojo series readers have been waiting for!

A spine-chilling and steamy romance between a Japanese sweets maker and the man who framed her mother for murder!

Following in her mother's footsteps, Nao became a traditional Japanese sweets maker, and with unparalleled artistry and a bright attitude, she gets an offer to work at a world-class confectionary company. But when she meets the young, handsome owner, she recognizes his cold stare...

THE SWEET SCENT OF LOVE IS IN THE AIR! FOR FANS OF OFFBEAT ROMANCES LIKE *WOTAKOI*

Sweat and Soap © Kintetsu Yamada / Kodansha Ltd.

In an office romance, there's a fine line between sexy and awkward... and that line is where Asako — a woman who sweats copiously — meets Koutarou — a perfume developer who can't get enough of Asako's, er, scent. Don't miss a romcom manga like no other!

The boys are back, in 400-page hardcovers that are as pretty and badass as they are!

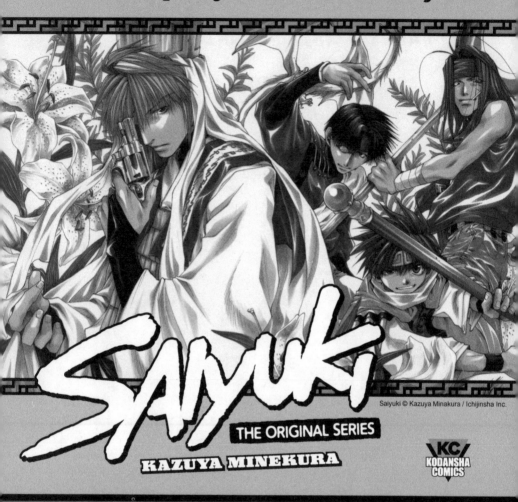

Saiyuki © Kazuya Minakura / Ichijinsha Inc.

SAIYUKI

THE ORIGINAL SERIES

KAZUYA MINEKURA

"AN EDGY COMIC LOOK AT AN ANCIENT CHINESE TALE." —YALSA

Genjo Sanzo is a Buddhist priest in the city of Togenkyo, which is being ravaged by yokai spirits that have fallen out of balance with the natural order. His superiors send him on a journey far to the west to discover why this is happening and how to stop it. His companions are three yokai with human souls. But this is no day trip — the four will encounter many discoveries and horrors on the way.

FEATURES NEW TRANSLATION, COLOR PAGES, AND BEAUTIFUL WRAPAROUND COVER ART!

A dark and sexy body-horror action manga perfect for fans of *Prison Scho*
and *High School of the Dead!*

Shuichi Kagaya is a smart kid, and most smart kids his age would be thinking about college. Shuichi is also a monster, and he's smart enough to know that monsters don't go to college. But after he uses his monstrous form to save his classmate Claire Aoki, it doesn't matter what his plans for the future were, because he's not the one making the decisions anymore Now that the seductive, sadistic Claire knows Shuichi's secret, she's got her own ideas about what a monster is good for—because he's not the first monster she's met...

KC
KODANSHA COMICS

GLEIPNIR

"You and me together...we would be unstoppable

EDENS ZERO
エデンズゼロ

HIRO MASHIMA IS BACK! JOIN THE CREATOR OF *FAIRY TAIL* AS HE TAKES TO THE STARS FOR ANOTHER THRILLING SAGA!

A high-flying space adventure! All the steadfast friendship and wild fighting you've been waiting for...IN SPACE!

At Granbell Kingdom, an abandoned amusement park, Shiki has lived his entire life among machines. But one day, Rebecca and her cat companion Happy appear at the park's front gates. Little do these newcomers know that this is the first human contact Granbell has had in a hundred years! As Shiki stumbles his way into making new friends, his former neighbors stir at an opportunity for a robo-rebellion... And when his old homeland becomes too dangerous, Shiki must join Rebecca and Happy on their spaceship and escape into the boundless cosmos.

KC KODANSHA COMICS

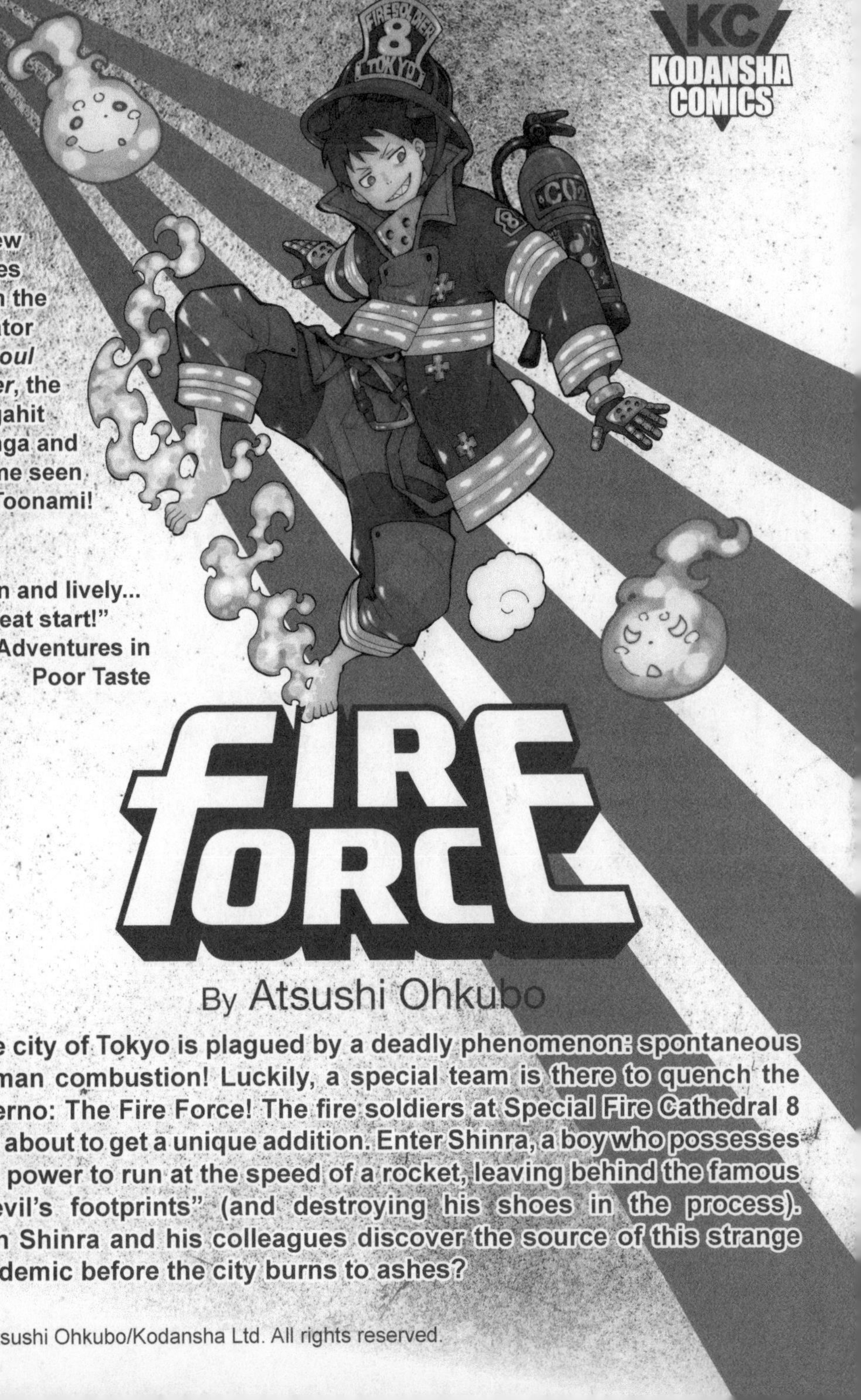

FIRESOLDIER
8
TOKYO
CO2

KC
KODANSHA COMICS

A new series from the creator of *Soul Eater*, the megahit manga and anime seen on Toonami!

"Fun and lively... a great start!"
-Adventures in Poor Taste

FIRE FORCE

By Atsushi Ohkubo

The city of Tokyo is plagued by a deadly phenomenon: spontaneous human combustion! Luckily, a special team is there to quench the inferno: The Fire Force! The fire soldiers at Special Fire Cathedral 8 are about to get a unique addition. Enter Shinra, a boy who possesses the power to run at the speed of a rocket, leaving behind the famous "devil's footprints" (and destroying his shoes in the process). Can Shinra and his colleagues discover the source of this strange epidemic before the city burns to ashes?

Young characters and steampunk setting, like *Howl's Moving Castle* and *Battle Angel Alita*

Beyond the Clouds © 2018 Nicke / Ki-oon

A boy with a talent for machines and a mysterious girl whose wings he's fixed will take you beyond the clouds! In the tradition of the high-flying, resonant adventure stories of Studio Ghibli comes a gorgeous tale about the longing of young hearts for adventure and friendship!

PERFECT WORLD

Rie Aruga

A TOUCHING
NEW SERIES
ABOUT LOVE AND
COPING WITH
DISABILITY

An office party reunites Tsugumi with her high school crush Itsuki. He's realized his dream of becoming an architect, but along the way, he experienced a spinal injury that put him in a wheelchair. Now Tsugumi's rekindled feelings will butt up against prejudices she never considered — and Itsuki will have to decide if he's ready to let someone into his heart...

"Depicts with great delicacy and courage the difficulties some with disabilities experience getting involved in romantic relationships... Rie Aruga refuses to romanticize, pushing her heroine to face the reality of disability. She invites her readers to the same tasks of empathy, knowledge and recognition."
—Slate.fr

"An important entry [in manga romance]... The emotional core of both plot and characters indicates thoughtfulness... [Aruga's] research is readily apparent in the text and artwork, making this feel like a real story."
—Anime News Network

KC
KODANSHA
COMICS